Festschrift
A TRIBUTE
TO
DR. WILLIAM HORDERN

DR. WILLIAM HORDERN, Th.D., D.D.

Festschrift

A TRIBUTE
TO
DR. WILLIAM HORDERN

Edited by

WALTER FREITAG

UNIVERSITY OF SASKATCHEWAN

CONTENTS

Greeting... vii
Foreword ix
William Hordern: Curriculum Vitae xi
Roster of Institutional Sponsors............................... xiii
Roll of Congratulators..xv
Contributors to the Festschrift xix

PART ONE
Studies in Systematics/Ethics

Perspective
    Marjorie Hordern, Saskatoon 3

The Question of God and the Trinity
    Carl Braaten, Chicago 6

Karl Barth, Juergen Moltmann and the Theopaschite Revolution
    Ronald Goetz, Elmhurst................................ 17

Narrative Theology: Translation or Transformation?
    Millard Erickson, St. Paul 29

Black Theology: It's Origin, Method and Relation to
    Third World Theologies
    James Cone, New York 40

An Update on Liberation Theology in the Canadian Context
    Benjamin Smillie, Saskatoon 51

Lubricating the Camel: Clement of Alexandria on Wealth and
    the Wealthy
    Walter Wagner, Allentown 64

Realism and Freedom Within a Penitentiary
    Gary Watts, Mission.................................. 78

Luther's Attitude Towards Poverty: Theology and Social Reform
    Richard Hordern, Regina 94

Is the Emperor Naked?: Religions and Religion in Theological
    Education
    Roland Miller, Regina................................. 109

PART TWO
Biblical/Historical Studies

Righteousness as Relationship
Adrian Leske, Edmonton 125

Luther in the Thought of Bultmann
Walter Freitag, Saskatoon 138

The Courage of Faith at the Eucharist According to Martin Luther
Egil Grislis, Winnipeg 147

Martin Luther in the Writings of Eugen Rosenstock-Huessy
Eugene Tate, Saskatoon 162

Printing and the Reformation
George Forell, Iowa City 178

Henry Melchior Muhlenberg's Canadian Connections
Helmut Lehmann, Philadelphia 185

Canada's Lutherans in a Mediating Role?
E. Theodore Bachmann, Princeton 194

The Search for Christian Unity
Otto Heick, Waterloo 216

Footnotes 227

Publications of William Hordern 257

Index 268

GREETING

In this volume, a number of your friends and colleagues present a tribute as you retire after more than 40 years of teaching, preaching, and lecturing. It seems fitting that one who has written so much and thereby contributed so much to stimulative and reflective thought should be honored in this way.

The writing of essays, engagement in scholarly discourse, indeed the whole enterprise of teaching and academic interchange, seems to many an exercise in abstraction. You have the special gift of wedding thought and the life situation. The essays collected in this volume ranging, as they do, over a wide assortment of subjects, honor your own research and your unusual capacity for analysis and interpretation of many facets of theology and our contemporary life.

The production of a Festschrift such as this is, of course, much more than a salutation of academic achievement. There is implicit here as well, a recognition and congratulation of your human achievements. You are not to us a disembodied intellectual toiling in the mythical and isolated ivory towers of academia. Rather, we salute you as one who has lived, walked and played in the world of ordinary humanity. You have felt and responded to the needs and hurts of those whom governments, corporations, institutions and even the church have tended to leave by the wayside. You have not stood aloof from the day to day flow of our local and national life.

We appreciate and pay tribute also to your capacity to cherish and learn from your own family. Far from standing at some remove from your thought and reflection, Marje and your children have always been a part of your work and you have readily acknowledged that. It is most appropriate that Marje has given us some insight into this in this volume.

You have many friends, both in Canada and the United States, who join in saluting you with respect and affection. Not all could contribute essays. However, colleagues at the Seminary and the University, hundreds of friends from the churches, former students, members of congregations, together with friends from the community want to express appreciation for what you have meant to us. We know you will continue to walk with us and help us reflect on what it means to bear the name of Christ in this world.

We hope and pray that your release from formal responsibilities will give the opportunity to follow through on pursuits which have been hampered by the constraints of time.

God bless and keep you.

Roger W. Nostbakken

FOREWORD

It is a matter of deep pleasure for me, on behalf of the essayists who have contributed to this volume, to pay tribute to Dr. William Hordern upon the occasion of his retirement from the office of president of Lutheran Theological Seminary at Saskatoon. This is a book in the tradition of the European Universities, a Festschrift or Book of Tribute, in honor of an esteemed colleague in the academic world and our word of appreciation for his contribution to it. It is all the more gratifying that the international and ecumenical influence of Dr. Hordern is exemplified in this volume through those who have contributed to it. We have been beneficiaries of Dr. Hordern's work as a theologian in Lutheran circles and in other Christian churches both in Canada and in the United States and that whether as students under his guidance or as colleagues in the academic disciplines. This is our salute to him. We wish him many more years of living by grace!

This publication would not have been possible without the sponsorship of a number of church jurisdictions and educational institutions. When I decided to embark on this venture, I had nothing in financial support except a lot of hope. I was overwhelmed by the instant willingness and magnanimous spirit with which all of these sponsors wanted to support this project in honor of Bill Hordern. I am very pleased and grateful to them all. To each and every one of them, my own personal word of thanks. It is equally appropriate here to express my profound appreciation to that host of Congratulators who wanted to express their support and to be listed among those who remember Bill as a teacher, colleague and friend.

I am conscious of the fact that I have left the essayists who submitted articles without remark. Let me say that I can scarcely find the words to thank them not only for their readiness to come to my aid, their willingness to participate, but for the latitude they have allowed me as editor. More still, they have shown me a spirit of cooperation and support which I shall long remember. They have made this endeavor a festive task for me.

A book such as this depends upon the assistance and help of a good number of other people, and I wish to acknowledge them as well. To Mr. Guy Aho, who prepared the list of publications of Dr. Hordern, and to Mr. Sterling Bjorndahl, who assisted in proof-reading, my thanks! Your help was as needed as it was important. An especial word of gratitude is extended to Mr. Davis Hordern who did yoeman service not only in proof-reading but a variety of other matters; at a time when I had to reduce my workload for a while, he took over many of the tasks still outstanding on the Festschrift. I know that he spent many hours at the work and carried it out carefully. It was indeed well-done!

Mrs. Anne Wright and the staff of the Printing Services, the University of Saskatchewan, were unfailingly courteous in the face of my questions and requirements, always prepared to be of service, and to bring this enterprise to completion. They made my tasks easier both with sound counsel and efficient work.

I trust that I shall be forgiven if I single out one individual, the secretary at our seminary, Mrs. Laurie Parenteau. I don't know what would have happened if she had not been available to deal with letters, with the reproduction of materials, with financial accounting, with the answering of telephone calls and of making them on my behalf. For that, and more, I am in her debt. She is a person of competence and ability, able to work under pressure and still give you a smile. Thank you, Laurie!

I am particularly pleased that Marjorie Hordern has contributed her own piece to this volume. She does so, she says, as a lay theologian but I think what she has to tell us is more than that. In truth, we should also be rendering her tribute on this occasion. Bill would not have become the Bill he is but for Marj, as he himself would attest, but the seminary also would not be what it is today but for Marj's service in an administrative capacity at our school. Thanks, Marj.!

Whatever failings may appear in the book, up to and including the printer's devils or spelling mistakes, those must be assigned to me; whatever it's merits, those should be granted to those who made the volume what it is.

Walter Freitag, Editor

CURRICULUM VITAE

William Hordern

Born at Dundurn, Saskatchewan

Married to Marjorie Joyce, 1944

Children - Richard, Joyce, Davis

ACADEMIC DEGREES

B.A. (with Great Distinction), Univ. of Sask. 1941
(Major in Political Science and Economics)

License in Theology, St. Andrew's, 1943

B.D., St. Andrew's College, 1945

S.T.M. (Magna cum Lauda), Union Theological Seminary,
New York, 1946 (Master's Thesis: "The Theology of the
Social Gospel")

Th. D., Union Theological Seminary (Christian Ethics and
Theology), 1951, (Thesis: "Marxian and Christian Views of
History")

POSITIONS HELD

1943-45, Pastor, Marsden-Neilburg United Church

1945-49, Assistant to the Pastor, St. John's Lutheran Church,
Richmond Hill, N.Y.

1946-47, Class Assistant to Reinhold Niebuhr (Union Theo.
Sem.)

1947-48, Tutor Assistant to Paul Tillich (Union Theo. Sem.)

1949-57, Teaching in Philosophy and Religion Department,
Swarthmore College, Swarthmore, Pa.

1957-66, Professor of Theology at Garrett Theological Seminary,
Evanston, Illinois

1961-66, Assistant Pastor (part-time), Trinity Lutheran Church,
Skokie, Illinois

1966-85, President, Lutheran Theological Seminary, Saskatoon

1973- Board of Directors, Lutheran Life Insurance of Canada

MEMBERSHPS
American Academy of Religion (Vice-President 1964-65, President 1965-66)
Saskatoon Golf and Country Club (since 1966)
New Democratic Party of Saskatchewan (since 1966)

HONORS RECEIVED
Doctor of Divinity Degree from St. Andrew's College, 1968
Listed in *Who's Who in America* since 1962

ROSTER OF INSTITUTIONAL SPONSORS

Evangelical Lutheran Church of Canada,
Saskatoon, Saskatchewan
S.T. Jacobson, President

Central Canada Synod, L.C.A.,
Winnipeg, Manitoba
L. Luetkehoelter, President

Board of Governors,
Lutheran Theological Seminary,
Saskatoon, Saskatchewan
C. Satre, Chairperson

University of Saskatchewan,
Saskatoon, Saskatchewan
L. Kristjanson, President

Friends of
Lutheran Life Insurance Society of Canada
Waterloo, Ontario
H. Dietrich, President

Good Samaritan Society,
Edmonton, Alberta,
G. Hennig, President

Western Canada Synod, L.C.A.
Edmonton, Alberta
D. Sjoberg, President

Luther College,
Regina, Saskatchewan,
M. Anderson, President

Waterloo Lutheran Seminary,
Waterloo, Ontario
R. Crossman, President

Central Pentecostal College,
Saskatoon, Saskatchewan,
H. Faught, President

Camrose Lutheran College,
Camrose, ALberta,
G. Johnson, President

Alumni Association,
Lutheran Theological Seminary,
Saskatoon, Saskatchewan,
R. Hordern, President

St. Andrew's College,
Saskatoon, Saskatchewan,
J.R. Donnelly, President

College of Emmanuel and St. Chad,
Saskatoon, Saskatchewan,
R. Brown, President

St. Thomas More College,
Saskatoon, Saskatchewan,
J. Hanrahan, President

Board of Education,
Evangelical Lutheran Church of Canada,
Saskatoon, Saskatchewan
L. Heinemann, Chairperson

Students Association,
Lutheran Theological Seminary
Saskatoon, Saskatchewan,
M. Anderson, President

Concordia Lutheran Seminary,
Edmonton, Alberta,
W.T. Jantzow, President

Eastern Canada Synod. L.C.A.,
Kitchener, Ontario,
W. Huras, President

Manitoba-Saskatchewan District,
Lutheran Church-Missouri Synod,
Regina, Saskatchewan,
R. Hohm, President

ROLL OF CONGRATULATORS

Guy Aho,
Minneapolis, Minn.

Jose H. Ariza,
Westlock, Alta.

John Anderson,
Calgary, Alberta

Vernon Begalke,
Grand Prairie, Alta.

Wolf Belzing,
Edmonton, Alta.

Norman Berner,
Kitchener, Ont.

Herman Bickel,
Victoria, B.C.

Ernst Bittner,
Regina, Sask.

Sterling Bjorndahl,
Saskatoon, Sask.

Arthur Boen,
Saskatoon, Sask.

Arild Borch,
Saskatoon, Sask.

Jim Bork,
Lloydminster, Sask.

Ole Bruun,
Ashern, Man.

Arthur G. Buckley,
Saskatoon, Sask.

Hans Burmeister,
Brandon, Man.

Robert Byhre,
Shaunavon, Sask.

Brian Chappell,
Lipton, Sask.

Henrik Cherland,
Winnipeg, Man.

Gunner Christiansen,
Edmonton, Alta.

J. Ralph Donnelly,
Saskatoon, Sask.

Ray Ducholke,
Lacombe, Alta.

Lowell Eckert,
Edmonton, Alta.

Larry Ehrhardt,
Williamsburg, Ont.

Henry Enns,
Sudbury, Ont.

Wilton Ernst,
Delta, B.C.

George Evenson,
Camrose, Alta.

Ronald Flamand,
Grand Prairie, Alta.

William Flath,
Melville, Sask.

Walter Freitag,
Saskatoon, Sask.

Fred Gaertner,
Osoyoos, B.C.

Martin Garber-Conrad
Edmonton, Alta.

Leon Gilbertson,
Winnipeg, Man.

Doug Giles,
Winnipeg, Man.

Volker Greifenhagen,
Saskatoon, Sask.

Ken & Kathy Grambo,
Brooks, Alta.

Egil Grislis,
Winnipeg, Man.

Allan Grundahl,
Saskatoon, Sask.

Jean Hackborn,
St. Jacobs, Ont.

Cindy & Jim Halmarson,
Saskatoon, Sask.

Kendall Harris,
Richmond, B.C.

J. Fred Haugen,
Weyburn, Sask.

Irwin Hohm,
Calgary, Alta.

Reinhold Hohnsbein,
Olds, Alta.

Wayne Holst,
Calgary, Alta.

Randy & Joyce Hordern-Zutter,
Sherwood Park, Alta.

David Hunter,
Saskatoon, Sask.

S. Theodore Jacobson,
Saskatoon, Sask.

W.T. Jantzow,
Edmonton, Alta.

Gordon Jensen,
Swift Current, Sask.

David Jobling,
Saskatoon, Sask.

Alfred Johnson,
Victoria, B.C.

Tim Johnson,
Lanigan, Sask.

Charles Johnson,
Saskatoon, Sask.

Orville Kaminski,
Fairy Glen, Sask.

Herbert Keil,
Surrey, B.C.

John Kleiner,
Saskatoon, Sask.

Lois Knudson,
Archerwill, Sask.

Walter Koehler,
Saskatoon, Sask.

Roger Koester,
Meadow Lake, Sask.

Karl Kuskevics,
Hamilton, Ont.

Tim LeDrew,
Davidson, Sask.

Martin Leeseberg,
Saskatoon, Sask.

David & Karen Lefsrud,
Saskatoon, Sask.

John Lefsrud,
Edmonton, Alta.

Edwin Lehman,
Edmonton, Alta.

Fred Lenz,
Saskatoon, Sask.

Lorne Lissel,
Morden, Man.

Carl Listoe,
Saskatoon, Sask.

Herbert Loddigs,
Minneapolis, Minn.

John Lokken,
Outlook, Sask.

Lee Leutkehoelter,
Winnipeg, Man.

Pauline Marshall,
Saskatoon, Sask.

Peter Mikelic,
London, Ont.

Don & Mary Mitchell,
Saskatoon, Sask.

Doreen & Gerald Mitchinson,
High Level, Alta.

Edward Mitchler,
Dauphin, Man.

Randolph Mohr,
Calgary, Alta.

Les Nelson,
Cloquet, Minn.

Ronald Nelson,
Victoria, B.C.

Erland Nord,
Wetaskiwin, Alta.

Paul Nostbakken,
Saskatoon, Sask.

Roger Nostbakken,
Saskatoon, Sask.

Rolf Nosterud,
Prince Albert, Sask.

Willy Olesen,
Fort St. John, B.C.

O. Donald Olson,
Edmonton, Alta.

William Ott,
Bridgewater, N.S.

Barbara Ove,
Saskatoon, Sask.

Ernie Paetsch,
Wetaskiwin, Alta.

Laurie Parenteau,
Dalmeny, Sask.

Gustav Piir,
Saskatoon, Sask.

Tim Posyluzny,
Saskatoon, Sask.

Roy Pudrycki,
Edmonton, Alta.

Vernon Raaflaub,
Camrose, Alta.

Dan Repo,
Atikokan, Ont.

Cliff Reinhardt,
Coquitlam, B.C.

Henry Reitze,
Radisson, Sask.

William Riekert,
Nepean, Ont.

Brian Ross,
Islington, Ont.

Olaf Rostad,
Burnaby, B.C.

Eric Rosenquist,
Morrisburg, Ont.

Curtis Satre,
Calgary, Ont.

Erich Schultz,
Waterloo, Ont.

Phillip Schwindt,
Winnipeg, Man.

Frank E. Scribner,
Gimli, Man.

Donald Sjoberg,
Edmonton, Alta.

Dan & Brenda Skaret,
Saskatoon, Sask.

Paul Sodtke & Marion Tenkins,
Whitecourt, Alta.

Arnold & Marjorie Tiefenbach,
Regina, Sask.

Wolfgang Tillmanns,
Eatonia, Sask.

Roger Uitti,
Saskatoon, Sask.

Howard Ulmer,
Southey, Sask.

Kennett Verasammy,
Saskatoon, Sask.

CONTRIBUTORS TO THE FESTSCHRIFT

Bachmann, E. Theodore
> B.A., Haverford College, M.A., Harvard, Ph.D., Chicago, S.T.M., Luth. Theol. Sem., Philadelphia; Lutheran World Federation Visiting Professor, Faculdade de Teologia, Brazil (1954). Executive Secretary, BTE, LCA; Pacific Luth. Sem., Berkeley, Professor Emeritus.

Braaten, Carl E.
> B.A., St. Olaf, B.TH., Luth. Theol. Sem., St. Paul, Th.D., Harvard; Fulbright Scholarship, Guggenheim Fellow. Professor of Systematic Theology, Luth. School of Theology, Chicago.

Cone, James H.
> B.A., Philander Smith College, B.D., Garrett Theol. Sem., M.A., Ph.D., Northwestern, L.L.D., L.H.D.; Rockefeller Foundation Fellow (1973/74). Charles A. Briggs Professor of Systematic Theology, Union Theol. Sem., N.Y.

Erickson, Millard J.
> B.A., Minnesota, B.D., Northern Baptist Theol. Sem., M.A., Chicago, Ph.D., Northwestern. Vice-Pres. & Dean, Professor of Theology, Bethel Theol. Sem.

Forell, George W.
> B.A., Philadelphia, Th.M., Princeton, Th.D., Union Theol. Sem.; D.D., L.H.D., Litt.D., LL.D.; Fulbright Scholar (1957/58), NEH (1975/76). Carver Distinguished Professor of Religion, Univ. of Iowa.

Freitag, Walter H.P.
> B.A., Carthage, M. Div., S.T.M., Chicago Luth. Theol. Sem., S.T.D., Luth. School of Theol., Chicago; Franklin C. Fry Fellow. Professor of the Church in Historic Witness and Biblical Theology, Luth. Theol. Sem., Saskatoon.

Goetz, Ronald
> B.S., Northwestern, S.T.B., Harvard, M.A., Ph.D., Northwestern. Professor of Theology & Religion, Elmhurst.

Grislis, Egil
> B.A., Gettysburg, B.D., L.T.S., Gettysburg, Ph.D., Yale; Sterling Fellowship, Yale; Social Sciences and Humanities

xix

Research Council of Canada Fellowship. Professor of Religion, University of Manitoba.

Heick, Otto W.
B.A., B.D., Hamma, M.A., Ph.D., Nebraska; D.D., Litt. D. Waterloo Luth. Sem., Professor Emeritus.

Hordern (nee Joyce), Marjorie
Teaching to 1944; church schools, scouts, school and church women's activities to 1977. Administrator, Luth. Theol. Sem., Saskatoon.

Hordern, Richard, P.
B.A., St. Olaf, M. Div., S.T.M., Luth. Theol. Sem., Saskatoon, M. Phil., Ph.D., Union Theol. Sem.; Canada Council Doctoral Studies Fellowship, Allen Schendel Award. Assistant Professor of Religious Studies, Luther College, Regina.

Lehmann, Helmut T.
B.A., Saskatchewan, Dip., Luth. College & Sem., Saskatoon, Th.D., Freidrich-Alexander Univ., Erlangen. Luth. Theol. Sem., Philadelphia, Professor Emeritus.

Leske, Adrian, M.
M. Div., S.T.M., Th.D., Concordia Theological Sem., St. Louis. Professor of Religious Studies, Concordia College, Edmonton.

Miller, Roland E.
M. Div., Concordia Theological Seminary, St. Louis, M.A., Ph.D., Hartford Seminary Foundation; Visiting Scholar, Harvard. Academic Dean and Professor of Islam and World Religions, Luther College, Regina; Coordinator of Religious Studies Programs, Univ. of Regina.

Smillie, Benjamin G.
B.A., Hon.-Phil., M.A., Toronto, B.D., Emmanuel College, Toronto, S.T.M., Andover Newton, Ed.D., Columbia. Professor of Church and Society, St. Andrew's College, Saskatoon.

Tate, Eugene, D.
B.A., Hamline Univ., B.D., Garrett Theol. Sem., M.A., Northwestern, Ph.D., Michigan State. NDEA Fellow, Dep't of Communication, Michigan State U. Professor of Sociology, St. Thomas More College, Saskatoon.

Wagner, Walter H.
B.A., Gettysburg College, M. Div., Luth. Theol. Sem., Philadelphia, Ph.D., Drew Univ.; LCA Fellowship for Graduate Study, Faculty Fellowship, Upsala College. Chaplain and Associate Professor, Muhlenberg College. Allentown.

Watts, Gary

B.A., Univ. B.C., B.D., S.T.M., Luth. Theol. Sem., Saskatoon, Ph.D., McGill, B.H.J., Univ. of Regina. Protestant Chaplain, Matsqui Institution, Abbotsford.

PART ONE

Studies in Systematics/Ethics

PERSPECTIVE

M. Hordern

A number of theologians and colleagues of Bill have contributed scholarly articles to this book. I cannot do the same. However, I have had the advantage of reading in original text and galley proof all of Bill's articles and books over a period spanning some forty years. It is my intention to put into perspective Bill's career as an author.

When Bill and I were at university together, the fundamentalist-liberal controversy was in full swing. At meetings of the I.V.C.F., the S.C.M., and in church groups and small gatherings, interested people became involved in heated discussions on such subjects as evolution, predestination, the Virgin Birth and transubstantiation. This sort of involvement continued during our years at Union Seminary, New York City, where Bill was enrolled for his doctoral studies and I was working at Dr. Fosdick's Riverside Church, and also in the library at Union.

As it happened, I had a distinct advantage over many student wives due to a pattern which had been established in the two years before we had moved to New York. During that period of our married life, Bill was serving the Marsden-Neilburg parish in Saskatchewan. Every morning, at 10:30 a.m., while I was preparing the meat, vegetables and dessert for the noon meal, Bill would sit in the ancient arm chair in the kitchen reading to me excerpts and articles from *The Christian Century*, *The Pulpit*, other magazines and journals of a social or theological interest, or from current books. Then, too, every Sunday evening Bill read the Scriptures for the following Sunday and began thinking about the sermon. By midweek he had put his thought to paper; I would then read his text and respond to it. This pattern of dialogue gave me an excellent introduction to the language, ideas and content of the discussions that went on at informal gatherings in the homes of such professors as Reinhold Niebuhr, Paul Tillich, John Bennett and Paul Scherer. When the "at homes" were over, the discussions continued far into the night in the men's washroom. Bill would give me the highlights the next day.

The United States, during those years, was in the throes of the McCarthy era and Bill became very interested in understanding the differences and similarities between communism and Christianity. This led to his choice of that topic for his doctoral thesis. He roamed New York

3

from bookstore to bookstore searching for materials which would then be read on the lengthy trips to and from St. John's Lutheran Church in Richmond Hill where he served as the youth director and, later, as assistant to the pastor. It was difficult to avoid the knowledge that Bill's area of study could make him suspect and liable to deportation. That, however, did not occur and his dissertation was finally completed. The text of *Christianity, Communism and History* was entered, later on, in a religious book contest, in which it won first prize. There was a monetary award, but the real bonus was the access thus made available to the world of publication.

In 1949, Bill became a teacher of religion at a Quaker school, Swarthmore College, in Pennsylvania. There, the weekly seminars in our home gave me opportunities to listen to students at coffee break. It was also the practice of the Quakers to hold a forum every week preceding their First Day Meetings and Bill was soon in demand as a leader for such discussions. It was to one of these groups that Bill gave a lengthy series of lectures on a number of theological topics; from this there evolved the widely read *Layman's Guide to Protestant Theology*. His interchange with these learned Quakers and the feedback he received contributed enormously to the clarity of the book and to its success. This book also brought Bill one of his prized letters – from an elderly woman who had once been Niebuhr's Sunday School teacher. In it, she said that she had been certain she would die before she understood what her pupil was saying; now, however, she had found it interpreted in a way that made it clear to her.

In the fifties and sixties, various theological trends vied for attention. These furnished the material for a number of articles, for the *case* books, *New Directions*, and more. The controversy aroused by the *God is Dead* movement came and went. Another theme was gaining his deeper attention. At Swarthmore Bill was the lonely theologian on staff, and he was placed in the philosophy department. His interest was evoked in the frequent discussions of the place and role of language in philosophical discourse. That stimulus remained with him after his move to Garrett in Evanston, Illinois, in 1957. There the philosophers were members of the Northwestern faculty. The result – *Speaking of God*, a book which I had a tough time reading, both in first draft and in galley. This work was well received.

Bill was elected President of the Lutheran Theological Seminary, Saskatoon, Saskatchewan in 1965, and assumed that office in 1966. The most vital trend in the period thereafter was that of the *Theology of Hope*. One summer was devoted to the writing of a book on this subject, but before it was completed, Bill decided that enough had been written on the topic. That manuscript rests in his files.

The *Laymen's Guide* needed revising and the arduous business of bringing it up to date became Bill's next task. That was accomplished and the text is still selling well. His efforts to change its title to *Layperson's Guide* proved fruitless. The last volume, *Experience and Faith*, is a book intended to speak to the lively interest in our time of the place of experience in one's own religious life.

I have not mentioned one book up to this point; it is out of place in the sequence since it is not the last of the books Bill has had published. *"The Grace Book"*, as we call *'Living by Grace'* in our family, is very special to each of us, and to those who know Bill as a person. It is not a trend book nor is it an interpretation of current theology. *This is Bill's own book, born out of his faith, an expression of the Christian way of life as he sees it and an expression of the way he lives.* Grace makes every person equal and wishes each and every person to be treated with respect and dignity. Those who have come to Bill for help have never been turned away. "Talking it over with Dad" is a way of life for his children. This book was dedicated to his only brother, Bob, who died in 1974. They were brothers and friends.

What will come next? A volume on the many aspects of liberation theology? A history of seminary trends from 1966-1985? A book of sermons? Whatever it is, this layperson will be receptive.

Thank you Bill,
for sharing your career with me
as you have with all your students;
Thank you, too,
for all the enrichment this has brought to us;
Thank you
for being you.

THE QUESTION OF GOD AND THE TRINITY
Carl E. Braaten

I. THE RELIGIOUS QUESTION

The common opinion is that God and religion go together, that they belong to the same subject matter. When Dietrich Bonhoeffer prophesied in his prison cell that religion was dying in the modern secular age, many believers prayed to God it would not be so. In previous ages people understood that religion was normative in human life. Prophets and priests, emperors and plebians lived within the same religious world-view. Only a rare fool or village idiot dared to say there is no God. But now fools and idiots seem to be legion, and many of them are tenured professors in our most prestigious universities.

It was not so long ago that atheism emerged within the space of Christian theology. Personally I spent quite a few days on university campuses debating the proposition of Christian atheism with the "Death of God" theologians. I enjoyed it very much, because I had always detected a certain "death of God" streak within my own experience. In my earliest days of theological study, I was stunned by the Ritschlian aphorism: "If I were not a Christian, I would be an atheist." The "gods" of all the natural theologies had died in my experience, but still I was a Christian. If that happened to me, coming from a world of humanistic rather than scientific studies, I could imagine that perhaps millions of modern people no longer had any vivid sense of the *mysterium tremendum et fascinosum* (R. Otto).

Apologetics is one of the major tasks of the Christian theologian. However, apologetics is a very odd business. In the nineteenth century, Friedrich Schleiermacher, whom Karl Barth called the "father of modern Protestant theology," defended Christianity by showing how "religious" it is. In contrast, in the twentieth century those following Bonhoeffer tried to defend the Christian faith by showing how thoroughly "secular" it can be. Bonhoeffer was influenced by Karl Barth, who claimed that the essence of Christianity, contrary to Schleiermacher's view, has nothing to do with religion. It is a matter of sheer revelation. When I was in my twenties, nurtured by the teachings of the great theologians, I first learned to despise religion. Although I had grown up on a mission field, and observed first-hand many abominations of religion, I had been taught the difference between true and false religion. Of course, without question my teachers taught me that Christianity was the true religion, all others being false and leading to perdition. But now it was Christian theologians of the stature of Barth and Bonhoeffer who were saying that religion itself was false, just one of the "Golden Calves" or "Towers of Babel" that the biblical prophets and the Protestant Reformers had tried to demolish. But we were assured that we had nothing to lose! In exchange for human religion, we would get divine revelation. With one blow we could shatter the alliance between Christianity and religion in a secular age, and thus with good apologetic intent preserve a place for Christianity beyond the reach of the modern scientific criticism of experience, reason, history, morality, society, nature or anything else that might previously have served as a point of contact for the Christian religion. The uniquely Christian access to God is invulnerable to all post-Enlightenment criticisms, because the essence of Christianity is a matter of sheer revelation.

There was an internal connection between the Barthian theology of pure revelation and the "Death of God" theology. Both asserted that Christianity lies totally beyond religion. For the Barthians the essence of a Christianity beyond religion was the pure revelation of God; for the "Death of God" theologians it was an authentic morality for a secular age. Now the "Death of God" controversy is over, and there seem to be few takers for a pure Barthian theology of trans-religious revelation. Nevertheless, we are still left with the same questions. How do we confront God in modern secular society? Where do we meet God in our common human world? Do we not all live as practical atheists, conducting our everyday business "as though God did not exist?" Having lost the innocence of adolescent humanity, do we not live in an age of the "broken myth" (Tillich), understanding the word "God" to be perhaps a mythological expression of a profoundly existential event like "love?" One German theologian called this event *"Mitmenschlichkeit"* (H. Braun). Have we not complained, with Gabriel Vahanian and others, that our modern technological culture has performed a kind of lobotomy on our capacity for God, which explains why so many people are romantically dabbling in the Eastern cults? Even serious theologians have talked about the "eclipse of God" or the "silence of God" or the "sacred void." All of these things are signs that the problem of God has become acute in our time.

As a Lutheran I responded to the problem of the "death of God" in terms of Luther's idea of the "hidden God" (*deus absconditus*). I felt some empathy for a generation that was raising the question of God from an experience of God's absence. Somewhere along the line I had been taught that the experience of God's absence does not mean that God is not present. God may be anonymously present within the universal structures of life, whether we feel it or not. God may be known as the hidden drive within people to do justice, whether they like to or not. God may be exerting a pressure "behind the backs" of all persons and institutions to secure the common good, against their own interests. God may be acting on the demands of conscience without our acknowledgement of their ground and source in him. God may be working as a driving force behind the demand which human beings make on each other in every social situation. This is the point that Gustaf Wingren makes in stressing the first article of the creed, belief in God the Creator of all things. This creed does not mean that once upon a time God created things; it means rather that God is now hiddenly at work in our natural life, that God is the directing power at work in our everyday encounters, that God meets us under the guise of masks, and not face to face. There is no escape from God, from the hidden God anonymously at work behind the backs of all the secular structures that seem to live and move and have their being without mediating any direct experience of God. Luther's idea of the "hidden God" had come to my rescue during the controversy over the "death of God," but of course it is not sufficient by itself. I saw this as at best a partial answer, which must drive theologians to re-open the question of God in a thoroughgoing way.

II.   THE QUESTION OF GOD

The first thing that seems to have become clear is that the question of God is a religious one, and that the attempt to salvage God-talk on the basis of pure revelation from above, while surrendering the category of religious experience, has proved to be a failure. Whatever else Christianity may be, it is at least a religion among the religions of the world. The case for Christianity must be made within a theology of the religions, and cannot exempt itself from the critical scientific study of religious phenomena.

A second thing that seems to be clear is that Bonhoeffer's prophecy of the end of religion in a secular age seems to have miscarried. We can say about the obituaries on religion what Mark Twain once quipped: "The reports of my death have been grossly exaggerated." I can imagine that when the ruins of our civilization are uncovered a few thousand years from now, the archaeologists will be saying: "Those twentieth century people were nuts about their religion. Look at all the wars they fought in the name of religion. And consider the millions of dollars they must have spent on their crystal cathedrals."

A third point is that an enlightened criticism of religion, whether in the line of Comte, Feuerbach, Marx, or Freud, does not guarantee its demise. We might paraphrase Whitehead's statement about metaphysics, "The only alternative to religion is bad religion." The reason for this is that religion cannot die, although it can appear in many forms. The reason religion cannot die is that it springs from the nature of human being in the world. The core of the religious question lies at the heart of the human self. It is not the case that a human being merely asks religious questions, or that only some people ask religious questions of no interest to others. This is not the case because religion is a structural dimension of human existence. The root of the religious question lies in the heuristic character of human being, for religion arises on the boundary between question and answer.

What is the question? The truly religious question? This is the question of the ultimate meaning and aim of human existence. Statements and symbols about God function to answer questions concerning the nature of ultimate reality. Through analysis of the human subject it can be shown that humans do strive to transcend all the givens of empirical reality, to discover what lies beyond the limits of human existence. Analogously, just as humans inquire into the meaning of their own existence, they also inevitably inquire into the meaning of the world as such. Every science deals with only a part of the whole of reality. No science can deal with it all. Theology, in the sense of *logos* of *theos*, can be defined as that mode of inquiry which goes beyond partial meanings, seeking an answer to the question of the final and total meaning of all events in the world of nature and history. Can it not be shown that the human spirit is inherently concerned, not only about its own interior meaning, but also about the totality of meaning? Does not the human spirit transcend in an infinite direction every partial disclosure of meaning, not only in the realm of religious experience, but in the world at large? The religious quest for God is meaningful within the framework of the ongoing process of inquiry into the transcendental conditions of the possibility of meaning in human life and of the world as such. Wherever this inquiry into meaning is stifled, as in countries where Marxist socialism is in control of things, the religious quest itself is thwarted.

The kind of inquiry we are referring to may be called a "new style of natural theology." This kind of theology stops short of claiming to possess definitive knowledge of God and his will unto salvation, on which the life of faith, hope and love can be based. But it does ground the meaning of the idea of God in the structures of common human experience. It is starting theology "from below," from the side of the human subject inquiring into the possibilities of meaning in existence and history. It does not begin "from above," from the sheer assertion of a positive revelatory datum blitzing us like a bolt of lightning.

Speaking of a "new style of natural theology" requires a word of contrast with a presumable "old style." The "old style" would attempt to arrive at a definite description of the real internal constitution of God, proceeding inferentially from what lies within our human world of experience and knowledge to the nature and attributes of God as such. The Harvard theologian, Gordon Kaufman, has written the following verdict on this approach: "It is not only logically dubious to attempt to speak of God on the basis of a 'natural theology'; it seems strangely archaic as well. Such an approach is both irrelevant to the situation of modern man, and theologically misguided. To *this* man, God must *reveal* himself if he is to be known at all."[1] I agree with Kaufman's objection to the "old style of natural theology." In classical natural theology virtually everything contained in the first article of the creed would be established: that there is a God, that God has created, governs, and preserves all things, and that many of God's attributes of power and glory can be known from the Book of Nature. But, of course, it is conceded that all this natural knowledge of God does not lead to the supernatural mysteries of faith. For such knowledge the Book of Holy Scripture is requisite.

It is a long story, but ever since the critical epistemology of Immanuel Kant, the confidence in reason's capacity to know so much about God has been severely shaken. We humans live within the limits of our finitude, in a kind of prison. We can bump against those limits, kicking and screaming for all we are worth. It's as though we had wings to fly like a bird out the window, but we cannot escape. We know about these limits, and we are bound to dream about what lies beyond, and long for passage, but we can not really know the infinite reality outside our finite world. We know only that we must ask about it, and we long for real knowledge about the nature of the reality that lies beyond. We can make statements about our limits, but we do not really know thereby the nature of the One who sets those limits. We do not know God unless and until he reveals himself under the conditions of these very limits.

It is not only on account of modern skepticism and secularism that we would question the older approach of natural theology, but also because the "God" of natural theology and the living God of Israel are not on friendly terms. Very early among the Church Fathers some difficulty was detected in equating the God of metaphysical theory with the God of Christian worship. Although I cannot subscribe Blaise Pascal's formula: "The God of Abraham, Isaac, and Jacob is not the God of the philosophers," their simple identification is equally problematic. There will never be a negotiated peace between Jerusalem and Athens. I would expect the quest for a settlement to continue, and an occasional more or less successful attempt at a workable coalition between metaphysics and faith. In the present situation I would opt for a theological coalition with a philosophy that helps to formulate the question of God in the most meaningful way. It is a form of anthropology oriented to religious questions and the quest for God. But it seems dubious to me that one could reach a satisfactory answer from this side of the question. Starting with natural theology, one may reach for God and grasp an idol, or seek the Ground and land in the Void.

The "Myth of Sisyphus" depicts human beings as condemned to strive for the top. Augustine said that "Our hearts are restless until they find their rest in God." Christian doctrine asserts that human beings are made in the "image of God." Godwardness is built into the shape of human existence. The religions are filled with stories and symbols of what it is like on "the other side." Human beings are on a journey to where the gods live. That may be the kingdom of heaven in Jesus' message, or it may be Olympus, Empyrium, Atlantis, Elysium, Valhalla, Nirvana, or some other place that promises human fulfillment. The logic at work behind all these stories and symbols is what Tillich calls the "negation of the negative." This is coupled with the "analogical imagination" (David Tracy) which posits the positive. The history and phenomenology of the religions confront us with a myriad of conflicting images, symbols, metaphors, stories, legends, and myths about the nature of the reality above and beyond the realm of earthly life. What are the criteria by which we can discern which of these ways of telling the story of God is most meaningful and true for us today?

III. THE CRITERION OF CHRIST

The Christian tradition has unanimously pointed to the event of Jesus the Christ as the answer to the question of where God has revealed himself in a definitive way. Jesus of Nazareth is the person in whom the promises of the God of Israel intersect with the human quest for meaning and fulfillment. There are many "Gods" in the pantheon of the world's religions. For Christians Jesus is the One who identifies the God of Israel as his Father. The identity of God is revealed in the history of Israel and the person of Jesus. The question of who and what and where God is in the world is answered by his self-identification in Jesus Christ. For Christian believers, even though the classical proofs for the existence of God seem unnecessary and the media of a general revelation of God seem less transparent than they presumably used to, the identity of God and his will for humanity are revealed in a unique and definitive way in Jesus of Nazareth. The Christian doctrine of God stands or falls with his self-revelation in Jesus of Nazareth. Jesus Christ is the sole medium through whom God reveals himself as the finally valid answer to the question of which God in a world of putative gods we are prepared to worship and trust regarding our future hope and destiny. Jesus the Messiah is for us the exclusive medium of the divine self-revelation and the decisive event of salvation. He is the One in whom the final destiny of each individual and the ultimate future of all reality are represented. And since Jesus is the revelation of God's true self-identity, we do not look for another such revelation. Jesus is unique —the one and only eschatological communication of the true identity of God.

Since we can no longer identify God by way of natural theology, and the leading symbols of other religions have gained no power over us, we must come to the Father through Jesus of Nazareth. Jesus' God will be our God, or we will simply have no clear focus for our ongoing quest for God. If we bring our question of God to Jesus of Nazareth, we may let him show us the Father. "He that hath seen me hath seen the Father." Jesus Immanuel represents God to us. Jesus defined God for us in acts and words that declared the coming of the kingdom of God. God's kingdom is not something outside himself; rather, the being of God is identical with the power and glory of his coming rule. After the events of Easter and Pentecost the communities founded by the apostles became convinced that the kingdom of God was present and active in the ministry of Jesus in a unique way. The powers of the kingdom in the person, acts and sayings of Jesus constitute a real presence and union of God with him. None of the contemporaries of the historical Jesus called him "God," not even his closest disciples, but in the light of Easter and within the matrix of worship the confession of the Godhood of Jesus came to be made.

The classical Christian doctrine of God developed the kind of christological connection we have been pointing out in the dogma of the incarnation, as this was formulated at the Councils of Nicaea and Chalcedon. Within the last decade we have witnessed an attack on the principle of christocentricity in the doctrine of God. James Gustafson[2], John Hick[3], Paul Knitter[4], Gene TeSelle[5], Tom Driver[6], and a growing list of others have mounted a vigorous attack on the christocentric principle. They allege that this christocentric impulse has made the God of the universe and of the world's religions too Semitic, historically limited, and anthropocentric. The pendulum has swung from the Jesus-centered death-of-God theology of a decade ago to a God-centered Jesus-is-dead theology of today. They call it a "Copernican revolution in theology." They count as their older ally H. Richard Niebuhr's attack on every "unitarianism of the second article." Christocentricity is allegedly incompatible with the "radical monotheism" of biblical faith. It allegedly makes of Christ a "second God" alongside the One God behind the universe of faiths, and it turns a "mere man" into an object of faith and worship. Tom Driver, pulling out all stops, refers to the Christ-centeredness of classical Christianity as "Christofascism." The revolution called for would put God back into the center of the cosmos and the universe of religions, thus dislodging Christ from the central position he has held in the old Ptolemaic scheme of things. Away with the narrow anachronistic parochialism which links the special self-revelation of God and the salvation of the world to the event of Jesus the Christ! Only then will Christianity be able to get on to the super-highway of ecumenical openness, theological pluralism, and inter-religious dialogue.

In my view the underlying premise of this attack on christocentricity is the old axiom: *finitum non capax infiniti*. (The finite is not capable of the infinite). God is supposedly too big and too busy to focus on humanity with all the passion and power of his innermost self. The old Lutheran formula, *finitum capax infiniti*, gave philosophical utterance to Luther's theology of the cross (*theologia crucis*). The old squabble between Lutherans and Calvinists on the real presence of Christ in the Holy Sacrament eventually became a christological issue with metaphysical implications for the doctrine of God. That old squabble is now reappearing under new guise.

Those who attack the christocentric line in theology from Luther to Schleiermacher and Barth hold as their first premise a definition of the infinite God as metaphysically incapable of expressing himself in a revelationally and soteriologically definitive way in the one finite particular event of Jesus the Christ.[7] They are hooked on an unexamined metaphysical *a priori* that links them to the Reformed principle: *finitum non capax infiniti*. One of these attackers asks whether the very concept of an incarnate being who is both fully God and fully man is really intelligible. Of course not, because after all, the finite is not capable of the infinite. Another is troubled by the idea of the incarnation, because it is intellectually impossible to make the ontological equation: Jesus equals God. There can be, it is assumed, no ontologically real incarnation and hypostatic union of God in his personal essence and human nature. Yet, most of these attackers make one concession. Even though the ontological linkage between God and Jesus is broken, there is nothing wrong for Christians to continue in their personal piety and worship to go on speaking of Jesus Christ "as if he were God for us." This is a renewal of the *"als ob"* philosophy of the nineteenth century, and recently David Tracy has reverted to it with his reference to Jesus Christ as the "supreme fiction."

When the linkage between the reality of God and the history of Jesus is shattered, as in this recent dyscarnational christology, the result is clear. A claim is being made that we can gain access to the true knowledge of God *outside* of his self-definition in the person of Jesus. The Word of God is *extra carnem Christi*, not totally embodied in the flesh and blood of Jesus. This flesh-less Word can freely roam the universe with only an occasional incidental connection to the Jew from Nazareth.

Luther once said that the author of the Fourth Gospel was not a Platonist but an evangelist. The metaphysical assumption of the new anti-christologists is Platonist or Neo-Platonist. Their underlying difficulty with the incarnational union of infinite and finite is the grace-less and face-less absolute of Hellenistic metaphysics, which found it ontologically impossible to live and move and have its being in history, in human form, in a state of humiliation. The metaphysical absolute of Hellenistic philosophy would never be caught dead in the person of Jesus and his destiny on the cross.

But what if God is not a prisoner of such a metaphysical strait jacket?! Luther said that God reveals himself *sub contrario*. The infinite is capable of the finite; it happened in the incarnation. It is not metaphysical nonsense but dialectical truth that the Infinite would mediate itself though the finite, life through death, light through darkness, victory through defeat. The timeless metaphysics of Hellenistic philosophy must be revised on the basis of biblical revelation. Then the history of Jesus becomes the key to the biography of God. The God of the gospel is capable of an intrinsic openness to the identity, attributes, and experiences of human being in the world, and this is neither conceptually unintelligible nor ontologically impossible.

IV. CHRISTOCENTRIC TRINITARIANISM

On the basis of christology a thorough revision of the doctrine of God will liberate it still further from the Greek metaphysical husks which accompanied the patristic development of the Trinitarian dogma. Diametrically opposed to the anti-christological trend is a movement to continue the Barthian initiative toward a new affirmation of the Trinity on the basis of christology. There are new books on the Trinity by Jüngel[8], Moltmann[9] and Jenson.[10] They represent a significant advance to a new conception of the Trinity, precisely at a time when most other theologians have raised the white flag of surrender. It is a regrettable fact that many theologians look upon the Trinity as a piece of moribund speculation, following Harnack's verdict in his *History of Dogma* that the trinitarian dogma is a product of the Hellenization of Christianity. The new theologies of the Trinity argue that so far from being a mere "memory-aid" to organize various topics of Christian belief (Schleiermacher's approach), the root of the Trinity doctrine lies in biblical soil, in the economy of divine revelation and salvation. The Trinity is an indispensable and integral part of the Christian apprehension of God, not an arbitrary set of symbols intending to say something else more fundamental. Trinitarian thinking is required by the ways in which God has revealed himself in the economy of salvation.

The doctrine of the Trinity, so essential to a positive understanding of Christian faith, serves also as a critique of various forms of mystical, philosophical, political and moralistic monotheism. Christian faith is not bound to a "radical monotheism," as H.R. Niebuhr misleadingly held. Instead, it stands for a trinitarian monotheism. I agree completely with Moltmann, who states in *The Crucified God*: "Christianity cannot be represented as a 'monotheistic form of belief' (Schleiermacher). Christian faith is not 'radical monotheism.' As a theology of the cross, Christian theology is the criticism of and liberation from philosophical and political monotheism."[11]

Only a new formulation of the Trinity can make clear the identity and nature of the biblical God, the God of the gospel and of Christian faith. This new formulation calls for the death of some ancient assumptions about God. The God of the great patristic synthesis had to be impassible and immutable. This was an assumption taken over from the metaphysical monotheism of Greek philosophical thought. The God of the gospel, in contrast, is one who suffers. Bonhoeffer put it so succinctly: "Only a suffering God can help."

Process theism has also challenged the patristic idea of the divine metaphysical attributes of impassibility and immutability, and calls upon the philosophy of A.N. Whitehead to make its case for the primacy of the category of becoming in God. However, the approach of process theology has led to a di-polar concept of God, and makes its identification of God apart from trinitarian dialectics. This is because for process theology the event of Jesus Christ is not constitutive of our knowledge of God, but is at best its exemplification. Only after it gets its doctrine of God rolling, does process thought at a later stage begin to worry about the sense of specifically Christian symbolism, so that Christology and Trinity appear as addenda to a theistic metaphysics. The approach of genuinely trinitarian thinkers moves in the oppositive direction. Pannenberg has said: "Wherever philosophical concepts are taken over, they must be remolded in the light of the history-shaping freedom of the biblical God."[12] Pannenberg has not yet written a full-scale doctrine of the Trinity, but the suggestions he has made so far indicate that he will be part of the movement to revise and renew trinitarian theology. I am convinced that this is the right direction to go in dealing with the most pressing theological question of who and what we are prepared to name God.

Why the Trinity, after all? The reason is that the identity of God is not separable from the integrity of his actions. We do not look for the inner nature of God in some remote sphere above and beyond the structure of his operations in and upon the world. A theology that begins its doctrine of God with trinitarian dialectics is a way of speaking faithfully of the God of the gospel of Good Friday and Easter Sunday.

The implications of trinitarian revisionism will be far-reaching. The political implications of trinitarian dialectics can be vastly different from the hierarchical relations presided over by the Sovereign Monad of the various unitarianisms. The God of the gospel is no comfortable being assigned a role at the top of the Constantinian pyramid, in which every class has its place and every person his/her task, promoting both an authoritarian and a class-structured society.

I believe that Luther's theology of the cross has awakened the imagination to discover new dimensions in the doctrine of God. The triune God and the crucified Jesus belong together. The identification of God with the crucified Jesus drives theology to be serious about the trinitarian distinctions in God as Father, Son, and Holy Spirit. Then it no longer makes sense to speak of God in a simple untrinitarian way. It is the Son, Jesus of Nazareth, who suffers and dies on the cross. But the Father suffers with him. And for this reason there is some truth to the old heresy "Patripassianism." We may speak of an infinite grief of the Father in the death of his Son, and this is a form of suffering just as intense as the suffering of dying.

One of the most difficult aspects of the doctrine of God is the relation between theodicy and Trinity. How can we think about God and evil at the same time? What should we do about evil? Should we take care of it by putting it in God himself? Should we say that not only the potentiality of evil comes from God as the source of all power, but all the actuality of evil itself is somehow contained in God? Thinking of the horrors of modern times, Moltmann, says, "Even Auschwitz is in God himself."[13] Personally, I do not have any way of knowing that. Those who cry out from the graveyards of death make it seem rather that history is left with an open wound that has not yet been closed. I see a trinitarian theology of the cross as a defense against any solution to the problem of evil that ends with the mystification of real history and a theology of glory.

KARL BARTH, JUERGEN MOLTMANN AND THE THEOPASCHITE REVOLUTION

Ronald Goetz

Theologically ours has been the century of the suffering of God—the Theopaschite Century. The rejection of the ancient doctrine of divine impassiblity and immutability among contemporary theologians has become epidemic. Apart from certain conservative defenders of older theological traditions, the vast majority of constructive theologians, silently or noisily, as the case may be, have throughout the century been abandoning the traditional view. Just as significant perhaps is the fact, even among those theologians who proving the rule by being exceptions to it have not embraced modern Theopaschism, that there has failed to develop a creative, modern restatement of the older dogma.[1]

The Theopaschite Revolution has occurred across all major denominational lines. Protestant, Catholic, and even Eastern Orthodox theologians of the highest importance have, in their own ways, contributed to its triumph. Nor is the revolution restricted to any school of theology; liberals and neo-orthodox find a curious coalescence at this point. Figures as diverse as Karl Barth and Alfred North Whitehead converge for a moment at the point of divine suffering before turning away once again in violently opposing directions. If there has been an emergent "orthodoxy" in our century, it lies in the new consensus that God suffers.[2]

The theological implications of the Theopaschite Revolution for Christianity are enormous. Every classical Christian doctrine—the Trinity, the two natures of Christ, creation *ex nihilo*, the atonement theories, sin (original or otherwise), predestination, etc.—was originally formulated by theologians who took divine impassibility to be axiomatic. Certainly, mainstream Protestantism inherited the orthodox tradition on the presupposition of God's impassible sovereignty. Even Luther, who in his theology of the cross affirmed the suffering of God even unto death, seemed to take back much of what he gave in his equally foundational doctrines of predestination and the *Deus Absconditus*. When contemplating the deterministic purposing of the hidden God, Luther portrayed an inscrutably impassible divine sovereignty which was even more severe than that of Calvin.

17

Eighteenth and nineteenth century liberalism, which generally rejected or radically reinterpreted the orthodox tradition, was also, with few exceptions (Hegel chief among them), under the sway of the dogma of divine impassibility. As Karl Barth, observed "The God of Schleiermacher cannot show mercy"[3]. There can be no suffering where there is no mercy.

Given the rejection of this century's old dogma, the task of contemporary theology must be to recast every Christian doctrine in the light of the modern assumption that God's being is a suffering being. No classical doctrine can look quite the same once the impassibility dogma is rejected. How can such a 180° turn on an assumption so basic to our understanding of God's very nature not cause a refocusing of every theological utterance? Generally, however, modern theologians who have committed themselves to the doctrine of divine passibility have done so on a piecemeal basis, without full recognition of the vast difference for the whole theological "language game" that this one move must make.[4]

However, Whiteheadian theologians cannot be faulted for having failed to provide a systematic reinterpretation of Christianity. The Whiteheadian metaphysic, grounded as it is in a concept of a limited deity, entails an inevitable rejection of the Almighty God of the Old Testament and creation ex nihilo. A full-blown Christology and the entire panoply of Christian doctrine (Trinity, Two Natures, Atonement, Election, Eternal Life, etc.) that flows from the event of Jesus Christ is rendered mere mythology by the rationalist side of Whitehead's thought. It is little wonder that in offering its version of the theological tradition (as the very salvation of Christianity from itself unto the modern world!) the Whiteheadian school should find it necessary to provide its alternative account of Christian theology across the board. For the burden of proof is on the process theologian to prove that Whitehead, in spite of the fact that he himself did not embrace Christianity, can nevertheless be best understood as a good and faithful servant of the Lord Jesus Christ.

From the more "orthodox" side clearly the century's most far reaching and monumental attempt consistently to work out the implications of the suffering, indeed the self-emptying—the kenosis (Phil. 2:17)—of God for every aspect of Christian doctrine is to be found in the Church Dogmatics of Karl Barth. As Donald G. Dawe observes:

> In Barth's theology, Kenosis assumes its place as a major motif of Christian Faith . . . Barth has grasped more clearly than any of his contempories the basic and all-pervasive importance of Kenosis in Christian revelation.[5]

For Barth, God does not suffer vis-à-vis the world because he is limited and cannot not suffer. Divine suffering is the result of a deliberate determination of the Almighty God who loves in freedom. It's precisely his insistence that both creation and redemption are free acts of God's self-emptying, even "self-humiliation," which marks Barth's irreconcilable difference from the Whiteheadian conception of a limited deity. For Whitehead God is ontologically, indeed congenitally, limited. For Barth, God is ontologically the Almighty Lord, who in loving freedom limits, or better, humbles Himself for the sake of His creation.

Karl Barth began his career in a deliberate attempt to foment a theological revolution which centered in his rediscovery of the awful sovereignty of God. Thus, the twentieth century revolution began by Barth might hardly seem to fit the revolution that this paper describes. In the *Letter to the Romans* God was portrayed as the "wholly other," as "death" and even as "the enemy." Commenting on Paul's statement of God's "everlasting power and divinity," Barth declared:

> ... and what does this mean but that we know nothing of God, that we are not God, that the Lord is to be feared. Herein lies His pre-eminence over all Gods; and this is that which makes him out as God, as Creator, and as Redeemer.[6]

It is God's sovereign "everlasting" power which gives Him pre-eminence over "all gods"; i.e., the false gods of human idolatry. The early Barth's vision of divine sovereignty might have appeared to lead to a hyper-Reformation sense of impassible divine determinism and double predestination.

By the time Barth began his *Church Dogmatics*, his sense of divine sovereignty was undergoing a radical change. Not that Barth would ever mitigate his affirmation of the utter majesty of God, but he came to hold that there is a greater sovereignty than the sovereignty of an imperious potentate; i.e., the sovereignty of a God who can even risk suffering at the hands of His creatures. God's "self-humiliation" becomes the first factor in the light of which "all the predicates of his Godhead" are to "be filled out and interpreted." The later Barth will say that it is in the light of God's self-humiliation that the "false gods" are revealed in their falseness. This is a far cry from his contention in *Romans* that God's claim to "pre-eminence over all gods" lies in the utter superiority of His power over our puny power—as if there were a contest.

> It is in the light of the fact of His humiliation that on this first aspect all the predicates of His Godhead, must be filled out and interpreted. Their positive meaning is lit up only by the fact that in this act He is this God and therefore the true God, distinguished from all false gods by the fact that they are not capable of this act, that they have not in fact accomplished it, that their supposed glory and honour and eternity and omnipotence not only do not include but exclude their self-humiliation. False gods are all reflections of a false and all too human

19

self-exaltation. They are all lords who cannot and will not be servants, who are therefore no true lords, whose being is not a truly divine being.[7]

If we are right in the contention that the most basic theological revolution of the twentieth century is the movement toward divine passibility, then Paul Tillich and others are wrong in contending that in Barth's movement from *Romans* to the *Dogmatics*, "Barthianism" underwent a shift from a revolutionary to a conservative, not to say a reactionary, stance.[8] In fact, the *Dogmatics* constituted a work of genuinely revolutionary import whereas in the *Romans* period Barth was still working with an older, indeed, philosophic concept of God's sovereignty, as he himself admits.

One can better appreciate the reluctance of the theology of past centuries to affirm the suffering of God if one considers the pitfalls that the doctrine faces in the contemporary situation. American theology, for example, has flirted with such grotesque parodies of Theopaschite faith as the Christian atheism of the "God is dead" movement and is presently much impressed by the attempt to which we've already referred—to pass off a limited deity as if such could be God.

Barth's greatest notoriety came when, in his attempt to avoid such theological disasters, his thought focused on negation, e.g., his attack on natural theology and apologetics, his Feuerbachian philosophy of religion, his purely theologically grounded oposition to Hitler. Only by first saying "no" to the dictates of the modern *Zeitgeist*, "no" to the anthropocentrism and ethnocentrism of "modern man," could the suffering of God be affirmed without its slipping into a call for atheism or the curious presumptuousness of a rationalistic reconstruction of Deity.

The widespread enthusiasm with which the English speaking theological audience embraced the "new" Barth of the *Humanity of God* was revealing in two ways. One, it indicated the degree to which in one form or another the Theopaschite Revolution was already a *fait à complet*. Two, in this general acceptance there was a tacit acknowledgment that Barth's supposedly newborn concept of God was acceptable only if the discomfort and pain of its delivery could be avoided. However, Barth's theology could only say "yes" the way it finally did, because it had established its prior "no." Further, the *Humanity of God* would be merely an aborted fragment, wholly without viability, if it were not supported by the fundamental theological undergirding of the *Church Dogmatics* and Barth's *kenotic* reinterpretation of such seminal Christian doctrines as the Trinity, Revelation, Predestination, Creation, and Redemption.

Barth's theological radicalism is often not noticed. If, for example, one gives too much emphasis to his often nearly fundamentalist approach to Scripture, his irritating "revelational positivism," or if one misconstrues his constant dialogue with and appreciation for the orthodox tradition, one could indeed interpret him as merely a maddeningly resourceful reactionary and his theology finally as a mere "*tour de force*." But this would fail to see that though Barth's appreciation of orthodoxy is genuine, his intimate use of it is finally in order to turn it on its head by changing the basic axis of every doctrine from divine impassibility to divine self-humiliation.

For example, Barth the Protestant partisan, the self-styled Calvinist, interprets the atoning death of Christ and the God's eternal decree kenotically, and thus, in the very teeth of Luther and Calvin: "Man is not rejected. In God's eternal purpose it is God Himself who is rejected in this Son . . . Predestination means that from all eternity God has determined upon man's acquital at his own cost"[9]. Such a reinterpretation of the saving import of the Christian faith from double predestination to a theology of divine suffering and sufferance which borders on universal salvation constitutes by itself, even if Barth had written only this, a drastic turning from the terrible inscrutability of the God of Luther and Calvin whose sovereign decree or secret will is shrouded in a mystery of awful darkness.

This movement toward a universalistic understanding of God's saving intention is certainly not original; it reflects the generous spirit of the very liberalism against which Barth so long contended. However, liberalism had claimed that the only way to affirm the universalism of God's love was to reject the orthodox tradition. For orthodoxy had long since seemed to exclude the universal self-giving love of God by its portrayals of the dark side of God's inscrutable will. Consider its doctrine of predestination, or its seeming celebration of the terrible wrath of God visited on his Son as that wrath is implicit in the classical substitutionary doctrine of the atonement. Liberalism's horror at the ferocity of the orthodox version of God's impassible exercise of His purpose, together with its rationalism and skepticism *vis à vis* the Trinity, the Incarnation, etc., lead liberalism to leave orthodoxy for dead.

Barth saw that only by coming to terms with the whole orthodox tradition, only by an interpretative reaffirmation of the Trinity, Incarnation, the Atonement, and even Predestination, could the generous concerns of liberalism be given a Biblical and, indeed, a rational grounding. Without such a revelational orientation, the liberal spirit has no foundation in divine reality. It is left hanging in the air by its speculative anthopocentrism. Barth in one bold stroke radically changed but a single fundamental orthodox assumption, a philosophic assumption imported from orthodoxy without Biblical foundation—divine impassibility, and in so doing he so drastically altered orthodox Christianity that that which resulted was neither orthodoxy nor liberalism. It became the most far reaching statement to date of Theopaschite Christian theology.

Juergen Moltmann has gained much of his reputation as a theologian from efforts to push Barth beyond himself unto a more radical working out of the implications of God's suffering relationship to the world. Clearly Moltmann, as a post-Barthian theologian, is radically indebted to Barth for his Biblically oriented Christocentric, Trinitarian, and, indeed, *Kenotic* theological perspective. Nevertheless, Moltmann contends that the Barthian stress on God's primordial sovereignty renders the Trinity merely a revelation of God's changeless eternity. This in turn precludes a recognition of the historical and eschatological character of God's being (*Theology of Hope*); it makes it impossible adequately to ground the cross of Jesus Christ in the very Being of God (*The Crucified God*); and finally it gives expression to a "nominalist," virtually totalitarianist version of the freedom of God (*The Trinity and the Kingdom*).

Although I have many reservations concerning Moltmann's theological program, I confess to sharing his fundamental instinct that despite his theology of the divine *kenosis*, Barth holds back from drawing the radical historical and eschatological conclusions such a theology logically entails. However, the root cause of Barth's hesitancy before the full logic of *kenosis* cannot be properly located in his doctrine of the Immanent Trinity, as Moltmann supposses.[10] In the final section of this paper I will try to show, over against Moltmann, that Barth's emphasis on the freedom of the one God in his doctrine of the Immanent Trinity is a necessary emphasis for a theology of divine *kenosis*. Indeed, in his refusal consistently to push his teaching on the divine *kenosis* into history and eschatology, Barth has to that extent turned away from the full logic of his doctrine of the Immanent Trinity.

For Moltmann, Barth's doctrine of the Immanent Trinity entails such a radically monotheistic conception of God that is in fact closer to a philosophic theism than it is to genuine trinitarianism[11]. Moltmann argues that Barth's unwillingness to speak of the "persons" of the Godhead, preferring the non-personal phrase "modes of being," reveals the typical "modalistic" tendency of Western Christianity[12]. It cannot be denied that for Barth the personhood of God is singular, as the eternal Trinity is "posited" in an act of free will by the one God. God wills His own nature as love; He wills eternally not to be alone, but to be the Father of the Son, and as such He generates forth "the Spirit of Love."[13]

Moltmann contends that such a doctrine renders the Triune love of God an act of simple divine will, which in turn entails that the sovereign will of the one person of God is ontologically prior to His Triune being. Thus, Moltmann argues that Barth, in spite of his "defining God as 'the One who loves in freedom,' " sees God's primordial nature as His free, essentially autocratic sovereignty and not His love. In radical opposition Moltmann argues that the Father generates the Son out of the demands of His nature, not by virtue of the freedom of His will.

The generation and birth of the Son came from the Father's *nature*, not from His will. That is why we talk

22

about the *eternal* generation and birth of the Son. "The Father begets and bears the Son out of the necessity of His being".[14]

Moltmann insists that there cannot be eternal love in God without relationship, and there can be no relationship without there being genuine persons who are *in* relationship. "Love cannot be consummated by a solitary subject"[15]. Therefore, "God is love" entails that primordially and eternally the Trinity is comprised of three distinct persons. "The three Persons are independent in that they are divine, but as Persons they are deeply bound to one another and dependent on one another".[16]

Moltmann is aware that such language might be read as tritheism. However, for Moltmann, while the "Persons" of the godhead are distinct "Beings," he insists that their divinity is one. "Father and Son are alike divine Beings, but they are not identical. The Son is other than the Father but not in essence"[17]. Notwithstanding his claim that the Father and Son are not other "in essence," the phrase "Father and Son are alike divine Beings" clearly retains a tritheist ring.

Moltmann runs this risk of incipient tritheism because he believes that only by radically stressing the personal distinctions between the Father, the Son, and the Holy Spirit can theology overcome Barth's tendency to subsume the significance of human history and human freedom in the primordial freedom of the one God. "An absolutist sovereign in heaven does not inspire liberty on earth"[18].

Moltmann is, therefore, particularily incensed by Barth's vision of God's primordial motive for Creation. For Barth, the creation is a reflection of the Trinity. Thus, it mirrors the absolute loving freedom of the one God who has eternally posited His own Triune nature. As God freely chose out of the graciousness of His Triune self-sufficiency to create the world, it follows that God might have chosen *not* to create. Moltmann vigorously rejects the contention that God might not have created the world, that before He created, God was eternally impassible and self-sufficient in the love of the Father for the Son through the Holy Spirit.

> "What concept of liberty is Barth applying to God here? Is this concept of the absolute freedom of choice not a threat to God's truth and goodness?" Could God really be content with His impassible glory? Does God really not need those in whom in the suffering of His love He loves unendingly?[19]

Moltmann calls the belief that God might have not created the world a "fictitious suggestion of arbitrariness in God" which "leaves behind it a residue of despotism in the concept of God"[20]. On the contrary Moltmann insists that given the fact that "creation is a fruit of God's longing for 'His Other' "[21], creation is necessary to God's very being. "In this sense, God 'needs' the world and man. If God is love, then He neither will nor can be without the one who is His beloved"[22].

For Moltmann, only a love that results from the eternal and necessary longing of the Father for the Son escapes the alleged despotism of Barth's schema and is worthy of humanity's free loving response. But why a love that is compelled by one's very nature and thus not free is more winsome than a love which in freedom is freely initiated and freely bestowed, Moltmann never satisfactorily explains.[23]

There are many problems connected with Moltmann's doctrine that God creates out of necessity, but in this context I will only underscore what I take to be his most glaring difficulty: his confusion of *eros* with *agape*. This error grows directly out of the very tritheistically tinged version of the Immanent Trinity which he hopes will preserve the love of God. In spite of his protests to the contrary[24], Moltmann's doctrine renders God a prisoner of His own need to love. For God's love toward us is not as the New Testament witnesses, an act of free loving divine condescension (*agape*); it is rather the necessary by-product of the Father's need for the Son (*eros*). Moltmann would try to have it both ways, that God *chooses* to create[25] and at the same time *must* create in order to complete His love[26]. This simply will not do. Either God creates in loving freedom, or He is in the thrall of a need to create which He cannot control, for creation is a function of His primordial, eternal, tri-personal need and desire.[27]

For Moltmann the oneness of God is achieved through the passionate relationship of the three personal Beings of the Godhead. Such language obviously has sexual overtones. His trinitarianism requires language of "bisexuality or transexuality"[28]. The creation is the "fruit" of Father's "longing for" the distinctly "other" person of His Son, and God's love could not be completed unless "the divine love presses even beyond the Trinity"[29]. Creation is the inevitable love child of the *eros* of the Father for the Son.

In denying the primordial loving freedom of God, Moltmann is flirting with a doctrine of an ontologically limited deity.[30] And even the suggestion of such a thing precludes the free graciousness spoken of in the New Testament. There can be no divine *agape* where there is not utter majestic sovereignty and self-sufficiency to undergird it. For there is no divine *agape* if there is divine need. Process theology holds that only if God is the limited "fellow suffer" of the Whiteheadian conception can God be love. This is true if by "love" *eros* is meant. But there is not the least shred of *agape* in either pole of the process concept of a bipolar deity. God in both His impassible and suffering modes—i.e., in His primordial or His consequent nature—is in the thrall of a prior necessity to create.

In the Bible, God is the sovereign Lord who limits Himself. Any act of God toward the creature entails a movement of divine condescension, of divine *kenosis*—i.e., of *agape*—for the terms are virtually synonomous. God loves not out of any need for an object to love, for in His own Triune life He is rich in love. God is not forced to create us, and given the fact that we are sinners, estranged and hostile, the graciousness of God in redeeming us can only be received as a miracle of dazzling grace. Indeed, it is so dazzling that were it not a miracle of sheer good will and graciousness, it would appear to be "arbitrary." Yet we could not resent such surprising grace or reject it as autocratic except as we resented the fact that we ourselves are not God, and, thus, that we are dependent for our very existences as well as for our salvation on a grace which we cannot earn or command. God is not arbitrary, God is God.

The sovereignty of God does not contradict the love of God; His sovereignty is the *sine qua non* of His love, of His *kenosis*. On this issue Barth was absolutely correct. Only one whose dominion is complete can actually be said to humble himself with respect to the creature. The coming of a limited God could not be an act of kenosis. It could only be the movement of one imperfection to another imperfection, and thus be no self-humbling at all.

Once the loving freedom of God has been firmly acknowledged, then it is possible to speak of God's sovereign *kenosis* in a way that would provide a solid basis for many of Moltmann's concerns. Of course, God "needs" the world. For He has, in His free condescending love, bound Himself, His eternity, His being, to the creation so completely that He can no longer be the God He has chosen to be without His dependence on His creation. Luther saw clearly the logic of the incarnation: "Mary suckles God with her breasts, bathes God, rocks Him, and carries Him . . ."[31]. God wills to be cared for by the very creature He creates and sustains. And once God has chosen to be our God, there is no turning back. "For the gifts and call of God are irrevocable" (Rom. 11:29).

Of course, the honor of God is tied to the freedom of the creature. Of course, there can be no despotism in God. However *eros* will not secure our freedom for it is not itself free. But *agape*, as the love of One absolutely free, must liberate, must set free the objects of its good will, or it is not *agape*.

On the other hand—and here the concerns of Moltmann vis a vis Barth must be carefuly acknowledged—*agape* is not paternalism. Like *agape*, paternalism is the love of that which is greater for that which is lesser, but it is finally alien to *agape* for it is offered so as to guarantee the rights and prerogatives of the lover. It is ultimately a self-serving philanthrophy. It cannot humble itself.

On the other hand, since genuine *agape* can be expressed only in acts of *kenosis*, it cannot but enrich its object with the gift of the very being of the lover. Agape is the absolute self-giving of the One who loves in freedom. It bestows on humanity not just love, but that attribute that makes love divine: freedom. In the words of Irenaeus, "Our Lord Jesus

Christ, the Word of God, of His boundless love, became what we are that He might make us what He himself is." The incarnation absolutely entails the promise of the deification of humanity.

Modern theology is confronted by a dilemma which threatens heresy on either side. It must steer a course between the Scylla of divine despotism and the Charybdis of divine impotence. Either is a philosophic distortion of the God and Father Jesus Christ. And as such, either constitutes an equally irrefutable ground for the widespread protest that atheism constitutes the reverse side of the Theopaschite Revolution. In the face of the problem of evil an ultimately limited, finally impotent deity who creates a world of suffering but cannot redeem it is no less contemptible than a despot who damns or saves by his incomprehensible decree. How dare a cosmic blunderer make a world in which there is anguish for most and death for all, in which He can only be a "fellow sufferer"? How dare the Creator of all plead diminished responsibility?

It is slim comfort to be told that while God cannot rescue us from death, we do have a certain survival since we are forever remembered by God, and as such contribute to "the self-creation of God. If the God who loves us is constantly enriched by the memory of His creatures who, notwithstanding such a God's sympathy, are all dead in the long run, how does His love differ from that love of a gourmet for a good meal?" The cannibalistic implications of Whitehead's conception of God makes the impassibility and apathy of the God of classical theism seem positively wholesome.

Moltmann could never finally be classed as an exponent of the concept of limited deity. Nevertheless, he tries to resolve the dilemma between despotism and impotence by qualifying the free Lordship of God in his doctrines of the Immanent Trinity and in creation. Yet, Moltmann's deeply eschatological faith brings him finally to affirm the all-sufficient power of God to redeem all things in the end. This triumphalism seems rather strange after all his attacks on Barth's triumphalism.

> If God exalts Christ alone to be Lord, then he 'must' reign over everything and everyone; otherwise God would not be God. That is why all other rulers have to be destroyed. The sole lordship of Christ is universal. And because he is 'Lord both of the dead and of the living' (Rom. 14.9) he cannot rest until death too be destroyed. But if death is no more, then Christ with his life-giving Spirit has made all the dead live. Then his rule is consummated. Then his goal is achieved. Then all promises and hopes are fulfilled.[32]

If in the eschaton God's triumph is assured, if God's reign will be over a "kingdom" in which His "friends" will achieve the complete bliss of perfect freedom, then the power to accomplish such a thing must have been in God in the beginning. "The sole Lordship of Christ" could not be "universal" if from the beginning the Lordship of the Father was not universal and free.

Barth, for his part, never tries to minimize the primordial sovereignty and power of the self-humbling God. Thus, he understands far more urgently than does Moltmann that there can be neither divine *agape* nor the eschatological redemption that God's *agape* necessitates (Mk. 12:26-27) without divine dominion (Mk. 12:24). Nevertheless, as Moltmann's protest indicates, Barth's theology does not always pass the litmus test of *agape* on the human side. *Agape* would not be *agape* if it were simply a display of divine condescension. The test of *agape* lies in the answer to the question: Does the love that begins in the free love of God create in the object of that love the very freedom of its source? It is "for freedom" that in His crucified love, "Christ has set us free" (Gal. 5:1).

It is precisely on the question of the historical significance of human freedom and, above all, on the question of the eschatological significance of human freedom that Barth's theology is most problematic. One example will have to suffice. The conservative Calvinist G.C. Berkhouwer, who was one of the earliest of Barth's critics to pick up on the Theopaschism of the *Dogmatics*, was extremely critical of Barth's expounding of the Christian hope of the eternal life as merely an "eternalizing" of our completed lives.[33] Thus, Barth takes the scriptural promise that in the end God will be "everything to everyone" to indicate that *our* finite life will be finished, that time will have ended and humanity will forever stand completed in the eternal impassibility of God. There can be no question of our developing in our ongoing redeemed life new enterprises in a hoped for "beyond." "Man as such, therefore, has no beyond. Nor does he need one, for God is our beyond."[34]

Barth's irenic and appreciative reception of Berkouwer's work is well known, but despite the urgency of Berkouwer's protest against Barth's doctrine of eternal life, it is perhaps revealing that in the *Dogmatics* Barth's only critical response to Berkouwer was over the question of his triumphalism *vis a vis* the problem of evil[35].

Though I would argue the matter differently and to a very different conclusion, Berkouwer was quite right that Barth's triumphant view of the problem of evil was further evidence of the same dynamic that inspires Barth's eschatology.[36] If "from the very outset" evil has been defeated, and human history has already been secured by God in election, does this not render history a "mere process" by which God can effect the inevitable triumph of His grace, with human beings little more than the passive beneficiaries of His boundless and irresistible good will and grace? Does not Barth's historical theomonism together with an eschatology that seems to render redeemed humanity frozen in eternity undercut the very agape that he elsewhere so eloquently defends? How can God's love be truly *agape* if we are so "swamped by grace" as to trivialize our contribution to anything?

God, in the freedom of His love, has determined to bind His very being to the creature and to raise the creature to His own life. God has determined that His own life be affected by the creature, indeed to tie His own destiny to human destiny so tightly that our suffering is His suffering and our growth in freedom is His growth in freedom. Luke tells us that under the care of Mary and Joseph "Jesus increased in wisdom and stature" (Lk. 2:52). If God was truly incarnate in Jesus, it was not His humanity abstracted from His divinity that was subject to development in fellowship with human beings. It was both natures of the inseparably, united God/Man that "increased." The paradox of God's love is that the all-great God wills to achieve even greater richness and glory by means of His humble dependence upon His creatures. A theology of divine *kenosis* must celebrate not minimize the fact that God wills to evolve His ever increasing glory by irreversibly binding Himself to His creatures in eternal and reciprocal relationship.

A final comment. There is, to be sure, a onesidedness in Barth's radically monotheistic Trinitarianism emphasis. The personhood of the Father, of the Son, and of the Holy Spirit is given insufficient witness in Barth's doctrine. For example, when Jesus prayed in terrible anguish in Gethsemane, the Scripture describes an I/Thou encounter between the Son and the Father. "Modes of Being" is a pale and abstract designation for the Father and Son, particularly when the relationship between these so called modes flairs up in such awful personal passion. Jesus' cry: "My God! My God! Why hast Thou forsaken Me?" reveals a profound personal tension between the Father and the Son for which Barth's doctrine cannot adequately account.

Nevertheless, Barth's onesidedness does not necessitate or justify Moltmann's counter onesidedness, especially in the light of the radical monotheism of the Old Testament and Jesus' own monotheism (Mk. 12:29-30). Neither a doctrine of the primordial oneness nor a doctrine of the primordial threeness gives sufficient witness to the radical mystery to which the doctrine of the trinity by its very paradox points. Any exposition of the one being of the Triune God that cannot or does not keep in finally unresolvable tension the Triune being of the one God and the oneness of the Triune God errs by virtue of its very resolution of the tension. Only by maintaining the mystery of the paradox can we give witness to the all-sufficient good will, unity, stability, power, and eternity of God, while at the same time witnessing to the complexity of God's personal self-giving unto death and even self-alienation which is portrayed in the human suffering of Jesus Christ.

NARRATIVE THEOLOGY: TRANSLATION OR TRANSFORMATION?

Millard J. Erickson

All of us who have had the privilege of studying with William Hordern were impressed with the understanding of contemporary theology which he shared with us. His keen analytical ability and his breadth of sympathies enabled him to understand the movements which were extant at that time. He gave us a perspective from which the theological scene made sense. But the world has changed over the years. In particular, the theological scene has changed at an accelerating pace. The lifespans of theologies have become progressively shorter. The old sets of understandings no longer apply. Yet it is here that the greater contribution of Dr. Hordern is evident. The categories of analysis and understanding which he imparted continue to bear fruit, for even with different theological content, these categories enable us to classify and thus to understand the new schools of thought. In this paper, we will review one of Dr. Hordern's sets of categories, then apply these to a contemporary theological movement.

I have chosen to work with the now familiar distinction between translators and transformers of the Christian faith. This was most fully expounded in Dr. Hordern's discussion of theological dialogue, in the introductory volume of *New Directions in Theology Today*.[1] Both groups of theologians believe that the world has changed since biblical times, so that a mere literal repetition of the biblical language makes the Christian faith irrelevant, if not unintelligible. If there is to be genuine dialogue with the world, the language must be contemporized, but there is difference of opinion as to how radical such change must be. Transformers are the more radical. They believe the world has changed so much that "modern man" and his thinking have been qualitatively transformed. Consequently, the only way to enable the contemporary person to accept the Christian message is to change it drastically, deleting major portions of traditional Christian teaching if necessary.[2] An example, perhaps extreme, of transformers, is the 'death of God' theology which is willing to surrender the idea of a transcendent or primordial god in order to make Christianity acceptable to modern persons.[3] Its representatives hold that the changes which have taken

29

place in the world had rendered belief in God impossible. If there is a willingness to abandon certain facets of the Christian tradition, thus making this view basically liberal, there is, however, a rather whole-hearted acceptance of the modern world, and all that that entails.[4]

Translators, on the other hand, according to Hordern, while agreeing on the need for dialogue, do not believe this dialogue requires a radical revision of the Christian faith. While the dialogue with the world informs the theologian *how* he must speak today, he does not look to the modern world to find out *what* he must say.[5] Modern man, in other words, cannot be the ultimate authority for what Christians may believe. It is necessary to challenge at some points the understanding which modern men have. If not, then Christian theology is merely telling non-Christians that they really are Christian without knowing it. But in that case, theological dialogue has actually become monologue, in which the modern world is speaking to itself.[6] By claiming that theology must say something to the world that the world is not saying to itself, it is raising the issue of truth, something that the transformers tend not to raise. Indeed, for the transformers, relevance rather than truth is the major issue. Langdon Gilkey accuses them of confusing psychological pressures with logical necessities.[7] Thus, the translators, taking seriously the challenges of modern learning and not willing merely to be fideists, generally engage in some form of apologetics. Hordern advocated an apologetic which began, not by assuming that it could utilize evidence accessible to all persons and demonstrate Christianity's truth to all rational persons, but by raising the question of the validity of the secularist's starting point. The aim of this type of apologetic is to show that the world and life make more sense from Christian premises than from those of atheism. Thus, Hordern was advocating an Augustinian, rather than a Thomistic, apologetic.[8]

This then is the classificatory system which we propose to apply to the cluster of views which have come to be called, "narrative theology." Is this theology a restatement in modern thought forms of the traditional Christian message, or is it actually an alteration of the message, for the sake of the contemporary person? We must begin this part of the paper by attempting to define narrative theology. Here we find certain problems of definition and delimitation, for many persons are in one way or another identified with such a movement. The widespread references to "narrative," "story," and "imagination" are indicative of this perva-sive influence. To be sure, not all who refer regularly to these terms do so in the same sense. But to the extent that theological discussion emphasizes the role of story rather than discursive analysis, it falls within the parameters of the movement which we are considering. Gabriel Fackre has observed that the "variety and imprecision of terminology in the discussion of narrative are striking."[9] In part, this is due to the influence of such diverse fields as literary criticism, psy-chology, linguistics, social ethics and communications theory. Fackre offers a definition which is wide enough to take into account this variety of views: "narrative theology is discourse about God in the setting of story."[10] If we would analyze narrative theology using Hordern's translator/transformer distinction, it will be necessary to distinguish different varieties of narrative theology. A helpful morphology here may be put in terms of the function which narrative or story is seen to perform. While the classification which we will employ is necessarily somewhat oversimplified, we may think of three general types of narrative theologies: those which focus upon the communicative, the hermeneutical, and the heuristic role of narrative.

1. The communicational role of narrative. Narrative theologians have recognized that the content of theology is by its very nature abstract and thus rather difficult to communicate. It is, on this basis, preferable to communicate theological truth through the telling of a story than through giving discursive lecture. Belden Lane contends that this is the way in which rabbis answer questions, at least insofar as they follow the tradition in the form of Haggadah (the way of story) rather than Halakah (the way of reasoned reflection on the law). So for example, the Haggadic tradition contains a story about a man who left his village, seeking a magical city where everything would be perfect. When he stopped for the night, he placed his shoes in the center of the path, pointing in the direction in which he had been travelling. During the night, however, a practical joker turned his shoes around pointing in the direction from which he had come. At the end of the second day he saw the city in the distance, but it was much smaller than he had expected, and it appeared strangely familiar. Finding a street much like his own, he knocked on a familiar door, entered, lived happily with that family, in the magical city of his dreams. One could express the meaning of the story by saying something like: "Happiness is not to be sought somewhere else, but in the place where God has placed one." How much more powerful, however, is the expression of this in story form.[11] One person who has demonstrated this very effectively is C.S. Lewis. His Narnia chronicles are vivid statements of Christian truth, having an appeal not restricted to children. Gilbert Meilaender suggests that while it is possible to think "about" a universal statement, doing so keeps us from experiencing the truth. A myth, however, enables us to transcend finite existence and actually taste reality.[12] In a sense, what this modest form of narrative theology is stating is that truth and particularly abstract truth, must be illustrated to be communicated effectively. Much preaching has found its effectiveness here: in the use of illustrations drawn from the common experience of the listeners.

2. A second role or function of narrative is the hermeneutical. Here narrative is considered actually to be the key to understanding the meaning of the biblical text. There is a mild and also a stronger form of this assertion. The mild form is the observation that the narrative portions of the biblical text constitute the normative factor, in the light of

which the remainder is to be interpreted. Essentially, biblical religion is understood as narrative faith.

This contention is actually asserting that not only the content but also the form of the Biblical story is significant. The Bible is therefore not to be read merely as an illustration. It is not meaningful in terms of the general idea that it illustrates. Rather, the story as such is of importance to the reader. What is needed in our disoriented age is not merely more information. Instead, the person's whole orientation and frame of reference need to be changed. Story as story has the capacity to form and influence the person's identity.[13]

This involves us further in the question of what it means to speak of understanding something. If hermeneutics is determining the meaning of the biblical teaching, or gaining understanding of it, then we must comprehend what it means to understand. George Stroup argues that understanding involves more than merely knowing. It involves the ability to engage in the activity that knowing describes. Beyond that, however, it includes an appreciation of the historicity and the horizon in which the language is embedded. Understanding also involves self understanding, in which the person's own history is understood in the light of the faith narratives of the community.[14] Since justification involves the person's own identification with and characterization by the relationship between God and his people,[15] the story is a particularly appropriate form of conveying the gospel message, since it releases the creative involvement of the listener.[16]

3. The final role of narrative, and perhaps the most radical, is what we might term the heuristic or epistemological. This is the suggestion that narrative or story is not merely a means for expressing or communicating the message of theology, once that has been arrived at by whatever means. Story is actually a means of discovering the message. And this, again, may take several forms. One form is to challenge the nature which theology itself has generally taken. It is not uncommon for theology to take certain basic timeless truths, frequently understood as deriving from the Bible, and formulate them in terms of a prevailing philosophy. A number of narrative theologians, however, argue that this is not the proper way to do theology, or at least ought not to be the only vehicle through which it is done. T. Patrick Burke, for example, argues that while theologians have traditionally attempted to translate stories into philosophy, this does not work, for neither the story nor the philosophy are preserved intact.[17] Both must be squeezed and cut and trimmed. One of the difficulties inheres in the fundamentally different natures and aims of a story and of a philosophy.[18] The purpose of a story is to show us life as it really is, and ourselves (or some aspect of ourselves) as we really are. It does not attempt to solve the puzzles of life. The role of a philosophy, on the other hand, is to resolve and explain the puzzles. Thus, a distortion takes place in the attempt to preserve the story so that it can be re-expressed.

Robert Roth's objection is somewhat more restricted. He observes that there has been a great value in expressing the Gospel in the prevailing philosophy of the day, especially from an apologetic orientation. With each such use of a philosophy, however, there also is an accompanying serious error: "the handmaiden begins to act as a wife, the philosophy begins to give orders to the theology."[19] Thus, these efforts have always failed to accomplish their purpose. Other disciplines which have been employed, such as history, sociology and psychology, while useful and informative, cannot be cross-fertilized with theology, either. Story, however, is particularly appropriate for understanding the Gospel, for the very nature of the Gospel is a story.[20] It is not a set of abstract truths; it is rather, a happening in which man is one character among others. He sees literature as supplementing philosophy, by showing us the questions being asked by our age, and by conveying some of the basic themes of the Christian message, such as freedom of action, the absurd, and conflict.

Probably the most extensive discussion of the heuristic potential of story or narrative is that given by George Stroup in *The Promise of Narrative Theology*. Stroup begins by noting a twofold crisis: the crisis in Christian identity and the confusion in Christian theology about the meaning of revelation.[21] He believes that these two issues are so closely bound together that one cannot be addressed without the other. A major factor in self understanding, whether by the individual or the Christian community, is knowing one's own story. The narrative of the Exodus and of the Cross are the means by which the Jewish and Christian communities respectively have understood who they are. But the narrative needs to be reinterpreted for different generations. The dialogue between tradition and situation is what leads to understanding. And revelation becomes an experienced reality at the point where an individual's identity collides with that of the Christian community. When the individual begins to reinterpret his or her personal tradition in the light of the Christian community's narratives, we may say that conversion has taken place. Indeed Stroup says, "To confess Christian faith is to say in effect, 'I understand who I am in the light of and by means of the faith narratives of the Christian tradition.'"[22]

This understanding of who one is in the light of narrative especially involves the imagination.[23] It is this conception that is perhaps the most emphatic statement of the heuristic aspect of narrative or story. According to Stephen Crites, imagination is a distinct activity of the psyche as a whole, a synthesizing activity whereby it attains religious meaning and truth.[24] Indeed imagination is seen by Crites as the primary faculty of theology.

We should not assume that the heuristic value of narratives is restricted to biblical narratives. McClendon emphasizes the role which Christian biographies play in theology:

> In or near the community there appear from time to time singular or striking lives, the lives of persons who embody the convictions of the community but in a new way...Such lives, by their very attractiveness or beauty, may serve as data for the Christian thinker, enabling him more truly to reflect upon the tension between what is and what ought to be believed and lived by all.[25]

McClendon speaks of the lives of persons such as Dag Hammarskjold, Martin Luther King, Jr., and Clarence Jordan as embodying "proto-typical" or "canonical" images. In living out one's life under the vision of certain dominant images, that life becomes the image of that vision for others. Thus, the study of biography is a means for discovering the truth of such things.[26] John S. Dunne speaks of a process which he terms "passing over." One can enter into the lives of others, understand what a "life-story" is and what is distinctive about the reader's own life story. In the midst of these life-stories, the reader discovers something besides the shape of the life story in the past and in the present: "God's time, the greater and encompassing time which is that of the stories of God, and he experiences companionship with God in time.[27]

One form in which the heuristic role of story is depicted has been developed at some length by Robert Roth. He observes that stories do not only give us insight into our times, but supply a clue to the very nature of reality.[28] Thus he examines some of the great themes found in stories around the world, from various periods.[29] In this model, the question regarding Christian stories is not primarily whether they are historically accurate or not.[30] Rather, the question to be placed regarding the Jesus of history is how he fits into the Messiah story.[31] It is not essential that the Christian story be exclusive of statements in a non-Christian tale.[32] Underlying this is a conception of the nature of reality. Reality is understood as "multifarious." It "includes many realms,...some are empirical and some are not, some are historical and some are not."[33] These themes run through stories of many difference cultures.

A number of writers within the general fold of narrative theology emphasize this power of biblical stories to relate us to more universal themes or structures of reality. So Amos Wilder, for example, speaks of the biblical apocalypse being grounded in and putting us in touch with "the nethermost piers and caissons of human being itself."[34] It appears that narrative has an inherent power to relate to and express certain universal themes of reality, these archetypal characters, which are the ultimate locus of truth or reality.

We need to face now the question which lies at the heart of this essay: is narrative theology a case of translating the gospel, or giving it a restatement in contemporary form, or is it a matter of transformation, of actually modifying the message for the sake of acceptability in the present age?

The answer, as one might suspect, is, "That all depends." There is no single unequivocal answer to the question. The answer really depends upon two considerations: which particular narrative theology or theologian one is talking about, and second, what one's criteria of transformation are. We may begin our evaluation with those narrative theologies which, on our morphology, emphasize the communicational role of narrative. It would appear that what these theologies are attempting to do is to communicate clearly a body of content, which they assume that they possess. There is an emphasis here upon the received body of truth, as something objectively existing.

An example of this approach is that presented by Gabriel Fackre in *The Christian Story*. In the introduction, he includes a section entitled, "translation." He emphasizes the "coring" task of the church, a term he has adopted from the writing of Martin Marty. Coring is a matter of clarifying what Fackre calls "the ABC's of faith."[35] Despite the widespread claim that there is a multiplicity of stories rather than *a* Christian Story, Fackre insists upon the core of the Christian message:

> There is an out-thereness of biblical truth which is to be seen, whatever the angle of vision, and however our view of it is affected by the glasses we are wearing. There is an object with which our subjectivity deals. There is a Story which our translation seeks to communicate. There is a hard core of affirmation at the center of our perceptions and interpretations.[36]

This core appears in the headings of the following chapters of the book: God, Creation, Fall, Covenant, Jesus Christ, Church, Salvation, Consummation, God. Fackre insists that the gospel is "always a norm to which we are accountable, never subservient to our agenda."[37] He says that "to know this critical line between translation and accommodation is the art of authentic communication."[38]

Clearly, Fackre is attempting to identify his position with the translators, even using that very terminology, and distinguishing it from that of the transformers, or as he terms them, accommodators. The statements on doctrines which he makes in the remainder of the book are in most cases, rather conventional in content, if not in form. Indeed, George Stroup complains that the concept of narrative does not really affect Fackre's formulations:

> His interpretation of doctrines such as creation and christology does not differ significantly from the interpretations usually given these subjects. The category of story does not seem to enhance or to alter traditional interpretations of Christian faith, nor does Fackre (sic) explain how the category illumines perennial theological problems such as the relation of the two natures of Christ or the meaning of 'God acts.'[39]

One might even go so far as to conclude that Fackre, at least in this book, is not engaged in doing narrative theology. A likelier hypothesis is that his is a different variety of narrative theology than that of Stroup.

The use of narrative as a means of communication appears to be a helpful means of translation. Its value is not merely that of clarifying meaning but of arousing and holding interest. An example mentioned earlier is C.S. Lewis' children's literature. One aspect of narrative that is particularly pertinent to the matter of interest is its plot and suspense. Once the parable of the prodigal son (for example) is read, everyone knows how it will end, and attention is lost. The use of narrative, like inductive sermons, helps maintain the uncertainty and thus the interest. It appears that the use of narrative in the communicational role is quite compatible with translation as a technique.

When we come to the use of narrative as the hermeneutical key to the Bible, the picture is less clear. To a large extent, the Bible is composed of narrative and is to be interpreted as such. There are, however, large portions of the Bible which simply do not fit the pattern, as James Barr has pointed out.[40] What is to be done with the poetical books of the Old Testament, or with the Book of Revelation in the New Testament? Either these are distorted in interpretation, omitted, or dealt with on a different paradigm. Either of the first two options will have a tendency to result in transformation, especially where crucial teachings are found only in these non-narrative materials.

To a considerable extent, the question of whether the hermeneutical use of story is translation or transformation will depend upon the type of hermeneutic that is involved. If the emphasis is upon determining the author's intended meaning,[41] there is a greater bias toward translation than in the "new hermeneutic." The latter emphasizes the object leading the meaning out of the interpreter, rather than vice versa, and hence tends more toward transformation of the message.[42]

What of the heuristic use of narrative? Here there will again be variation, depending on the particular theologian being considered. One version is to emphasize the role of imagination in the doing of theology. To the extent that imagination is simply a matter of insight into the meaning and application of biblical and doctrinal truths, there is no reason why this should not be understood as merely contributing to translation, since the first step in translation is necessarily a matter of properly and sufficiently understanding the concepts to be translated. If narrative theology can contribute to stimulating the imagination, it is serving a useful and needed function, for in our television age, as contrasted with the era of radio drama, little imagination is required.

If, however, imagination is seen as constitutive of at least part of the content of faith, as it appears is the case in the thought of Crites, then the potential for transformation is great. For here, unlike the work of Fackre, there appears to be an expressive role for imagination, which does not fully come to grips with the crucial question of the historical truth of the narrative.[43] Hartt maintains that as Christians we do not merely *believe* the Gospel is true, we *claim* that it is true. There is a fact-assertive (or as Hartt calls it, assertoric) mode of presumptive cognitivity, that cannot be reduced to the expressive, without changing the nature of the message.[44] There is, in other words, a difference in meaning between "Jesus rose from the dead" and "Jesus rose from the dead *and it really happened."*

The issue whether existence is a predicate has received a great deal of discussion in recent years, particularly in connection with the ontological argument.[45] That discussion appears to me to bear directly upon the issue under consideration here. For purposes of our discussion, I am willing to grant that the *concept* of the resurrection of Jesus is the same whether we are affirming or denying that it occurred. But we have learned from the analytical philosophers that the basic unit of meaning is really not the word (or the concept) but the proposition. Thus although the meaning of the expression, "resurrection of Jesus" is the same in each of the following sentences, the meaning of each of the sentences is quite different from each of the others:

1. "Did the resurrection of Jesus occur?"
2. "The resurrection of Jesus did not occur."
3. "The resurrection of Jesus occurred."
4. "I believe the resurrection of Jesus occurred."

The third sentence, for example, is falsified if the second one is true. Number four, however, can be true even if number two is true. Thus, any substitution of statement number four for statement number three is an alteration of the meaning of the theology involved.

There is a closely related issue, and one which can only be touched on within an essay of this scope, for it is a very large one indeed. It concerns the locus of the referents of theological language, in terms of Soren Kierkegaard's famous distinction between objectivity and subjectivity.[46] In many of the narrative theologians, there appears to be a rather strong shift of emphasis from the objective referent of the theological language to its subjective dimension. So, for example, Crites discusses the question of the resurrection of Jesus. He is willing to grant that a resuscitation of a certifiably dead man could count as a putative fact, although he is not optimistic about such a task being accomplished. The statement that God raised Jesus from the dead has a quite different status, for statements about divine agency really cannot be empirically verified. Crites then, however, makes a revealing statement about belief in such divine agency:

> Whether I assert it, or whether I assert my belief in it, is from a factual point of view a distinction without a difference. It does not suit the nature of the claim, on the one hand, that if I am to assert belief in this story I must undertake a moral responsibility for the assertion that is

never required merely to acknowledge a fact: a convergence of this story with my own story, at once a hermeneutical and a moral task.[47]

It may well be that the key to what Crites is saying is in the expression "from a factual point of view" — that he is merely emphasizing that theological statements, such as those referring to divine agency, cannot be empirically verified. But the point seems to go beyond this, to merging the objective referent and the subjective response, or the difference between the signification of a symbol and its significance for the knower or experiencer of it. This is apparent also in Stroup's concept of "collision."

It seems to me that if this is not transformation of the message, it at least opens the door rather widely to such transformation. When Friedrich Schleiermacher shifted the locus of piety from doctrines or actions to feelings, he transformed Christianity. The same was true of Rudolf Bultmann's emphasis upon *Geschichte*, as contrasted with *Historie*. While the shift is not as complete or radical with the narrative theologians as with these two other men, there is nonetheless a modification. For it seems to me that the biblical persons were asserting certain facts as true independently of their experiencing of them.

The other point at which the heuristic role of narrative jeopardizes the retention of the core of Christianity is with respect to the uniqueness of the message. This issue arises especially with someone like Roth, who finds certain archetypal themes in the Christian story as well as in a number of other stories found in other times and places. These classic stories seem to be the possession of the entire human race, as it were.

This suggestion seems, however, to modify the Christian tradition at one or both of two points. Either what is being said here is that the stories of different religions are the same, or that the uniquely Christian story can be known through different traditions. In the former case, Christianity's uniqueness soteriologically is dissolved into a type of universalism. In the latter case, the uniqueness of the events and messages which are usually thought of as Christianity's special revelation is lost. These truths can be found in other places in addition to the Bible. Thus, general revelation enlarges to the point where it virtually consumes special revelation.

Now, to be sure, there can be and are differences of opinion as to what constitutes the essence or the core of Christianity. But I believe I recall Dr. Hordern distinguishing liberal Christianity from liberal religion at this point of uniqueness. If Jesus was only different in degree, not in kind, from other humans who have lived, if the message of the Bible is found elsewhere than in the Bible, have we not modified Christianity to the point where we must speak of transformation rather than merely translation? Indeed, if even the lives of Christian believers since biblical times do not merely illustrate or confirm the biblical message but actually supplement it, must we not say that transformation has been at work in the matter of the normativity of the biblical narrative?

In conclusion, then, we have observed that some narrative theologians attribute to narrative a communicative, some a hermeneutical, and some a heuristic function. While there are variations among individual theologians, in general the first group tend to be translators, the third group, transformers, and the second group may be either.

BLACK THEOLOGY: ITS ORIGIN, METHOD AND RELATION TO THIRD WORLD THEOLOGIES

James H. Cone

The concept "black theology" refers to a theological movement that emerged among North American black people during the second-half of the 1960s. During the early part of the 1970s, the North American idea of black theology began to make an impact in South Africa. In this essay, I will limit my analysis to the origin and meaning of North American black theology,[1] with special reference to its methodology, as defined by its dialogue with the Third World theologies of Africa, Asia, and Latin America.

Origin of Black Theology

The origin of black theology has three contexts: (1) the civil rights movement of the 1950s and '60s, largely associated with Martin Luther King, Jr.; (2) the publication of Joseph Washington's book on *Black Religion* (1964); and (3) the rise of the black power movement, strongly influenced by Malcolm X's philosophy of black nationalism.

1. **Civil Rights Movement**. All persons involved in the rise of black theology were also deeply involved in the civil rights movement, and they participated in the protest demonstrations led by Martin King. Unlike most contemporary theological movements in Europe and North America, it is important to note that black theology's origin did not take place in the seminary or the university. In fact, most of its early interpreters did not even hold advanced academic degrees. Black theology came into being in the context of black people's struggle for racial justice, which was initiated in the black churces, but chiefly identified with such protest organizations as the Southern Christian Leadership Conference (SCLC), the National Conference of Black Churchmen (NCBC), the Interreligious Foundation for Community Organization (IFCO), and many black caucuses in white churches.

From the beginning black theology was understood by its creators as a Christian theological reflection upon the black struggle for justice and liberation, largely defined in the life and thought of Martin Luther King,

Jr. When Martin King and other black churchpeople began to relate the Christian gospel to the struggle for justice in American society, the great majority of white churches and their theologians denied that such a relationship existed. Conservative white Christians claimed that religion and politics did not mix. Liberal white Christians, with few exceptions during the 1950s and early '60s, remained silent on the theme or they advocated a form of gradualism that denounced boycotts, sit-ins, and freedom-rides.

Contrary to popular opinion, Martin King was not well-received by the white American church establishment when he inaugurated the civil rights movement with the Montgomery bus boycott in 1955.[2] Because black people received no theological support from white churches and their theologians (they were too occupied with Barth, Bultmann, and the death of God controversy!), black people themselves had to search deeply into their own history in order to find a theological basis for their prior political commitment to set free the black poor. They found support in Richard Allen (the founder of the African Methodist Episcopal Church in 1816), Henry Highland Garnet (a 19th century Presbyterian preacher who urged slaves to resist slavery), Nat Turner (a slave Baptist preacher who led an insurrection that killed sixty whites), Henry McNeal Turner (an AME Bishop who claimed in 1898 that "God is a Negro"), and many others.[3] When blacks investigated their religious history, they were reminded that their struggle for political freedom did not begin in the 1950s and '60s but had roots stretching back many years. It was also encouraging to find out that black people's struggle for political justice in North America has always been located in their churches. Whether we speak of the independent Northern churches (AME, AMEZ, Baptists, etc.), the so-called "invisible institutions" among slaves in the South (which emerged with the independent black churches after the Civil War), or blacks in white denominations, black Christians have always known that the God of Moses and of Jesus did not create them to be slaves or second-class citizens in North America. In order to make a theological witness of this religious knowledge, black preachers and civil rights activists of the 1960s developed a black theology that rejected racism and affirmed the black struggle for liberation as consistent with the gospel of Jesus.

2. **Joseph Washington's Black Religion**. When black preachers and lay activist Christians began to search for the radical side of their black church history, they also began to ask about the distinctive religious and theological contributions of black people. It was generally assumed, by most whites and many blacks as well, that black people's culture had no unique contribution to make to Christianity in particular and humanity generally. Indeed white liberal Christians understood integration to mean assimilation, and that meant blacks rejecting their cultural past by becoming like whites, adopting European cultural values. The assumption behind the white definition of integration was the belief that African

cultural values among North American blacks were completely destroyed during slavery. Therefore, if blacks were to develop a cultural knowledge of themselves, they had to find it in their identification with white American values.

Joseph Washington, a black scholar, wrote his book in the context of the hegemony of integration in black-white relations in America. Contrary to the dominant view, Washington contended that there was a unique black culture, a distinctive black religion that can be placed along side of Protestantism, Catholicism, Judaism and Secularism. Black religion is not identical with white Protestantism or any other expression of Euro-American Christianity. Washington, however, was not pleased with the continued existence of black religion, and he placed the blame squarely upon white Christians. He contended that black religion exists only because black people have been excluded from the genuine Christianity of white churches. Because blacks were excluded from the faith of white churches, black churches are not genuine Christian churches. And if there are no genuine Christian churches, there can be no Christian theology. Blacks have only folk religion and folk theology. In Washington's own words: "Negro congregations are not churches but religious societies — religion can choose to worship whatever gods are pleasing. But a church without a theology, the interpretation of a response of the will of God for the faithful, is a contradiction in terms."[4]

Although Joe Washington's *Black Religion* was received with enthusiasm in the white community, it was strongly denounced in the black church community. Indeed, black theology, in part, was created in order to refute Washington's thesis. Black preachers wanted to correct two misconceptions: (1) that black religion is not Christian and thus has no Christian theology; and (2) that the Christian gospel has nothing to do with the struggle for justice in society.

3. **Black Power Movement**. After the March on Washington in August 1963, the integration theme in the black community began to lose ground to the black nationalist philosophy of Malcolm X.[5] The riots in the ghettoes of U.S. cities were shocking evidence that many blacks agreed with Malcolm X's contention that America was not a dream but a nightmare.

However, it was not until the summer of 1966, after Malcolm X's assassination (1965), that the term black power began to usurp the word integration among many civil rights activists. The occasion was the continuation of the James Meredith "march against fear" (in Mississippi) by Martin Luther King, Jr., Stokely Carmichael, and other civil rights activists. Stokely Carmichael seized this occasion to sound the black power slogan, and it was heard loud and clear throughout the U.S.[6]

The rise of black power had a profound affect upon the appearance of black theology. When Carmichael and other radical black activists separated themselves from Martin King's absolute commitment to nonviolence by proclaiming black power, white churchpeople, especially clergymen, called upon their black brothers and sisters in the gospel to denounce black power as unchristian. To the surprise of white Christians, black ministers refused to follow their advice and instead wrote a "Black Power" statement that was published in *The New York Times*, July 31, 1966.[7]

The publication of the "Black Power" statement may be regarded as the beginning of the conscious development of a black theology in which black ministers consciously separated their understanding of the gospel of Jesus from white Christianity and identified it with the struggles of the black poor for justice. Radical black clergy created an ecumenical organization called the National Conference of Black Churchmen (NCBC) as well as black caucuses in the National Council of Churches and almost all white churches. Black clergy denounced white racism as the antichrist, and were unrelenting in their attack on its demonic presence in white denominations. It was in this context that the phrase black theology emerged.

Black Theology as Liberation Theology

It is one thing to proclaim black theology and quite another to give it theological substance. Many white Christians and almost all white theologians dismissed black theology as nothing but rhetoric. Since white theologians controlled the seminaries and university departments of religion, they made many blacks feel that only Europeans and persons who thought like them could define what theology is. In order to challenge the white monopoloy on the definition of theology, many young black scholars realized that they had to carry the fight to the seminaries and universities where theology was being written.

The first book on black theology was written by me under the title of *Black Theology and Black Power* (1969). The central thesis of that book was its identification of the liberating elements in black power with the Christian gospel. One year later I authored the second book, *A Black Theology of Liberation* (1970) and made liberation the organizing center of my theological perspective. I wrote: "Christian theology is a theology of liberation. It is a rational study of the being of God in the world in the light of the existential situation of an oppressed community, relating the forces of liberation to the essence of the gospel, which is Jesus Christ."[8]

After my works appeared, other black theologians joined me, supporting my theological project and also challenging what they regarded as my excesses. In his *Liberation and Reconciliation: A Black Theology* (1971), J. Deotis Roberts, while supporting my emphasis on liberation, claimed that I overlooked reconciliation as central to the gospel and black-white relations. A similar position was advocated by Major Jones' *Black Awareness: A Theology of Hope* (1971). Other black theologians

43

claimed that I was too dependent upon white theology and thus was not sufficiently aware of the African origins of black religion. This position is taken by my brother, Cecil, in his *Identity Crisis in Black Theology* (1975), and it is also found in Gayraud Wilmore's *Black Religion and Black Radicalism* (1972).

While my perspective on black theology was challenged by other black scholars, they supported my claim that liberation was the central core of the gospel as found in the scriptures and the religious history of black Americans. For black theologians the political meaning of liberation was best illustrated in the Exodus and its eschatological meaning was found in the life, death, and the resurrection of Jesus. The Exodus was interpreted to be analogous to Nat Turner's slave insurrection and Harriet Tubman's liberation of an estimated 300 slaves to freedom. Slave songs (often called "Negro Spirituals"), sermons, and prayers expressed the futuristic character of liberation found in the resurrection of Jesus.

Because many black male theologians were reluctant to take up the subject of sexism and others were openly hostile when black women raised the issue as a critical theological problem, a black feminist theology is emerging as an open challenge to the patriarchal nature of the current perspectives of black theology. Jacquelyn Grant and Pauli Murray are prominent examples.[9] While they accept the liberation theme of black theology, black feminist theologians reject the narrow limitations of that theme to racism, as if sexism were not an important problem in the black community. Because of the urgency of the problem of sexism, black women have begun to insist on doing theology out of their experience. Black feminist theology is both a challenge to the sexist orientation of black theology and a deepening of the black struggle against racism.

Black Theology's Method and Relation to Third World Theologies

During the beginning of the 1970s, black theologians of North America began to have some contact with other forms of liberation theology in Africa, Latin America, and Asia.[10] Black Theology in South Africa became a natural ally. Black and Latin theologies became co-partners in their identification of the gospel with the liberation of the poor, although one emphasized racism and the other classism. A similar partnership occurred with black, African, and Asian theologians regarding the importance of culture in defining theology.

In black theologians' dialogue with Third World theologians, the striking difference between the theologies of the poor and the theologies of the rich became very clear to us. As long as our dialogue was confined to North American whites who oppressed blacks and to European theologians whom our oppressors venerated, our understanding of the theological task was determined too much by our reactions to white racism in the United States. African, Asian, and Latin American theologians enlarged our vision by challenging us to do theology from a global perspective of oppression. Third World theologians urged us to analyze racism in relation to international capitalism, imperialism, colonialism, world poverty, classism, and sexism. For the first time, black theologians began to seriously consider socialism as an alternative to capitalism. We began to see the connections between the black ghettoes in the United States and poverty in Asia, Africa, and Latin America, between the rising unemployment among blacks and other poor people in the U.S. and the exploitation of the labor of Third World peoples, and between the racist practices of white churches of North America and Europe and the activities of their missionaries in the Third World. These discoveries deeply affected our political and theological vision, and we began to see clearly that we could not do theology in isolation from our struggling brothers and sisters in the Third World. As oppressors band themselves together in order to keep the poor of the world in poverty, the world's poor must enter into political and theological solidarity if they expect to create a movement of liberation that is capable of breaking the chains of oppression.

Early in our dialogue, black and Third World theologians realized the importance of building a common theological movement of liberation. Although we experienced several differences with each other (especially with Latins during the early stages of our dialogue regarding race and class analyses), our mutual commitment to do theology in solidarity with the poor held us together. We had too much in common to allow our differences to separate us. Furthermore, it became increasingly clear that our differences were largely due to a difference in contexts and to our mutual internalization of the lies that our oppressors had told us about each other. After black and Third World theologians' nearly seven years of dialogue under the auspices of the Ecumenical Association of Third World Theologians (EATWOT), including five major conferences, our differences have diminished considerably, and our similarities have increased to the extent that we are now engaged in the exciting task of creating a Third World theology of liberation that we all can support.[11]

When the question is asked, "how do we do theology?", black and Third World theologians agree that theology is not the first act but rather the second. Although our Latin American brothers and sisters, with the use of Marxist class analysis, were the first to explicate this methodological point,[12] it was already present and now re-affirmed in all our theologies.[13] The first act is both a religio-cultural affirmation and a political commitment on behalf of the liberation of the poor and voiceless people of our continents. Our cultural identity and political commitment are worth more than a thousand textbooks of theology. That is why we do not talk about theology as the first order of business in EATWOT. Rather our first concern is with the quality of commitments that each of us has made and will make for those about whom and with whom we claim to do theology. We contend that we know what people believe by what they do and not by what they say in their creeds, conference statements, or theological textbooks.

Praxis (i.e., a reflective political action that includes cultural identity) comes before theology in any formal sense. Therefore, the initial motivation that compels us to do theology is not our desire to place books in university and seminary libraries for professors and their graduate students. On the contrary, our reason for making theology arises form our experience in the ghettoes, villages, and churches of the poor in our countries. We do not believe that it is necessary for our people to remain poor. Something must be done about the misery of our people. Doing and saying are therefore bound together so that the meaning of what one says can only be validated by what one does. Theology for us is critical reflection upon a prior religio-cultural affirmation and political commitment to be in solidarity with the victims of our continents.

Because the starting point of black and Third World theologies is defined by a prior cultural affirmation and political commitment to be in solidarity with the poor, our theologies bear the names that reflect our affirmations and commitments. We call our theologies black, African, Hispanic-American, Asian, Red, Latin American, minjung, black feminist, and a host of other names that still sound strange to persons whose theological knowledge has been confined to European and white North American theologies. The identities of our theologies are determined by the human and divine dimensions of reality to which we are attempting to bear witness. We do not begin our theology with a reflection on divine revelation as if the God of our faith is separate from the suffering of our people. We do not believe that revelation is a deposit of fixed doctrines or an objective Word of God that is then applied to the human situation. On the contrary, we contend that there is no truth outside of or beyond the concrete historical events in which people are engaged as agents. Truth is found in the histories, cultures, and religions of our peoples. Our focus on social and religio-cultural analyses separates our theological enterprise from the progressive and abstract theologies of Europe and North America. It also illuminates the reasons why *orthopraxis* in contrast to orthodoxy has become for many of us the criterion of theology.[14]

Although black and Third World theologians have been accused of reducing theology to ideology by many European and North American critics, that criticism is misplaced because it camouflages the human character of all theologies and particularly the ideological option for the rich that our critics have made. Unlike our critics, we do not claim to be neutral in our theology, because the enormity of the suffering of our people demands that we choose for their liberation and against the structures of oppression. We cannot let the people who support the structures of oppression define what theology is. On this point, black theologians identify with the way Malcolm X expressed it: "Don't let anybody who is oppressing us ever lay the ground rules. Don't go by their game, don't play the game by their rules. Let them know that this is a new game, and we've got new rules."[15] The dominant theologians of Europe and North America want the same theological rules because they made them, and their rules will help to keep the world as it is —whites controlling blacks, men dominating women, and the rich nations keeping the poor nations dependent. But what most European and North American whites find difficult to understand is that we are living in a new world situation, and this requires a new way of making theology. Again, I like the way Malcolm put it:

> The time that we're living in ... and ... are facing now is not an era where one who is oppressed is looking toward the oppressor to give him some system or form of logic or reason. What is logical to the oppressor isn't logical to the oppressed. And what is reason to the oppressor isn't reason to the oppressed. The black people in this country are beginning to realize that what sounds reasonable to those who exploit us doesn't sound reasonable to us. There just has to be a new system of reason and logic devised by us who are at the bottom, if we want to get some results in this struggle that is called 'the Negro revolution'.[16]

In EATWOT, black and Third World theologians have been attempting to develop together a new way of making theology. In contrast to the dominant theologies of Europe and North America that are largely defined by their responses to the European enlightenment and the problem of the unbeliever that arose from it, our theological enterprise focuses on Europe's and North America's invasion of the continents of Africa, Asia, and Latin America inaugurating the slave trade, colonization, and neo-colonialism. Our primary theological question is not how can we believe in God in view of the modern, western confidence in reason, science and technology that seems to exclude the necessity for faith in God. Rather our theological problem arises from our encounter of God in the experience of the misery of the poor. How can we speak about Jesus' death on the cross without first speaking about the death of people? How can the poor of our countries achieve worth as human beings in a world that has attempted to destroy our cultures and religions? The chief contradiction out of which our theologies achieve their distinctiveness is the problem of the non-person. That is why our most important conversational partners are not philosophers of metaphysics and other socially disinterested intellectuals in the university; we are primarily interested in talking with social scientists and political activists who are engaged in the liberation of the poor.

Black and Third World Theologians' concern about the oppressed person forced us to establish links with the communities of the poor, and we experienced in their ecclesial life something more than a routine gathering of like-minded people. In poor people's worship life is revealed as a knowledge of themselves that cannot be destroyed by the structures that oppress them. The liberating character of their spirituality can be seen in the way poor people's faith in God evolves out of their cultural and political aspirations. It can be observed in the Basic Christian Communities of Latin Amercia, the black and Hispanic churches of North America, the indigenous churches and traditional religions of Africa, and in the religious life of Asia. In their worship, the God of grace and judgment meets the poor and transforms their personhood from nobody to somebody and bestows upon them the power and courage to struggle for justice. Worship, therefore, is not primarily an expression of the individual's private relationship with God. It is rather a community happening, an eschatological invasion of God into the gathered community of victims, empowering them with "the divine Spirit from on high," "to keep on keeping on" even though the odds might appear to be against them. In the collective presence of the poor at worship, God recreates them as a liberated community who must bring freedom to the oppressed of the land. Black and Third World theologies are being created out of poor people's ecclesial and religious life, and they seek to interpret the God encountered in their religio-cultural and political struggles to overcome Euro-American domination.

It has been within the context of the churches and the religions of the poor that black and Third World theologies have begun to re-read the Bible. In this re-reading many of us began to speak of the "hermenuetical privilege of the poor" and of "God's bias toward the poor." Although Latin theologians have done more exegetical work to demonstrate the biblical option for the poor than others,[17] a similar concern is shared by most Third World theologians. Suh Nam-Dong, an interpreter of the minjung theology of South Korea, may be quoted as an example:

> Theological activities do not end with the exposition of
> biblical texts on salvation or liberation of people by God.
> In the Bible, the Exodus, the activities of the prophets,
> and the event of the Cross offer new insights, but these
> texts ought to be rediscovered and re-interpreted in the
> context of the human struggle for historical and political
> liberation today.[18]

While acknowledging that the distinctiveness of black and Third World theologies is primarily defined by their particular contexts, their method of making theology may be summarized with the following emphases.

1. Black and Third World theologians make theology in complex religio-cultural contexts and with the political commitment to liberate poor people from oppression. Theology then is reflection upon the

meaning of God in solidarity with the poor people who are struggling to overcome cultural and political domination. The acid test of any theological truth is found in whether it aids the victims in their struggle to overcome their victimization. There are no abstract, objective truths that are applicable for all times and situations. Truth is concrete, and it is inseparable from the oppressed who are struggling for freedom.

2. Because the liberation of our people is the central motivation for us to engage in the theological enterprise, the second element of our method is social analysis. Social analysis is bringing to light that which is hidden. It is unmasking untruth so that truth can be seen in a clear light. Black and Third World theologians do not believe that the work of theology can be done unless the truth is known about the systems of domination. Racism, sexism, colonialism, capitalism, and militarism must be comprehensively analyzed so that these demons can be destroyed. We agree with Karl Marx's eleventh thesis on Feuerbach: "The philosophers have only *interpreted* the world, in various ways; the point, however, is to *change* it." In our use of the critical tools of the social sciences, as well as religio-cultural analyses, black and Third World theologians have been attempting to make theologies of liberation rather than theologies of domestication.

3. Through a political commitment that is informed by social and cultural analyses, a new hermeneutical situation is created. The Bible is no longer a mere ancient document whose meaning can only be uncovered by the historical criticisms of biblical experts. Political commitment, informed by social analysis provides an angle of vision that enables us to re-interpret the scripture and thus bring to light that message which European and North American biblical exegetes had covered up.

When the Bible is read in the community of the poor, it is not understood by them as a deposit of doctrines or of revealed truths about God. Rather it becomes a living book that tells the story of God's dealings with God's people. Its importance as a source for creating theology cannot be overstated for black and Third World theologians. Even feminist and South African theolgians, who question its authority (largely because of its sexist and racist misuses), do not ignore the Bible.[19] They wrestle with it, refusing to allow an abstract biblical authority, written by men and interpreted by whites, to negate the authority of their own experience. God, they insist, cannot be less than the human experience of liberation from oppression. We must not allow an abstract Word of God to usurp God's Word as Spirit who empowers people to be who they are — fully human in search of the highest beauty, love, and joy.

4. The meaning of the gospel that is derived from our re-reading of the Bible cannot be communicated with old European and white North American theological concepts. The truth derived from our people's

struggles must be communicated through the histories and cultures of our people. Truth is embedded in the stories, songs, dances, sermons, paintings, and sayings of our people. Since many of us have learned how to do theology in European and North American universities and seminaries, we have had to be converted to a radically new way of doing theology. How do we make theology using the history and culture of our people? What method is appropriate for these sources? The answer to this question is not clear to many of us, and that is why several EATWOT members wish to spend the next three to five years working on this methodological problem.

Because black and Third World theologians have been doing theology for a short time and doing it together even less, we do not have a fully developed method for making theology. These points represent my attempt to listen to what we have been saying to each other in our search to build a Third World theology that is derived from the religio-cultural and political struggles of our people to overcome Euro-American domination.

AN UPDATE ON LIBERATION THEOLOGY IN THE CANADIAN CONTEXT

Benjamin G. Smillie

It is a privilege to have received the invitation to submit an article in a Festschrift in honor of Dr. William Hordern. The editor reminded contributors that William Hordern is well known in contemporary theology, church and society issues and the theology of Luther. I have chosen the area of church and society to expand the focus that has brought William Hordern to considerable prominence in the last eight years. In 1977, at a Conference on "Political Theology in the Canadian Context" sponsored by the University of Saskatchewan,[1] and again in 1984, at the Prairie Christian Training Centre in Fort Qu'Appelle at a Conference on "Liberation Theology in the Canadian Context,"[2] Hordern gave two papers which outlined the distinctive characteristics of these two similar theologies, Political Theology and Liberation Theology, and the impact they have had on the contemporary theological climate.

In the introduction to his paper at the Fort Qu'Appelle Conference, Hordern said that he had been asked if Liberation Theology is not just another fad. His answer, which is emphatically reinforced in this paper, was that Liberation Theology is here to stay. This is a particularly important reality to have confirmed by William Hordern, because he has been one of Canada's most influential theologians. In his concise writing he has brought theological truths into the home of everyone who desires to have a better understanding of the Christian faith. He writes with the same clarity that was expected of the prophet Habakkuk, who heard God's call to "Write the vision; make it plain upon tablets, so he may run who reads it" (Habakkuk 2:2).

Because it would be an affront to Hordern's ability to explain theology with remarkable lucidity, I will not attempt to summarize the most able summarizer we have in Canadian theology. Instead, I will pick out themes from his work which need further development if we are to understand what "God is doing in the world to make and to keep life human"[3] in our Canadian context.

Many theologians, who have watched the actions of the established churches in Canada are excited at their involvement in facing politically sensitive issues. This brings an important dimension which has been too long ignored by Canada's theologians. The emphasis now is to examine "sinful social structures" rather than the 'sins of the dispositon' like anger, jealousy, pride, greed, and other 'sins' of private morality. It is important to notice that the social issues which are stressed do not centre on drug addiction, gambling, lotteries, "Lord's Day Observance," alcohol and others which are often circumscribed by middle class neighbourhoods. This shift in emphasis within the Canadian context is exemplified in the statement made by the Canadian Catholic Bishops in 1983, *Ethical Reflections on the Economic Crisis*.[4] Insisting that the concern about the economy was not based on "any specific political option, but by the gospel message of Jesus Christ," they cited two principles which are fundamental to the Christian Gospel:

> The first principle has to do with the preferential option for the poor, the afflicted, and the oppressed. As Christians, we are called to follow Jesus by identifying with the victims of injustice, by analyzing the dominant attitudes and structures that cause human suffering and by actively supporting the poor and the oppressed in their struggles to transform society. The second principle concerns the special value and dignity of human work in God's plan for Creation. It is through the activity of work that people are able to exercise their creative spirit, realize their human dignity and share in Creation....The importance of human labour is illustrated in the life of Jesus who was himself a worker, a craftsman like Joseph of Nazareth."[5]

The Bishops deplored the offence to the Gospel which is represented in 1.5 million people unemployed in Canada. In their statement, they came close to taking on the "principalities and powers" in their implication that the blame for their unemployment lies with the transnational corporations and banks who can move capital from one country to another in order to take advantage of cheaper labour conditions.[6]

The United Church of Canada, at the meeting of its General Council in 1984 at Morden, Manitoba, took up similar issues. Like the Catholic Bishops, the United church criticized the long term and chronic nature of the economic crisis in Canada, pointing out the tragedy of families and of community life caused by such endemic structural unemployment. They showed that 1.5 million Canadians unemployed was higher than 1939 levels of unemployment and suggested that the real rate of unemployment in Canada is 15.5% if we are to include those who have given up trying to find work because they have become totally discouraged with constant rejections. The General Council statement put the total figure at nearly 2 million Canadians unemployed.[7]

This excursion into economics in a paper on Liberation Theology may, at first sight, appear to be a diversion from the theological subject at hand. However, it is in this example that most of the basic ingredients of Liberation Theology are manifested.

Liberation theologians start with the premise of God's bias for the poor. In concrete terms, this means that they analyze the economic material base which effects the living possibilities of people. They point to Jesus' self understanding of ministry in the words of Isaiah:

> The spirit of the Lord is upon me, because [God] has anointed me to preach good news to the poor. [God] has sent me to proclaim release to the captives and recovering of sight to the blind, to set at liberty those who are oppressed, to proclaim the acceptable year of the Lord (Luke 4:18-19).

Liberation theologians, like the Catholic Bishops in their statement, do not emphasize private sin because they are aware that the preoccupation with the personal leaves the church person with a tunnel vision on wider issues. They are critical of the status quo which masks sinful social structures. Liberation Theology is 'concretely contextual' which means that it is grounded in human situations, not vacuous generalities. As well, Liberation Theology is ecumenical. This ecumenism is illustrated in the Bishop's statement which is similar to statements from the Protestant Canadian Council of Churches, particularly the United Church of Canada General Council report referred to earlier in this paper. In Liberation Theology, there is an avoidance of the old debate between conservative and liberal theologies which wracked the church in the 1920s and the 1930s, centering on the use of critical scholarship in the understanding of the background to the biblical text. Liberation theologians assume the insights gained from biblical critcism and, refusing to become preoccupied in ecclesiastical debates centering on biblical orthodoxy, they analyze the source of oppression to be in the economic power brokers of banks and of multinational corporations.

However, the Canadian Catholic Bishop's statement is remiss in one of the major hallmarks of Liberation Theology. Liberation theologians, particularly from Latin America where the disparities between wealth and poverty are not as well camouflaged as they are in Canada, recognize the importance of doing a class analysis in order to shed light on where the economic (hence political) power lies. The failure to do a class analysis is not unique to the Catholic Bishops. In both of Hordern's papers referred to, he states that "all theology reflected a class bias."[8] Yet in neither paper does he name the dominant class who is in control of production and who is doing the oppressing in Canada! All of us "middle class" theologians are very reluctant to do this kind of class analysis! Partly out of a sense of honesty, we avoid dividing economic sheep from economic goats because we know, through our own relatively affluent lives devoid of hunger and stark want, that it can appear hypocritical to try to divest ourselves of responsibility for our share of the greed and possessive individualism which leaves poor people poor. Our style of life leaves us objectively in closer identity with the wealthy capitalist than with the poor with whom our theologizing wants to seek identity. The task is to overcome our class interest in both our political analysis and our political practice.

Unfortunately, another common approach which avoids the necessity of doing a class analysis has been not to name the oppressors with economic power in Canada but instead, to concentrate on teaming up with the poor. Roger Hutchinson, a Canadian ethicist and advocate for progressive coalitions, suggests that it is possible for groups of concerned church people, native rights groups, the Task Force on the Church and Corporate Responsibility and the Inter church Committee on Refugees, to provide "a floor" on which all groups can stand in working to support marginalized people. This paper contends that, without a rigorous class analysis, the compromises in accommodating the views of the people who possess the economic power, reduce this "floor" to quicksand! Hutchinson suggests that this coalition would not have a mandate to lead churches to the left; it would be non ideological; it would avoid "unnecessary alienation" by refusing to attack right wing groups. As well, he criticizes those who take a stronger stand against corporate capitalism by quoting Leon Howell who, in the *Christian Century*, stated that issues today are "murkily ambiguous" and those who take a strong stand are "attacking the real and alleged errors of others, a relatively soft self-assignment."[10]

If Liberation Theology in the Canadian context is to be different from liberal optimistic idealism of the Social Gospel and if it is to have any impact on the life of Canada, it must do a class analysis of Canadian society. Specifically, it must expose the rich with economic power who control the political machinery of this country and whose wealth increases in direct proportion to the shrinking resources of the poor. The major task of Liberation Theology is to cut through the mystification which suggests that we live in a democratic, free and open society with equal opportunity for all.

In order to do this exposition and demystification, Liberation theologians and biblical scholars begin by examining the historical materialist base of society[11] which shapes the socio-economic conditions of the contemporary society under study and the socio-economic conditions of the historical period in which the biblical text was written. When an historical materialist analysis of Canadian society is done, it becomes obvious that the concentration of power is in the hands of the "super rich" who control the "modes of production." It should be noted that such an analysis does not concentrate on the millionaire hockey stars like Wayne Gretzky, nor on singers like Anne Murray and Gordon Lightfoot because, although all of these possess considerable wealth, none of them are in central positions of economic power. On the other hand, an examination of the "Canadian Economic Emperors" reveals not only how the wealth and power of these Emperors is directly responsible for the large unemployment this country lives under but also, it reveals how the economic power can spread over into the production of weapons for the arms race which draws Canada into the vortex of super power confrontation.

This linkage of economic power with the arms race is also important for those people in peace groups who see war as an extension of individual aggression. Consequently, they fail to see that if a record march against the Cruise testing brings out 3,500 protestors in Saskatoon in May of 1983 but two weeks later, a march in support of the Union of Unemployed Workers draws only a hundred attendants, the first huge march is, in fact, a failure because the linkage between the capital intensive arms industry and the lack of jobs for unemployed people has not been made!

But to do an historical materialist examination of Canadian society and, at the same time, to use an historical materialist hermeneutic of the biblical text, is (predictably) to invite criticism. Liberation Theology, which has come to be associated with a Marxist critique, is likely to elicit an instant reaction that this is too radical an economic political tool to use in analyzing Canada. In the view of these critics, if an historical materialist analysis of the Bible is used, it distorts the biblical text because it represents an ideological bias that has come to be associated with atheistic Communism. It should be noted that the reason the Marxian analytical method is used is because it is the only method which clearly exposes those whom the Bible calls "the rich" and "the poor!" All other methods available to date, unfortunately, leave these identities "murkily ambiguous!"

Many Canadian theologians, who profess a strong sympathy with Liberation Theology, tend to rationalize this recent theological shift with its Marxist economic analysis as 'being perfectly legitimate for Latin America but quite out of place for Canada' – a country with no military dictatorship, no secret police, no torture chambers, no arrests by night of members of families who oppose the government and who are never seen again, no feudal land owners and no censorship of the press.

These overt signs of democracy tend to mask the reality of a highly class structured Canadian society where nine families control 22 of the largest companies in Canada. Dan Westell, a financial analyst for Canada's national newspaper, the *Globe and Mail*, reports:

> Big business frequently seems faceless, owned by institutions and run by professional managers. But ultimately share certificates belong to people and a surprisingly large chunk of Canadian business is dominated by very few.[12]

He goes on to analyze the economic power on the Toronto Stock exchange in June 1984, with a listing of the 300 companies which make up the Exchange. Says Westell:

> ...Nine super rich families or individuals owned shares with market value of more then $9 billion out of a total index value of about $80 billion.[13]

E.M. Bronfman, Chairperson of the Board of Seagram's (the largest liquor company in the world) had a salary in 1981 of $1,064,288 which was a 20% increase over his 1980 salary. Also in 1981, the average salary of Canadians was $18,500 – a salary which was under the "6 and 5 wage and price control" of the federal government.[14]

The Bronfmans (whose financial fortune started with the father, Samuel Bronfman, bootlegging whisky across the Canadian/United States border during Prohibition in the 1920s[15]) have multiplied the family fortune in the present generation by becoming "a central agent in smuggling munitions to South Africa under the company name of Space Research Corporation." From 1968 to 1973, the Bronfman's Space Research Quebec was a company with 7,000 acres in Highwater, Quebec. In 1969, Space Research Corporation U.S., also owned by the Bronfman family, was incorporated with 1,000 acres of adjacent land at North Troy, Vermont. The United States branch of the company expanded into the manufacturing of inter ballistic missiles using the Carribean islands of Barbados and Antigua as a front for their operation – "Shells from Canada and Florida were shipped by Space Research to Antigua, where they were transferred to vessels bound for South Africa."[16] This highly lucrative export trade was carried on under the noses of the Canadian and United States governments even though, in 1963 and in 1977, a United Nations arms embargo called on all nations to stop all export of arms shipments to South Africa.[16]

How do Liberation theologians in Canada address these pyramids of economic power in the hope of building a more egalitarian, just society to which the biblical "kingdom of God" refers? That God's bias is for the poor is repeatedly substantiated as a central and recurring theme in both the Old and the New Testaments of the Bible. The biblical prophets, represented in the prophet Isaiah, say to the wealthy of Judah:

> "The lord enters into judgement with the elders and princes of his people: 'It is you who have devoured the vineyard, the spoil of the poor is in your houses'" (Isaiah 3:14).

An example where the exploiter is named is found in the instance where Elijah watched King Ahab covet and possess his neighbour Naboth's vineyard, with the scheming help of Ahab's wife, Jezebul. The prophet Elijah, having witnessed King Ahab engineer the death of Naboth and then take over his vineyard, confronts the greedy king with his ill gotten gains. Ahab asks Elijah, "'Have you found me, O my enemy?' He answered, 'I have found you, because you have sold yourself to do what is evil in the sight of the Lord'" (I Kings 21:30).

The same judgement is described in the New Testament. Jesus, confronting the righ young ruler who wants to become a disciple, says to him: "If you would be perfect, go sell what you possess and give to the poor, and you will have treasure in heaven; and come, follow me" (Matthew 19:21). Jesus' parable of the rich man who treats the beggar, Lazarus, as part of the misery which blends into the landscape, receives the judgement of hell for his callous indifference (Luke 16:19-31).

However, if we say that both the Old and the New Testaments point to God's bias for the poor and then our hermeneutic brings out proof texts which reflect this bias, we must also recognize that a large part of the biblical record appears not only to condone but also to adulate wealth. King Solomon, with his profligate life style and his undistributed wealth, is second only to King David in being described as the wise model king. The prodigality of his wealth is not condemned. Jesus socially fraternizes with the rich in Jerusalem. It is Joseph of Arimethea, a rich man who is a disciple, who provides a cemetry for Jesus' crucified body (Matthew 27:57). The woman with the alabaster box of ointment pours it over Jesus as a form of anointing at a Bethany dinner. When the guests are shocked at the wasteful act as an offence to the poor who would have benefited tangibly from the money, Jesus says to them, "For you always have the poor with you, and whenever you will, you can do good to them; but you will not always have me." (Mark 14:7)

This apparent ambiguity of matching proof texts has received, through the use of an historical materialist hermeneutic of the Bible, a break-through using a new heuristic device. This new approach uses a rigorous historical materialist hermeneutic of both the Old and the New Testaments. Biblical historian, Norman Gottwald, in a encyclopedic study of the tribal confederacy in the Old Testament, locates ancient Israel in its social matrix. In doing so, he presents the thesis that when the material economic base of Israel's history is examined, we do not have an historical exodus of a slave society coming out of the bondage of Egypt and engaging in a conquest of the Philistines and the Canaanites who are already residents in Palestine. Norman Gottwald, after a thorough examination of the historical material base of the texts of the early traditions of Israel, explains that what actually happened was a revolt within Palestine. Says Gottwald:

> [This revolt was engineered by]...a village based retribal-
> ism movement [which] broke away from the city states
> control and in the course of that historical project to
> enable economic and political emancipation through
> self-defense and mutual aid, the movement created its
> own culture. Central to that culture was the religion of
> Yahweh with a sharply etched symbol system and a

centralizing cult practice. This religion was a key factor in achieving unity and perseverance in the historical project of economic and political emancipation.[17]

When this historical material structural base produces a concretised theology in the reality of the biblical text, this theology affects the representative theological language we use to describe what is happening. Gottwald makes some important suggestions.

- "God" is an historical concrete power who establishes and sustains social equaltiy.

- "The Chosen People" is the distinctive self conscious- ness of a society of equals.

- "Covenant" is bonding of decentralised social groups in a large society of equals committed to cooperation without authoritarian leadership.

- "Eschatology" or hope for the future is the assurance that God's plan is committed to people who build a society of equals with the confidence and determin- ation that this way of life can be preserved against great environmental odds.[18]

The historical materialist hermeneutic of the New Testament also has distinguished scholars, particularly Fernando Belo, a Portugese lay theologian[19] and George Pixley, an American scholar who has made his home in Latin America.[20] In his historical materialist reading of the New Testament, Pixley draws parallels to Gottwald's Old Testament hermen- eutic. Pixley does this by examining the "Jesus movement" in Palestine and the political economic conditions which brought it to birth.

The principle source of oppression against the realization of God's kingdom in Palestine was seen by the Jesus movement to be the temple and the class structure which the temple supported. Because the Pharisees and the Sadducees were agents of the Roman conquerors and because their support amongst the people centered on the religious sacrifices in the temple, Jesus' challenge is not surprising:

> And he entered the temple and began to drive out those who sold, saying to them, "It is written, 'My house shall be a house of prayer'; but you have made it a den of robbers" (Luke 19:45).

Jesus' accusation was directed at the parasitic class structure represented in the Pharisees and the priests. Like the contemporay mercenaries who work for a foreign oppressive power, the Pharisees and the priests possessed the credibility of being local people. They insured the docility of those who were being oppressed because their privileged position had religious sanctification. As well, they made life simpler for those who represented the imperial power, because it cut down on the number of Roman legions needed to maintain control.

Pixley explains that the Roman Empire was dependent on a hinterland slave society which insured productivity for the wealth of Rome. Furthermore, this productivity was enforced by an army, but because slaves do not produce children whose allegiance can be assured, the Roman armies had to conquer new territories. The *quid pro quo* that was successfully established in Palestine was made possible not only by the surrogate king Herod but also by the religious freedom Rome offered those who upheld the sanctity of the temple.[21] Unlike the Zealots who wanted to preserve the temple, Jesus and his followers saw in the temple the reinforcement of a class structure which left a double oppression on the poor – taxes for Rome and taxes for the temple.[22]

This historical materialist interpretation by Pixley brings into focus the principal enemies who plotted Jesus' death – the Pharisees in Galilee and the priests in Jerusalem. In other words, Jesus' enemies were the principal beneficiaries of the class system. Also included among Jesus' enemies were the scribes and the priests who upheld the banking operation of the temple in Jerusalem, and the Roman authority personified in the procurator, Pontius Pilate.

The Gospels agree that Jesus was executed as a messianic claimant. This is understandable in the title on Jesus's cross, "the King of the Jews" (Matthew 27:37). Mark, the writer of the second Gospel, records that there had been an uprising with some casualities in "Holy Week" (Mark 15:7). This explains why those who were also crucified with Jesus were two *lestai*, a word that can refer either to common highway robbers or to armed insurrectionists.[23] In the light of Mark, they were probably the latter.

Since the Jesus movement died with Jesus' death on the cross, what was its subsequent history? Pixley says that this history has been lost to us. However, says Pixley: "Our interest remains because the Latin American popular movement of our day knows that it must learn even from historical failures if it is one day to succeed in establishing a just society."[24]

When Bible scholars start to identify the centrality of the Jesus movement as an heuristic device of looking at New Testament hermeneutics, it becomes obvious that when a passage of Scripture is chosen on the theme, "You must be born again," it is important to turn to the conversion of Zacchaeus described in Luke 19:1-10, rather than the conversion of Nicodemus described in John 3:1-15. Zacchaeus was a "chief tax collector and rich." In the eyes of Jesus' followers, when Jesus went into Zacchaeus' house, he was slumming with a "sinner," a man who was the agent of Rome and the temple. But the test of Zacchaeus' conversion shows that the most recalcitrant rich exploiter can be converted: "...Behold, Lord, the half of my goods I give to the poor; and if I have defrauded any one of anything, I restore it fourfold." In contrast, the problem with the conversion of Nicodemus is that it is too often interpreted in 'spiritual rebirth' terms. Thus interpreted, being "born again" becomes a blasphemous term on the lips of "born again" President Ronald Reagan whose nuclear brinkmanship threatens the world with annihilation.

By using historical and materialist analyses, Feminist Biblical scholars have brought important insights to our understanding of the socio-economic conditions of women in the biblical period. Feminist theologians, however, face the double oppression of living in a patriarchal society and of having this society sanctified by partiarchal biblical texts. This makes the work of Feminist biblical exegetes very difficult, although challenging.

Elizabeth Fiorenza, an historical Feminist biblical scholar who examines the Feminist historical base, provides important clues to understanding women in the early Church. She points out that women of considerable prominence and wealth founded house churches in the Church of the "Diaspora." This new Church (called the "Christian Movement," which took over from the "Jesus movement" as Christianity spread through the Roman Empire) was not patriarchal, says Fiorenza. In this "Christian movement," house churches were founded by women and its egalitarian life style stood in contrast to the highly class structured Greco-Roman society.[25]

Elizabeth Fiorenza, as a Feminist theologian and Bible scholar, gives strong impetus to the solidarity of all oppressed people when she says, "The basic insight of all liberation theologies, including feminist theology, is the recognition that all theology, willingly or not, is by definition always engaged for or against the oppressed."[26] However, in the conclusion of her book, she refers to the "ecclesia of women" (past, present and future) as a "...Catholic sisterhood that spans all ages, nations and continents..."[27] and then she suggests that this bonding is necessary to face patriarchal and androgenous oppression. With this approach, the issue of class becomes obscured.

Marlene Dixon, a Feminist sociologist makes incisive criticism of this approach which treats all women as an oppressed class. She says:

> ...It attacks the development of class consciousness in working class women, serving to strengthen the bourgeois ideology of "men as the enemy" and "women as caste," which is so destructive to the struggle for the emanicipation of women."[28]

Dixon points out that "sisterhood is the root of bourgeois feminism" which subverts the economic class struggle by dividing the poor women and the poor men into alienating camps.

All people, women and men, can rejoice at Fiorenza's historical analysis which calls for greater equality within the church. Her analysis raises the place of women in the life of "the ecclesia" and, at the same time, exposes the oppression of women which has resulted from a sanctified Biblical male God. But although patriarchy has indeed been the cause of much of the oppression suffered by women throughout history, is it the only or even the main cause of women's oppression? Would liberation from patriarchy liberate for example, our native women or those living in the third world? When Feminist theology does not do a class analysis (and in some cases it does), does it now run the risk of itself being an agent of oppression? As I see it, women live under the double bondage of patriarchy and class, hence Feminist theology must answer to both. But this also means that Liberation Theology in the Canadian context must provide not only a class analysis but also the Feminist perspective which means something more than merely using inclusive language! It means that Liberation Theology that does do a class analysis must also be rigorous in its exposure of patriarchal oppression. "To set at liberty those who are oppressed" (Luke 4:19) demands answering the question of "who?" and "why?"

The thesis of this update on Liberation Theology in the Canadian context is that an historical materialist class analysis, which examines the historical economic social political conditions of Canadian society, exposes an oppressive class structure in Canada. This class structure, reinforced by a pernicious economic ideology called "supply side monetarist economics" (designed by the American economist Milton Friedman, and endorsed by Ronald Reagan, Margaret Thatcher, and Brian Mulroney), conceals the oppressive nature of our social economic and political structures. This economic ideology assumes that if you give the super rich and the companies they control tax breaks, and leave them free to spend their money, they will come forward with public philanthropy by establishing businesses for the public good which will create jobs. Contrary to popular belief, the huge unemployment statistics in Canada (as well as in Britain and in the United States) reveal both the cruelty of this economic vice and that it is a massive hoax.

If Liberation Theology is to provide any alternative through this historical materialist method, it must first expose the sanctimonious idealism in our churches which presently legitimate those who hold economic power. To do this will require serious 'soul searching' and thorough analysis of the liberal theology which permeates our smug middle class churches and consequently, makes of the church, a haven for the economically powerful and their minions who accept their domination as inevitable. A German New Testament scholar, Walter Stegemann critiques church services in which an idealistic interpretation of the parable of the Pharisee and the tax collector psychologize and rationalize the story. He says:

> The parable needs only to be altered slightly, namely in good Lutheran – Pauline tradition it would help to tell of a wealthy Christian who no longer points with pride to his or her religious "achievement" but confeses their

sinfulness before God. Of course one would immediately include the [paupers] besides oneself in the confession of guilt and accuse him of being a sinner also. The master accuses the servant of a similar abstract sinfulness instead of repenting of [one's] own sin and refraining from sinning in the future by directly or indirectly participating in the pauperization of the servant. This treatment of rich and poor, master and slave, as equal in relation to sin, is itself sin "before God," since "before the world" it is paralleled by an often cruel reality of nonequality.[29]

The searing truth of this quote not only exposes the hypocritical theology in our 'comfortable pews' but also, it provides an enormous challenge as the implications of historical materialist class analysis of our society and the biblical witness are brought into prominence.

To restore confidence of poor people that the church is on their side and intends to work for a more equitable and just Canada, demands implementation of two political requirements which are fundamental to the mandate of the Gospel of our Lord Jesus Christ.

The first is a just tax structure.[30] At present eighty-one per cent of all Federal Personal Income Taxes is paid by workers who earn less than $18,000 per year. Since 1979, 740 Canadians with incomes of over $100,000 paid no taxes at all. The recommendations of the 1967 Carter Commission on Taxation are still to be implemented. Canada needs a surtax on all incomes of over $50,000; it needs to remove the 50% tax holiday on Capital gains; it needs an Inheritance Tax. As well, Canada needs much closer scrutiny of Canadians who escape taxes through having their money in "off shore tax havens" which are often in the Carribean.

The second political requirement has long term implications – the need in Canada to develop an economy of self-reliance. Such an economy will require careful stewardship of our natural resources in order to avoid environmental pollution. Self-reliance will require giving preferential low interest loans and trading opportunities to countries which need to develop their own appropriate technology. Self-reliance will require a Canadian population with full employment for those who want to work outside the home. The implication of self-reliance is reduced physical dependence upon international production and trade. Above all else, self-reliance will mean freeing the economy from the grip of multinationals who transfer capital and close down company towns as they move to poor third world countries with sweat shop labour.

Although these may appear to be bold suggestions, they have been taken up by church groups and now they appear in important resolutions by church courts. However, they still need to be implemented.

William Hordern has been a theological catalyst in Canada on most of the issues which have been discussed in this paper. Although he retires from theological teaching, his incisive mind is ever present in a collegial enterprise to engage these theories. He is needed with his fresh insights because our Canadian society is polluted with the terrible injustices of undistributed economic wealth. At the same time, the theological noise from the "Immoral Majority"[31] sanctifies laissez-faire theological and economic imperialism. Within our main line churches, both Protestant and Catholic, there appears to be a spiritual awakening made evident in the statements by the Canadian Catholic Bishops and the Canadian Council of Churches acting as tribunes for the poor. Regrettably, at the same time, there is an anti-intellectualism within the church which stifles dissent. In this, our contemporary situation, we need Hordern's unshakable faith and prophetic vision, as well as his theological expertise!

As we bid him farewell, our prayer should be: "Would that all the Lord's people were prophets. [like William Hordern] that the Lord would put [God's] spirit upon them"! (Numbers 11:29)

LUBRICATING THE CAMEL: CLEMENT OF ALEXANDRIA ON WEALTH AND THE WEALTHY

Walter H. Wagner

Wealth creates problems. For the poor the problems are not only the lack of necessities, money and possessions. Poverty, "unwealth," reaches deeper: it is a state of mind and a social reality. Being poor is linked to being powerless, marginalized, oppressed. In addition, Euro-Americans have tended to blame the poor for being poor, associating poverty with being crude, lazy, immoral and inferior. Times and tones, however, are changing. Since World War II, especially in the last twenty years, criticisms by and on behalf of the poor have aimed at wealth and the wealthy, together with the systems and structures which produce them. Among Christians this shift is evident in documents such as Vatican II's *Gaudium et Spes*, terms like "preferential option for the poor," and various movements often called "Liberation Theology."[1] Regardless of our political, economic or religious positions, we are acutely aware of the plight and pent-up power of the poor, and of some of the problems and limitations involved in alleviating poverty.

At the other end of the spectrum the problems of the prosperous are more than getting, keeping and passing on what they have. Wealth, too, is a state of mind and a social reality. Its links and associations are the obverse of poverty's: power, importance and authority, sophistication, diligence, propriety, and superiority. The stakes for the wealthy, personally and collectively, are high. How are money, prestige and power gained and used? What are the prices paid by the environment, society and individuals for some to become and stay affluent? When and to whom are the "haves" accountable for their attitudes and actions? Can a person be rich *and* moral? For those of even modestly tender conscience, being wealthy may engender feelings of anxiety and guilt in a world of desperate and suffering people. Subjected to inner and outer pressures, the prosperous may be tempted to protect themselves by closing ranks, clenching their fists and hardening their hearts. Outnumbered and often resented, the prosperous may feel rejected by the wider human community.

Wealth creates peculiar problems for Christians. Although we are spread across the economic spectrum, substantial numbers of new and re-evangelized Christians are poor persons living in Africa, Asia and the Americas. Many of these brothers and sisters in Christ are neither slow nor soft-spoken in addressing wealthy Christians in their own lands and the North Atlantic nations. Together with persons of other religious and ideological convictions, they pose significant questions about being wealthy and Christian.

Rich Christians themselves are hooked on a dilemma. One horn, sharpened by biblical references and theological traditions, regards wealth as a gift of God, a sign of divine approval for faithfulness and a call to responsible action toward one's neighbors. The other, also sharpened by biblical references and theological traditions, suspects that wealth rarely is gained by the just, but ensnares the wealthy and obstructs their salvation. Perhaps a nimble rich Christian might skirt Ecclesiastes' and Ecclesiasticus' pessimism, hurdle James' condemnations, and hold on to a full platter in spite of the Magnificat. Perhaps the mighty and the affluent in the Church are able to discuss dispassionately the merits of cutting health care, closing factories, revising Native Peoples' treaty rights, and putting up with acid rain. Nevertheless, no matter how adroit in action or conversation they may be, wealthy Christians are a problem to themselves, the Church and the society. There is need for an authentic theological and pastoral understanding of wealth and wealthy believers. The point of entry into such a development may be one of the most difficult sayings attributed to Jesus:

> And Jesus looked around and said to his disciples, "How hard it will be for those who have riches to enter the kingdom of God!" And the disciples were amazed at his words. But Jesus said to them again, "Children, how hard it is to enter the kingdom of God! It is easier for a camel to go through the eye of a needle than for a rich man to enter the kingdom of God." And they were exceedingly astonished, and said to him, "Then who can be saved?" Jesus looked at them and said, "With men it is impossible, but not with God; for all things are possible with God."
>
> Mark 10:23-27

The passage is too plain to be open to hermeneutical debates as is Matthew 25:31-46 and too well attested to be considered a later interpolation of the Church as might be Mark 10:2-9. Neither can its obvious thrust be relegated to examples of oriental hyperbole, e.g., cutting off offending limbs and casting mountains into the sea. Nor is anything gained through supposing that otherwise sensible merchants tugged unburdened camels through narrow gateways on the way to market. Moreover, the account of the rich man who occasioned Jesus' statement along with the passage moved Antony, Peter Waldo, Francis of Assisi and others to decisive, literal obedience. At stake here is not biblicistic imitation but a perspective on life, a summons and response to discipleship, a relationship to self and society. How might wealth be connected to discipleship? What status do wealthy believers have, if any, within the Christian community? Can a person be both rich and a Christian? Is it possible for a camel to pass through the eye of a needle?

The passage and the questions raised could be taken from the stances of the synoptic authors and their putative communities.[2] We, however, will examine one Christian's treatment of the issues and the specific text along with some implications—plus and minus—which he presents to us. Clement of Alexandria, widely regarded as the first self-conscious Christian theologian-author, considered the place and conduct of rich Christians with critical yet sympathetic detail.[3] His extant writings disclose an unusual, even odd, figure, at least in the light of later creeds and dogmas. Clement's positive and frequently expressed concern for the wealthy seems unique in the early Church. He obviously knew and cared about prosperous Christians and pagans. His descriptions of social life and banquets indicate first-hand experience of such events and close association with the participants, yet he keeps conscious distinctions between them and himself.

The study begins with comments about Clement's theological perspective. The main section deals with his views on wealth and the wealthy, including his sermonic-essay, *Who is the Rich Man Being Saved?* In conclusion I venture some reflections on the inherent opportunities and risks for Christians and the Church today when camel and needle are brought together.

1. Clement's Theological Perspective

While the faith and life of the Church described by Clement are recognizably rooted in and derived from the first Christian communities and the New Testament, obviously there were changes.[4] An essential change was in the reigning motif of salvation. The shift might be summarized as a transformation of an age-ending cosmic act to an eternal and essentially individual process. The earlier apocalyptic-eschatological expectation was for the imminent triumph of God in history and the establishment of his kingdom. Existing cosmic, social and political orders would be wiped out in the day of resurrection, judgment and new creation. Salvation was deliverance; deliverance from divine wrath, demonic enslavement, sin and death. How works, grace and right belief related to salvation were open to discussion, but entry into the kingdom was limited to a faithful, morally strict remnant. Discipleship for individuals and communities was a matter of urgent, immediate action.

For Clement and those whom he addressed, discipleship was no less urgent, but salvation was construed differently. The apocalyptic-eschatological action was transformed into an education-developmental process. An individual was led through this earthly and then various heavenly learning places until she reached the mansion prepared for her.[5] Salvation was still deliverance, albeit deliverance from defiant ignorance, willful disobedience and destructive habits. God's wrath and Satan's torments were only pedagogical threats intended to prod stubborn learners to greater efforts. Salvation was both the educational process and its goal, the soul's becoming fully the image and likeness of the *Logos*. Put another way, salvation was the consummation of God's creative plan, that is, for all humans eventually to become gods.[6]

Although Clement did not eliminate a dissolution of the present cosmos, he seems to have reserved speculation about it and descriptions of heaven to esoteric teachings shared among the most advanced in the process, i.e., the "true gnostics." A person's physical death appears to have an eschatological function in that such a death ends the earthly level of instruction. The period before death acquires an urgency in that physical structures, social position and economic status fall away from the soul as she moves on in the process of fulfillment.[7] Time on earth for the proper development and formation of mind, will and habits is short, and is to be used under proper guidance and appropriate discipline.

Construing salvation as the educational-developmental process of fulfillment required imaginative and articulate applications of allegorical-typological methods of interpreting Scripture, pagan literature and philosophy. Clement's concept of salvation and the way of life which led to it was supported by his emphasis on wisdom literature (Greco-Roman as well as Jewish) and a wisdom-oriented hermeneutic to virtually everything from the structure of the cosmos to bathing. Logically, the epitome of the divinely inspired speaker and doer of the Word of God was not the prophet-apostle but the wiseman-teacher.

Whether Clement's theological perspective is to be regarded now as a corruption of the gospel or a rationalization to cope with the failure of the parousia or a creative interpretation of Christian teachings is beside the point. The point here is how his position relates to the issue of wealth and wealthy Christians. Clement's understandings have been used by the Church more unknowingly than deliberately and more selectively than judiciously.

2. Clement on Wealth and Wealthy Christians

Familiarity with the trappings of wealth and wealthy Christians was not unusual for the Church in Alexandria and perhaps elsewhere.[8] At least such is the impression given by Clement. That the Alexandrian congregation included members of ample means and upper class tastes is scarcely surprising in light of the city's size, prosperity and religious-philosophical bent. What is surprising is the attention Clement devoted to the wealthy and their ways of life. Affluent persons are not only *in* his audience; they *are* his audience. In sharp contrast to Tertullian, his Latin African contemporary who addressed some of the same topics, Clement does not resort to insult and condemnation. His attitude and rhetoric presuppose educated, sophisticated readers. On closer examination, whole sections of his works consist of broad principles, specific applications, apt illustrations and persuasive paradigms directed toward wealthy Christians. All these plus his supposed digressions are artfully integrated into his overall theological framework.

Obviously Clement did not address multi-million member international ecclesial bodies or rich believers with great political-social influence. He spoke to individuals or small groups of concerned persons. Presenting some underlying concepts and much practical guidance, he discussed personal development for salvation in the context of problems and risks encountered by affluent sisters and brothers in Christ. He did not consciously seek to widen the needle's eye, that is, to ease the requirements for the discipleship to fulfillment. He might admit, however, to lubricating the camel or proposing how the rich person could enter the kingdom. Whatever other position Clement may have had at Alexandria, when he counseled the wealthy he was a pastor, a wiseman-spiritual director. His *Who Is The Rich Man Being Saved* is openly pastoral in style and content. Basic positions in the *Paidagogos* and *Stromateis* also are crucial to understanding Clement's theological-ministering perspective and procedures. In his wiseman-pastor role Clement dealt with at least three closely linked issues which are still pertinent. Initially, he assured rich Christians that they could be saved and implicitly advised other believers about their relations with the wealthy. Then he provided a responsible approach to possessions and their uses. Finally, he gave practical direction and encouragement to the wealthy and those who ministered to them. In handling these issues Clement relied on the harmonious interplay of creation, soul and salvation within God's comprehensive purposes.

First, the camel can pass through the needle's eye—but only when willing, disciplined and active. In *Who Is The Rich Man* Clement addressed specifically the issue of wealthy Christians.[9] His reflections on average members' reactions to prosperous fellow believers indicate that there were serious tensions. Some were insolent and rude toward the rich, while others fawned over and flattered them. These contradictory reactions had a common result: they impeded the salvation of the wealthy. On the one hand those who were treated gruffly despaired of being loved by God and included in the plan of fulfillment. Exclusionary conduct and harsh words by the economically humbler members seem to have been based on literalistic understandings of the Scripture. The same sort of understanding demoralized the rich who took the biblical criticisms and personal rebuffs to heart. If God favored some people with love and acceptance but rejected others on the basis of their economic and social standing, then salvation was beyond the reach of the rich. Indeed, it seemed that only the penniless and destitute could be righteous. On the other hand, there were wealthy Christians who interpreted the Scripture differently and so were not bothered by the literalists. They, however, responded to the admiration and praise of obsequious believers. These wealthy Christians became careless about what the Lord required of them in their education to salvation. Instead of leading disciplined lives they basked in the attention given them and ignored the legitimate harshness of the biblical warnings. If one type of rich person despaired of salvation, the other presumed it would be bestowed as a matter of course.

Clement's response was based on a pair of tenaciously held assumptions. He was convinced that salvation was a matter of eternal not temporal, heavenly not earthly fulfillment. And he adamantly maintained that God loved humans and determined to save them all. These assumptions were combined in his hermeneutic of Scripture and life. Because salvation concerned the development and discipline of the soul, the fullest meanings of biblical passages were to be sought in their applications to the soul. Yet, since God made the world through the Logos, the physical creation was not to be disparaged. The creation served both as a setting and instrument for the soul's education. On such grounds, the Bible—especially the words of Jesus the Paidagogos—presented a range of divinely-wise lessons and directions for the soul's improvement. The range extended from praise and promise to criticism and condemnation, but the latter served as goads to progress, not as actual descriptions of God's dispositions and intentions. Literalists erred in applying the Bible to the present world and bodily existence in it, while the careless ignored the biblical demands and exhortations to discipline their souls' habits, actions and passions.

As the learner requires an appropriate learning context and an instructor, so the soul now needs the creation and the Paidagogos. The problem for humans was in their souls, not their bodies. Essentially, wealth and poverty were issues of the mind, will and appetite. Here his interpretation of the Marcan passage about the rich man is both consoling and pointed. The Saviour's words to divest oneself of all possessions cannot be taken with physical literalness for they apply not to worldly possessions but to the soul. Clement pointed out that if salvation were based on total poverty, "... those men who have nothing at all, but are destitute and beg for their daily bread, who lie along the roads in abject poverty, would, though 'ignorant' of God and 'God's righteousness' be most blessed and beloved of God, and the only possessors of eternal life, by the sole fact of their being utterly without ways and means of livelihood and in want of the smallest necessities. Nor again is it a new thing to renounce wealth and give it freely to the poor, or to one's fatherland which many have done before the Saviour's coming. . ." (*Rich Man*, 11).

Instead of limiting himself to the man's possessions, Clement noted that he also was a good man, one who fulfilled the Law. Goodness, however, is not perfection; the works of the Law do not save, only grace does. For Clement, the Saviour knew that the rich man needed not "to fling away the substance that belongs to him and to part with his riches, but to banish from the soul its opinions about riches, its attachment to them, its excessive desire, its morbid excitement over them, its anxious cares, the thorns of our earthly existence which choke the seed of true life" (*Rich Man*, 11). The allusions to the Sermon on the Mount and the Parable of the Sower are deliberate. Clement consciously conflated passages in instructional chain references to make the Logos' point that true treasures are in heaven, not on earth. Naturally, then, rich persons were being saved. Clement observed realistically that '. . . it is no great or enviable thing to be simply without riches."

Nevertheless, Clement knew that between the soul and riches there would be a destructive dynamic,

> Wealth, in fact, seems to me like a snake; unless a person knows how to grasp it properly, dangling it without harm from just above the tip of the tail, the snake will twist about to the hand and strike. Wealth, too, twisting in the grasp, whether experienced or not, can cling to the hand and bite unless a man rises superior to it and uses it with discretion; that is to say, he may train the beast by the invocation of the Logos and remain unharmed.
>
> *Paidagogos* III, 6, 35

The rich may be saved but they need more caution, discipline and effort than others. Wealth is not a reward; it is a severe test. As will be seen, the rich need affirmative and critical support from persons within the Christian community. To mix metaphors in Clement's style, the camel can pass through the needle's eye but only when anointed as an athlete trained by the Logos-Paidagogos.

A responsible approach to possessions and their use, our second issue, links Clement's hermeneutics to his view of human nature. Clement cannot be pinned down to either Platonic or Stoic or any consistent doctrine of the soul, because he is not concerned about the "parts" of the soul and their functions but about developing a relationship between the divine and the human. He proceeds in a two-fold manner. What may be called the biblical-theoretical framework is based on Genesis 1:26, humanity in the image (*eikon*) and likeness (*homoiōsis*) of God, and John 1:1-18, the work of the Logos. Clement took the word God in the Genesis passage to mean the supreme deity who created the cosmos through Logos. Whether Clement held the Logos to be of the same or similar substance to the supreme God is not germane to the present issue. Logos, the agent through whom all was made, is uniquely the *eikon* and *homoiōsis* of God. Logos and God are in total communion (*koinonia*), sharing all perfection; e.g., perfection in love, incorruptibility, immortality, passionlessness, etc. Logos alone can properly be called *aner*, man, because Logos is the only one who is in God's image and likeness. For purposes here, Logos may be termed the heavenly Human. The heavenly Human is the father (and even mother!) of creaturely humans, men and women. Their destiny is to develop fully into being in the image and likeness of Logos. So, the heavenly Human is the origin of, pattern for, guide to and, broadly speaking, goal for all creaturely humans. To be saved is to be in the *eikon* and *homoiōsis* of the Logos who, in turn, is the *eikon* and *homoiōsis* of God.

Clement pushed further by distinguishing between the image and likeness. Logos implanted his image as a gracious gift into all humans. The *eikon*, called the mind and a love charm, establishes a bond of communion between the heavenly Human and creaturely humans, and among the creaturely humans. *Homoiōsis* is the capacity to grow into being like the Logos apparently in those aspects of life especially related to motivations and actions. The many faceted pedagogical process to salvation may be described as bringing the *eikon* to full externalized expression along with actualizing the potential of the *homoiōsis*. Even if there were no problems in Eden, Adam and Eve were immature children who needed further discipline and improvement before they could take their places among the heavenly beings. Yielding to the serpent was an act of defiant ignorance which made their souls sickly weak, and disordered their minds, will and passions. Thereafter, creaturely humans were tied to the earth and became more brutish than the beasts, entrenching themselves in customs that only reinforced their ignorance, disobedience and feebleness.

In such a condition, women and men encounter and use possessions. Ordinarily, it is not the things in themselves which are troublesome, but the soul's disorientations which turn wealth and associated activities into snares and burdens. Never one to leave his children in the lurch, Logos becomes the wise and loving Paidagogos. As instructor-guide he intends to raise the soul out of its bondage to passion for things and to train the soul in the proper use of wealth so that the person will be prepared to be initiated into the secrets of heavenly knowledge. In that process the Logos—and his already-initiated representatives—offer instruction, discipline and guidance on the basis of individual needs and circumstances. Possessions then can become instructional materials in the lessons which lead to salvation.

Within his biblical-theoretical framework Clement developed a psychological-practical mode of ethical precepts and directions, again working through the communion between Logos and creaturely humans. As encouraging exhorter (Protreptikos) and disciplinary trainer (Paidagogos), Logos seeks to lift up, train, heal, instruct and improve the soul in order to become ultimately its Teacher (Didaskalos) who imparts the divine wisdom. To reach the final stage of development the soul must have proper habits, engage in good works and have self-controlled dispositions. Clement's "psychology" or understanding of the soul might have been flexible in the formal sense, yet he held that habits, actions and passions were crucial areas no matter how many parts or functions the soul had. While habits sometimes referred to pagan traditions to be jettisoned through the urgings of the Logos-Protreptikos, they were also deeply pervasive in the personality structure of the individual. As such, habits were ingrained, and could be changed only through discipline and practice, a re-programming of conduct patterns. Clement was quite specific about the Logos-Paidagogos's role in applying healing, advice and instruction to the soul's actions and passions.

Because the Logos created the cosmos and is the source of all truth and goodness wherever these may occur, Clement drew freely and frequently, although selectively, from pagan culture. The general principles (katorthomata) and specific duties (kathekonta) of Stoic ethics formed a useful set of guidelines for his psychological praxis. A panoply of tones used by the Logos-Paidagogos in instructing and training Christians is laid out in *Paidagogos* I. It is applicable to all Christians regardless of economic status and social condition. These, plus the remainder of the *Paidagogos*, portions of the *Stromateis* and the *Rich Man* deal in long drawn out, sometimes humorous, detail with the lives and times of the wealthy.

At first glance it appears that Clement treats the rich so leniently that their way into the kingdom is broad and easy. For example, he seems to expect that after their baptisms wealthy Christians will continue their social rounds and styles in much the same way as before their conversions. They will keep attending lavish feasts, wear luxurious garments, have jewelry, use cosmetics, own slaves, live in richly furnished homes, and enjoy the company of worldly non-believers. Concessions about items such as rings and cosmetics as well as actions like the etiquette of laughing and belching decorously at banquets, taken out of context, could earn Clement a reputation as toady to the rich. In context, however, Clement prescribes a rigorous process of intensifying discipline for the soul which benefits the community if followed. Every habit, act and feeling is subject to the Paidagogos's all-encompassing, strict attention. No object owned—even cups and chamberpots, or private moment—including sleep and bathing, or food eaten or thought about escapes the Paidagogos's training program. The more a person has, the more likely he or she is attached to possessions; so the more pervasive and intense are the exercises imposed by the Logos. Since the problem of wealth is a problem of the soul rather than of the things that are owned, the resolution of the problem is in correcting and training the soul.

Giving away external property or even ceasing certain actions is not what the Saviour enjoins the rich man to do,

> He who has cast away his worldly abundance can still be
> rich in passions even though his substance is gone. For

his disposition continues its own activity, choking and stifling the power of reasoning and inflaming him with its inbred desires. It is no great gain then for him to be poor in possessions but rich in passions. For he has cast away not the worthless things but the indifferent (*adiaphora*), and while depriving himself of what is serviceable, he has set on fire the innate material of evil by the lack of material things. . . the Lord admits the use of outward things, bidding us to put away, not the means of living, but the things that use these badly; and these are. . . the infirmities and passions of the soul.

Rich Man, 15

Possessions, as will be indicated below, may have quite positive roles in the salvation of the wealthy. Effective, enduring instruction is that which penetrates to and throughout the soul. That kind of education takes time and patience for both trainer and trainee. Clement knew that education proceeds rather than leaps. Souls need to absorb new ways willingly and make the new patterns of habits, actions and strivings their own. Plainly immoral and idolatrous conduct, of course, was not to be tolerated. More common and more difficult to reach were the attitudes and dispositions which society endorsed and which persons, here rich persons, had acquired during years prior to responding to the Logos-Protreptikos. Those attitudes and dispositions struggled to maintain their places in directing the soul, so it would take time and steady, careful exercise to redirect the soul. Clement's concessions were temporary expedients to be given up by the person as her or his soul advanced in being more fully the Logos's image and likeness. Constant pressure on and supervision over the rich—freely accepted and acted upon by them—were required if the rich were to pass through the needle's eye. While the camel could get through, the passage took hard, thorough work under the disciplining voice and hand of the Logos.

Clement's third issue, that of practical direction and encouragement to the wealthy and those who minister to them, seems at first far from practical and fraught with risks, but may still be apt. Logos is not a platitudinous or absentee Paidagogos. In order to carry forward the educational plan of salvation, to show creaturely humans what their heavenly future will be, the heavenly Human became incarnate. Whatever else the earthly career of the enfleshed Logos was for Clement, he takes it as a revelation of the Logos as Protreptikos and Paidagogos, and as an opening to know Logos as Didaskalos. Some creaturely humans then and now have made such rapid progress in the Logos's plan for consummation that they have been initiated into his heavenly mysteries. To reach that level and to advance further in being in the Logos's image and likeness, they completed and successfully mastered the curriculum by which their souls' habits, actions and strivings were renovated, indeed, recreated. They now no longer desire nor need wealth or possessions.

Such rare individuals are far from being detached from earth because they are attached to heaven. They engage in *therapeia*. Toward God through Logos, *therapeia* is proper worship in the wisdom and truth that makes them free from things and free to advance further toward divinity. Through Logos toward their creaturely brothers and sisters, *therapeia* entails their being the Logos's images and likenesses, his pedagogical representatives, trainers and discipliners for those still struggling with their souls' greater immaturity. They are the true gnostics, the ones wise in the ways of the Lord. Clement includes himself in their ranks, but nowhere even hints that they have a particular rank in the church. They are teachers, mentors, guides, models, disciplinarians, personal spiritual directors yet are not called presbyters or deacons. While they appear to be servants for the whole Christian community, Clement singles them out for a special function with regard to the rich.

Clement proposes that a rich person or family regard such a wise one as instructor-discipliner. There are obvious parallels between the ancient practice of having a live-in paidagogos for the children of the wealthy. Clement's paidagogos, however, would be for adults and not be a slave. This paidagogos would be an authoritative counselor, knowing about and speaking out, bluntly when necessary, on the intimate details of family, business and social life. The paidagogos-gnostic would scarcely be a household chaplain who offered prayers at mealtimes and sermons at special events. Given the full range of the Logos-Paidagogos's arsenal and medicine cabinet of tones and tactics, including both public and private measures, Clement's proposal calls for levels of discipleship among the rich and perhaps the wise as well which are rare in any age. It appears clear, moreover, that wealthy Alexandrian Christians were open to the proposal and probably acted on it.

Whether or not the paidagogos-wise one was in residence is less germane than the relationship between the rich and the guide that is suggested. The prerequisite of the relationship is to have persons who will enter into it. There are affluent Christians, but what about the guides? Clement places the relationship in the context of the Christian community so if there are to be such persons, the church is summoned to identify and develop them. The guide is to be more than highly knowledgeable about the Scripture and tradition. The guide is to be a mature, devout person who has struggled with and achieved not only substantial self-understanding but has given himself or herself to the transforming power of the Logos in the details as well as the major points of life. Further, the person is expected to be understanding, skilled, alert to the ins and outs of human personalities and social realities. As is the Logos, the person is to be loving, patient and persistent. The paidagogos does not have to be adroit in the affairs of business any more than in giving parties. What is required is the ability to penetrate the obscuring mists of the external conditions and lures of things to the essential ethical and theological issues at stake. The penetration is not for academic purposes but directed toward the educational plan of wholeness among God's creatures. In other words, the guide should be able to discern the core concerns beyond profit and appearance, articulate these concerns, and point the ways to use situations and things for the purposes of justice and fulfillment.

Wealth involved more than a state of mind which required transformation; it was also a tangible social reality. What were the rich to do with their affluence? Clement's response stresses the communion which exists among humans, their unity as God's children, with a priority given to Christian fellowship,

> Thus he declares that all possessions are by nature unrighteous [after quoting Luke 16:9], when a man possesses them for personal advantage as being entirely his own, and does not bring them into the common stock for those in need; but that from this unrighteousness it is possible to perform a deed that is righteous and saving, namely, to give relief to one of those who have an eternal habitation with the Father . . . you should not yield to a request or wait to be pestered, but that you should personally seek out men whom you may benefit, men who are worthy disciples of the Saviour.
> *Rich Man* 31

Sharing is the motif of using wealth. For Clement ". . . love bursts forth into good works" (*Rich Man* 28). As God's love has burst forth in creating humans and all things, so human love bursts forth to respond to God and to love what God created in love. To love one's neighbor, indeed, is to love the Logos-Saviour who came to be our neighbor. The Logos-Neighbor loves us as himself, raising us to life with him. In response, love for the Saviour includes caring for and sharing with those who are growing into his ways and likeness. Sharing also involves how and what is shared are acquired. It is plain hypocrisy to get wealth dishonestly and then to legitimate acquiring it by giving it to others. Honesty, frugality, integrity in gaining wealth are expected. What is acquired provides Clement with opportunities to compile lists of luxuries and to comment on luxury-loving attitudes, especially in *Paidagogos* II. His maxim is "We should possess wealth in a becoming manner, sharing it generously, but not mechanically nor with affectation" (*Paidagogos* II, 6, 34). Reasoning that when all outer trappings are removed people are all equal, "it is not he who possesses and retains his wealth who is wealthy, but he who gives; it is giving, not receiving that reveals the happy man. Generosity is a product of the soul; so true wealth is in the soul" (*Paidagogos* II, 6, 36).

3. Conclusions

Can the camel go through the needle's eye? Clement's response may not be exegetically sound, but it contains theological-pastoral elements which can be constructive and destructive. Some trends current in liberation theology appear to restrict God's love, acceptance and salvation to the poor. This is the long delayed reaction to the drift among affluent Christians which identifies the redeemed with the rich. Taking only parts of Clement's position while muting or silencing altogether other portions leads to distortion. His affirmation of the rich was carefully developed. Only lubricated camels can go through the needle's eye into the kingdom. The lubrication is composed of the gracious tough love-discipline of Logos and the sweat of the rich. A close reading discloses that Clement persisted in an educational-guiding model which requires substantial sacrifice and risk on the part of the wealthy. The program was varied but consistent in focussing God's love and wisdom on self-control and service by the believer.

Is there anything positive which the Church today may consider and even develop? At least four areas come to mind.

First, recognize the need of the rich for a ministry to the rich. Clement's pastoral approach need not be taken as antagonistic to the prophetic voices about the abuse of wealth and power. Neither does it encourage a fawning over the rich in the hope of being bequeathed some of their riches or sharing in the glow of their supposed power. A pastoral approach realizes the deep and complex human dilemmas faced by the wealthy, their sense of need to give, and their willingness to be disciples.

Second, recognize the theological issues and tensions connected with wealth and the wealthy in Scripture, history and present circumstances. The Church is experienced in developing statements about economic and political issues related primarily to corporate and governmental authorities. Another factor in this field is the theological examination of and perspectives on wealth, as well as poverty. The theological connections between justification by grace and the place of discipline are pressing at least the Lutheran Church for open discussion.

Third, as Clement highlighted education, so may the Church. An aspect is the development of discipleship formed by love and lubrication, by God's grace and our responses to his discipline. The linkages between how money is gained, from whom and at what cost, with our faith are being made public as in the speeches of Pope John Paul II in Canada (1984) and elsewhere. Another aspect is Clement's suggestion of a paidagogos-guide. Does theological education—either during or after seminary graduation—prepare persons to be guides to the rich? Fraught with dangers and difficulties, the idea may merit further discussion.

Fourth, the issue of the ministry of the whole people of God runs throughout discussions of wealth and the wealthy. The respective roles of lay and ordained persons as advisers, counselors, helpers in a ministry to the rich is clear. Yet the ministry of the rich through sharing, how those in positions of authority in economic and corporate areas make decisions are matters connected to the responsibility of all Christians to be agents of reconciliation.

Wealth can generate problems, be a state of mind and a social reality. Whether or not camels can pass through the eyes of needles will not be really known until the consummation of God's plan for salvation. In the meantime we have the liniment of discipline and the anointing of grace.

REALISM AND FREEDOM WITHIN A PENITENTIARY
Gary Watts

I) From Seminary to Prison

My first year at Lutheran Theological Seminary, Saskatoon, was also Dr. William Hordern's first year there. Apparently he was someone who had studied and taught in "the States" and then decided to come home. Having come through the secular educational system in the province of British Columbia, I was curious about this new president of the seminary, who seemed both academically competent and firmly confident about the Christian faith. I encountered Bill Hordern in various ways. For instance, whenever my fellow first-year students had a grievance or petition to present to the President, they would often ask me to present our case. I was usually gullible enough to do so, and remember Hordern once remarking as I entered his office: "So again you are the mouse to bell the cat!"

Hordern never seemed to me to be a warm counsellor-type, nor a zealous evangelist. However as I got to know him during that first year and the years following, I found him to be very personally concerned about each student and staff member, and he expressed this in numerous quiet, practical, ways. Also I found him to be vitally concerned about proclaiming the basic "good news" to our changing society. Usually my meetings with Hordern resulted in a theological debate! That was great. Here was a man who shared my concerns about communicating the basic gospel message to the contemporary world. I wanted seriously to grapple with the theological issues of the church in society before going to the parish. I immensely enjoyed the class discussions in his ethics and theology courses. Actually Hordern usually was quite evasive about giving his own "answers" to an issue, but was always ready to engage a student in a lively search for biblically-based answers for twentieth-century man. I felt that the Christian faith was becoming more relevant for me, given my previous experience and education.

I enjoyed studying the theology of Paul Tillich but found his systematic thought easy to put aside once I had explored it. Another theologian who had influenced Hordern was Reinhold Niebuhr. Niebuhr, still living at that time, was concerned about the need to apply the love of God to concrete social situations. Hordern was always realistic. Although he appreciated the idealism of youth in the sixties, I recall him saying in one chapel sermon: "Our youth don't realize that you cannot go back to the Garden!" Niebuhr was concerned about the responsible use of power in a fallen world. An American, Niebuhr certainly was not a social reactionary, since he opposed his nation's military involvement in Viet Nam. Yet I balked at Niebuhr's call for Christians to use power responsibly. Was the responsible use of power genuinely possible? If so, was not there a danger in morally justifying the misuse of power?

I was then drawn to an emerging German theologian whose *Theologie der Hoffnung* (1965) was published in English in 1967. Juergen Moltmann's *Theology of Hope* appeared at a time of theological ferment. But as Hordern correctly predicted upon reading the book: "Theology of hope is not just another fad." Indeed it was not. Moltmann was calling upon "main-line" Christians to reconsider the importance of biblical eschatology. For him eschatology meant the doctrine of Christian hope. Interestingly, some students in evangelical/fundamentalist seminaries were stating that they were no longer interested in biblical eschatology. Moltmann found biblical teachings about eschatology to be central to the Christian faith and relevant to our twentieth-century world. He regretted that the Christian faith had "banished from its life the future hope by which it is upheld . . . whereas the biblical testimonies which it handed on are yet full to the brim with future hope of a messianic kind for the world."[1]

Moltmann served the Christian Church well in retrieving eschatology from its position as a mere appendage to systematic theology. He said:

> From first to last, and not merely in the epilogue, Christianity is eschatology, is hope, forward looking and forward moving, and therefore also revolutionizing and transforming the present.[2]

Moltmann's theological concern did not pass unheeded. In 1969 a former American student of Hordern wrote:

> If the gospel of Christ, as Moltmann suggests, frees a man to be for those who labor and are heavy laden, the humiliated and abused, then it would seem that for twentieth-century America the message of Black Power is the message of Christ himself.[3]

Moltmann focussed on Scriptures such as Colossians 1:27, "He is our hope."[4] Moltmann's purpose was to remind us that the "Christian faith lives from the raising of the crucified Christ, and strains after the promises of the universal future of Christ."[5]

Nearing the completion of seminary, I filled in the appropriate form for church leaders, expressing my desire to become a) an assistant pastor in an urban congregation, or b) a teacher-missionary, or c) a military chaplain. Instead I became the pastor of a northern rural parish, and then a chaplain in a maximum-security penitentiary. What I had learned in seminary proved to be very meaningful in my prison ministry. Extremely few inmates knew the meaning of "theology". Not even the best-educated correctional worker I met had heard of Niebuhr and Moltmann. But I became convinced that all people stand in a broken or healing relationship with God, that the God we may choose to ignore or repress is, in some sense, always there. In prison, one cannot avoid inner questions of hope/hopelessness, and of love/justice. Staff are also in prison, though not for 24 hours a day. A prison is a microcosm of the world. It is like the outside world, only more so. In prison one finds man, and hopefully God.

Under the terms of the British North America Act of 1867, the Federal Government of Canada was authorized to administer correctional institutions for convicted offenders sentenced by the courts for imprisonment of two years or more. The federal agency which administers the sentence of such offenders while they are incarcerated is Correctional Service Canada. So the primary role of corrections, whether federal or provincial, is to administer the sentence of the courts. The federal correctional institutions are called "penitentiaries". C.S.C. is divided into five geographical areas: Atlantic Region, Quebec Region, Ontario Region, Prairie Region, and Pacific Region. The penitentiaries in each Region are classified into three basic security levels—"maximum", "medium", and "minimum". The sentenced persons are called "inmates". The other day when I asked an inmate to sign his request form for a religious diet, he said, "Let's be honest." Under his signature, he stroked out the word "inmate" and wrote in "prisoner".

Some government officials are proud that Canada has an imprisonment rate of only 111 per 100,000 citizens (or 150 per 100,000 adult population). South Africa and the United States are known throughout the world for their ability to imprison great numbers of their citizens. Canada's rate of 111 is small in comparison to the American imprisonment rate of 270 per 100,000. However the imprisonment rate in England/Wales is only 87; France is 68; Australia is 65; Norway is 52; Japan is 46; and the Netherlands is 28. Out of the adult Canadian population of 18.4 million, 1.9 million have criminal records. On the average day in 1984, 27,406 people were imprisoned in Canada. The total number of staff employed by federal and provincial correctional services last year was 23,592.[6] Prisons are very much a part of Canadian society. And of course we must remember that our prisons hold only our unsuccessful criminals. Furthermore criminologists agree that prison populations do not reflect the real percentage of "white color crime", industrial crime, or even "organized crime".

In prison ministry, the Christian is confronted with the concrete implications of his belief that man is created in the image of God. Try explaining to staff that each inmate is a unique creation of God after a guard has been beaten nearly to death. How does the inmate believe in this when (contrary to regulations) a staff person merely throws a scrap of paper into his cell which casually states that his mother died three days ago? Questions arise in prison. What is genuine "justice"? What constitutes "punishment"? Can a person really be "rehabilitated"? Is "amazing grace" anything more than a happy song to sing? Can a "psychopath" ever change? Does the Bible support the "system"? Basic theological questions keep surfacing. The chapel volunteer wonders, "How is God's love revealed to cold or hidden hearts?" The inmate asks himself, "How can God the Father be loving when my father was cruel?" To live in a maximum-security institution is to know the human condition in its rawness. The inmate must usually deal with intense interpersonal pressure, and the struggle between good and evil is always close at hand. To live in prison is to run further from the Father, or to find freedom through the risen Lord.

II) Ethical Realism

I will examine only two aspects of the theology of Reinhold Niebuhr and Juergen Moltmann—Niebuhr's emphasis on the need for ethical realism, and Moltmann's emphasis on discovering freedom through Jesus Christ. Although the word "love" has little specific meaning in the English language, the original Greek language of the New Testament uses several words to express love. Most of all, what the Bible says about God's love for man is expressed in the two words "Jesus Christ".[7] The New Testament word *"agape"* expresses a giving of oneself for others, a willingness to show love in action. It is this form of love which Niebuhr refers to as the "impossible possibility". He believes that God's love, as revealed in Jesus Christ, is the ethical norm for which we are to strive. He describes this perfect love as existing in the realm of transcendence.[8] Our task, according to Niebuhr, is to relate God's ideal love to the moral action of this world. Niebuhr believes that the love of God's kingdom is relevant to every relationship of social justice, no matter how complex.[9]

Early in his ministry, Niebuhr concluded that it is important to know what is possible, and what is impossible, in the moral demands under which all people stand.[10] He states that no limits are to be set within history for the achievement of more universal brotherhood.[11] He says:

> The uneasy conscience of man over various forms of
> social justice, over slavery and war, is an expression of
> the Christian feeling that history must move from the
> innocency of Adam to the perfection of Christ, from the
> harmony of life with life in unfree nature to the perfect
> love of the Kingdom of God.[12]

Niebuhr refers to Paul's vision of universal love expressed in Galatians 3:28, saying that although it is meant primarily for the church, it is relevant to all social relationships. Niebuhr maintains that even the purest form of *"agape"* (love of one's enemy and forgiveness towards the evil-doer) does not stand in contradiction to historical possibilities. More specifically he says:

> Penal justice can achieve more and more imaginative forms; and these more imaginative and generous treatments of the evil-doer can be historically justified by the reclamation of the criminal.[13]

Although he understood love as possible for man in society Niebuhr had many reservations. He was heavily influenced by Reformation theology and Luther's theology in particular, but found in the Lutheran Reformation a weakness in dealing with the problem of law and grace. He says this weakness becomes apparent "when the issue is transferred from the inner life to the complexities of culture and civilization, and all expressions of the collective life of man."[14] When Niebuhr speaks about programs for reclaiming the criminal, he quickly adds:

> But they cannot be initiated purely by considerations of their social value; for a considerable risk is always involved in such treatment. Furthermore every society will mix concern for the safety of society and sinful elements of vindictive passion with whatever elements of forgiving *agape* may be insinuated into its penological procedures. But there is no limit to the possible admixture of forgiving love in criminal justice, except of course the absolute limit that no society will ever deal with criminals in terms of pure forgiveness or achieve a perfect relation between justice and forgiveness.[15]

One could examine Niebuhr's theological concern about relating biblical love to the present criminal justice system in Canada. We could consider the re-emergence of the political and moral issue of "capital punishment" in the light of Niebuhr's theology. It would also be profitable to apply his thought to the moral issues interwoven with the life of correctional staff, or even of the federal civil servant in general. Niebuhr believed that no present "justice" can be regarded as normative. "The higher possibilities of love, which is at once the fulfillment and the negation of justice, always hover over every system of justice."[16] Niebuhr also commented:

> Very frequently the judge, who condemns the profligate, has achieved the eminence in church or state from which he judges his dissolute brethren, by the force of a selfish ambition which must be judged more grievously sinful than the sins of the culprit.[17]

Here however we will examine Niebuhr's call for ethical realism only in regard to the inmate community.

After working in a penitentiary for a number of years, I dropped in for coffee with Hordern at the Seminary. I said, "I'm struggling even more with the question about using power responsibly." Hordern replied: "I'm still struggling with that question too. On Mondays, Wednesdays, and Fridays I think it can be done. But on Tuesdays, Thursdays, and Saturdays I am convinced it cannot be!" (I should have asked him: "What do you think on Sundays?") Actually inmates in a prison are much more involved in issues of power than are most staff, for from the minute a new inmate ("fish") walks through the front gate he is involved in a power struggle. Who are his friends, if any, going to be? Who are his enemies? A middle-class person, or a first offender, or young teenager, may find himself in a very vulnerable position. He is walking into a sub-culture within our society which has very definite values, rules, and leaders. Where is he going to fit in? At what point does he "draw the line" in terms of power and morality?

Many times, as I sat in a counselling session with an inmate, a story of Niebuhr's came to mind. It expresses well the ethical dilemma of the average inmate. Hordern mentions the story in *A Layman's Guide to Protestant Theology*:

> In his [Niebuhr's] Detroit pastorate, while he still held a liberal theology, he was teaching a Sunday-school class about the Sermon on the Mount. Having expounded eloquently upon turning the other cheek, he was challenged by one of the boys in the class. This boy made a living for his widowed mother and family by selling papers. Each day, he said, there was a fight among the newsboys to see which one would get the best corner upon which to sell papers. Was he, as a Christian, to turn the other cheek, allow another boy to take his corner, and thus reduce the support that he could give to his family? Niebuhr found that his [liberal] theology had no answer.[18]

Hordern uses this story to illustrate how Niebuhr came to realize that society never confronts us with simple moral alternatives, that "the tragedy of social life is that one must choose the lesser of two evils rather than an abstract absolute good."[19] Certainly that describes the situation in which the Christian prisoner finds himself. Should he turn the other cheek? (Recently a Christian inmate I know did so literally and was severely beaten by his fellow inmates.) A new inmate usually does not have the opportunity of slowly coming to objective, absolute decisions. (Neither, for that matter, does a police officer.) As soon as a "friend" quietly slips him a "gift" of illegal drugs, he had better make some fast decisions.

If a new inmate is a young teenager, will he resist when propositioned by homosexual men seeking to have sex with him? Will he, and can he, violently defend himself? Or will he accept the protection of a "heavy" inmate, and be willing to live with the consequences of that decision? If "turning the other cheek" means passivity, then he is headed quickly to the bottom of the inmate power structure where he will probably remain for the length of his sentence. His reputation will follow him wherever he goes in the prison system. The worst situation is for the inmate to be labelled a "rat" (an informer) or a "skinner" (sex offender). Then his life will be in constant danger, and his killer need not fear reprisals from other inmates. A penitentiary inmate, whether Christian or not, must be aware of the social realities of his incarceration.

I recall one middle-aged man who came to us with a life sentence (25 years before parole) for fatally shooting an R.C.M.P. officer. Such an offence should have made him a hero among inmates with power. However, he was a very ordinary middle-class family man who had previously believed in the philosophy of "lock 'em up and throw away the key." Now his family, his friends, and society in general, turned against him. Suddenly he was socially untouchable. Newspapers were filled with letters-to-the-editor which mentioned him by name and called for a return to "capital punishment". One person cared. An unknown person mailed him a Bible. Sitting alone in his cell, he started reading it.

This man began to realize, as he had not known before prison, that he needed and wanted the acceptance and guidance of God. He began coming to our church services and Bible studies. "You know according to the Bible we are all the same," he said to me after one Bible study. Another day, at the door of the chapel, I heard him get angry at some inmates who had been condemning "skinners" as totally undesirable. "Look, we have all done something wrong or we wouldn't be in here," he said. "As far as I am concerned, those guys are no worse than we are. We are all sinners needing God's forgiveness." I immediately became concerned for his future safety. "I agree with you," I said, but added: "*I* can say that, but I think it would be wise for you to keep such comments to our private conversations, and perhaps the Bible study group." The inmate did not agree. He rapidly lost credibility within the inmate population. Increasingly he found himself in encounters with tough-talking younger inmates. First he got a cup of coffee in the face, then a couple of beatings. He was transferred to another institution. There he was stabbed and nearly died. Reluctantly he "checked in". That is to say, he joined the "PC's", the Protective Custody inmates who are held separately within a prison for their own protection. Within a few months, he had gone potentially from the top of his new sub-culture to the bottom.

Setting aside the question of what he should or should not have done, we can see that the inmate was probably unaware of the serious consequences of his biblically-based statements in his social situation. Compare his attitude to that of another inmate I know. The inmate was not openly a Christian. He basically adhered to the "inmate code" (the unwritten value system known by most inmates of a maximum-security penitentiary) and this was common knowledge. He also built up his body so that he could physically defend himself against anyone. One night while the men gathered in the gymnasium, an inmate was stabbed. In such situations other inmates will see nothing and know nothing. As the victim lay squirming on the floor, blood pouring from him, the inmates quietly began leaving the area. However, this inmate walked over to him, and dragged him a considerable distance to a metal gate where he yelled at the guards to call an ambulance. Obviously he saved the bleeding man's life. As a "heavy" inmate he could do that without unfortunate consequences.

Many similar examples of ethical decisions come to mind. (I realize that all the motives and facts are not known.) I recall one young man who became a Christian through the influence of a provincial jail chaplain before he came to us. He had committed a burglary with another youth, but was shocked when the other deliberately murdered a night watchman. He went to trial first and received a very heavy sentence as an accomplice to murder. Now he was being asked to testify at the trial of the other youth who did the shooting. He explained that he had found the other person shockingly dangerous, but he did not hate him. He honestly felt that as a Christian he should go to court and tell the truth. His sentence had already been given, so there was nothing to be gained in "a deal". Yet he had a lot to lose, very likely his life. Was he naive, stupid, idealistic? Perhaps. He went and he honestly testified. For his own safety he was transferred to another part of the country. There he is steadily growing in his Christian faith, and maturing to manhood. For a couple of years he lived in constant fear. In the back of his mind, he still half wonders if someone will identify him. He is not sure he would make the same decision again.

Niebuhr said that the world does not need ethically pure people; but it needs people who dare to undertake responsibility. Indeed he regarded theologians either as pure or as responsible.[20] It was this realistic ethical approach that caused Niebuhr to insist on the necessity of using power to check power, and of using power to serve justice whenever possible.[21] He believed it was very important for Christians to consider the harsh realities of social power when seeking ethical relevance. Although critics considered him too pessimistic about what is morally possible, Niebuhr maintained that the highest ethical level possible for a group of people is justice, not love. Niebuhr realized that most individuals adapt to the bigotry of their particular group. In this process, the individual loses his ethical insight and objectivity. That is why the individual person can restrain his egotism more than the total group to which he belongs. Niebuhr points out that most people in a group will indulge in impulses of envy, jealousy, pride, and greed, and that this is what causes conflict between groups.

One fascinating aspect of prison life is the visit to an outside hospital. The inmate and his escorting officer slowly start to converse on the way to the city hospital. As they sit perhaps for hours at the hospital, the inmate and officer usually first share their views about neutral topics, and then about some of the frustrations of their daily life. If the inmate is held overnight, the two of them often share their views about society today, about marriage, and even about the meaning of life and death. A genuine appreciation of each other as unique persons seems to spring up. But, as they are driven back to the penitentiary, a visitor would see a uniformed guard firmly directing a downcast prisoner in handcuffs. Down the corridors they go, past electronically controlled gates to the large domed room in the centre of the prison. After being thoroughly searched (a "skin frisk") the inmate walks down his "range", past the other inmates in their cells. His escort officer, having a cigarette with several of his fellow officers back in the large domed room, is talking about "these no-good inmates getting better treatment than they deserve." The inmate, entering his cell, swears aloud about the "dirty bulls". Neibuhr would understand their situation perfectly.

To be sentenced to imprisonment is to enter a social group which has over the years developed a definite value system. This value system provides the group with solidarity, protection, pride. If the individual member wants to survive or prosper within the group he would be wise, for example, not to steal from another inmate, and not to give information (or even appear to give information) to opposing groups. (Interestingly people involved in organized crime and its rigidly enforced "code of ethics" seldom come to prison.) If an inmate lacks the intelligence to understand, he may be tolerated but will not have access to information. If he is mentally unstable (and therefore unpredictable) he may be humoured, but definitely not depended upon. As a penitentiary inmate, it is valuable to know what is "coming down" ahead of time. It is helpful to know what is happening in terms of the power struggles within one's own inmate group, and to a lesser degree of any power struggles occurring with the staff group. Not many inmates can afford the luxury of being "loners".

In attempting to relate the gospel message of God's forgiving love within such social realities, Niebuhr concluded that Christians must always take into account the law of self-love as well as the law of love. In other words, God's love must be implemented in a pragmatic manner if it is going to be relevant for a particular social situation. Accepting the reality of self-love, says Niebuhr, gives the Christian a foundation for "a pragmatic ethic in which power and self-interest are used, beguiled, harnessed, and deflected for the ultimate end of establishing the highest use and most inclusive possible community of justice and order."[22] For example, he replied to a Canadian pacifist that we must be willing to make moral discriminations which cause us to favour one side over another in a war—even if this involves us in guilt.[23] It would seem that Niebuhr's understanding of group egotism and his call for ethical pragmatism is more relevant to prison life than the eschatological hope of Moltmann. Yet inmates long for a message of freedom, freedom from more than iron bars.

III) Freedom In Christ

Biblical eschatology, says Moltmann, begins with the historical reality of the resurrection and "announces the future of that reality, its future possibilities and its power over the future."[24] He does not believe we can understand eschatology in terms of our common, reoccurring experiences. He centres his theology of hope on the resurrection of Jesus Christ. "Eschatology is the passionate suffering and passionate longing kindled by the Messiah."[25] For Moltmann, the second coming of Christ means that we can live now in hopeful expectation. He explains that "parousia" does not simply mean the arrival of someone who has departed. It means "imminent arrival", and refers to the presence of Christ. It is a presence which "must be awaited today and tomorrow."[26]

Niebuhr did not reject, of course, the importance of biblical eschatology. On the contrary, he wrote *The Destiny of Man* in 1943 when most theologians were giving little importance to doctrines of the "last things". Niebuhr believed that the biblical proclamation of the return of Christ, of the last judgment, and of the resurrection, expresses the ultimate sovereignty of God. Although love does not triumph in this present world, the vindication of Christ and his triumphant return express "faith in the sufficiency of God's sovereignty over the world and history, and in the final supremacy of love over all the forces of self-love . . ."[27] Nonetheless, Moltmann gives greater emphasis than Niebuhr to what the "last things" can mean for man in society right now. Although present social realities contradict the intentions of God for us, Moltmann finds in eschatology a solid basis of hope. His hope in the crucified and risen Christ speaks to prison society.

After writing *Theology of Hope*, Moltmann turned increasingly to the negative aspects of social reality. He knows full well that there is much in our society which contradicts God's promises of redemptive power in Christ. Moltmann spoke of "the suffering and the dissatisfaction with the present in which man cannot become man as he hopes."[28] However Moltmann does not call upon Christians to exercise ethical pragmatism. Rather he proclaims Christian hope, a resurrection hope which has the power to contradict social reality as we presently experience it. Niebuhr (born in 1892) was pastor of a church in Detroit during World war I, and it was that parish experience that prompted him to seek the ethical relevance of the gospel in an increasingly industrial American society. In the following years he was influential in the theological, social, and political issues of his nation. While he was delivering theological lectures in the United Kingdom during World War II, German bombs were falling. Meanwhile Juergen Moltmann, born in 1926, was becoming old enough to enlist in the German army. At the end of the War, Moltmann and his fellow prisoners, languishing in a prisoner-of-war camp, struggled with despair and hope as they waited to be returned home.

In an English prison camp, Moltmann discovered the biblical God of hope. Upon his eventual return to Germany, he entered theological studies. As with Niebuhr, Moltmann's theological concerns were heavily influenced by his personal experiences. He once remarked: "A liberal bourgeois theology would never have gotten through to us."[29] Looking back on his prison years, Moltmann says he experienced "an unorganized, uneducated, imprisoned, and suffering mass of people without a face, without a freedom, without history." He says: "It seems to me that as a P.O.W. I was in the people and nothing more than one of the people."[30] Moltmann states that in his theology he strives to give words about hope "of" the people, and not hope "for" the people.[31] He believes that Christians are to resist institutional stabilization and to raise questions about things which are assumed to be certainties. He calls upon Christians to break through social stagnation. Hope alone, he says, keeps social life "flowing and free".[32]

Moltmann's theology of hope provides a powerful presentation of God's redemptive possibilities in Christ for all people. The Hebrew word meaning "redemption" derives from the practice of a person buying back something which had once belonged to him. The biblical concept of redemption emphasizes that God acts decisively on our behalf. We allow ourselves to become slaves, but God through Jesus Christ acts to liberate us, to grant us our freedom. Moltmann calls upon man to allow God to be God, to cease making himself, "the unhappy and proud God" of himself and his fellow man. The death of Jesus frees us. It changes us from slaves to become free sons of God.[33] Reinhold Niebuhr's writings show a general movement toward an explicit expression of the central significance of Jesus Christ. He took exception to criticism that he does not do justice to God's initiative and action in human history.[34] Niebuhr does not deny the power of God in our world, but he is more concerned about our own responsibility to create a more just society. At age 75, Niebuhr commented that the mixture of motives in all people "refutes the doctrines both of total depravity and of saintliness."[35] Nevertheless it is Moltmann who clearly proclaims the freeing power of Jesus Christ, of his Spirit and his Church.

Different theoretical models have been followed in the correctional service during the past decades. At present we seem to be shifting out of an "opportunities model", which is a variation of the rehabilitation model. There is a basic flaw involved in the concept of "rehabilitation". How can a person be "rehabilitated" if he has never been "habilitated"? What social norm is there for him to go back to? Rarely, for example, does one meet an inmate who grew up with his two parents living together. (This is the trend of our whole society.) In fact, if he grows up via the normal pattern of foster homes, juvenile facilities, and provincial jails, he is much better prepared than the average citizen to cope with the social environment of a maximum-security penitentiary. (Sometimes orphanages or mental hospitals are also part of his socialization.) Many costly programs have been instituted by Correctional Service Canada in the past two decades to give the inmate the opportunity to receive counselling, learn a trade, etc. In the institution in which I am now a chaplain, it is even possible for inmates to receive a university degree. Chaplains in each institution are just one or two staff persons within a whole "Socialization Department". Yet the fact remains that a person adjusts to his immediate social environment. Historically, the paradox of prisons has been that they are "a school for crime". Even with all the "socialization" opportunities provided in contemporary Canadian penitentiaries, the inmate usually lacks the motivation to change.

Yesterday one of our inmates "O.D.'ed", overdosed on illegal drugs. Tattooed on his arm were the words, "Born to Lose". That slogan, a popular "jail house" tattoo, is often a self-fulfilling prophecy. The inmate was nearing the end of a fairly lengthy sentence. He was liked by both inmates and staff. However he was addicted to drugs, and it had ruined his life. Why did he not change? Why live and die in prison? Last night I toured, with the children of our congregation, the local police station. The police officers had put up a large sign for themselves which read: "This is Cold Turkey Day". During the past week, health authorities had been warning people to quit smoking. Callers to "talk shows" had expressed their frustrations and small victories in attempting to conquer their addiction to nicotine. Why did these people find it so difficult to make such a small change in their life-style? Many of us at least border on addiction to coffee, despite the medical facts known about the drug, caffeine. If a person comes from a broken home, has poor education, has never held a steady job, has spent most of his teenage years in jail, and has a low self-image, it will be difficult for him to make a big change in his life-style when he completes his sentence. It is not impossible, but it is difficult.

An ex-inmate who had become a Christian toward the end of 25 years in federal penitentiaries came to speak at my chapel service. As we walked through the corridors, I introduced him to old Bill. Bill was very old for an inmate. He was about 60 years old, while the average age for an inmate at that institution at that time was 21. (Prison ministry is a youth ministry.) Old Bill was not highly respected by the other inmates, but was never harmed by them either. A couple of years earlier, staff had encouraged Bill to accept parole. They even drove him downtown to show him around, but he seemed glad to get back to the institution. An enthusiastic "born again" ex-convict said to Bill: "You would like to get out. Believe me, Jesus is the answer. Look at me. I was in prison for 25 years. Praise God I now have a wife, children, and a home. This can be true for you too!" Old Bill looked at him in amazement and replied: "Did you see the headlines in the newspaper yesterday? Millions are unemployed in our country. Violence in our society is increasing. You were in 25 years. Well I have been in for 30 years and I say 'No thanks. I'm staying right here'."

Most penitentiary chaplains recruit volunteers from local churches to assist them in their chapel programs. Usually it is Christians from the "evangelical" churches who volunteer. Much could be said, positively and negatively, about evangelical Christians (and para-church organizations) involved in prison ministry. The strength of most evangelical volunteers is that they do care about individual inmates, and they do see the need for a deep change, a rebirth, within the inmate. Although it is not a major theme of his theology, Moltmann firmly endorses the biblical concept of rebirth, meaning that a person may be born again to a living hope by the mercy of God through the resurrection of Jesus. "In the rebirth of life, the new creation of the world into the kingdom of God in an individual life is already experienced *here*."[36] Moltmann maintains that this rebirth is only possible because of the mercy of God, and is manifested in the resurrection of Jesus. It happens through the power of the Spirit which points the faithful person to the living hope.

Inmates take as their motto, "Born to Lose". Many people outside of prison take as their motto, "Born to Win". A Christian alternate motto could be "Born from Above", based on Jesus' words to Nicodemus in John 3:7 in the Greek text. (The phrase "born again" in the King James Translation has been so overused and misused that even the evangelist Billy Graham hesitates to use it anymore.) Most inmates, whether they admit it openly or not, come to a point in their incarcerated life where they sense a need for a deep inner change. However even "evangelical" Christians in prison ministry need to realize that there are a few inmates who may never "make it on the street", may never be socially "rehabilitated". Jesus did not speak about becoming socially adjusted; He spoke of being "born of water and the Spirit" and entering the "kingdom of God". (John 3:5) In the prisoner one sees more plainly the condition of fallen humanity—of all of us. It is a spiritual conflict of enslavement and freedom. Where is the source of the power to change? In Ephesians 1:10, Paul speaks of "the immeasurable greatness of [God's] power in us who believe, according to the working of his great might . . ." Niebuhr certainly acknowledges the Spirit of God dwelling in man, and the Spirit's work of love and forgiveness.[37] Moltmann, however, gives much greater emphasis to the Spirit and his power. To speak of "the resurrection of the crucified Jesus" and "the cross of the risen Christ," says Moltmann, "would be incomplete without a similar emphasis on the sending of the Spirit."[38]

Moltmann reminds us that although the experience of rebirth through the Spirit is an individual's own experience, it should not isolate him from his society. The reborn person, living under the influence of the Spirit, has a future orientation which "opens him for the community, and for the world."[39] Moltmann wants Christians who speak about the forgiveness of sins through Jesus Christ to recognize that this liberation can have dangerous results in experience and practice.[40] He understands God's redeeming forgiveness of man within a social dimension, believing that in Jesus Christ people discover power as they are seized by the Spirit of freedom. The believer can celebrate the "freedom of the risen Christ." The Spirit of Christ lifts away "the spell of destiny and the feelings of personal helplessness."[41] The creative Spirit of God opens up new possibilities and powers. Niebuhr warns of that which is socially impossible, but Moltmann's pointing to that which is possible through the Spirit also applies to those in prison. He says:

> The Spirit of God makes the impossible possible; he creates faith where there is nothing else to believe in; he creates love where there is nothing lovable; he creates hope where there is nothing to hope for.[42]

The Spirit of the risen Christ exists within our penitentiaries. Some inmates discover the power of God's Spirit and grow in fellowship with other Christian inmates. The peace found is not a passive avoidance of the ethical issues of the prison community. Parole Board members sometimes refer to a Christian inmate's faith in Christ either as insincere, or as an escape from his problems. That may be. Yet the genuine Christian knows that his daily life can become more difficult. He adheres less to the moral standards of his immediate social environment. He might, for instance, be seen talking to Christian guards. He might welcome an undesirable inmate to church. He might privately share his faith with an inmate leader. The Christian inmate soon begins to wonder about the moral standards of society in general. He may, for example, stop going to see some of the rehabilitative(?) Holywood movies. He may struggle with feelings of self-righteousness and the desire to impose his new ethical standards on others. Observed closely by other inmates, he reminds them to look, not to him, but to Jesus Christ. He does not claim the perfection which some inmates and staff now expect of him. He does identify himself as a member of the Christian community within the walls, and in practical ways shows concern for others.

The role of the Christian, Moltmann says, is to be a witness of the gospel, of the love and freedom of Christ.[43] He adds that the Christian is to pray that the Spirit will make him sensitive to social injustice. The average penitentiary inmate, actually quite socially conservative, is happy to speak at length about the "injustice of the system." (Because of their involvement with police agencies and law courts, inmates are often more aware of social inequities than the average citizen.) He does not speak so easily about his own contributions to injustice in society, nor about examples of injustice among inmates. The mature Christian inmate grows in his awareness of injustice done to others, not himself. He becomes less accepting of the "inmate code", but sometimes disappoints staff members, and people outside of prison, because he does not completely endorse their social codes either. While Niebuhr might understand this in terms of ethical realism, Moltmann would understand this in terms of becoming identified with Jesus Christ and his future. Peace with God, says Moltmann, means conflict with the world.[44]

Moltmann is convinced that the Christian Church stands or falls with "the gathered congregations", which he also describes as "the open friendship of Jesus."[45] Look around you at the prison worship service. You see a 16-year-old boy trying to make sense of what he learned about Jesus in Sunday School. Beside him is a man with already "five years in" of a 25-year sentence. He has become a Christian while incarcerated, and until the year 2005 hopefully will be a positive influence upon other inmates. A third man is still playing games with God—he will commit himself totally to God if He will mend the broken relationship with his wife. A fourth man, in his forties, has been battling with the power of alcohol. He looks back on a wasted life, but is happy to have found God as the "Higher Power" and does not hate himself anymore. Beside him quietly sits the theology student who killed his wife. A young Cree Indian struggles with the "white man's" message about good news in Jesus Christ, and his desire to rediscover the pride and spirituality of his own people. An authoritative inmate comes in late and sits by the back door of the chapel. After 10 turbulent years, he is accorded respect (if not fear) by inmates and staff. He feels trapped in his manly role and longs for the courage to accept what God offers. Each of these inmates has experienced a crisis of hopelessness. Some have attempted suicide. At times, each has been very demanding and critical of others.

Yet among these inmates and others, one can find the Body of Christ as prisoners are being set free from what enslaves them. Moltmann would understand. He says that when the Christian, personally and in community, lives his life with Christ's life, his life-history becomes a small part of God's great history of liberating the world.[46] Moltmann, more than Niebuhr, is aware of God's possibilities for man within any social environment. Moltmann realizes that man's liberation by God is firmly fixed in the suffering, resurrection, and future of Jesus Christ. This perspective of freedom in Christ is essential in prison ministry. Of course these men are living only within a sub-culture of Canadian society and they will not stay in a penitentiary forever. Upon release, they will find at least initially that it is very difficult to cope with daily living. It is Niebuhr who addresses Christians who are able to exercise leadership in our society as a whole, and he more concretely links his theological perspective to social morality.

IV Conclusion

A penitentiary is man in society. The inmate lives within an intense social environment. Niebuhr's ethical realism speaks to such a situation. Moral decisions must be made, which seldom approach purity. His emphasis on ethical realism, which takes into account power conflicts and group egotism, is directly applicable to the dilemma of the Christian inmate. Yet Niebuhr's ethical approach borders on pure pragmatism. God has shown Himself within history in Jesus Christ, and the risen Christ (as stated in Matthew 25:36) can be found in prison. No one can take Christ to a penitentiary—because He is already there. Moltmann's view of man in society centres on the reality of the presence of Jesus Christ and his imminent future. Therefore Moltmann calls for individual and social rebirth, not an acceptance of present realities. The penitentiary inmate need not despair. Jesus Christ and the power of his Spirit opens up for all of us new possibilities of freedom. What *has* been in our personal lives and our society need not continue to be. As we read in Psalm 146:7, "... The Lord sets the prisoners free."

LUTHER'S ATTITUDE TOWARDS POVERTY: THEOLOGY AND SOCIAL REFORM

Richard P. Hordern

Luther's teachings on poverty and wealth are at the core of his theological program. His views on poverty, along with the related questions of capitalism, usury, social welfare, and the problem of the rich, are integral aspects of his development of "the theology of the cross," the Incarnation, the presence of Christ in the neighbor, the concept of community, and Christ as revealed in community. It is Luther's concern for the poor that connects these theological themes to concrete historical reality, thereby preventing his theology from becoming abstract speculation unrelated to human life.

The Medieval Background

Luther's theology of poverty is a protest against the development of the theme during the Middle Ages. Towards the start of the medieval period the church was facing a dilemma: how to continue the Apostolic affirmation of God's special option for the poor, yet accommodate the wealth and power of the Roman Empire?[1] A compromise was articulated whereby only the monks and clergy, who were to seek a higher state of perfection, were obliged to live a life of "poverty" without private material possessions; while the laity, living at a lesser level of perfection, were exempted (they, of course, would need to do a bit more in the way of good works to make up for this shortcoming). This framework was the basis for the ensuing Middle Ages.

This led to an attitude, which haunts the Roman Catholic Church to this day,[2] whereby poverty was no longer seen primarily as an injury to the human spirit but rather as a virtue to attain. There was a threefold practical consequence from this during the Middle Ages. First, the monks who had taken a vow of poverty were seen as being more spiritually perfect than the laity who still had private possessions. Second, those who were outside the monastery, yet poor, were also seen as being in a blessed state, leading to a blasphemous acceptance of poverty: if someone were poor and hungry, why damage that person's spiritual blessedness by providing that person with a decent standard of living? Third, one of the most important good works for the laity was to give alms to the poor. Thus, in the context of the merit system, it was essential to have poor beggars around in order for people to be able to perform the good work of assisting them! An abolition of poverty would have ended this opportunity for doing a good work and gaining merit! Thus professional beggars were both accepted and commonplace in the cities and countryside, including monks practicing their voluntary poverty and also laity who were involuntarily poor.

Rich Church, Poor People

With Luther's restructuring of theology it was inevitable that he would see through the sham of the existing system and see poverty in a new light. After realizing that justification is through faith alone, and that good works merit no special status before God, the significance of poverty had to be reexamined. As a monk and priest, Luther had taken the vow of poverty, but found that his vows did not give him a favored relationship with God. Indeed, as he often later remarked, the monks claimed to be "poor" and yet lived in comfort and idleness at the expense of the common people and the poor. Large sums of money had to be raised from the commonfolk in order to keep the monks in their "poverty"! But if the key to acceptance with God was faith, why should monks sit around, doing nothing, living off the poor, and yet claim that their poverty put them in an exalted state before God? Why the exaltation of the "poor" monk while, in the real world outside, there were people who were involuntarily poor yet forced to impoverish themselves even further by supporting the monasteries? Luther saw the false poverty of the clerics and the real poverty of the people, and in this tension between a rich church and the poor people found another clue that the church had strayed from the teachings of the Bible.

The special concern for the poor is present in the official starting-point of the Reformation, Luther's *Ninety-Five Theses* of 1517. Prompted by a local sale of indulgences, Luther opens the theses with a statement on the radical nature of repentance and the total claim that God makes upon human life. Luther next addresses some of the contradictions within the penance system and the power of the Church (Pope) to forgive sins. Then he looks at the positive side, at what Christians ought to be doing: works of love, works of mercy. For Luther, this means primarily works of compassion towards the poor:

> 42. Christians are to be taught that the pope does not intend that the buying of indulgences should in any way be compared with works of mercy.
> 43. Christians are to be taught that he who gives to the poor or lends to the needy does a better deed than he who buys indulgences.

44. Because love grows by works of love, man thereby becomes better. Man does not, however, become better by means of indulgences but is merely freed from penalties.

45. Christians are to be taught that he who sees a needy man and passes him by, yet gives his money for indulgences, does not buy papal indulgences but God's wrath.

46. Christians are to be taught that, unless they have more than they need, they must reserve enough for their family needs and by no means squander it on indulgences.[3]

Luther saw in the sale of indulgences not only a false presentation of the proper works of the Christian life but also a rich and wealthy church hierarchy robbing the common and poor people of their limited financial resources. At this point of his career Luther felt that the problem lay more with the local indulgence salespeople than the Pope, and so Luther expressed the belief that the Pope, as a true Christian, would agree that it was immoral to sell indulgences at the expense of raising money from the poor:

50. Christians are to be taught that if the pope knew the exactions of the indulgence preachers, he would rather that the basilica of St. Peter were burned to ashes than built up with the skin, flesh, and bones of his sheep.

51. Christians are to be taught that the pope would and should wish to give of his own money, even though he had to sell the basilica of St. Peter, to many of those from whom certain hawkers of indulgences cajole money.[4]

But perhaps Luther did have some suspicions about the Holy Father since, after all, Luther had seen the splendor of Rome and knew the economic situation of the people in his parish. A bit later he seems to get angrier and returns to the topic of papal wealth:

86. Again, 'Why does not the pope, whose wealth is today greater than the wealth of the richest Crassus, build this one basilica of St. Peter with his own money rather than with the money of poor believers?'[5]

Luther's indignation comes from the spectacle of a wealthy church robbing the poor in order to build a monument of human grandeur.

While in 1517 he objected to the church raising money from the poor, a few years later he stated that no one, rich or poor, should contribute to the institutional life of the church out of proportion to their giving to the poor:

It would be satisfactory if we gave the smaller proportion to churches, altars, vigils, bequests, and the like, and let the main stream flow toward God's commandments, so that among Christians charitable deeds done to the poor would shine more brightly than all the churches of wood and stone....Beware, therefore, O man! God will not ask you at your death and at the Last Day how much you have left in your will, whether you have given so and so much to churches - although I do not condemn this - but he will say to you, 'I was hungry, and you gave me no food; I was naked, and you did not clothe me' (Matt. 25:42-43). Take these words to heart, dear man! The important thing is whether you have given to your neighbor and treated him well.[6]

Early in 1518, because of the debate over the *Ninety-Five Theses*, Luther, in finalizing his *Explanations of the Ninety-Five Theses*, amplified his comments:

I would say this to people: Look, brothers, you ought to know that there are three types of good works which can be done by expending money. The first and foremost consists of giving to the poor or lending to a neighbor who is in need and in general of coming to the aid of anyone who suffers, whatever may be his need. This work ought to be done with such earnestness that even the building of churches must be interrupted and the taking of offerings for the purchase of holy vessels and for the decoration of churches be discontinued. After this has been done and there is no longer anyone who is in need, then should follow the second type, namely, contributing to the building of our churches and hospitals in our country, then to buildings of public service.[7]

(What would happen today if we did not spend another penny on church buildings until "there is no longer anyone in need"?)

Beginning with this early debate, Johann Eck became Luther's primary theological opponent for many years. Eck wrote refutations of Luther's theses, and one of Eck's arguments was that alms should be given to the needy, instead of going to the church, *only* in situations of extreme want, for unless the need is extreme, poverty remains a virtue.[8] Luther later gave the following reply:

So we learn neither to help nor to give to the needy until they are perishing, starving, freezing to death, or fleeing because of poverty and debts. But this infamous gloss and supplement is confounded by a single word. 'What you wish another to do to you, do so to him.' No one is so foolish, however, as to be unwilling that anyone should give to him until such time as the soul is leaving the body or he has run away from his debts, and then help him when he is beyond help. But when it comes to churches, endowments, indulgences, and other things which God has not commanded, then no one is so keen or so diligent in figuring out whether we should give to the church before the tiles fall off the roof, the beams rot, the ceiling caves in, the letters of dispensation molder, or the indulgences rot with age; although all these things could wait more easily than people who are in need.[9]

We are not called to a virtue of poverty: we are called to abolish poverty.

The Common Chest

During 1518 and 1519 the debate centered around the power of the Pope and, therefore, the doctrine of the Church. In 1520 Luther published a series of tracts that generally outlined all of the essential points of his developing theology. We find that a reform of theology and the church must include economic reform for the poor. Luther did not want simply to "assist" the poor, he wanted to achieve "the complete elimination of poverty in the town and in the nation."[10] In his *Long Sermon on Usury* of 1520[11] he called for the abolition of begging. In his appeal *To the Christian Nobility of the German Nation* he called upon the political rulers to bring about needed reforms in church and society, including his proposal to establish a "common chest" for the relief of the poor.[12]

Luther opens his appeal to the nobility by attacking the riches and wealth of the church as represented by the Pope and others in the hierarchy.[13] Then, in contrast to the present wealth of the church, there stand the beggars. "One of the greatest necessities is the abolition of all begging throughout Christendom," writes Luther. "It would even be a very simple matter to make a law to the effect that every city should look after its own poor, if only we had the courage and intention to do so."[14]

Luther envisioned a structural means of dealing with poverty, in as much as individual and private acts of charity always fall short of solving the problem, more extensive than local parish charity. He also felt that a common program would identify abusers of the system, for Luther suspected that many of the beggars were idle and slothful monks. A centralized system of welfare, operated on a city-wide basis, would make it possible to ensure that assistance would go to the truly needy.[15] In terms of a theological basis for the system, Luther comments, "there is no greater service of God than Christian love which helps and serves the needy, as Christ himself will judge and testify at the Last Day, Matthew 25 (:31-46). This is why the possessions of the church were formerly called *bona ecclesiae*, that is, common property, a common chest, as it were, for all who were needy among Christians."[16]

98

It was during Luther's exile (1521-22) that the "common chest" was first implemented by Karlstadt at Wittenberg.[17] Within a few years the practice had spread to many of the other cities of Germany.[18] Funding was based on an annual tax plus confiscated church property.[19] The system eventually had some problems, which Luther tended to blame on the incompetence of the church administrators,[20] although penny-pinching city councils were hardly free from blame. But the basic system remained intact and is recognized as perhaps the first of the government sponsored welfare programs which we have today.

Usury and Early Capitalism

The feudalism of the Middle Ages was based on an agricultural economy. The way to accumulate wealth was by possessing large amounts of land, which was then parceled out to peasants who would pay the landowner annual rents. By owning a large amount of land it was possible for the landowner to have a good income while performing no real work on the land. At the same time, a complex system of mutual obligations had been developed to ensure that goods were sold at a "just price" and that everyone made a "fair living."[21] However, trade and manufacturing also were growing in importance. In financing trade ventures a money economy was used. It didn't matter how much land you owned, the important question was whether you had some money to invest. A person could invest money and then receive a profit or interest on the money loaned. The "money economy" provided the essential basis for capitalism to replace feudalism: the important way to obtain more wealth no longer came by owning land but by having surplus wealth (capital) which could be invested to yield profit or interest. This allowed those with surplus capital to increase their wealth without actually doing the work involved in the venture.

Luther was strongly opposed to this early form of capitalism. He believed it was impossible for money to make money: only work, said Luther, could increase wealth.[22] You were born rich or poor, that was your station in life given by God, and it was impossible to become richer than was allowable within the limits of your station — unless you robbed or stole from someone else. Luther saw the growing trade of his day, and the related financial institutions, as symptomatic of greedy people essentially stealing from others, stealing either from those doing the actual work or from the gullible consumer persuaded to buy a luxury not truly needed.

Furthermore, the financial institutions, especially the Fuggers, were deeply involved with the papal office since the high cost of Rome's splendor required constant loans. The church availed itself of the financial institutions despite the fact that the unanimous testimony of the Bible and even the laws of the church were opposed to usury, namely, of lending money and charging interest on it. As Luther saw it, if your neighbor needed to borrow something, why should you charge interest and thereby profit from your neighbor's misfortune? If your neighbor needs something, give a loan and don't complain if the neighbor is unable to pay you back![23] Luther's views were not ameliorated by the fact that his antagonist Johann Eck was a consultant to the wealthy Fugger banking house (which financed the fateful sale of indulgences in 1517). Eck assisted the Fuggers in finding theological loopholes to avoid the church's restrictions on charging interest.[24]

Luther's position that money cannot produce money, and therefore that loans should primarily be considered a form of charity, has been traced back to Aristotle, among other sources.[25] But it would be wrong to dismiss his general views on economics as "mere philosophy", as some have done. The arguments Luther presents in support of his position derive from his theological understanding of poverty and from the scriptures. While some of his specific examples and concerns are contextually dated, underlying his discussion is the theme of the absolute priority of helping the neighbor rather than profiting from the neighbor. For example, in commenting on the business idea (still common today) that the seller is justified in charging as much as the market will bear for a product, Luther comments:

> Thus occasion is given for avarice, and every window and door to hell is opened. What else does this mean but this: I care nothing about my neighbor; so long as I have my profit and satisfy my greed, of what concern it is to me if it injures my neighbor in ten ways at once? There you see how shamelessly this maxim flies squarely in the face not only of Christian love but also of natural law. How can there be anything good then in trade? How can it be without sin when such injustice is the chief maxim and rule of the whole business? On such a basis trade can be nothing but robbing and stealing the property of others.[26]

The economic concern for the neighbor cannot be put into a secondary position as "application" rather than theory, for it is integral to Luther's theological themes pertaining to the Gospel. Karl Holl has commented: "Since the warnings of the Sermon on the Mount had laid hold of his conscience, the contradiction between it and the current money economy could not be concealed by the arts of the exegete.... the whole spirit of this capitalism...seemed to him to be irreconcilable with Christianity."[27] As another scholar has concluded, Luther's "views of economics, while temporally conditioned, were biblically determined, and must be seen in the light of his entire social ethics."[28]

Material Possessions

Part of Luther's position on poverty reflects his reaction against the moralizing hermeneutics (biblical interpretation) of the Middle Ages. That hermeneutic found moral imperatives and virtues throughout the Bible. Moralizing distressed Luther as a way in which the Gospel of grace was hidden, being replaced by a religion of doing good works to merit salvation. He especially attacked the conclusion that the Bible saw the lack of material possessions as a virtue for Christians to attain rather than being a scandal to abolish. He despaired, "now there is so much begging that it has even become an honor....I think it would be more fitting if there were no more begging in Christendom under the New Testament than among the Jews under the Old Testament."[29] When Luther commented on the text from Luke, "Blessed are the poor," he noted that Jesus "is not teaching me where to build the foundation of my salvation, but giving me a promise that is to console me in my sufferings and in my Christian life."[30]

In later years Luther's position was also shaped by the Anabaptist view of poverty and possessions. Anabaptism can be understood as a full acceptance of the monasticism of the Middle Ages, for, with the exception of celibacy, the other vows and virtues of the monastery were extended to become a requirement for all Christians, including individual poverty and the communal ownership of possessions. Luther rejected the position, for in both monasticism and Anabaptism there was the underlying assumption that the material and secular world was evil and inferior to the "spiritual world." Against this, Luther argued that Christians should not hesitate to use the material goods that God has given in trust for the neighbor, provided we have no more than we actually need to conduct our affairs in life.

> We are not to run away from property, house, home, wife, and children, wandering around the countryside as a burden to other people. This is what the Anabaptist sect does, and they accuse us of not preaching the Gospel rightly because we keep house and stay with wife and children....In our heart we should be able to leave house and home, wife and children...we should be able, if necessary, to give them up at any time for God's sake....But when the necessity arises, then let him do so in God's name, not because he would like to get away from wife and children, house and home, but because, as long as God wills it, he would rather keep them and serve Him thereby, yet is also willing to let Him take them back.[31]

Luther directed many of the same criticisms against Anabaptism as he had against the monasteries. For example, there was the claim to be "poor" yet the community in general did not normally suffer want. They felt they were giving away all their possessions to the poor, but all they were doing was keeping their possessions for themselves, said Luther. Luther saw possessions as a trust held until needed by the neighbor — it is only through sharing that possessions have value, but how can we share if we have given away everything?[32] The reason for "having" is to help those who "have not."

This draws attention to the attitude one should have towards possessions. Luther follows the Biblical concept of *anawim* piety where, in some instances, the term "poor" refers to a special kind of trusting disposition towards God. Luther interpreted many of the Biblical texts in this twofold sense, both in terms of literal meaning of material poverty and also in terms of poverty as an inward disposition of humility towards God. Since the Reformation principle was justification apart from the "riches" of "merits" it was easy for Luther to identify true Protestant faith in God as an example of "poverty" before God (because the poor must have a total daily trust in God for their survival in a threatening world). Likewise "the rich" are those who have an inward disposition which Luther identifies as greed, regardless of whether or not the person has many possessions: "a man is called 'rich' in Scripture, even though he does not have money or property, if he scrambles and scratches for them and can never get enough of them."[33]

Because of the inward meaning associated with these terms, some interpreters have concluded, erroneously, that external possessions do not matter in God's sight, the important thing is your attitude towards material possessions; one could be as wealthy as one liked and still be a good Christian if your heart were not tied to possessions. Luther would not agree at all with this position. He did not believe that anyone needed wealth except for princes (and others charged with political governance) who needed a greater amount to run the affairs of state; there was no other reason for a person to be rich. Even for a prince, if wealth exceeded that which was truly need, then it was to be given to the poor.[34] Luther did not support "private property" in the sense that we could do as we wish with our possessions — our wealth is a trust for our neighbor.

When discussing the "inward" dimension of poverty and riches, it is essential that the definition of these terms be grounded in historical reality. When the Bible speaks of the "poor in spirit" the term is defined by the materially poor. When Luther speaks of poverty he speaks both of its inward and external reality. To translate the Bible's references to the "poor" as indicating a spiritual state that all can attain regardless of material possessions is to read the Bible allegorically, a method of interpretation strongly resisted by Luther. The inward disposition of poverty can only be defined with reference to the materially poor: "Humility, therefore, is nothing else than a disregarded, despised, and lowly estate, such as that of men who are poor, sick, hungry, thirsty, in prison, suffering, and dying."[35] Luther's method of interpretation is not allegorization but the construction of symbolic meaning: "spiritual poverty" can only be defined in light of the materially poor.[36]

Theology of the Cross

Appreciating the relevance of Luther for our present day situation consists of understanding his Biblical and theological insights and studying them in light of our own context, just as Luther spoke to specific situations in his context. Some of the Biblical and theological themes that intersect in his views on poverty and economics are: Christ in the neighbor; Christ as encountered in community; the Incarnation; and the "theology of the cross."

Luther is known for his strong emphasis on the Incarnation and the humanity of Christ that counter-acts the distant and remote Christ too often portrayed during the Middle Ages. Luther emphasized theology as anchored in the realities of life, rather than abstract speculation. Christ is to be found in this world. The bread and wine of communion are the body and blood of Christ in more than merely a "spiritual" sense. The infinite God was fully present in the finite person of Jesus, and thus all finite human beings have direct access to God through Christ. It is Jesus' entry into the human condition that makes it possible for Christ to be "our representative" before God, thereby assuring the possibility of forgiveness and salvation.

But the human condition is a diverse reality, and we cannot identify Christ with any aspect of it that we choose. In his "theology of the cross" Luther makes it clear that our understanding of Christ, and our relationship with God, cannot be mediated through patterns of human wealth, power, and privilege; that is what was erroneously projected into the "theology of glory" during the Middle Ages. Instead, said Luther, it is through human weakness, suffering, humility, oppression, and poverty that we find God and truly understand Christ and the nature of Christ's salvation through the cross. The poverty and low estate of Jesus do not direct us to human wealth and power to find God, but to human suffering and oppression.

> He (God) lets the godly become powerless and to be brought low, until everyone supposes their end is near, whereas in these very things He is present to them with all His power, yet so hidden and in secret that even those who suffer the oppression do not feel it but only believe. There is the fullness of God's power and his outstretched arm. For where man's strength ends, God's strength begins, provided faith is present and waits on Him. And when the oppression comes to an end, it becomes manifest what great strength was hidden underneath the weakness. Even so, Christ was powerless on the cross; and yet there He performed His mightiest work and conquered sin, death, world, hell, devil, and all evil. Thus all the martyrs were strong and overcame. Thus, too, all who suffer and are oppressed overcome.[37]

Luther used the theology of the cross and the reality of poverty to relate God to the depths of the human condition. This theology, unfortunately, has often been spiritualized in the Lutheran theological tradition, being used to support an escapist, other-worldly individualistic faith. The cross of Christ too often becomes a sentimental neon light on a church altar or steeple, a sign of human escape from the misery of life rather than being God's entry into the hardships of human oppression. As James Cone has commented,

> Modern-day Lutheran scholars...appear to turn the cross of Jesus into a theological idea, completely unrelated to the concrete historical struggles of the oppressed for freedom....But when the poor of the Third World and of North America read of Christ's passion, they do not view it as a theological idea but as God's suffering solidarity with the victims of the world. Jesus' cross is God's election of the poor by taking their pain and suffering upon the divine person.[38]

The theology of the cross is not so much another "doctrine" as it is a viewpoint from which to regard all doctrines and all of life.[39] William Hordern has stated,

> All theology is done from an ideological political perspective. The only question is what shall that perspective be. If we take the Bible seriously, then it must be from the perspective of justice for the poor and the oppressed wherever they are. No church and no theologian can pretend to be faithful to the God revealed in Jesus Christ if they pass by on the other side of those who are victims of injustice, discrimination and oppression.[40]

We are reminded that it is only from the perspective of the oppressed that we can understand both the human need facing our neighbor and also the work and presence of Christ in society. We encounter Christ in our neighbor. Luther's theology of the cross directs our gaze to those who are on the "underside" of history.

Community and Vocation

Nor are human beings isolated individuals. Luther's concept of community is an essential assumption that underlies his theology. It is an understanding we need to recover today because the rampant individualism of Western society has already caused this concept to disappear from many surveys of Luther's thought.

Luther saw society as an organic whole, a unity under God. Just as there are many members of the body of Christ, likewise there are many members in human society, yet there is one organic whole or community. Community is a gift of God whereby we are placed into a network of mutual inter-dependencies and obligations with all other members of the community. People perform different functions in the community but all the functions are intended to serve everyone.

There are different vocations, or callings, that people undertake, such as pastor, theologian, farmer, miner, prince, laborer, parent, and so forth. In the concept of vocation all callings are from God, and therefore sacred, so Luther thus unifies society into an even greater unity than that achieved in the thought of the Middle Ages when the sacred versus secular distinction of occupations separated the vocations. We should regard our own calling as a task which God wants us to perform well for the benefit of our neighbor (all other members of the community). It is the height of selfishiness and greed to live our lives on our own, because for Luther society is not the sum total of individual members: society is a pre-ordained entity into which individual people find themselves placed by God. We are to serve our neighbor as we fulfill our own particular calling in life whatever it may be. Consequently, it is concluded, "the best way to serve one's neighbors is to do well the task that is assigned to him."[41]

The callings of life are not seen by Luther as human constructions, nor is the existence of community the aggregate result of human effort. Community and the vocations have been planned and pre-ordained by God. For Luther, that means that the agricultural and small town society of the Middle Ages is God's one design for human society. This reflects his unfortunate assumption that the orders of society are not so much a part of human history and endeavor but more a part of God's created world of nature. People must accommodate themselves to the social system just as they must to weather or disease. Luther found it impossible to conceive of human transformation bringing in a better or different kind of society, whether through democracy or revolution. He saw tampering with social structures as analogous to tampering with the very laws of God's creation - hence any program of social change would be perceived as anarchy, literally, going against the laws that establish the status quo.

The placement of human society under the realm of nature, rather than history, probably accounts for much of the reactionary element in Lutheran social ethics, whether we think of Luther's fanatical concern for order and law during the peasant uprising at the expense of a more just social arrangement (which is the only basis for order and law), or more recent events in South Africa. Luther could not envisage a different form of economy, government, occupations, politics, and so forth, and so he assumed that any changes in the social structure could only bring about anarchy.

Thus we see one reason why Luther and Lutheranism have tended simply to support the status quo of society. On the other hand, Luther did speak about social abuses, notably poverty and usury and the early capitalism, and his comments make it clear that he felt change within social structures was both possible and a mandate for Christians. From his perspective, usury and poverty and free enterprise trade represented greedy and unjust distortions of the divine social system, and what was needed was not so much a new system but a restoration of the ordained patterns of the past.[42] Today's problem would be to ascertain what "orders" are essential in light of the many transformations of society that have occurred since the Reformation.

Interwoven in these themes is Luther's constant emphasis on love for the neighbor. Luther does not see love for the neighbor as a "law" of God but as the natural disposition of loving concern characterizing every Christian who has been justified freely by God's grace. Conversion to Christ means, at the same time, conversion to the neighbor, for we are to find and serve Christ in and through our neighbor, thus building and sustaining the community. More precisely, our neighbor is Christ for us. We encounter Christ through relationships. The Incarnation and the theology of the cross direct us to Christ in the neighbor, in particular, neighbors in need. In Luther's concept of community, the Christian is never to work for personal gain or opportunity, nor to amass private possessions that exceed legitimate needs, rather everything is to be done in the name of serving the neighbor.

The Peasant War and Luther's Limitations

I have intentionally delayed mentioning Luther's position during the "Peasant War" of 1525 until the end of this topic. When most people think of "Luther's attitude towards the poor" they think immediately of the Peasant War and Luther's strong and cruel rejection of the peasants in favor of the princes. But Luther's writings during the uprising yield no information about his attitude towards the poor. He did not understand the desperate plight of the poor peasants and did not see the uprisings as poverty riots. We do learn about his theory of the "two kingdoms" wherein he treats the social realm as an aspect of nature, and some of the other assumptions of his cultural framework which made it impossible for him to understand the dimensions of the peasant revolt and the issues at stake. To this day the Peasant War hangs as an albatross around the neck of Lutherans, for it was during the Peasant War that the lower social classes of Germany largely departed from Lutheranism, with the result that to this day the dominant ethos of Lutheranism is middle upper class. Still, his writings of 1525 are a poor starting point for understanding Luther's ongoing approach to poverty, both prior to and following the peasant revolt.

Some have tried to ameliorate Luther's stand, yet when all is said and done, Luther cannot be excused for his strong and totally unnecessary encouragement of the princes to stab, smite, slay, and mutilate the peasants — who had already lost the battle when Luther's words appeared. Although his initial writings are sometimes described as "blaming equally" both sides, it remains that an estimated 100,000 peasants were put to death, unknown thousands more disfigured and maimed through the princes' application of Luther's "justice." But how many princes died? This was scarcely a situation in which "equal blame" did anything but give total support to the militarily superior princes.

Here we see clearly Luther's limitations as a Christian theologian. It is to his credit that he was a "man of his times," rooting theology in his cultural and social context, but it is to his detriment that, as a "man" of his times, he allowed some of his cultural limitations to become theological limitations. By making biblical exegesis subordinate to such ideas as his theory of the two kingdoms, the created orders of a static society, and the placement of society within the framework of the natural world governed by unchangeable laws of nature, he developed many points where his thinking must be discarded in constructing a valid theology for the modern day context. Luther was perhaps momentarily correct in sensing that the survival of the Reformation might be at stake in the peasant uprisings, but eternally wrong in not appreciating the human dimensions of the plight of the peasants and their allies, both before and during the uprising. He said that no one should have more than they "need" in light of their calling, and so had little sympathy for the "dumb peasants," as they were frequently referred to at the time, who from his point of view needed next to nothing in the way of material comforts in order to survive. Even in his early writings he was frequently condescending towards the poor and the peasants, seeing them more as objects of charity than as human beings. He also saw "needs" in a crassly materialistic way, not recognizing, for example, freedom from slavery as a legitimate "need" of the poor. As with his rejection of early capitalism, so here Luther opposed individual initiative in fighting for social justice in favor of a passive reliance on the "system" to provide justice.

Thus he imputed selfish motives to peasants demanding their rights; in other words, Luther was content to have the foxes guarding the hen house! Perhaps too many years in monasteries and princes' castles had dulled his consciousness of the world and his ability to identify with the ordinary people.

When we today articulate a theological approach to society, we must begin with the assumption that the working structures of society are human creations which people can transform for better or for worse. While certain fundamental structures may be necessary for human civilization, we must avoid the danger of associating the humanly constructed systems of society with God's plan of creation. Democracy, freedom, the industrial revolution, our complex economy, and the recognition of human rights are crucial modern assumptions of which

Luther had no awareness. Where Luther treated society as an aspect of nature, we must treat it within the context of human history: we recognize no divine sanction for the status quo.

Bearing in mind such limitations, many of the insights of Luther's theology need to be upheld. We can see in his writings the importance of grounding "social concerns" within an over-all theological framework of the Gospel. In a day when government supported social assistance programs are being slashed by politicians who do not understand the cross of Christ, we are reminded of the inter-relatedness of society and that the obligation for social relief and development must transcend individual and private acts of charity. We need to rediscover and appreciate Luther's concept of community which contrasts sharply with the individualism of our society that distorts our perception of many of Luther's teachings (as well as the teachings of the Bible which likewise are unaware of individualism). We are challenged by Luther in our personal lives regarding our solidarity with and support for the poor and the oppressed, offering everything we can. Our possessions, privileges, and talents are a gift, a trust from God which we have until our neighbor needs them. The Christian community is only faithful to Christ insofar as it is in solidarity with the poor and the oppressed of the world, and today's world has structures of injustice far more cruel than Luther knew in his day. Luther calls us to solidarity and compassion, not as a "law," not as a "virtue," but simply as an aspect of living under and by the grace of God.

IS THE EMPEROR NAKED?: RELIGIONS
AND RELIGION IN THEOLOGICAL EDUCATION

Roland E. Miller

The place of the study of religions and religion in theological education
has not been finally determined. To that extent, there exists a perceptible
sense of incompleteness, of something missing in the total picture.[1]
Surely, it would seem, the subject matter of religion belongs to
theology!...And yet the precise nature of that belonging remains
unresolved. Seminaries and divinity schools have attempted to deal with
the situation in a variety of ways. Attention has been given to religions
and religion within the traditional disciplines, brief survey classes have
been introduced, and there have been some laudable efforts to deal
more creatively with the issue as a whole. In general, however, the
approach, especially within denominational seminaries, has been a very
tentative one, and it may be suggested that in the main the discussion of
the fundamental issue has barely begun.

The failure to develop fuller clarification of this matter is the
combination result of several factors. Our present situation reflects a
long historical development, the current state of the art in theology itself,
and surely also the conviction that the present approach is relatively
adequate given the mandate of theological education and the needs of
the church. Where the immediate context of the church in contemporary
society is not perceived as being primarily a religious one but rather a
religious vacuum, there may be a lack of a sense of relevance. Further,
the current situation may also reflect the belief that such a need, if there
is one, should be dealt with at undergraduate levels, or it may reveal the
practical restraints of funding, time and energy that inhibit dealing with
a need even when it is deeply felt. Finally, it may also point to the
well-known tendency in all academic processes to develop forms of
disciplinary self-perpetuation and curricular inertia, that merge with
respect for tradition and resistance to "trendiness" in theological
education.

Whatever the reasons, this coat of many colours barely conceals a
nakedness. The reality of the situation is clear: the role of the examination
of religions and religion within a theological curriculum remains
undecided. Since un-wholeness has a possible corollary of un-

wholesomeness, it may be useful to engage in some reckoning and reflecting on this issue. To do so is to pay tribute to William Hordern whose interest in the subject began very early in his career, and who has been consistent in allowing the spirit of theology to carry him to new horizons, rather than setting arbitrary limits to the range of its compass and concern.

I propose to deal with the topic in two sections: an historical overview and an analysis of the need.

A. A Look at the History of the Issue

From earliest times the church has had an interest in religions, but from widely differing points of view. A full study of that interest has not been done.[2] At each stage the context in which the people of God were situated was a critical factor.

In the Biblical period the relation has been described as being primarily one of "exclusivism and intolerance."[3] The terms conviction, encounter, engagement, witness, judgment more positively capture the essence of that relation. The Old Testament focussed on the reality of Yahweh. In comparison to that reality and the convenant established by the Almighty, the gods of the nations were non-sense. "For all the peoples walk each in the name of its god, but we will walk in the name of the Lord our God forever and ever" (Mic.4,5). Anything within the individual or society that detracted from the sole Lordship of the Almighty was to be abandoned and overcome. There is also revealed, however, the liveliness of the religious context of the children of Israel and their awareness of it. The gods may have been unreal as far as the people of God were concerned, but their religions were very real and presented an ongoing challenge. Thus Israel's theological insight and apprehension were worked out in the crucible of religious encounter. Old Testament studies have not only helped us to understand that context, but they have also contributed largely to the understanding of the general religious history of humanity.

New Testament Christians were in continuity with the Old Testament mood. Not only that, they were directly involved in the newly received and accepted task of proclaiming Christ to the Gentiles and bringing about the obedience of faith. They were not set down in a religiously pluralistic world as its observers or analysts, but they were rather sent to it to disclose the Unknown and to reveal the mystery of redemption through the Gospel. Yet here again, the awareness of the religious context was an ever-present factor, nuancing their theological sensitivity and colouring their communication. Whether it was reflected in the cosmic Logos of the fourth Gospel, or in Jesus' own knowledge of Gentile religiosity (Mt.6,7), or in St. Paul's empathy with those involved in the Jewish dilemma and the Greek quest (1 Cor.9, 19ff.), or in John's awareness of Hellenistic mysticism (1 Jn.2), the religious context was a conscious reality for the people of God in New Testament times.

After the first wave of the Christian movement its scholars had to deal with that reality in a more disciplined fashion. In His gracious economy God provided unusually able minds to engage in that effort. The purpose and task of the apologists and fathers were clear — to address the issues raised by the religions and to clarify the Christian faith. In opposing the gods of the religions, they had to account for their origin and to explain the resemblance of some elements to Christianity; at the same time, they had to demonstrate the supernatural origin of the Christian faith and to communicate it intelligibly into an atmosphere dominated by popular religion, Greek philosophy and Roman law, all of this amidst chronic persecution. Men of the calibre of Justin Martyr, Irenaeus, Tertullian and Augustine in the West, and Clement of Alexandria and Origen in the East took up the task with great intelligence and vigour. They were contextual and missionary theologians, knowing and dealing with the religions of their time, and their theological works remain as exciting sources for the Christian understanding of the doctrine of God.

The period between the early church and the later medieval church, the 8th to 10th centuries, was dominated by Islamic intellectual genius. In this relatively dull period of the church's development there were few to emulate John of Damascus (675-749), whose personal knowledge of Islam was drawn from his years of service in the Ummayad government, prior to his becoming a priest. While John's apologetic helped to establish the polemic and scholastic mode of disputation between Muslims and Christians that continued to modern times, his writings reflect a living dialogue with Muslims, and they provide a continuing resource for those concerned with both guarding the unity of God and communicating the Christian understanding of that unity. It is not insignificant therefore that his *Orthodox Faith* became a standard manual of doctrine in Eastern Christianity. Theodore Abu Qurra (d. ca.820), John's disciple who wrote in Arabic, and the conciliatory Nestorian Patriarch Mar Timothy I (780-823) were of similar ilk.[4]

As time moved on in the Middle Ages the presence of Islam became overwhelming. Judaism had been rendered silent and fearful. Islam, however, was alive and forceful. Christian theology and action were compelled to have reference to that reality, for as R.W. Southern points out, it was "the most far-reaching problem of medieval Christendom." It was so not only from the practical side since it "called for action and discrimination between the competing possibilities of Crusade, conversion, coexistence and commercial interchange," but also because it raised a host of theological questions.

> As a theological problem it called persistently for some answer to the mystery of its existence; what was its providential role in history—was it a symptom of the world's last days or a stage in the Christian development;

a heresy, a schism or a new religion; a work of man or devil; an obscene parody of Christianity, or a system of thought that deserved to be treated with respect? It was difficult to decide among these possiblities. But before deciding it was necessary to know the facts, and these were not easy to know.[5]

The well-documented tragedy of this period, of course, is that the facts were seldom known. Ignorance, imagination and emotion dominated, and the theological failure to acquire religious facts led to massive distortion and an unhappy history. In the eastern church Christian doctrine was being formulated with some reference to Islam, Hellenism and dualism. The church's definition of itself "was determined not by internal struggles within Christendom, Eastern or Western, but by the necessity to state in brief compass the heart of the gospel."[6] In the West, however, the major tone of Christian response to Islam became that represented by the Crusades, and their influential heritage of misunderstanding, misconception and malice is not yet fully diffused. There was a strong minor tone, however, that forced theology to be aware of religion in a different way.

The first element in that minor tone was produced by the Graeco-Muslim cultural movement which, transmitted through Spain, finally led to the Renaissance and Reformation. This drift of thought is one of the most remarkable and important events in intellectual history. What Islam took from the Greek philosophers with the help of Syrian and Persian Christian translators, it read, learned, marked and inwardly digested, and in the frame of Islamic religious philosophy it then passed on its gift to the West. Ibn Sina (Avicenna) and Ibn Rushd (Averroes) led the way. The briliant Ibn Rshd (1126-1198) more or less compelled Western Christianity to contend with Aristotle and his principle of active intelligence. In the end, theologians of the West led by Thomas Aquinas rejected Averroeism and its apotheosis of reason, but they accepted the gift of Aristotle, who was virtually elevated to the rank of a church father. The fact that orthodox Muslims themselves were in the process of rejecting much of what western Christians were accepting was not known, though a matter of far-reaching consequence for Islam and later history.[7] As theology was worked on in relation to philosophical Islam by a process of both absorption and reaction, the freeing of the Christian mind had begun.

The other important aspect of the minor tone was that represented by the missionary movement of the church, which has spear-headed the church's theological engagement with religion. Giants among them were Peter the Venerable, Francis of Assissi and Ramon Lull. Lull (1235-1315) was Europe's apostle of reason who became its fool of love. With almost inexhaustible energy and in more than 200 works he engaged himself in the task of rationally demonstrating the truth of the Christian faith. Along the way, he immersed himself in Arabic and Islam, especially the philosophy of Ibn Rushd which he vigorously opposed. He spent years of lonely effort attempting to persuade princes and popes to establish schools of oriental learning for missionaries and chairs in Arabic and other languages in universities, and his principle was finally conceded by the council of Vienna in 1311. In later years he was persuaded that not the path of reason but the path of love must prevail. His spirit was kindled and inflamed with the love of the Crucified, and in works like *Book of the Lover and the Beloved* his heart poured forth profound hymns of love.[8] In 1315, at the age of 80, he sealed his testimony in blood in the streets of Bugia, Tunisia, martyred as he proclaimed the Christ. Theology *habitus practicus est*!

Peter the Venerable (1092-1156), Abbot of Cluny, had actively reflected on the religion of Judaism and Islam, despite his heavy administrative tasks as the director of a far-flung monastic domain. He pioneered a new attitude and a new approach, and thereby became a milestone in history. In regard to attitude, he declared that Muslims have a place in salvation, and that therefore Christians must strive for their conversion, not their extermination. In regard to approach, he argued that while Islam must be refuted, in order for that to happen it must be accurately known and understood. He therefore gathered a group of translators, including a Muslim member, and oversaw the translation into Latin of five major Islamic works, one of which was the Qur'an itself! Let us go to the Muslims, he declared, not "as our people often do, by arms, but by words, not by force, but by reason, not in hatred, but in love."[9] Here was a new hermeneutic for the study of Islam. It was in that same spirit that Francis of Assissi engaged the Sultan of Egypt in dialogue (1219) with his gospel of friendship and love, at the very moment that the soldiers of the fifth crusade were massacring the Muslim inhabitants of Damietta. When Malik al-Kamil dismissed St. Francis with the words: "Pray for me, that God may reveal to me which faith is more pleasing to him,"[10] he was unconsciously underlining the need, and perhaps even an inchoate appeal, for theological engagement with religion.

The engagement of the early and medieval church with its religious environment, theologically and missiologically, establishes the main themes which we must address with respect to the place of the study of religions in theological education. We may therefore hasten past the period of the Renaissance, with its humanistic concerns and glorification of the past, and the Reformation, with its freshly uncovered evangelical criterion for dealing with religion. We may pause to note Martin Luther's awareness of the religion of Islam, which was set in the highly charged political and polemical context of his time. Instead of raging at the Turks who were besieging Vienna in 1529 (in fact, many "Lutherans" at first welcomed the incursion of Suleiman the Magnificent and his Ottoman forces as a distraction for the Catholic emperor, Charles V!), Luther interpreted the Islamic military penetration into Europe as an expression of God's judgment upon the Christianity of his day. Similarly, he utilized the Muslim theological approach, as he understood it, to illustrate the theme of work-righteousness which was pervasively infecting the church. More startling is the fact that in 1542 he encouraged Thomas Bibliander's publication of Robert of Ketton's old translation of the Qur'an, came to the rescue against the city council of Basel when Bibliander was jailed for his temerity, and joined with Melanchton in preparing a foreword for the new edition. His interest, trenchantly expressed, was to expose untruth, but he intended to do it accurately. To that extent he followed in the train of Peter the Venerable.

It was the Catholic Reformation, however, expressed through its missionary expansion, in particular the "discovery" of Confucianism by the Jesuit missions in China led by Matthew Ricci, that opened a new religious world to Western Europe and presaged a major change for the study of religions. The earlier reports of travellers who had signalled the existence of a larger religious world were now confirmed by the more intimate and knowledgeable experience of missionaries. Ricci, Robert de Nobili, Bartholomaeus Ziegenbalg and William Carey stood at the borders of new religious dimensions. Theirs were minds as able and hearts as large as the heroes of the early church, but there was a greater sense of threat in the unfamiliarity, vastness and content of the new materials from eastern religion. How would the church respond to the new situation? The signs were not very promising; in fact, the philosophers of western culture intercepted the pass and ran with the ball.

Matthew Ricci (1552-1610) conducted a skillful, trail-blazing ministry to the sophisticated Chinese court. Essentially equating Confucius (Kwang Fu Tze) and Aristotle, he perceived them as standing at the highest point in natural theology and as a true *praeparatio evangelica*. He therefore composed a catechism which drew on Confucian writings to illustrate Christian truths. It was a road-levelling kind of methodology, dedicated to the ultimate goal of rooting Christ in Chinese soil. His penetrating vision, not to speak of his physical endurance and courage, as well as the fact that he successfully planted the church, were all to no avail. Ricci was castigated for his approach, and it was not until the mid-1700's that the storm over his views abated in Western Europe. Robert de Nobili (1577-1656) engaged in a more dramatic form of identification with Brahmin Hindus in South India, and his experiment likewise met with considerable disapproval.

Bartholomaeus Ziegenbalg (1683-1719) was one of the first two Protestant and Lutheran missionaries to reach India, landing in 1706 in Tranquebar with his colleague, Heinrich Pluetschau. Like many of those who would follow him Ziegenbalg would die young, but with zeal and energy he planted the church, and in the process worked out fundamental missiological principles. Holding that the preaching of the Gospel must be based on an accurate knowledge of the minds of the people, he supplemented his other activities with linguistic and cultural studies. One of the products of his effort was a careful study of the religious beliefs of South India, which he dispatched to his superiors in the West. For his temerity in engaging in this activity he was rapped on the knuckles by his mission board, which suggested that he had been sent to root our Hinduism, not to study it. His work, the *Geneology of the Malabar Gods*, was not published till 1867. William Carey (1761-1834), the remarkable cobbler-scholar and first Protestant missionary to Bengal, whose achievements are almost epic in scope, received church commendation for many contributions; he was not thanked, however, for his thousand page Sanskrit grammar, or for his translation of the Ramayana.[11] The ambience between religious awareness and theological perception, which had been partially apprehended in the West through the interaction with Judaism and Islam, was not being transferred to the new and wider religious context, except in rare cases.

In the end, it was not nervousness regarding the missionary endeavour, nor the cumulative increase of global knowledge that accompanied the colonial expansion of the West, which provided the major factor in the changing approach to the study of religions. It was the Enlightenment that provided the key element. The Enlightenment was an intellectual revolution that followed upon the Renaissance and Reformation, which affirmed a virtually unlimited confidence in human capacity and the power of reason. Through the application of this approach to the totality of life the movement eventually led to the scientific age and our technological era. The totality of life also included the area of the religions and religion. The thinkers of the Enlightenment did not hesitate to deal directly with religious questions, and their intellectual energies produced the foundation of the disciplines now associated with the academic study of religion. But their basic approach, which was to separate knowledge and belief, also initiated a division between theology and religion that persists to the present.

The bifurcation did not take place as a formal split but as a complex process. Up to the time of the Enlightenment religions and religion —whatever may have been known about them and however they may have been viewed — were the province of the church and its teaching. Many of the leading thinkers of this period, however, were not only interested in religion but were at the same time at odds with the classical positions of Christian theology; the fact that they ordinarily remained within the church merely served to complicate the matter further. In the end, the study of religion became a victim of this tension. As critical thinkers more and more expounded on religion from their points of view, the church more and more set itself the task of defending its theology. The critics viewed religion from the perspectives of philosophy and history, leaving aside traditional theology (which, for many, was equated with superstition). The church, sensing danger, drew back. Its defence against the radical interpretations of religion led to ambivalent attitudes toward the subject itself. The final result was a kind of continental divide in Christian intellectual history; the study of theology minus religion became the task of the seminary, while religion minus theology was to become the province of the academy.

> Those engaged in religious studies sought credentials in the secular university in a time in which theology was not only dethroned but forced to maintain a separate identity. Hence, religious studies came to see itself not as a "discipline" *for* true believers, but *about* them.[12]

We must hasten to add that this development varied greatly from region to region, and from institution to institution. As late as the mid-point of our century Heinrich Frick (d.1952) occupied the chair of systematic theology at the University of Marburg, at the same time being in charge of the history of religions and of missiology![13] Especially in Holland theologians took a lead in the study of religion. In North America, however, the pattern of separation was sharper and more consistent. For a period of time in the second half of the nineteenth century and the early years of the twentieth century interest in the study of religions was evident in both seminaries and universities, but thereafter there was a drifting apart.[14]

We have gone ahead of our story and must return briefly to the Enlightenment. The Enlightenment period may be divided into two major streams: the stream of rationalism (late 17th and 18th c.) and the stream of romanticism (18th and early 19th c.). The two streams crossed one another, influencing each other, and were at times indistinguishable. Yet each stream provided a critical factor in the development of the study of religion. Rationalists emphasized the concept of natural religion, which was held to correspond to rational religion, and which was further regarded as the universal religion of humanity. The positive religions are not the important thing. What is important is to call humanity to awareness of the essential and true religion, which has a set of basic, rationally-acceptable notions that are common to all humanity. Since God is rational and humans are rational, religion must be rational. What reason discovers from the book of nature are basic universals such as God, existence of soul, the need for worship and virute, reward and punishment, and immortality. Revelation, if there is any, can only confirm natural rational knowledge and cannot go beyond its grasp or be in disharmony with it. All dogmas and mysteries must therefore be critically judged in the pure light of reason and if found incompatable with it, be discarded.

Many rationalists remained in the church, arguing that Christianity properly (i.e. rationally) understood is the truest expression of this natural and reasonable religion, and in that sense the fulfillment of all religious aspirations. David Hume (1711-1766) and others like him, however, shattered the deist complacency, demonstrating that even the argument from first cause for the existence of God is not supportable by reason. He saw no alternative to agnosticism and atheism. We need not marvel that the church and theology began to lose touch with — nay fear! — religion.

The romantics, like orthodox Christians, also reacted against the rationalists and what appeared to be a cold, proud and arid intellectualism. They shared the new-found confidence in reason, but they held in equal reverence the elements of human intuition and feeling. They were marked by a sense of, almost "in love with", the nobility of nature and humanity. Since nature is revelation, all that it produces, all its luxuriant branches must be respected. The varieties of religion are therefore to be accepted — and wherever possible admired — as expressions of the warm and wonderful history of the human race under the guidance of the Eternal Spirit. Ideas in general, and religious views in particular, are to be viewed in terms of relationships rather than absolutes, for there is relative good and truth in every reality. But we may be assured that under the education of God the human race is mounting ever upward to the heights of religious expression, where a final reconciliation and unity will be realized.

This was, indeed, a different spirit, but not less difficult for traditional Christian faith. Many romantics, too, remained in the church, arguing that Christianity properly understood *was* that final height of ethical monotheism to which all religion was tending. As rationalism, however, had its Humes and Voltaires, so romanticism had its Rousseaus and Herders. The church, which had faced the bogy of critical rationalism, now encountered the menace of historical relativism. Gotthold Lessing (1729-1781), who bridges the movements, declared: "Not the truth of which a man is—or believes himself to be—possessed, but the sincere effort he has made to reach it, makes the worth of a man."[15] Threatened again, the church drew back, and its study of religion once more suffered by association.

The two streams of rationalism and romanticism met together and created the delta of a new science at the beginning of the modern era. In 1867 in his *Chips from a German Workshop* Max Muller of Oxford (1823-1900) called for an autonomous discipline to study religion in and for itself, naming it *allgemeine religionswissenschaft*, the scientific study of religion, and Conrad Tiele (1830-1902) of Groeningen established its basic orientation. Thus the new discipline of religious studies was born. Its very considerable development since that time is another story. For the moment it is sufficient to say that university acceptance was not immediate; for a period of time the study of religion followed an uncertain course, caught between the suspicions of theology on the one hand and the doubts of the academy on the other hand, while simultaneously contending with the particular interests of other academic disciplines. Gradually, however, its position as an independent discipline was recognized. In universities across the world the field was taken up with vigour and a series of brilliant scholars have assidously examined and reported on the realm of the sacred. The educational legacy of the development is impressive; in North America alone, there are over 900 departments or programs of religious studies in various institutions. At the same time, seminaries and divinity schools on the whole avoided the areas of religions and religion as a special field of interest in theological education. In theology itself there were notable scholars, from Nathan Soederblom and Rudolf Otto forward, who made highly significant contributions to the study, but in general the discipline wandered rather infrequently and haphazardly across the terrain of religion. In the present time various theological institutions have made adaptations to take into account a perceived unwholeness in their educational program, but the fundamental direction has remained the same.

Shall we accept our heritage and leave the matter alone, or shall we somehow seek to redress the situation? There is an argument for restoring religions and religion to theological education.

B.   A Look at the Place of Religion in Theological Education

The need and value of dealing with humanity's religions as a normal part of theological education may be dealt with in terms of two major areas:

1.   The Area of the Preparation of the Church for Mission

The sending church should be an understanding church. It is the task of a learned ministry to create that understanding.

We have already seen that a church which is involved in mission is in a contact situation with the religions. The truth, however, is interactive. An educational program that puts people in understanding touch with the adherents of other faiths generates *missio* and make it intelligent. It is clear that whatever vacuum exists between the concepts of sending church and understanding church become filled with a combination of non-involvement attitudes and mission myths. In the case of the former, the result is flatness in the church, while the latter produces outright danger, as we have seen. The failure to understand and the failure to support the mission of the church are two pieces of the same cloth, and both are at least partially derived from the difficulty of the clergy to adequately apprehend the religious and cultural context of the church's mission and to communicate it realistically to the members of the church. If nothing else, a deeper engagement with the religions in the training period would ease the problem of uninformed and at times embarrassing homiletics and pedagogy. Both Zoroaster and the pew need some saving! In sum, there is a need to deal with religions and religion[16] at seminary levels so that the clergy may better understand the mission of the church to the world and may be enabled to share that understanding.

The sending church should not only be an understanding church, but it should also be an equipped and *ably* witnessing church. This truism becomes an urgent reality for two reasons. The first is the penetrating infusion of unfamiliar religious philosophies in our society (often in corrupted forms), the increasing activity by missions of other religions that are carrying out their own spiritual obligations, and the regular influx of people of other faiths — frequently the intelligentsia — through the process of immigration. All this has combined to move the frontier of mission into our immediate neighborhood. The second factor is the vast, world-wide diaspora of western Christians engaged in business and other activities abroad, at a time when nationalism and resurgent religions block the traditional forms of Christian mission. Thus, not only has the "foreign" religious world moved to where we are, but we have also moved to the traditional homes of the great religions. In both cases, the interaction of large numbers of congregation members with the members of other religious movements has become a normal pheno- menon. Clearly this demands both a ministry of consciousness-raising and practical equipping. We therefore deal with religions and religion at seminary levels so that clergy may be personally enabled to witness to Buddhists, Hindus and Muslims, and may in turn enable and inspire others to do the same.

2. The Area of Development of Theological Competence

As every Christian must be able to think missiologically about religious people, so Christians must be helped to think theologically about religious experience. It is the task of a learned ministry to give that help.

A minister who is a religious semi-illiterate is a contradiction in terms. While the image of the minister as a jack-of-all-competences is shrinking to a more realistic figure, one focal point of the image will probably always remain, namely, the assumption that a minister is a person who is skilled in religion. This expectation – which, it must be conceded, is a quite natural one – is sharpened by the fact that the religions of humanity are commanding striking attention from modern society, not only at studied levels, but in every day life. The media are forcing the issue, at the same time as they demonstrate their inadequacy to deal with it. Competence in religion, that is, an understanding of the phenomenon of religion itself that exceeds a merely superficial grasp and an informed awareness of the major religous options of humanity, is fundamental for a ministry for our age.

We must move to a less obvious point, but one of great significance for theological understanding. The theological heritage of the Christian faith may be sustained without exposure to a major alternative system of theology, but only at severe cost. We may not full agree with Max Mueller's stark declaration: "He who knows one religion, knows none." The starting-point for this famed declaration was at truth derived from Mueller's own field of specialization, the linguistic world: "He who knows one language, knows none."[17] Those who recognize degrees of knowledge will hesitate before the absoluteness of this statement. Yet all will recognize the important intellectual reality that is being testified to: one who has no comparative base, is not only unable to generalize about religion, but is also limited in his or her appreciation of the uniqueness of that which is possessed. A qualified "yes" may be given to the question: "Is it possible to teach Christianity effectively without another religion?" But it is quite clear that the depth knowledge of one of the other great systems of theological thought sharpens and refines existing Christian insights, points to the fact that the task of constructive theology is not complete, and above all, highlights the contrast between the Gospel and all religions, including Christianity, and underlines the critical centrality of the person of Christ. Observers watched Paul Tillich struggle with this awareness in the later years of his life. Tillich said,

> My own Systematic Theology...had another intention, namely, the apologetic discussion against and with the secular...But perhaps we need a longer, more intensive period of interpenetration of systematic theological study and religious historical studies. Under such circumstances the structure of religious thought might develop in connection with another or different fragmentary manifestation of theonomy or of the Religion of the Concrete Spirit. That is my hope for the future of theology.[18]

The development of theological insight in relation to another system of thought occurs both by contrasts and parallels. It is well known that the world of non-Christian religions offers a host of pertinent and contemporary parallels to the religious milieu of Biblical times, a fact of considerable significance for Biblical theology. The contribution may also come, however, through lively and positive content. We may argue that all such positive spiritual insights are either explicit or implicit in the Bible and in Christian tradition, but minimally it must be recognized that the experience of other religions may serve to re-engage us with certain aspects of Christian truth. Anyone who has drawn near to the Islamic emphasis on the majesty of God will also sense the value it can have in restoring to Christianity that dimension of awe and surrender which is its own birthright. The late highly-respected German Lutheran missiologist, Walter Freytag (1898-1959), put it well when he said: "There is no understanding of other religions which does not yield new Biblical insight."[19]

The skills that grow out of this kind of engagement with the religions further assist the future clergy of the church to understand the theory and method of theologizing in context, thereby enabling them to be practically involved in ongoing theological thinking in the church. It may be that the average minister's life experience in North America will be largely with the pseudo- or quasi-religions of humanity, such as humanism, naturalism, secularism, materialism, nationalism, scientism, communism, and so on.[20] However, the skills that are developed in a theological education that trains men and women to deal with the varied expressions of the sacred, will also go a long way in assisting them in their dealing with the secular philosophies of our time. Thus the church of Christ, that is not of the world and yet is in the world, will be constantly refreshed with a new stream of missionary theology related to the context of the day. It should also be noted that the knowledge of how the people of other faiths are facing the challenges of the secular religions, how they are dealing or failing to deal with them, is itself immensely instructive for Christian thought and life, and equally productive of sympathy for our fellow human beings, who are caught in the same situation as we are and who are living in hope and fear.

Finally, the study of religions at the seminary level will enable the development of theological competence in an area of growing complexity and concern in the church at large, namely the question of truth as it relates to the religions and the trend toward universalist views in the church. Here there is no place for lazy or uninstructed minds. The issue has a sublimal reality for Christians that affects attitude and comitment to a far greater extent than is normally recognized or admitted. The nature and extent of God's revelatory action among human beings must be determined not only from Scripture but from the empirical evidence available in the religions of humanity. Only on the basis of real data can we face responsibly the theologically difficult questions of the nature of truth in the religions, the possibility of learning from them, the need for continued missions, and associated questions that perturb many minds and trouble many hearts. The currently massive interest in "dialogues" with other religions, and the assumptions, limitations and purpose of that enterprise, merely underline the urgency that is here for theological education. Is it carrying out its task, not only to study the living religions, but to do theology of religion itself?

Conclusion:

Let us clothe the emperor!

The following garments may be suggested for the theological education today:

a. A survey knowledge of the major religious options of humanity.

b. A depth knowledge of at least one of the major living religious traditions other than Christianity; this exposure should be not merely to the classical system of thought, but to the living contemporary expressions of faith and practice.

c. A study of theology of religion at a senior level as a concomitant to theology of mission and systematic theology.

How this kind of tailoring is to be achieved through the standard structures of seminaries and divinity schools is a matter that must be considered from within the perspectives of individual institutions, bearing in mind the inevitable restraints that are involved.[21] There can be no common answer, but there can be a common goal.

In thus reclaiming a portion of its birthright, theological education will not take away from but will rather contribute to the noble discipline of *religionswissenschaft*, to which it owes so much, both for its dedicated and disciplined study of the whole field of religion, and for the valuable materials it has produced that may now be gratefully used by the church in relation to its theological and missiological tasks. In return, it will give what it has to give — its own hard research and contributions to scholarship, the Lullian spirit associated with the fools of love, and its theological insight. From the perspective of Christian faith it is affirmed that humanity in religion can only, in the ultimate sense, be understood theologically, for humanity is under God. The God who is revealed in Jesus Christ as the seeking and finding Saviour has always been in salvific search of human beings, that is, of religious people. The history of religions in theological perspective may therefore be viewed as "the fight of God against religion within religion,"[22] for those whom He loves. The Gospel is the story of how that struggle is resolved. We may suggest, then, that the study of religions in the setting of Christian theological education must itself be living history of the salvific struggle of God's people for their fellow humans who stand in fascination and trembling before the Mystery.

PART TWO

Biblical/Historical Studies

RIGHTEOUSNESS AS RELATIONSHIP
Adrian M. Leske

One of the most important terms in both Old and New Testament theology has always been the concept "righteousness" (*sedeq, sedaqâ* in Hebrew, *dikaiosynè* in Greek). Its continual use in the prophetical writings and in the Psalms and its pivotal use in the message of Jesus and in Paul make it essential that this term be understood in the fulness of its meaning in its various contexts. It is not sufficient to translate the term variously as "deliverance," "victory," "triumph," "justice," or "right conduct" as has often been done in the past in numerous Bible translations and scholarly writings. "Righteousness" is a much more dynamic and all-embracing concept than the above interpretations allow. Martin Luther struggled a long time with this concept and the new insights he gained in studying Paul's discussion of righteousness became central to the theology of the Reformation. Protestants since then, however, have not always understood the term so clearly. William Hordern has pointed that out only too well in his fascinating book, *Living by Grace*, and with deep insight has recognized that righteousness must always be defined in terms of the right relationship with God.[1] Over the years my associations with Dr. Hordern have led me to a deep appreciation of the enormous contribution he has made to our theological understanding in so many ways. It is a privilege for me to contribute this article to a collection honouring him.[2]

Righteousness as a Covenant Term in the Old Testament

Israel, from her beginnings, saw herself as bound in a special relationship with Yahweh her God, in which he had delivered her from oppression in Egypt, chosen her to be his people, and given her the promise of land, peace and security under his kingship. Israel entered into this covenant relationship as his elect, accepted Yahweh's rule and his stipulations that they live together under him and with one another in the bond of covenant love. In this special relationship it was a profound privilege for Israel to be under Yahweh's gracious rule and not under the oppressive power of earthly kings. In this covenant relationship they committed themselves never to oppress one another, as was common in the feudalistic societies of their day, for they were all equal under Yahweh, their King. The people of Israel knew that it was *only* through maintaining this special relationship with Yahweh and with one another that they and their children could have peace and be blessed. Faithfulness to the covenant relationship was therefore absolutely essential for their living in the land in peace and prosperity.

The term which came to be used as an overall expression of faithfulness to this covenant relationship between Yahweh and Israel was *sedeq, sedaqâ*, "righteousness." Israel was perceived as being righteous when she committed herself to Yahweh and lived according to the covenant stipulations and the laws set up to safeguard the covenant relationship with one another, when she acted according to the covenant relationship of love towards God (Deut. 6:5; 19:12; Ps. 31:32) and towards neighbor (Lev. 19:18). Yahweh was spoken of as righteous when he acted in accordance with the covenant promises to give Israel his royal protection and guidance, justice, peace and prosperity in the land. He exercised his righteousness primarily not only when he showed his mercy and love toward Israel but also when he gave judgment. God's judgment was always so important to Israel for it insured that the covenant relationship could be maintained. In other words, Yahweh was seen as righteous when he carried out both the blessings and the curses invoked in the covenant ceremonies as expressed in Deuteronomy 11:26-29; Deuteronomy 27-28, and elsewhere. Throughout Israel's history the righteousness of Yahweh was most evident when he executed judgment with Israel and for Israel, and when he delivered his people from all forms of injustice, suffering, and oppression.

"Righteousness" is, therefore, primarily faithfulness to a relationship in which both parties are committed to one another. This is borne out by the terms most closely associated with *sedeq/sedàqâ* in the Old Testament. They are all relationship terms— *emunû*, "faithfulness"; *emet*, "steadfast faith" (being faithful in upholding the relationship); *hesed*, "steadfast love"; *meysàr*, "equity"; *rahamîm*, "mercy", "compassion" (a plural word derived from *rehem* "womb" indicating parental love for offspring or brotherly love for those born of the same womb); and *mispàt*, "judgment, justice." This last term, used so often together with "righteousness", has the meaning of carrying out God's judgment according to the covenant relationship. The function of the "judges" (*sopetîm*) in Israel's early history was to do just that on Yahweh's behalf. In this covenant between Yahweh and Israel, Yahweh was always seen as faithful and therefore "righteous", whereas Israel often became faithless and consequently transgressed the covenant stipulations. However, when she turned again to Yahweh, sought the covenant relationship and responded to Yahweh's steadfast love she was considered "righteous". As Elizabeth Achtemeier has pointed out, in the Old Testament the fulfilment of the law itself is not seen as constituting righteousness but the one who is righteous seeks to fulfil the covenant law because he accepts it in faith as God's gracious guidance to him.[3]

Righteousness as loving faithfulness in a relationship was really put into dramatic focus by the prophet Hosea. He depicted the covenant relationship between Yahweh and Israel as wedded faithfulness. Israel had been unfaithful and gone after other gods, but Yahweh yearned to bring her back to him, to take her back to her beginnings in the wilderness, to "the days of her youth, as at a time when she came out of the land of Egypt" (2:15) — back to the honeymoon. Then Israel would once again call Yahweh "My husband", and Yahweh would make a universal covenant giving Israel peace and security. Yahweh promised (H 2:21-22; E 2:19-20):

> I will betroth you to me forever: I will betroth you to me
> with righteousness (*sedeq*) and with justice (*mispat*),
> with steadfast love (*hesed*), and with mercy (*rahamîm*). I
> will betroth you to me with faithfulness (*emunà*), and
> you shall know Yahweh.

In this statement it is God's righteousness which is seen as the power to transform Israel to a life of faithfulness. It is also important to note that *sedeq* and *emunà* are seen here in synonymous parallelism.[4] The use of the verb *yada*, "to know" with all of its implications of sexual union and intimacy completes the whole concept of the intimate relationship of the covenant between Yahweh and Israel.[5] Later on, when Hosea upbraided Israel for forsaking Yahweh and putting her trust in other gods and nations he again used "knowledge" to express an intimate life-giving relationship. He charged that Yahweh had a covenant lawsuit (*rîb*) with Israel because "there is no faithfulness (*emet*), and no steadfast love (*hesed*), and no knowledge (*da at*) of God in the land....My people are destroyed for lack of knowledge, because you (O priest) have rejected knowledge "(4:1,6). However, for those who found the sexual connotations a little heavy, Hosea also offered another image of close relationship, that of a father and son: "When Israel was a child I loved him, and out of Egypt I called my son" (11:1).

The intimacy of the covenant relationship expressed in the imagery of a husband-wife relationship was taken up again later by Jeremiah. He, too, compared the establishment of the Sinai covenant with Israel to the taking of a marriage vow: "I remember the devotion of your youth, your love as a bride, how you followed me in the wilderness..." (2:2). But while Yahweh remained ever faithful, Israel sought other lovers (2:32-37). Jeremiah described the destruction of the Northern kingdom of Israel in terms of a divine divorce! (3:6-10) and the Southern kingdom of Judah should have taken warning from that, yet still proved to be just as faithless. He called Judah to repent and promised: "If you swear 'Yahweh lives' with steadfast faith, with justice and with righteousness, then nations shall bless themselves in him, and in him shall they glory" (4:2). This was a call to the renewal of the marriage vow but there was no response. Judah continued in her adulterous ways and would experience the faithlessness she had shown to Yahweh. She would suffer the ignominious death of a prostitute rejected by her lovers after they had abused her! (4:29-31). However, Yahweh remains faithful even when he carries out the curses of the covenant by chastizing them in judgment. This is clearly part of God's righteousness, his faithfulness to the covenant relationship, in the thinking of Jeremiah. This was made clear when Jeremiah called upon God's righteousness to bring vengeance upon those who had plotted against his life (11:20; 12:1). Isaiah used it the same way when he proclaimed: "Destruction is decreed, over-flowing with righteousness" (Is. 10:22) from which only a remnant shall return.[6] Yet God's righteousness always includes his *hesed*, his ever-lasting love, so there is always deliverance and restoration to the ideal relationship of husband and wife. That idea was foremost in Jeremiah's famous statement about establishing a new covenant to replace the one broken. In this new covenant there will be no need for written codes for it will be in their hearts:

> And no longer shall each man teach his neighbour and
> each his brother, saying, 'Know Yahweh,' for they shall
> all know me, from the least of them to the greatest, says
> Yahweh; for I will forgive their iniquity, and I will
> remember their sin no more. (31:34; cf. vv. 31-33)

Sometimes in this relationship Israel was called upon first to show righteousness towards Yahweh and then to experience the abundance of Yahweh's righteousness towards her, as in Hosea 10:12:

> Sow for yourselves righteousness,
> reap the fruit of steadfast love;
> break up your fallow ground,
> for it is the time to seek Yahweh,
> that he may come and rain righteousness upon you.

But more often Yahweh was seen as taking the initiative in the relationship with his righteousness in the hope that it would cause a righteous response in Israel, as in Isaiah 45:8:

> Shower, O heavens, from above,
> and let the skies rain down righteousness;
> let the earth open, that salvation may sprout forth,
> and let it cause righteousness to spring up also.

The prophets were continually exhorting Israel to keep her part of the covenant relationship and to "let justice roll down like waters and righteousness like an everflowing stream" (Amos 5:24), but just as often they were accusing the people of having "turned justice into poison and the fruit of righteousness into wormwood" (Amos 6:12).

The appeal to the people to show "justice and righteousness" was a common one among the prophets. But just as common was the expression of the hope of experiencing Yahweh's justice and righteous-ness. With the coming of the monarchy, the king of Israel was understood to be Yahweh's earthly representative through whom Yahweh's judgment and faithfulness to the covenant relationship would be maintained. However, when these kings again and again proved inadequate in that regard, the hope was projected forward to a future king, a Messiah, as Yahweh's true representative. This chosen one would bring about God's righteousness and judgment for all forevermore:

> He shall not judge by what his eyes see
> or decide by what his ears hear;
> but with righteousness he shall judge the poor,
> and decide with equity for the afflicted of the land...
> Righteousness shall be the girdle of his waist,
> and faithfulness the girdle of his loins. (Is. 11:3b-5; cf. 9:7; 16:5)

The result of this divine righteousness expressed through his Messiah would be peace and quietness and trust forever (Is. 32:16, 17). In the midst of his gloomy predictions of destruction Jeremiah gave this messianic oracle:

> Behold the days are coming, says Yahweh, when I will raise up for David a righteous branch, and he shall reign as king and deal wisely, and shall do justice and righteousness in the land. In his days Judah will be saved, and Israel will dwell securely. And this is the name by which he shall be called: "Yahweh our Righteousness." (Jer. 23:5-6; 33:14-16)

In II Isaiah that messianic doer of righteousness was understood to be Cyrus of Persia. His victories over Israel's enemies and oppressors were seen as fulfilling God's righteousness (Is. 41:2; 45:1,4,13). Even though he did not *know* Yahweh (45:4) he was used as Yahweh's agent to bring judgment for Israel. In this context and throughout II Isaiah there is always a close association of the concept of righteousness with the idea of salvation and deliverance. Yahweh is depicted as demonstrating his covenant faithfulness, his "righteousness" by delivering Israel from her oppression. He is therefore a "righteous God and Saviour" (45:21), and it is because of his own faithfulness to the covenant that he acts:

> Hearken to me, you stubborn of heart,
> you who are far from righteousness:
> I bring near *my* righteousness, *it* is not far off,
> and my salvation will not tarry;
> I will put my salvation in Zion,
> for Israel my glory. (46:12,13; cf. 51:1-8)

Yahweh's righteousness meant Israel's salvation in spite of her failure to practise righteousness. Israel had been tried in the "furnace of affliction" (48:10) because of her transgressions and the people "swear by the name of Yahweh and confess the God of Israel but not in steadfast faith and not in righteousness" (48:1). The righteousness of Yahweh was clearly Israel's *only* hope of salvation according to 51:1-8. For only "in Yahweh shall all the offspring of Israel be made righteous (*yisdequ*) and make their boast" (45:25). Like Hosea, Jeremiah, and Ezekiel (16:1-63; 23:1-49) before him II Isaiah depicted the covenant relationship as that of the love between husband and wife:

> For your Maker is your husband,
> Yahweh of hosts is his name;
> and the Holy One of Israel is your Redeemer....
> For Yahweh has called you
> like a wife forsaken and grieved in spirit,
> like a wife of youth when she is cast off, says your God.
> For a brief moment I forsook you,
> but with great compassion I will gather you.
> In overflowing wrath for a moment I hid my face from you,
> but with everlasting love I will have compassion on you,
> says Yahweh, your Redeemer....
> For the mountains may depart and the hills be removed,
> but my steadfast love will not depart from you,
> and my covenant of peace shall not be removed,
> says Yahweh who has compassion on you...
> In righteousness you shall be established....
> This is the heritage of the servants of Yahweh
> and their righteousness from me says Yahweh.

After the return from exile, in the reform instituted by Ezra, the exile and the subsequent poverty and political subjection of the post-exilic community was seen as Yahweh's punishment on Israel's failure to keep the covenant laws. This had a strong and lasting influence on Israel's theology from here on. In Ezra's prayer of covenant renewal Yahweh was addressed as "the great and mighty and terrible God, who keeps covenant and steadfast love" (Neh. 9:32), and who "has been righteous in all that has come upon us, for you have dealt faithfully and we have acted wickedly" (Neh. 9:33). All the people, therefore, "enter into a curse and an oath to walk in God's law which was given by Moses the servant of God and to observe and to do all the commandments of Yahweh our Lord and his ordinances and his statutes" (Neh. 10:29). From this time on, covenant righteousness was understood primarily as obeying the collected law codes, separating from non-Jews, keeping the Sabbath, and maintaining worship in Jerusalem. In the years of persecution that followed under the Seleucids, covenant righteousness was exemplified in maintaining the Torah, observing the sabbath, and practising circumcision, as well as doing prescribed acts of piety such as the giving of alms, prayer and fasting.

Covenant and Righteousness in Rabbinic Judaism

In Rabbinic Judaism the emphasis on obedience to the Torah exemplified in Ezra's reform was continued. As the people of the covenant (*benè berît*) that was their primary focus in terms of their covenant relationship.[7] It was, of course, presupposed that God carried out his part of the relationship, being bound especially in relation to Israel through his covenant with Abraham with its strong element of promise.[8] He had chosen Israel and would remain faithful to the covenant and would vindicate the righteous in this life and in the life to come so that Israel might be blessed and become a great nation. But the main concern of the Rabbis was how *man* could best be faithful to the covenant. That faithfulness was to be evidenced by obedience to the commandments and by repentance when there was failure. In this way the Israelite could remain in the covenant relationship and have a share in God's promises. As Ed Sanders puts it,

> Obedience is rewarded and disobedience punished. In case of failure to obey, however, man has recourse to divinely ordained means of atonement, in all of which repentance is required. As long as he maintains his desire to stay in the covenant, he has a share of God's covenantal promises, including life in the world to come. The intention and effort to be obedient constitutes the *condition for remaining in the covenant*, but they do not *earn* it.[9]

So the Rabbis constantly instructed the people to be righteous, that is, faithful to the covenant by obeying the Torah and atoning for transgressions. To be disobedient and to reject the Torah would be a rejection of the covenant relationship and consequently a rejection of God's saving grace.[10] In the Rabbinic literature, while *sedeq* retained the meaning of "righteousness", *sedaqà* took on more the extended meaning of giving alms or charity when referring to man's action. The giving of alms was a demonstrable action taken to fulfil the requirements of the covenant relationship under the law, and in the contemporary literature almsgiving, prayer and fasting came to be regarded as exemplary deeds of righteousness and atonement for sin. Such was the advice given in Tobit (12:8-9):

> Prayer is good when accompanied by fasting, almsgiving and righteousness. A little with righteousness is better than much with wrongdoing. It is better to give alms than to treasure up gold. For almsgiving delivers from death, and it will purge away every sin. Those who perform deeds of charity and of righteousness will have fulness of life.[11]

So the emphasis in the Tannaitic literature was always on man's keeping the law and doing acts of piety. But it was understood that God is always faithful to the covenant, a faithfulness which he demonstrated by showing justice and mercy. Particularly from the time of the exile it was understood that God carried out his justice by punishing transgression. He demonstrated his mercy by bringing the righteous through the refining fires of suffering and affliction (seen as punishment for sin in this life) to the Kingdom of God or the world to come.[12] For the party of the Pharisees, the coming of the messianic era was dependent on there being a sufficient number of righteous people in Israel to establish the Kingdom of God. This righteousness was to be gained through the strict keeping of the law. Their claims to righteousness on the basis of the law led to a form of religious elitism. It was this elitism and their understanding of righteousness that brought Jesus into sharp conflict with them as he began his proclamation of the Kingdom of God.

Covenant and Righteousness in the Teaching of Jesus

In the synoptic gospels the word for righteousness, *dikaiosyne*, is found only eight times. It is used once in the Gospel of Luke in the Blessing of Zechariah (Lk. 1:75). The other seven are all found in the sayings of Jesus in Matthew's Gospel — two of them in relation to the activities of John the Baptist who announced the coming of the Kingdom of God and the other five in the Sermon on the Mount where Jesus ushered in that Kingdom and described what membership in the Kingdom means.

It is clear that Jesus saw the establishment of the Kingdom in terms or reestablishing the intimate covenant relationship between God and his people intended in the original Sinai covenant and proclaimed by the prophets. In this sense Jesus had not come to abolish the law and the prophets but to fulfil them (Matt. 5:17). The basis of this relationship, as Jesus described it in the Sermon on the Mount, was love for God and for one another, just as God loves (5:43-48; cf. 22:34-40). Members of the Kingdom were invited to address God as "Our Father" (6:9), and constantly throughout the Sermon, Jesus encourages his hearers to see themselves in a father-son/daughter relationship with God and to think and act towards one another on the basis of that relationship, reflecting the love of their Father in their lives. When that kind of love relationship is established, it becomes the sole motivating force in the person's life so that he/she fulfils the law not by the act of carrying out the requirements of the law but by being motivated by the love that comes from his/her relationship with God to act in a meaningful way that often goes beyond the law's requirements. It is in this context that Jesus used the term "righteousness."

The first two references to righteousness in the Sermon are in the opening beatitudes which are the proclamation of the Kingdom in terms of covenant blessings. Each one of these blessings announces the

Kingdom to those who have been waiting faithfully for the fulfilment of God's righteousness through his Messiah as expressed so often in the prophets. Matthew 5:6 is no different. It announces: "Blessed are those who hunger and thirst for righteousness, for they shall be satisfied." To Jesus' Jewish audience who were familiar with the prophetic writings, such a pronouncement would immediately have called to mind that invitation to satisfy spiritual hunger and thirst in Isaiah 55 with it's hope of the coming messianic age and the promise in 56:1: "Keep justice and do righteousness for soon my salvation will come and *my* righteousness be revealed." Those who had been waiting for God's righteousness to be revealed were now having their hopes fulfilled! The messianic age had come and righteousness would be evident among them through his Messiah. Righteousness here is God's covenant faithfulness in keeping his promises.

Matthew 5:10 ("Blessed are those who are persecuted for the sake of righteousness, for theirs is the Kingdom of heaven.") rounds out and expresses the unity of the beatitudes by recalling the same blessing as given in the first. The Kingdom of God belongs to those who have sought to remain faithful to their covenant relationship with God and have suffered because of it. Those who are persecuted for the sake of righteousness are the same as the "poor in spirit" — those who were afflicted and oppressed and waiting for the good news of God's act of righteousness — deliverance. Here the reference is to the faithfulness of human beings to the covenant relationship.

In Matthew 5:20 Jesus mentions "righteousness" in the context of his discussion of the law. Having announced the Kingdom, it was vital for Jesus to deal with the question of the law since, in popular opinion, obedience to the law was the means of entry into the Kingdom. The Pharisees were of that opinion and prided themselves on their "righteousness" which they understood as "fulfilling the requirements of the law." In this context Jesus makes this startling statement: "I tell you, unless your righteousness exceeds that of the scribes and Pharisees you will not enter the Kingdom of heaven." It is obvious that Jesus here gives *dikaiosyne* a meaning different from that held by the Pharisees. The Pharisees could carry out the requirements of the law purely from the motivation of self-interest; but that could not be understood as "righteousness." Nor was Jesus advocating a stricter interpretation of the law here.[13] For him, the law can only be fulfilled when one has entered into that faithful relationship with the Father and reflect his glory. The righteousness he is speaking of here is that kind of relationship.

After having dealt with the law and its interpretation Jesus turned to those traditional deeds of righteousness — almsgiving, prayer and fasting — and warned: "Beware that you do not do your righteousness before men to be seen by them." (6:1) Just as he had done with the law so here Jesus puts these acts of piety into the right perspective — they are meaningless unless they are motivated by a sincere and faithful relationship with God.

The final reference in the Sermon comes near the end of Jesus' saying on anxiety. The whole point Jesus is making in this saying is that being under God's rule means that one enters into a trusting relationship with him recognizing his steadfast love and his faithfulness to take care of his people. Jesus concludes: "But seek first his kingdom and his righteousness, and all these things shall be yours as well."(6:33) The righteousness of God here is the same as that mentioned in 5:6. It is God's covenant faithfulness by which he carries out his promises of blessing and restoration.

In the light of all this Jesus' willingness to undergo John's baptism —"For thus it is fitting for us to fulfill *all* righteousness" (3:15) — takes on deeper meaning. While Jesus may be recalling the words of Isaiah 53:11 ("By his knowledge shall the righteous one, my servant, make many to be accounted righteous") he is nevertheless expressing his solidarity and unity with all seeking the Kingdom. But it goes further than that. In the person of Jesus, whose baptism is seen also as his enthronement as Messiah, both God's righteousness and that of human beings are being brought together and fulfilled as he draws all into that relationship with the Father. John was preparing the way for this by calling all to undergo the baptism of repentance and thus to express their desire to be part of God's new people. So Jesus refers to John coming "in the way of righteousness" (Matt. 21:32). For Jesus, righteousness is certainly a relationship term.

Covenant and Righteousness in Paul

Like the Rabbis of his day Paul hardly mentions the term "covenant" yet it is quite obvious that the whole covenant relationship between God and his people is basic to his thinking. However, God's act of righteousness in Christ has had such a powerful impact upon the whole of faith and life for Paul that the traditional concept of a covenant with chosen Israel identified by circumcision and the keeping of the law has been blown wide open so that that special relationship could now include Gentile sinners recreated by God's indwelling Spirit. In the past God's righteousness had been understood to include deliverance from injustice and oppression for the righteous through his representative Messiah. But for Paul that messianic deliverance had been so absolutely thorough and complete through Christ's atoning sacrifice that it was deliverance even from sin and death. No longer could any person again become bound down to the letter of the law. Sin had been atoned for once for all. Man had been set free to live the new life in Christ. God's law would now be written in man's heart through the abiding presence of the Spirit (II Cor. 3:1-6) as Jeremiah had prophesied (Jer. 31:33). In this new covenant (I Cor. 11:25; II Cor. 3:6) faithfulness to the Torah, exemplified in keeping the purity laws and submitting to circumcision which the Judaizing Christians regarded as necessary to fulfil the covenant relationship, is superseded by faithfulness to God evidenced by the spontaneous fruits of the Spirit (Gal. 5:22-26).

Even the imagery of the intimate covenant relationship of God and Israel as husband and wife has been superseded by the new intimate relationship of being "in Christ", of the church as being the "body of Christ", a new creation altogether (II Cor. 5:17; Gal. 6:15). Of course, the intimate relationship of Christ and the church is still pictured as the husband-wife relationship in Ephesians 5:21-33 but it is given even greater intimacy and oneness in the overarching concept of the head-body relationship. Paul also uses the imagery of the father-son relationship and, for the Gentiles, adoption as sons (Gal. 4:1-7) but, once again, it is a relationship which is established by God's reconciling love through his Son, Jesus Christ. The intimacy of this relationship, this oneness in the body of Christ is so complete that the Christian as a member of that body dies and rises together with Christ to newness of life (Rom. 6:1-11), and even *becomes* the righteousness of God in him (II Cor. 5:21).

According to Paul's view in the practice of Pharisaic Judaism and even in the practice of some in Jewish Christianity faithfulness to God in the covenant relationship has really degenerated essentially to faithfulness to the Torah. For them the Torah, which originally was only to be understood as the instrument of God's authority, had become an authority unto itself demanding the position and worship which belonged only to God. While the law itself is not evil, its power, its authority, its spirit had become so in desiring to usurp its function of being simply a custodian (*paidagogos*, Gal. 3:24). In Christ, however, its authority (*exousia*) has been conquered so that it is now part of the "weak and beggarly elemental spirits" of the universe (Gal. 4:8-10).[14] In Christ, the old Sinai covenant as Paul saw it in Rabbinic theology has been surpassed and the believer has been brought into that immediate covenant relationship with God experienced before Sinai by Abraham, and in which the believer becomes an heir to the promises to Abraham (Gal. 3:29).

In this relationship Paul could still maintain the validity of the *intention* and *spirit* of the law, particularly for himself and other Jewish Christians, as long as it was understood as a custodian and not as an authority and power unto itself. In his understanding of this new covenant, however, Paul was concerned about the same thing of which the prophets of the Old Testament spoke — faithfulness in the covenant relationship. So when he deals with such vexing questions as Corinthian Christians practising immorality or eating meat offered to idols, he does so on the basis of their union with Christ and not on the basis of transgression of God's law (I Cor. 6:12-20; 10:14-32). The relationship is all important. For Paul, therefore, the law is dethroned because it seeks to make righteousness as covenant faithfulness dependent on man's works rather than God's promises and grace so clearly demonstrated and fulfilled now in Christ. This is what Paul is saying in Romans 10:1-4

—many of the Jews do not submit to or even know the righteousnes of God because they are so busy seeking to establish their own. The Gentile question is only secondary to this.[15] With the emphasis on God's grace there is no room for the exclusivism of the Torah in Israel — no more for Paul than it had been for II Isaiah.

The righteousness of God for Paul is that same divine loving faithfulness in the covenant relationship which God had established with his people from the time of Abraham.[16] But now that covenant faithfulness has been demonstrated in all its fulness in Jesus Christ. And although it has now been manifested apart from the law through the faithfulness of Jesus Christ for all who believe, the law and the prophets did bear witness to it (Rom. 3:21-22). As proof of his righteousness, his covenant faithfulness, God put forward Jesus Christ as an atoning sacrifice and so has passed over former sins. In this way he draws people to faithfulness in him by his grace, as a gift. *God's* faithfulness draws human beings to faithfulness in Christ. This is why the gospel is the power of god unto salvation for everyone who accepts in trust, because it is the righteousness of God which is revealed *ek pisteos eis pistin* —from God's faithfulness to faithfulness in human beings (Rom. 1:16, 17). This interpretation seems to be borne out by Paul's quotation of Habakkuk 2:4: *ho de dikaios ek pisteos zesetai*, "the righteous by faithfulness shall live." I take the *ek pisteos* to refer to God's righteousness in this context. This is borne out by the Septuagint version of the verse: *ho de dikaios ek pisteos mou zesetai*; although the Masoretic text has: "the righteous shall live by *his* faithfulness;; (Cf. the same quotation in Heb. 10:38 with its variant readings). The word *pistis* is a difficult word to translate, and the translation "faith" does not really do it justice. It bears more of the sense of faithfulness and trust, particularly in the context of covenant. It is faithfulness and trust which is contrasted with carrying out the law, a relationship of faithfulness and trust engendered by God's own faithfulness. This refers to the original relationship between God and man even before the law was given, Paul argues. Abraham trusted in God's promises and it was reckoned to him as righteousness (Rom. 4:3; Gal. 3:6). Now, that original relationship of faithfulness and trust has been restored, and it is not something of which anyone can boast because God has newly created it and maintains it by his Spirit.

Righteousness by faith, then, is not simply a forensic declaration but a new relationship with God to be identified by *faithfulness* as a God-given, Spirit-inspired *response* to God's perfect and complete covenant faithfulness in Christ. Man is made righteous, that is, brought into that intimate relationship of faithfulness with God on account of Christ's atoning sacrifice, the proof of God's faithfulness to human beings.

W.D. Davies is only partly correct when he argues that the doctrine of Justification by Faith is really only peripheral and not at the centre of Paul's thought.[17] It is not righteousness by faith that is central but the righteousness of God — God's covenant faithfulness fulfilled in Christ.

Nevertheless, righteousness by faith is an essential and integral part of that in that the righteousness of God brings about in human beings that vital response of faithfulness in the covenant.

Concluding Remarks

It is always hard to define relationships. In fact, they probably never should be defined but rather lived and experienced. Our relationship with God is like that — it is personal yet an experience we share with everyone, it is variable, it is dynamic. To attempt to define it really has the consequence of confining and limiting it. Down through the ages, particularly from the time of scholasticism, theologians and scholars have had an obsession for defining, analysing, and systematizing Christian doctrines, concepts, and ideas in order to present a neat, orderly system of faith to which everyone might conform. That may be necessary to some degree but it can be both limiting and deadening. It can change a concept which is essentially dynamic and vital into something static and lifeless and less than what it should be. Certainly, terms like "righteousness", "faith", and "justification" have suffered in the process. But these are relationship terms and as such defy ultimate definition. They cannot be intellectualized; they can only be experienced.

LUTHER IN THE THOUGHT OF BULTMANN
W. Freitag

It is ironic that Bultmann, both as a New Testament scholar and as a systematic theologian is acclaimed at one and the same time to be the most illustrious and the most notorious savant of the Christian church in the twentieth century. Many Lutherans find his demythologizing scandalous; many others are offended by his Lutheran radicalism. Barth writes: "Bultmann's work is inconceivable apart from his Lutheran background. Of course, this is not the whole story."[1] The question is, just how much of the story is it?

The article "New Testament and Mythology"[2], the classic formulation of Bultmann, published in 1941, propelled him into the centre of theological controversy.[3] Yet that piece itself needs to be interpreted if we are to discern Luther's thought in it, and so other books and articles of Bultmann will have to be consulted.

When that is done, however, it comes as something of a surprise how infrequently, if discriminately, Bultmann cites Luther. He quotes passages from the Genesis and Galatians commentaries, but his favorite source is plainly J. Ficker's critical edition in 1908 of Luther's Lectures on the Epistle to the Romans, 1515/16.[4] Of scholars who have written on Luther, he refers if I mistake it not, only to P. Althaus[5] and H.W. Beyer;[6] after 1948, also to Gogarten.[7]

On the other hand, for anyone whose eyeteeth have been cut on Luther's theology, it is utterly tantalizing to read Bultmann's works; time and again, one seems to hear Luther himself talking and a conscious effort must be made to distinguish his voice from that of Bultmann. Bultmann himself claims that his knowledge of Luther is inadequate[8] though that should, I would suggest, be taken with a grain of salt. Elsewhere, he asserts the Luther too must be re-interpreted[9] although he has not, to my knowledge, anywhere suggested that Luther's theology has to be demythologized.

All of which says that Bultmann's relation to Luther is rather more subtle that one might expect. Just how subtle becomes apparent in a famous statement in 1952 in which Bultmann makes the claim that demythologizing "is a task parallel to that performed by Paul and Luther in their doctrine of justification by faith alone without the works of the law. More precisely, demythologizing is the radical application of the doctrine of justification by faith to the sphere of knowledge and thought."[10] The interpretation of that declaration sets our agenda.

Bultmann is a dialectical theologian, a kerygmatic theologian, a theologian of the Word of God. In this sense, he is a disciple of Martin Luther. Nevertheless, Lutheran and other Christian scholars find themselves at odds with him. The position taken by him apparently constitutes a threat both for systematic theologians and for biblical scholars. Indeed, the fear has been expressed that Bultmann is responsible not only for dismantling biblical theology, as traditionally understood, but also of dedogmatizing systems of theology. In this regard, Bultmann has been no better understood than has Luther.

Yet if there are those who think that Bultmann has reduced these areas to rubble, others argue that he has made a real contribution and that he is remarkably consistent in his position from start to finish – and that no less than Luther. Whether or not Bultmann is really Lutheran may be left to others to assess but the role of Luther in his thought remains crucial if we are to understand him.

On What Faith is Not

> We always understand our own work before it is done.
> But we never understand the work of God before it has happened.[11]

In common with dialectical theologians, Bultmann is fully conversant with the description of God as the "Wholly Other".[12] While that is meant to express the utter contrast between God and man, it remains that this is a way of talking about God, as though God were an object rather than God the subject. In Bultmann's view, there is a crucial distinction between "fides quae creditur",[13] the faith which is believed, and "fides qua creditur",[14] the faith by which one believes. The former is talk about God, the latter is the act of God.

Accordingly, faith is not a trust in God in general, a confidence that God will help me here and there, in this and that.[15] Nor does faith insist on the direct identity of God's action with worldly events. Were that the case, faith would be no more than a "pantheistic pietism or conviction in advance or a worldview which holds every event in the world to be the work of God because of his immanence in the world."[16] Nor is it assent to ethical teaching for that would amount to a secularization of the faith. On the basis of the moral commandments, there is no specifically Christian ethic; anyone can know what is demanded before the proclamation is heard. Further, if when God's forgiveness is announced that promise is allowed to be put into the hands of psychological counselors who seek to liberate humans from their past, that vitiates faith. Faith also is not the acceptance of dogma since dogma is neither address nor authoritative Word engendering faith.[17] Faith is not some sort of certitude deriving from an inner spiritual life, a life which seeks assurance that submission to Jesus as the Word is justified. Bultmann calls that pietism, the experience of Jesus as an emotion of the heart rather than of the Word; at bottom, such a faith is faith in myself.[18] In 1925,[19] equally pointed issue is taken with liberalism and, later, with humanism. The point is transparent, however uncomfortable for those who read him, namely, that no one can come before God with anything at all in his or her hands. Christian belief asserts that any such speaking about God is sin. "For it is necessary that a work of God be hidden and not understood at the time when it is done. But it is not hidden otherwise than under the contrary aspect of our conception or way of thinking."[20]

On What Faith is

> And so God brings it about that we go into ourselves through his going out from himself; and through knowledge of him be brings us also knowledge of ourselves.[21]

Faith cannot generate itself in man; it is never self-evident or natural; it is miraculous. This belief that God is the Father and we his children is not an insight which can be gained directly for it is not an insight at all. On the contrary, it must be believed, ever and again, as the miraculous act of God.[22] "Therefore, faith can only be the affirmation of God's action upon us, the answer to his Word directed to us. For if the realization of our own existence is involved in faith and if our existence is grounded in God and is non-existent outside God, then to apprehend our existence means to apprehend God."[23] But we can know his reality only in so far as we speak of his Word spoken to us, of his act done to us. Bultmann here cites Herrmann: "Of God we can only tell what he does to us."[24] If speaking of God is not speaking about God, then such speaking is from God and can only be the gift of God himself. Faith is simple surrender to God's grace in renunciation of one's own desire for recognition. And God's grace is simply his goodness which recognizes me just as I am, and does not demand that I should myself be a better creature and more worthy of recognition, but makes me a new and better creature by its acceptance of me as I am.

God's grace is radically understood for the first time when his transcendance is seen to be his constant futurity, his absolute freedom, which not only excludes every laying hold on him by men and women, every constraint or obligation upon God through the fulfilment of conditions which human beings can perform, every claim upon God, but also every rational comprehensibility of the divine action.[25] That is to say, faith is the radical surrender to God's will which is unknown to me or anyone before it happens. Such faith which embraces obedience and trust is therefore a person's decision against himself or herself and for God. As such, faith is an act.[26]

At this point, we need to comment on an apparent contradiction: between faith as God's act and faith as an act of human decision. Bultmann has expressed himself on this more than once. Faith has to do with God not as he is in himself but only with God as he is significant for every individual, for the individual's responsibility and for the individual's salvation. It does not deal with people as they are in themselves but always with them in their relation to God. Faith is constituted by God's acting in history and by the response of the human being to God's doing. So, faith as God's act is simultaneously faith as an act of human decision. God's act gives human beings a new existence and the new persons are always persons of the "Beyond" whose identity with themselves as people of the world can only be believed. Faith is thus God's act which gives us eschatological existence, that is, existence not of this world yet nevertheless in it.[27]

On the Word of God

Faith in God sticks to the Word, which is God himself: trusts and honors the Word, not because of the person who speaks it, but because faith feels it to be so certain and true no one could tear faith away from it...The Word in itself, without respect to person, must be enough to move the heart, must so capture and hold a person that he is imprisoned in it, feels how true and right it is – even if all the world, yes, even if God himself says otherwise.[28]

The Word stands at the very hub of Bultmann's thought, and is as fundamental for him as it was for Luther. The Word is the Gospel which proclaims Christ in the Predigt or Sermon.[29] The position is lucid, clear and unambiguous. Yet some critics of Bultmann take issue with him on just this fundament. On the one hand, there are those critics who are desperately afraid that Bultmann has irrevocably severed the historical Jesus from the Christ of faith and who are determined to re-establish some sort of continuity whether by history, ontology or other avenue with him; it requires only a step to the charge that Christ has risen into the kerygma according to Bultmann.[30] On the other hand there are those who say that Bultmann's use of the Word reduces it to a myth which does not relate to me and my life but which must nevertheless be accepted in faith. Still more extreme is the demand that Bultmann should go all the way to dekerygmatizing the Word because it is a myth.[31]

All that this discloses is the distance that has been travelled away from Luther and the insights of the Reformation during the intervening centuries. A relapse has occurred – back into that way of thinking which supposes that all that is needed for faith is the knowledge and assurance, mediated by tradition, doctrine or piety, that Jesus once lived, suffered, died and rose on our behalf. The church says so; doctrine says so; the bible says so; those are the facts. Believe it! To which Luther and Bultmann say a resounding "No!" For such a faith would only be an historical faith, not a living faith. Bultmann does not deny that the Christ of faith is at the same time the historical Jesus; however, faith cannot be based on the historical Jesus nor can the Christ of faith be made an object of investigation. We are left with the Word which proclaims and conveys the Christ of faith, with the kerygma and that is more than enough. His critics have not understood the meaning of the "once" of Jesus life, death and resurrection and the "once-for-all" significance of it. The objections lodged against him rest upon the age-old yearning to provide a guarantee for faith and salvation.[32]

Bultmann is prepared to agree that Christ rose into the kerygma provided that that is rightly understood, for that is indeed where Christ is to be found and heard. The Word who is Christ proclaimed becomes the Word for me in my historical situation when once I realize that I believe in Christ. That is to say, the Word of proclamation is self-validating; we "must abandon absolutely every attempt, every search for the Word of proclamation, whether external proof or proof within ourselves." "We can only acknowledge the Word, only believe it in faith and obedience."[33] Bultmann says:

> Wholly fortuitously, wholly contingently, wholly as specific event, the Word enters our world. No guarantee comes with it by virtue of which it is to be believed. No appeal to authority can have a preferential claim on the belief of others, whether it be made for Paul or for Luther. Even for ourselves, our own faith can never be a standing ground on which we can establish ourselves. Faith is continuously a fresh act, a new experience.[34]

Luther makes the point in another way. "Therefore we must be on our guard, for if we try to preserve the gospel, not by its own power, but by our own strength, then the cause is lost. For whatever is most ably defended by human beings, crumbles. Let us stop worrying. The gospel does not need our help. It has strength enough of its own. Let God take care of it by himself. It is his and he will maintain it. Therefore I leave it to him, however many and great are the attacks against us."[35]

Justification by Faith alone

> Faith does not make a man pious and justified before God by being itself our work and belonging to us but by accepting the promised and proffered grace which is given unearned from the rich treasure.[36]

It should be evident by now, from what has already been said, that Bultmann is not trying to talk about ideas, systems, doctrines or philosophies about God, man and redemption. He is "at pains to talk about the God in whose hands our time is held and who encounters each of us in our time."[37] The meaning of the Word of God as the act of God upon us is this, that God constituting our existence makes righteous persons of us sinners, that he forgives our sin and justifies us. It means that he accepts us as justified even while we are separated from him and can only talk about him or ask questions about him. "It is not that some special, demonstrable change happens in our lives, that we are imbued with special qualities and can do special things or speak special words which are of a non-human kind. What could we ever do or say that would not be human! But this has happened: all our acts and words are freed from the curse of dividing us from God. Our speech or action always remain sinful, since it is always something undertaken by us. But as sinful, it is justified, that is, justified by grace."[38]

In "The Problem of Ethics in the Writings of Paul", Bultmann writes that for Paul "justification, deliverance from sin is an eschatological benefit ..It is an event, an occurrence which results from God's action and constitutes God's judgment."[39] Justification is "God's new saving act."[40] So faith is a person's obedience in submission to God's saving deed and also the renunciation of any claim to be able to establish on one's own terms a right relationship with God. It is the belief that a person is justified only by God in Christ Jesus. That is why righteousness, or sinlessness, paradoxically, represents not a change in a person's moral qualities, nor something which is mystically experienced. It is something that can only be believed.

In this connection, Bultmann argues that the old quarrel whether God only regards the justified person as righteous or that the person is righteous should be abandoned. In the same way that sinners, as a result of Adam's sin really are sinners and not merely so regarded, so are the righteous really righteous. Misunderstanding can only arise when "to be declared righteous" is idealistically interpreted in ethical terms; on that basis, the distinction is both valid and necessary.[41] For Bultmann the issue is patent. God declares a person righteous and holds him or her to be so for the sake of Christ; human beings may not make that claim for themselves nor hold it to be a possession. Bultmann follows Luther here in maintaining the position that the righteousness which God bestows is a *iustitia aliena*,[42] a righteousness which is not one's own. It is a righteousness not of works, of whatever sort, but a righteousness of faith in and through the Word by the grace of God. To be justified through grace by faith alone means that God chooses to see us not as the sinners that we are but, through and for the sake of his son, Jesus Christ, as righteous. We are righteous and are so declared for Christ's sake only in relation, God's relationship to us through Christ. God remains the subject and only in that relation may one speak of justification. We cannot claim it for ourselves; that would be self-glorification.

Justification by faith alone does not mean the metamorphosis of a sinner into a saint. "Justus" does not imply a quality but a relation and therefore always stands in a paradoxical relationship to "peccator". "That is to say, therefore, that I, the peccator, am such as I stand in God's presence – precisely as I have emerged from my past – as a sinner, and not only as I commit actual sins from time to time. In other words, my new being has overcome the old, only in such a way that it imports the old into every conceivable situation, so that I am never holy, even when I have ceased to transgress any commandments, but I live always and only by forgiving grace."[43]

The Demand for Decision

> For such a man must have died to all things, recognizing that as far as good and bad, life and death, and heaven and hell are concerned, he can do nothing in his own strength.[44]

Perhaps before many of his contemporaries, Bultmann sensed that much of biblical interpretation, theology and proclamation as then understood would be reduced to the level of superstition, if not of pious humbug, in the twentieth century; and that that would happen no matter how intrinsically genuine, orthodox and sound they might have been. Rather was it the case that a new kind of person was emerging in his time, the person he called the post-mythological, secular individual conditioned by the scientific way of thinking, and living in a world so altered by that disposition that traditional Christian teaching and preaching would and could only appear to be hopelessly archaic and primitive.[45] That his prescience has since been confirmed by the utterly astounding advances on the frontiers of knowledge and the application of it in our time scarcely needs confirmation.

The question is: how are we to proclaim the gospel persuasively to people such as these? It is not simply a matter of understanding that certain claims of traditional Christian churches on such matters as the six-day creation, the virgin birth, nature and healing miracles and a literal resurrection have become unbelievable for such persons, but that the whole of conventional Christian teaching and preaching has become ineffectual and inefficacious for them.[46]

It is to Bultmann's credit that he takes just this challenge seriously. The effort must be made to understand the new breed of human being, and Bultmann utilizes the philosophy of Heidegger to ask the right questions to arrive at an existential theory about modern people.[47] But he is all the more concerned with reaching such persons, with preaching that confronts them with the need to make an existential decision, i.e., a decision upon which they are ready to stake their very lives.[48] On the one hand, as we have already seen, this involves the vertical relation between God and human beings, and in that connection a radical critique of traditional exegesis and theology; on the other, it has to do with the individual in his or her own personal history as well as relation with others.

The proclamation of the gospel, of Christ as God's eschatological act, puts individuals before the ambiguities of their own existence – the disjunctions in their lives, the contrarieties in their relation to themselves and their being-at-odds with themselves.[49] That is to say, the proclaimed Word challenges modern men and women to face the truth about themselves. Their striving to be somebody never quite succeeds and their pursuit of recognition never fully satisfies. The personal history of any one of us – our past – represents our reliance upon this-worldly standards, our confidence in our own achievements and also the failure of such commitments to truly make us happy. The past of each of us exhibits our enslavement to the power of sin, and the burden of our guilt, no less than the harsh reality of our living and our existing as a matter of quiet desperation.[50]

The same proclamation puts us before the existential decision to die to all those things which have enslaved us, to be freed from our pasts, to surrender our lives to Christ. Douglas Hall aptly puts it this way:

> A theology of the cross is not a theology of answers; it is a theology of the question. Besides, the whole thing is offered, not as light, but as a way into the darkness; the darkness that *is*, the darkness that must become the *known* context in every search for light.
>
> Let us be quite clear: only the light is final. We have no lasting interest in the darkness as such, and certainly no desire to court it. It is necessary to think about it and to enter into it only because it is already there. It is already our condition; and the true light that lightens our darkness can only be apprehended by us as we stand, honestly and knowingly, exactly where we are. Indeed, the true light will lead us into our darkness, unlike the false lights of religions and world views. For it is known that only as we become accustomed to the night, the deepening gloom, are we able to see the light that is specifically light for this darkness. Otherwise we are simply deluding ourselves with artificial light.[51]

Luther says the same thing just as trenchantly:

> We need here the greatest good sense, that is, to be wise not in regard to what is visible (for then we would have to despair) but in regard to what is to come and what is known and invisible...Hope turns its eyes to the unknown, and the hidden, the inner darkness, so that it does not know what is hopes for, but yet does know what it does not hope for."[52]

Once the existential commitment is made then, "(1) the believer lives constantly (only) in hope, that is to say, not on the basis of what he possesses, but by reason of what he will receive – he lives in relation to the future. (2) But it is this that is the fruit of faith – the ability to regard what is present as something passing. It is freedom from present reality, immunity from the tribulations which plunge the unbeliever into anxiety. It is freedom from the anxiety that constantly threatens life; it is being open to the future."[53]

Conclusion

We have now come full circle in interpreting Bultmann's program of demythologization, that is, of existential analysis. "Like the doctrine of justification, de-mythologization destroys every longing for security. There is no difference between security based on good works and security built on objectifying knowledge."[54] Indeed, one may say with Bultmann, "let those who have the modern worldview live as though they had none."[55]

The theology of Luther is part and parcel of Bultmann's thought radically applied to the world of knowledge, and of the scientific way of thinking, which characterizes the new breed of modern men and women. It is well to remember that it was no less a figure than Karl Barth who said that "those who throw stones at Bultmann should be careful lest they accidentally hit Luther, who is also hovering somewhere in the background."[56] In the light of our inquiry, that declaration must be considered a classic example of understatement!

THE COURAGE OF FAITH AT THE EUCHARIST ACCORDING TO MARTIN LUTHER

Egil Grislis

Martin Luther thought and wrote with immense energy and great personal conviction, paying intense attention to all the major insights of the Holy Scripture.[1] But as in the Holy Scripture so also in Luther's writings, the concern for faith in Jesus Christ supplied the existential[2] centre of the inquiry. Hence it is with faith[3] as the focus of our study that we shall attempt to describe Luther's life-long concern with the meaning of Christ's eucharistic presence.[4] More precisely, we shall attempt to assess those dimensions of faith which Luther accented more forcefully as he wrestled with the correct proclamation of the eucharistic presence of Jesus Christ.

I

To begin with, Luther's short, incisive, and immensely rich treatise of 1519 will provide for us an outline of Luther's key insights. We know the lengthy title of that treatise: *The Blessed Sacrament of the Holy and True Body of Christ, and the Brotherhoods*. The opening paragraph informs us that the sacrament of the altar has three parts: "The first is the sacrament, or sign. The second is the significance of this sacrament. The third is the faith required with each of the first two".[5] In actual exposition parts one and two overlap, necessarily must overlap, because the sign is not a mere illustration, but effectually brings into existence the reality which it has signified. In other words, the eucharist "signifies the complete union and the undivided fellowship of the saints".[6] Therefore, "the *significance* or effect of this sacrament is the fellowship of all the saints".[7] What Luther has in mind is not a mere social gathering, but rather such an existentially close sharing of faith and life that it is possible to claim that "Christ and all saints are one spiritual body".[8] As a citizen is assured of his citizenship by an actual document, so the eucharistic elements are a sign attesting to the union with Jesus Christ. And as a citizen partakes of all the duties and privileges connected with the citizenship, so also does the believer now participate in the saving benefits of Christ's atonement. In this way the eucharist serves to "strengthen and to encourage", namely, as Luther puts it:

> God gives us this sacrament, as much as to say, "Look, many kinds of sin are assailing you; take this sign by which I give you my pledge that this sin is assailing not only you but also my Son, Christ, and all his saints in heaven and on earth. Therefore take heart and be bold. You are not fighting alone. Great help and support are all around you.[9]

Thus even the very act of approaching the altar can be seen as an expression of trust and joy in gratitude that in the midst of life's dangers and sins such effective help is available. Luther continues the analogy: "a citizen whose property has suffered damage or misfortune at the hands of his enemies makes complaint to his town council and fellow citizens and asks them for help".[10] Likewise, the believer who has experienced both sin and misfortune can nevertheless make a resolve: "I will go to the sacrament to receive a sign from God that I have on my side Christ's righteousness, life, and sufferings, with all holy angels and the blessed in heaven and all the pious men on earth."[11] In their own respective ways, both the citizen and the Christian receive assistance, and at the same time are drawn deeply into their newly experienced fellowship.[12]

The basis of this Christian fellowship, so the believer perceives, is love.[13] Luther explains:

> As love and support are given you, you in turn must render love and support to Christ in his needy ones. You must feel with sorrow all the dishonor done to Christ in his holy Word, all the misery of Christendom, all the unjust suffering of the innocent, with which the world is everywhere filled to overflowing. You must fight, work, pray, and - if you cannot do more - have heartfelt sympathy.[14]

Clearly, Luther is recording more than a list of duties. Rather, he is convinced that the reciprocal experience of receiving and giving, being forgiven and forgiving others, being loved and loving others, is the marvellous effect of the eucharistic gift. Put another way, faith then is understood as a totally new life-style of the believer who has been transformed from a "timid" and "terrified" self into a courageous and brave one. If traditionally in Roman Catholic thought the eucharistic miracle had been described in terms of the change of substance of the bread and wine into the substance of Christ's flesh and blood, then Luther is now attempting to record the miraculous change in terms of the renewal and transformation of the believing individual. Luther writes:

> In this way we are changed into one another and are
> made into a community by love. Without love there can
> be no such change.[15]

Even the traditional concern with the eucharistic elements can emphasize this new dimension of personal transformation. Namely, notes
Luther:

> ...there is no more intimate, deep, and indivisible
> union than the union of the food with him who is fed. For
> the food enters into and is assimilated by his very
> nature, and becomes one substance with the person
> who is fed. Other unions, achieved by such things as
> nails, glue, cords, and the like, do not make one
> indivisible substance of the objects joined together.
> Thus in the sacrament we too become united with
> Christ, and are made one body with all the saints, so that
> Christ cares for us and acts in our behalf.[16]

At the moment, writing in 1519, Luther is not as yet denying the
doctrine of transubstantiation.[17] He has only moved the accent from
objective to subjective concerns, and instead of the eucharistic substance underscores the role of the self. Moreover, Luther also criticises
attempts at philosophical, notably Aristotelian, speculation in the
eucharistic realm. Suggests Luther:

> ... what becomes of the bread when it is changed into
> Christ's flesh and of the wine when it is changed into his
> blood and how the whole Christ, his flesh and blood, can
> be encompassed in so small a portion of bread and
> wine[18]

are really not significant concerns. What matters instead to Luther is the
tremendous opportunity to "exercise and strengthen your faith."[19] Thus
in the midst of life's struggles the holy eucharist[20] offers not only
consolation, but transmits authentic strength, *viz.*, the certainty

> that Christ and all his saints are coming to you with all
> their virtues, sufferings, and mercies, to live, work,
> suffer, and die with you, and that they desire to be
> wholly yours, having all things in common with you.[21]

At the same time, as Luther sees it, the recipient cannot remain
passive.[22] The very process of reception takes place precisely as the
believer attempts to "exercise and strengthen his faith".[23] Apparently,
trust is learned through trusting, and both confidence and love grow in
situations of risk and daring. In the end Luther does not speak so much
about the abstract notion of the faith, but pays special attention to the
heart, the authentic self, which has now become a new being:

> Then your heart will become truly free and confident,
> strong and courageous against all enemies [Ps. 23:5].

> For who will fear any calamity if he is sure that Christ
> and all his saints are with him and have all things, evil or
> good, in common with him?[24]

In this perspective Luther does not suggest that faith will somehow rescue the believer from all danger. Rather, the continued presence of dangers, difficulties, and real calamities will continue. Yet the believer, having matured in faith, will now possess the courage to confront the world in redemptive love — and therefore will not count the cost. In this way, notes Luther, "the sacrament is for us a ford, a bridge, a door, a ship, and a stretcher, by which and in which we pass from this world into eternal life."[25]

Thus understood, the sacraments, as a means of grace, are not magical; a mere partaking of them does not insure automatic results. Rather, Luther has selected his illustrations with obvious care, as each one of them portrays a situation that is seen as an opportunity for advance by the faithful and courageous. The ford enables the crossing of the river, but only to those who make the effort and take the risk. Similarly, both a bridge and a door can potentially provide an entrance unto a road that leads forward, but the individual must have the courage to walk toward the as yet unkown. Also a ship, or a stretcher, will carry forward, but only those who avail themselves of this means of transportation. Having provided such expressive illustrations, Luther immediately continues:

> Therefore everything depends on faith. He who does
> not believe is like the man who is supposed to cross the
> sea, but who is so timid that he does not trust the ship;
> and so he must remain and never be saved, because he
> will not embark and cross over.[26]

Without the courage of faith, the eucharist, obviously, is not put to its proper use. At the same time, it is precisely the eucharist which engenders such a courageous faith. Luther's reasoning is not necessarily circular. Rather, looking back to the very first eucharist, instituted by Christ, as the starting point, Luther appears to regard the entire Christian life as a grace-sustained spiral, wherein even the response is actively enabled by the grace of God.

In this way, Luther's early and relatively brief treatise sums up a rather weighty contribution to the subject matter of such centrality for the Christian faith. The least controversial in terms of inner-Protestant struggles, this statement has at times served as a common platform - as well as evoked the regret by Gustaf Aulén that subsequently Luther neglected the emphasis on communion contained in this treatise.[27] Without fully sharing that regret and assuming that controversy could not be avoided, I shall attempt to sketch several lines of Luther's development.

II

In his most controversial[28] Reformation tract, *The Babylonian Captivity of the Church*, 1520, Luther sought to explore further the significance of faith within the eucharistic context. Acknowledging his own dependence on St. Augustine,[29] Luther appealed to one of the very widely known insights of the saint, formulated with picturesque candor: "Why do you make ready your teeth and your stomach? Believe, and you have eaten".[30] Namely, reflecting at length on John 6, [31] and asserting that in this chapter we do not find a eucharistic discussion, Luther formulates the general principle, that authentic faith actually partakes of the flesh and blood of Jesus Christ. One further appeal to St. Augustine served to legitimatize this insight:

> Thus Augustine, in his *Contra Julianum*, Book II, proves from Innocent that even infants eat the flesh and drink the blood of Christ without the sacrament; that is, they partake of them through the faith of the church.[32]

That the mature believer would receive the flesh and blood of Christ in the eucharist, Luther simply takes for granted:

> I rejoice greatly that the simple faith of this sacrament is still to be found, at least among the common people. For as they do not understand, neither do they dispute whether accidents are present without substance, but believe with a simple faith that Christ's body and blood are truly contained there, and leave to those who have nothing else to do the argument about what contains them.[33]

And delivering one more salvo against the philosophical attempts to explain the eucharistic presence of Christ, Luther concludes with the observation that "the real body of Christ is present by virtue of the words"[34] — i.e. the words of the institution.

Although Luther desired to view John 6 apart from the eucharistic passages strictly so considered, he clearly regarded faith as the common means whereby the true body and blood are partaken. In this way the role of faith insured the unity of the Christian existence: whether in ordinary believing or in specifically eucharistic devotion, faith maintains such a close fellowship with Jesus Christ that it is appropriate to speak about partaking of His flesh and blood. If we did not know Luther's Catholic roots or his later explicit statements, it would be possible to regard his present understanding of flesh and blood as metaphorical, that is, as an especially colorful and emphatic way of describing the believer's union with Jesus Christ. Such a reading, of course, would also be unfair to Luther insofar as it would overlook his real intent which at this moment is not to describe how Jesus Christ can be present in the eucharist, but rather to confess how powerful is the saving Word of God!

To a society which had been accustomed to appreciate the holy mass as the quintessence of good works,[35] dressed in liturgical splendour, and to value its step-by-step dynamic, Luther bluntly declared:

> We must turn our eyes and hearts simply to the institution of Christ and this alone, and set nothing before us but the very word of Christ by which he instituted the sacrament, made it perfect, and committed it to us. For in that word, and in that word alone, reside the power, the nature, and the whole substance of the mass.[36]

The power of Christ's word, eucharistic or otherwise, was not historically tied to one event. Rather, although given once in a specific setting, the word now continues to exercise its effectiveness. Luther illustrates this creative dimension of the word by pointing to both "testament" and "promise".[37] Now "a testament," defines Luther, "is a promise made by one about to die in which he designates his bequest and appoints his heirs".[38] The bequest which Christ has left through his vicarious death is "the forgiveness of sins", applicable to all those who believe in Christ.[39] In this way the testament is a divine promise, available to "faith alone" — rather than to works or merits. The perspective in which Luther continues to approach the eucharist is that of *sola gratia*. The testament/promise are not obtained just because a person desires to have such a gift; the power of acquisition does not rest with us. The miracle happens not because we choose, but because the word is so powerful that it evokes, indeed creates our faith.[40] While truly ours — therefore faith can be denied and rejected — it is a gift. Now this faith-evoking miracle does not stop at one occasion, but continues. And from faith, evoked again and again, love proceeds, and love is followed by good works. Luther puts it in this way: "First of all there is God's Word. After it follows faith, after faith, love; then love does every good work...".[41] And in the process from faith to love and to good works, faith itself matures. It becomes now "a faith that relies confidently" on Christ's promise.[42]

When this all important centrality of faith is not grasped, the mass becomes merely a liturgical act in which every step must be carried out with minute precision — and every error, mistakenly, regarded as a destruction of its essence. Assuming that in his own day such a perversion of the mass[43] has occurred only too often, Luther exclaims with obvious disgust: "O worthless religion of this age of ours, the most godless and thankless of all ages!"[44] By contrast, convinced that God offers no "empty promises", Luther notes the biblically recorded fact that divine promises are ordinarily confirmed by a special sign.[45] While Luther regards the eucharist as such a sign, he nevertheless continues to subordinate the sign to the word, insisting that "there is greater power in the word than in the sign".[46] Namely, it is the word which assures the recipient of the divine largesse and at the same time consoles the sinner so that he does not need to worry about his unworthiness.[47] In this way, the Word, understood as God's saving promise in Jesus Christ, continuously brings to light the essential dimensions of faith:

> Who can receive or apply, in behalf of another, the promise of God, which demands the personal faith of each one individually! Can I give to another the promise of God, even if he does not believe? Can I believe for another, or cause another to believe?[48]

Precisely because God's promise of salvation is so distinctively personal,[49] the individual recipient of the promise, by definition, is risking everything. He must in an act of stalwart courage renew his response and his commitment to Christ. The basic model which Luther has in mind when describing this act of courage is analagous to that in justification, where the sinner-to-be-justified also turns from Law to the Gospel, from Wrath to Love, precisely as the sinner experiences his incapacity to turn and in the confession of such incapacity receives the gift of God-given capacity. As in justification, so also here in receiving the saving promise: the Word indeed evokes faith and enables assent, yet at the same time the courage of faith which has been brought into existence must be put to use by the individual. *He* must believe for himself — and so he must also reach out for the promise. In this way the very centre of Luther's eucharistic discussion remains grounded in soteriology. The quest for a merciful God has not come to a close once the doctrine of justification by grace through faith has been formulated, but continues throughout Luther's writings. Therefore Luther's occasional glimpses into his past ought not to be read as mere recollections, but may also serve to illumine Luther's mind at the time of his writing. A good case-in-point is a passage from *The Misuse of the Mass*, 1521. There Luther recalls:

> How often did my heart quail, punish me, and reproach me with its single strongest argument: Are you the only wise man? Can it be that all the others are in error and have erred for so long a time? What if you are mistaken and lead so many people into error who might all be eternally damned?[50]

The main answer, which ultimately helped Luther the most, was his discovery of a merciful God in Christ, infallibly[51] assured by the Scriptures. As Luther put it:

> Finally, Christ with his clear, unmistakable Word strengthened and confirmed me, so that my heart no longer quails, but resists the arguments of the papists, as a stony shore resists the waves, and laughs at their threats and storms![52]

The ultimate source of the courage of faith then was neither a matter of great personal daring nor a special inspiration, but of the ordinary and yet miraculous effect of the Word of God — bringing into existence faith which, if authentic, is always courage-filled.

III

While in a measure present in Luther's writings from the very beginning, his outspoken critique of philosophical thinking[53] — the so-called *speculatio* — begins to assume a prominent role in his anti-sacramentarian writings, notably beginning with *The Sacrament of the Body and Blood of Christ - Against the Fanatics*, 1526. Luther's outspoken affirmation of the real presence of Christ's body and blood in the eucharist had resulted in the charge "that we are eaters of flesh and drinkers of blood and that we worship a baked God".[54] While subsequently Luther took up this challenge and arrived at a theologically cogent explanation of the precise manner of Christ's eucharistic presence, his more immediate concern here was to protect the role of faith in the celebration of the eucharist. Luther writes: "Now God is the sort of person who likes to do what is foolish and useless in the eyes of the world..." (appealing to I Cor. 1:23 and 21).[55] In other words, it is Luther's deepest conviction that revealed doctrine in its ultimate meaning is beyond human grasp; precisely because it is so lofty, it may have the appearance of folly. To demand that human understanding should serve as a standard for God's wisdom, will result, Luther thinks, in the refusal to give credence to anything that God does or says. Luther's opponents, namely the Swiss in general and Oekolampadius in particular, whom he labels "the fanatics"[56], are therefore in error not only about their own eucharistic formulations (that is, that the eucharist is "mere bread, or a batch of bread")[57] but above all, in respect to the general understanding of faith. Notes Luther:

> Just as when someone is on the point of drowning, whether he drowns in a brook or in the midst of a stream, he is drowned just the same. So I say of those fanatics: if they let go of the word, let them believe whatever they like and squabble as long as they like. It has already happened that six or seven sects have arisen over the sacrament, but all of them under the delusion that Christ's flesh and blood are not present.[58]

In this way Luther makes it clear, that at the moment his intent is not to explain and to defend a particular theory of eucharistic presence. The real controversy is not, believes Luther, over his explanation of the real presence of Christ in the eucharist, but whether God's clear word[59] will have the final authority. Luther thinks that these "fanatics" "have not adhered to the words" of the Holy Scripture, and thus have "followed their own thoughts." Luther vividly reports his views of the situation: "...they have a colored glass before their eyes, and therefore the words must mean what they think".[60] Coloured glass, in Luther's day, presumably blurred one's vision; the on-looker was guessing more than actually seeing. Therefore, according to Luther's evaluation, these "fanatics" have not reflected on actual reality, but merely on the fruits of their own imagination. By contrast, true faith arises in faithfully listening to what is taught by the word of God. Then it is God's word that evokes both the understanding and the courageous trust to believe what has been understood. Of course, Luther knows that the understanding of the word of God is always dialectical: each insight includes the awareness that that which God offers is always beyond our understanding. While subsequently Luther will come to underscore that measure of insight which has been possible, his earlier statements prefer to elaborate the mystery of faith, e.g.:

> But whoever derives the right faith from the words will believe like this: Whether Christ enters into the bread or the cup or into whatever he will, God grant that as long as I have the words, I will not seek or speculate any further; what he says, I will keep. Thus the believer envelops himself in the Word, will not let himself be turned aside from it, and is always thereby sustained.[61]

Such a steadfastly courageous commitment to the Holy Scripture was the source of Luther's great personal strength - as well as the obvious cause for annoyance among those who questioned Luther's interpretation of Scripture in the very first place. Namely, to the so-called "fanatics" Luther's position could not help but appear to be intransigent: having made an exposition, Luther then insisted that it could not and need not be discussed any further, because it is utterly faithful to the text! Luther asserted:

> For we are not so simple-minded that we do not understand the words. If these words are not clear, I do not know how to speak German. Would I not understand, if someone were to place a roll before me and say: 'Take, eat, this is white bread?' Or again, 'Take and drink, this is a glass of wine'? Therefore, when Christ says: 'Take, eat, this is my body,' even a child will understand perfectly well that he is speaking of that which he is offering. It is a natural way of speaking that when someone points to a thing, we know what he is saying.[62]

Luther concludes by observing: "We know what Christ's body is, namely, that which was born of Mary, suffered, died, and rose again".[63] How the eating of such a body and drinking of such blood is not a cannibalistic procedure Luther does not consider. The explanation which Luther does supply follows his already acknowledged line of argument which insists that God's acts are ultimately beyond full human grasp. Luther supplies a powerful analogy:

> ...it is not reasonable that God should descend from heaven and enter into the womb; that he who nourishes, sustains, and encompasses all the world should allow himself to be nourished and encompassed by the Virgin. Likewise, that Christ, a king of glory [Ps. 24:10], at whose feet all angels must fall and before whom all creatures must tremble, should thus humble himself below all men and allow himself to be suspended upon the cross as a most notorious evil-doer, and that by the most wicked and desperate of men.[64]

Admittedly, Luther's powerful theology of the cross[65] does bring to light a clear and central biblical theme. Through the saving acts of God in Christ mankind receives its salvation - yet remains thoroughly baffled. The full meaning of the mystery of salvation we do not comprehend.

Now while the eucharist, no doubt, appropriately serves to point to this larger context of the theology of the cross, Luther's presentation of the words of institution - "Take, eat, this is my body" - at the moment bypasses the kenosis perspective and, instead, underscores that "the body" is a word which even a child can understand. It seems, on the surface, that Luther is placing "the body" alongside other objects, such as the "white bread" and the "glass of wine". If so, Luther may appear to be teaching a mere physical eating and drinking of Christ's body and blood - and hence defending cannibalism.

That was not Luther's ultimate intention. Many years later Luther acknowledged that, as he reflected on his debate with Zwingli at the Marburg Colloquy"[66]:

> Zwingli had a long, absurd talk with me about local inclusion, that the body of Christ could not be in the bread as it would be in space or in a vessel, just as if we taught that Christ's body was in the bread like straw in a sack, or wine in a barrel. After that some of them excused themselves and said that they had understood that we and the papists taught that Christ's body was in the sacrament locally, like straw in a sack. Oh, that was a useless, insignificant, lame excuse! For they knew very well that neither the papists nor we had taught that.
> (*Brief Confession of the Holy Eucharist*, 1544)[67]

In other words, in retrospect, Luther took for granted that his theological opponents should know that the real presence was not a literal presence of two objects - body and blood. Luther, rightly, knew that Rome had not taught a physical presence of Christ in the eucharist -and if he was suspected for holding a Roman Catholic view, then he, too, would likewise be free from a charge of literalism (and cannibalism). Yet in knowing the truth, Luther's immediate efforts at clarifying his position were not entirely successful. Namely, having celebrated the miracle of redemption in Christ,[68] Luther underscored the mystery of all created existence:

> Look at a grain of wheat in the field, and tell me how it comes about that the stalk grows out of the earth from a single seed and bears so many kernels on the ear, and gives each one its own form. Moreover, in a single kernel there are many, many miraculous works, which they neither perceive nor pay any heed to.[69]

Luther's next example is even more complex, showing how it is possible that a mere human word, which is just a sound, can nevertheless rule entire countries and capture many human hearts. Luther notes that even his own "small voice" could reach

> ...several hundreds or thousands of ears, yet every single ear perceives the complete and entire voice. I do not distribute it, so that each ear has only a part of it, but each one has all of it.[70]

Then Luther observes:

> Now if my voice can accomplish this so that it fills all ears, with each one receiving as much of it as the other, and my word is distributed so widely, should not Christ be able to do so all the more with his body?[71]

Certainly, this was a picturesque and highly insightful way of reflecting on the manner of Christ's real presence. Yet concrete and abstract examples stand side-by-side; the objectivity of the presence of kernels, originating all from one, and the infinitely more sophisticated presence of the spoken words in the minds of many hearers are, though impressive, at the same time also confusing examples.

In his own mind Luther was not really confused, and had the so-called "fanatics" continued to read his text with care, they would have been enlightened by the following statement:

> Just as little as you are able to say how it comes about that Christ is in so many thousands of hearts and dwells in them —Christ as he died and rose again — and yet no man knows how he gets in, so also here in the sacrament, it is incomprehensible how this comes about. But this I do know, that the word is there: "Take, eat, this is my body, given for you, this do in remembrance of me." When we say these words over the bread, then he is truly present, and yet it is a mere word and voice that one hears. Just as he enters the heart without breaking a hole in it, but is comprehended only through the Word and hearing, so also he enters into the bread without needing to make any hole in it.[72]

Indeed, Luther's continued insistence on the inexplainability of the presence of Christ's body and blood in the eucharist should have assured any careful and thoughtful reader that he could not have been thinking of locally present physical objects, because local presence could always readily be explained. In any case, Luther's sustained assertion of the mystery of the real presence serves to indicate the positive direction of Luther's thought, at every step challenging people to courageous faith in the miracle.

At the same time, necessarily, Luther remained mainly concerned about the role of God's word within this dynamic of faith. Only "foolish reason and flesh" could imagine that the words of institution, when spoken, "draw" Christ "down" from heaven. Rather, the words of institution serve to assure that Christ is really present in the eucharistic elements:

> Although he is present in all creatures, and I might find him in stone, in fire, in water, or even in a rope, for he certainly is there, yet he does not wish that I seek him there apart from the Word, and cast myself into the fire or the water, or hang myself on the rope. He is present everywhere, but he does not wish that you grope for him everywhere. Grope rather where the Word is, and then you will lay hold of him in the right way.[73]

Understood in this way, the existential struggle, the wrestling and the seeking, are continuously co-terminous with faith itself. Luther's faith is never blind, but always active and filled with the readiness to risk.

IV

In order to appreciate the full dynamic of Luther's groping in courage as he sought to understand the eucharistic presence of Christ, we need to recall how seriously — and at times literally — Luther took the role of the devil.[74] Therefore for Luther the contest and the struggle had to do not merely with human weakness and error, but with evil forces greater than the sum total of all human opposition. Luther began his tract *That the Words of Christ, "This Is My Body," Etc. Still Stand Firm Against the Fanatics*, 1527, with the following observation:

> How very true is the proverb that the devil is master of a thousand arts! This he proves beyond question in all the stratagems by which he rules his world, as in outward, palpable deeds of guile, intrigues, wickedness, sins, murder, destruction, etc. But especially and supremely does he demonstrate his craftiness in spiritual, inward matters which concern the glory of God and conscience. How he can slither and squirm, twist

and turn in all directions, and hinder and thwart us on all sides, that no one may be saved and persevere in the Christian truth.[75]

The entire tragic course of Christian history, from disagreements over Scriptural interpretations in the Early Church to the subsequent appeals to various councils and to arguments among the reformers, appears to Luther as the general and effective handiwork of the devil. Indeed, where the other reformers disagree with Luther — and hardly anywhere else more than in the interpretation of the holy eucharist — Luther is prepared to call them "fanatics", that is, to regard them as people who have fully succumbed to the wiles of the devil. With all seriousness Luther insists:

It is precisely the same devil who now assails us through the fanatics by blaspheming the holy and venerable sacrament of our Lord Jesus Christ, out of which they would like to make mere bread and wine as a symbol or memorial sign of Christians, in whatever way their dream or fancy dictates.[76]

Without a doubt, on the one hand, Luther's unwavering conviction that he is opposing the evil one with all his cohorts, heightens his own sense of commitment in faith. The making of eucharistic assertions is no mere exercise in thinking, but a clear exhibit of being a Christian on the battlefield of faith struggling with unbelief. At times Luther admits:

Therefore I do not fix my attention as much upon them, as upon him who speaks through them — the devil, I mean — just as they regard me as full of devils.[77]

Yet, on the other hand, the pre-judgment that his opponents possess no Christian insights, but only demonically inspired errors, precludes Luther from having any positive appreciation of anything that his opponents might have had to offer. Nevertheless, it remains a fact that Luther continued to converse with his opponents - notably at Marburg in 1529 in person, and subsequently, at length, in his writings.[78] In these conversations, and even more precisely, in his attacks on the "fanatics", Luther seeks to be scrupulously honest. He does not distort their views. Yet his attitude continues to be negative. Having re-stated a disagreeable argument, Luther could on occasion exclaim: "Oh, how the devil's pants stink here."[79] Or, Luther would charge that they "follow the fancy of reason, which they expect to lead them aright" (37:53) and therefore are "dumb as a clod".[80] On occasion Luther addresses the opponent: "Listen now, you pig, god, or fanatic, whatever kind of unreasonable ass [Esel] you are..."[81] Inevitably, the very courage of faith, expressed in aggression and controversy, prevents Luther from perceiving any spiritual riches — or even redeeming features — in the writings of his opponents. Though personally humble and willing to confess his many limitations, the very act of formulating his eucharistic theology displays

Luther's violence most explicitly, and therefore, to modern readers, least acceptably. While not always able to appreciate Luther's violence, we may, nevertheless, at least record the understanding that it was not Luther's bad temper which caused it - the courage of faith was the ultimate source of his outspokenness.

V

Yet while outspoken, Luther also spoke, risked and formulated a cogent explanation of the eucharistic presence of Christ's body and blood. Without detracting from Luther's accomplishment, it may nevertheless be in order to acknowledge that the exact manner of Christ's eucharistic presence was not Luther's main concern. He affirmed the real presence and celebrated the faith which courageously partook of the Lord's Supper - but only marginally offered an exposition of the manner of the presence. What Luther, however, does say, is eminently clear and may be, briefly, summed up in four steps.

First, Luther begins with an uneasy acceptance of transubstantiation,[82] only, soon enough, to declare it to be one of the captivities under which the church suffers.[83] Clearly, Luther prefers the Occamist category of consubstantiation.[84] Yet even when doing so, Luther's concern is not about philosophical niceties but the reality of Christ's presence.[85]

Therefore, secondly, Luther turns his major attention to the Word, as the means which transmits the true content of eucharist.[86] The influence of St. Augustine is explicit and cherished. Clearly, the Word outranks the signs, but the true presence of Christ is what really matters. As we have already noted, insofar as the Word generates faith, it is the concern with faith as the true means of receiving Christ to which Luther devotes his entire attention.

Thirdly, particularly during his struggles with the Zwinglians and Anabaptists, Luther underscores the presence of the real body and real blood of Christ. Luther's formulation of how he comprehends "real" is not clear. There are passages in which Luther singles out phrases that are bound to enrage his opponents, rather than to clarify the issue, e.g. "What if I eat Christ's flesh physically in the Supper...?"[87] At the same time, he also often refers to spiritual partaking. The main point, apparently, is a concern to sustain the real paradox: true faith must trust the unknown and the uncomprehended. Hence those who are believers are not to worry about the exact manner of Christ's real presence, but rather, with their whole beings, to commit themselves in stalwart obedience to Christ's command: "Take and eat..." Luther recognizes that the Word can never be adequately evaluated by humankind. Our true response is acceptance with joy.[88]

Fourthly and finally, in his *Confession Concerning Christ's Supper*, 1528, Luther, maintaining all of his preceding emphases, and particularly appreciating the insights provided by Occam, suggests that Christ is repletively present. Namely, Christ "is simultaneously present in all places whole and entire, fills all places, yet without being measured or circumscribed by any place... This mode is altogether incomprehensible, beyond our reason, and can be maintained only with faith, in the Word."[89] Among the several illustrations which Luther supplies for this view, I find the following especially moving:

> I have seen crystals or jewels within which was a kind of spark or flame, as in an opal, or a little cloud or bubble; and yet this little bubble or cloud shines as if it were at every side of the stone, for whichever way the stone is turned, the bubble can be seen as if it were at the very front of the stone, though it is really in the center of it... Do you not suppose that God in a much truer and more miraculous way can set forth Christ's body in the bread, even if he were at a certain place in heaven, than show me the spark in a crystal?[90]

Of course, Luther's primary interest is not in gems or jewellery. It is the glory of Christ, risen and personally real that attracts Luther's attention; here true presence becomes available, indeed, miraculously both evokes faith and sustains the same in this partaking. In obedient partaking, the Christian fulfills not only his responsibility but also enjoys the highest joy. Here the divine gift, the human courage, and the vivid experience of salvation all converge.

MARTIN LUTHER IN THE WRITINGS OF
EUGEN ROSENSTOCK-HUESSY

Eugene D. Tate

Both Martin Luther and Eugen Rosenstock-Huessy were the fore-runners of a new age in the history of Western society. As the one who gave focus to the social revolution known as the Reformation, Martin Luther gave new shape to the life of people in Europe and North America. Eugen Rosenstock-Huessy proclaimed the existence of a new Millenium brought about by a revolution as dramatic as that introduced by Martin Luther. He was one of the great scholars of this century, yet few persons have paid careful attention to his work.[1] In this article I wish to expand on work I have been doing in Communication Theory.[2] I will first examine how Rosenstock-Huessy treated Martin Luther in his examination of the history of Western Civilization. Then I would like to suggest some parallels between these two seminal thinkers where our understanding of both Luther and Rosenstock-Huessy are strengthened by the relation-ship between their work. Before I begin let me introduce to you the work of Eugen Rosenstock-Huessy, a man who W.H. Auden called, "One of the truly seminal thinkers of the Twentieth Century."

An Introduction to Eugen Rosenstock-Huessy

Although he is not well known on this continent Eugen Rosenstock-Huessy is well known in Europe and there are several centres focussing on his life and thought in Germany and Holland. The German Sociologist Dietmar Kamper is only one of many European scholars influenced by Eugen Rosenstock-Huessy. In the United States Harold Stahmer, Professor of Religion at the University of Florida, has been a major interpreter of his work. Rosenstock-Huessy's influence is understood by other major scholars of our day including Harvey Cox and Martin E. Marty and especially by those who studied with him at Harvard and Dartmouth. Generally, however, Eugen Rosenstock-Huessy is not known by scholars working on this continent even though he taught and lectured here from 1932 to his death in 1973. There is not space in this article to give a detailed account of his life and work; however, some brief comments are in order.[3]

Eugen Rosenstock-Huessy was born in 1888. He received his Doctorate in Law from the University of Berlin at the age of 20. He taught constitutional law at Leipzig University from 1912 to 1914. In 1914 he married Margrit Huessy and added her surname to his own in the European custom. During the First World War he served as an officer in the German Army on the French front.

In 1913, Rosenstock-Huessy met a young Hegelian scholar by the name of Franz Rosenzweig. Eugen Rosenstock-Huessy had converted to Christianity and during their conversations convinced Franz Rosenzweig to do the same. Rosenzweig went home to tell his parents of his decision and decided to attend the Yom Kippur services at the synagogue for one last time. It was here that he "converted" to Judaism. During the war Franz Rosenzweig served as a German soldier on the Macedonian Front. The correspondence between Franz Rosenzweig and Eugen Rosenstock-Huessy as soldiers during 1914 - 1918 was influential on both men. These letters have been published as, *Judaism Despite Christianity*.[4] While writing to his friend, Rosenzweig developed the book which became his seminal work, *The Star of Redemption*. Similarly Rosenstock-Huessy sent Franz Rosenzweig an early copy of his book *Angewandte Seelenkunde (An Applied Science of the Soul)* which was published in Germany in 1924.

After the war Rosenstock-Huessy went to work for the Daimler-Benz automobile factory in Stuttgart where he developed adult education programs for the workers. In 1921 - 1922 he founded the Academy of Labour in Frankfurt. In 1923 he returned to teaching at the University of Breslau as Professor of the History of Law and Sociology. Between 1923 and 1933 he helped found voluntary work camps for farmers, industrial workers, and students, to create a '"universitas' in the wilderness where [participants] attempted through their common labors and conversations to bind together people in... a common social enterprise."[5] It was in this enterprise that he met Helmuth James, Count von Moltke and his wife Freya. Helmuth von Moltke became leader of the Kreisau Circle and died in a Nazi prison. Freya von Moltke became housekeeper for Eugen Rosenstock-Huessy in 1959 after the death of his wife and worked with him on his two volume work, *Sociology*, as well as serving as a translator for many of his books.

Between 1910 and 1930 Rosenstock-Huessy was a member of a small group of friends who sought to work out their understanding of the necessity for a new perspective on human existence together. The people were all involved in the Patmos Press and their periodical, *The Creature*. Among them were Franz Rosenzweig, Martin Buber, Joseph Wittig, with whom Rosenstock-Huessy wrote the three volume *Alter der Kirche* [The Age of the Church, 1928], Victor von Weizsacker, Hans Ehrenberg, Karl Barth, Leo Weismantel, Werner Picht and Rudolf Ehrenberg. Writing in an unpublished autobiography about this experience Rosenstock-Huessy said:

> From 1915 to 1923 this group of friends felt as though living on Patmos. And Patmos we called the publishing house founded in 1919 for the purpose of giving us a first opening into the official world of books. In the main, we remained extra mundane, so to speak. But all the seed of my later work, and if I may say so, of my peculiar

contribution, stems from this period of total renewal and overhauling. If any period may be called one of emigration, this was it. When I immigrated to the United States with my wife in 1933, it was nothing like our inner immigration upon Patmos achieved after 1915. After that year, we lived totally unconcerned with the prevalent departments or divisions of existing social order and thought. The niceties of the antitheses faith and science, capital and labor, object and subject, Protestant and Catholic, lost their vitality. We entered a much more open situation. I suppose that any crisis brings this experience. We, however, were dedicated now to never going back behind it and to devoting the rest of our lives, instead to a return to normalcy, to the new norm of this extraordinary experience.[6]

When Hitler came to power in 1933 Eugen Rosenstock-Huessy left Germany with his family and went to Harvard University where he taught for two years. In 1935 he joined the faculty of Dartmouth University where he taught social philosophy until his retirement in 1957. While at Dartmouth in 1939 helped to organize Camp William James as a leadership training camp for the Civilian Conservation Corps.[7] During the 1950's he lectured at the German universities of Goettingen, Berlin and Muenster. During the 1960's he lectured at Columbia University and the University of California. He continued to live and write at Norwich, Vermont, until his death in 1973. In his introduction to *The Origin of Speech* Harold Stahmer credits Eugen Rosenstock-Huessy with 150 books and articles published in Europe beginning in 1910 in the fields of law, history, political science, psychology and sociology.

The Thought of Eugen Rosenstock-Huessy

The thought of Eugen Rosenstock-Huessy points the way to a new understanding of human communication and experience. It is best described as an *intellectual breakthrough*. Kuhn's[8] understanding of the paradigmatic development of the social sciences requires that a new paradigm replace the old. Axelrod[9] has pointed out that true revolutions in the social sciences take place as intellectual breakthroughs. He has shown that an intellectual breakthrough occurs with estrangement between the individual and the group. This is very different from Kuhn's understanding of continued communication between the group and individual so that the group eventually accepts the new scientific paradigm. As Axelrod explains:

> For Freud, Simmel and Buber breakthrough begins with this estrangement — this relatedness to the tension between the individual and group. But they express this

164

estrangement in a certain way; not by escaping or declaring indifference, but by attempting to generate more relevant and crucial possibilities for inquiry. They choose to struggle with the restrictive conditions suitable to their own experiences of theorizing. And in order to amend or dissolve the accepted paradigm, they articulate their critiques and provide a higher rationality — one that allows their work to reach an audience and to re-enter the community of discourse.[10]

Martin Buber admitted he had no teaching and the intellectual community could find no new paradigm in his work.[11] Eugen Rosenstock-Huessy wrote, "I do not enlarge on the academic premises; I contradict them."[12]

The work of Eugen Rosenstock-Huessy does not present a new paradigm for the social sciences because it is not confined to one academic discipline. It ranges over all disciplines from Communication to Theology, Philosophy, History, Psychology, Sociology and Anthropology. In this respect it is threatening to the intellectual establishment with their organized areas of specialization.

In *Out of Revolution*, Eugen Rosenstock-Huessy expressed his estrangement for the intellectual community in the following passage:

My generation has survived social death in all its variation, and I have survived decades of study and teaching in scholastic and academic sciences. Every one of their venerable scholars mistook me for the intellectual type which he most despised. The atheist wanted me to disappear into Divinity, the theologian into sociology, the sociologists into history, the historians into journalism, the journalists into metaphysics, the philosophers into law, and — need I say it? — the lawyers into hell, which as a member of our present world, I never left. Society is a hell as long as man or woman is alone. And the human soul dies from consumption in the hell of social catastrophe, unless it makes common cause with others.[13]

Rosenstock-Huessy understood that a generation which had been through the experience of two world wars could not accept the old paradigms or processes of thought. He came to this realization in the trenches of Verdun. A student of his, Clinton Gardner, came to this realization as he took over command of the just liberated concentration camp at Buchenwald towards the end of the Second World War.[14] A generation which has experienced the slaughter of Viet Nam, Lebanon, and El Salvador should also understand that the old paradigms of thought are useless. A new starting point must be found for a meaningful understanding of communication and human behavior. This new starting point must take seriously the Planetary Revolution which has occurred during the past century.

> The two world wars were the form of world revolution in which this new future reached into everybody's life; the nationalist and communist ideologies with their dreams of revolution were checkmated and are mere foam around the real transformation. The real transformation was made by the wars and it made the Great Society final. She is the heiress of State and Church.[15]

In *Out of Revolution* Rosenstock-Huessy traced the four major revolutions which have formed the life of persons on this planet. Rosenstock-Huessy showed that society was formed by four kinds of speech. Tribal speech oriented people to their ancestors, their past. Templar speech, such as arose in the Egyptian empire, oriented to the stars, the world outside people. Greek speech oriented to the inner self through poetry and philosophy. Finally, the speech of Israel oriented to the future by way of prophecy.

> With the coming of the Christian era, these four ancient modes of speech were fused. After Christ, men no longer felt bound by a single orientation. They felt free to participate in all four forms of speech. They discovered the rhythm which moves a person from listening to the imperative of prophecy; to the subjective questioning of his response; to the narrative listening to how others, in the past, have responded; finally to the objective or outward speaking which is his particular response to the reality which he had first heard in the imperative form.[16]

These four forms of speech have made the four revolutions experienced in Western society necessary. We are heirs of each of these great revolutions. The French Revolution freed the people from the monarchy. The British Parliamentary Revolution gave the people the right to rule along with the aristocracy. The Reformation freed people from the Church and turned their attention to their calling in life. The Russian Revolution is to be seen as the natural successor of the other three freeing the worker from the power gained by Bourgeoisie in the French Revolution. Each revolution does not rise from the others but builds on the success of the others.

During the Battle of Verdun it became clear to Eugen Rosenstock-Huessy that another revolution was necessary to free us from the rigorous scientific method brought about by Cartesian thought. He then understood that Descartes was wrong when he said, *'Cogito ergo sum'* (I think therefore I am). Modern science has been built on the Cartesian principle that thought is the basic reality of life. Cartesian philosophy has given us five hundred years of advances in Chemistry, Physics, Biology and Botany.

Rosenstock-Huessy's breakthrough was that he understood that one cannot build a social science on Cartesian principles. It is necessary to break with Descartes. The corollary to *Cogito ergo sum* is I exist therefore I will be measured. Overagainst these Rosenstock-Huessy placed his new grammar: *Mensuror, quia existo, respondeo etsi mutabor*. (I hear so that I may come to exist; I respond although I will be changed).[17]

In Anselm's [*Credo ut intelligam* — I have faith in order that I may come to understand] statement the emphasis is on the hearing, as the organ for inspiration by truth. In Cartesius', it is on the doubting as the organ for transformation of this divine truth into human knowledge. In our phrasing, the emphasis shifts once more, and now to the process of making known, of speaking out at the right time, in the right place, as the proper social representation. We no longer believe in the timeless innocence of philosophers, theologians, scientists; we see them write books and try to gain power. And this whole process of teaching again needs the same century-long self-criticism applied by Anselmists and Cartesians to the processes of detaching us from God and from nature. In society, we must detach ourselves from our listeners before we can teach them.

Both the *Credo ut intelligam* and the *Cogito ergo sum* worked very well for a time. However, finally the *Credo ut intelligam* led to the Inquisition and the *Cogito ergo sum* into an ammunition factory... When Joan of Arc was questioned under torture, her theological judges had ceased to believe. When Nobel Prize winners produced poison-gas, their thinking was no longer identified with existence.

Our formula *Respondeo etsi mutabor* reminds us that human society has outgrown the stage of mere existence which prevails in nature. In Society we must respond, and by our response we bear witness that we know what no other creature knows: the secret of death and life. We feel ourselves answerable for life's "Renaissance." Revolution, love, any glorious work, bears the stamp of eternity if it was called into existence by this sign in which Creator and creature are at one. "*Respondeo etsi mutabor*," a vital word alters life's course and life outruns the already present death.[18]

Rosenstock-Huessy's Treatment of Martin Luther

Since Martin Luther was the leader of one of the four major revolutions which have shaped Western society, Eugen Rosenstock-Huessy discussed Luther's work in great detail in *Out of Revolution* and in relevant portions of his other major books. Martin Luther's accomplishment was deemed, by Rosenstock-Huessy, to be more important and lasting than that of the other revolutions because even to this day all History books accept the Lutheran division of the Christian era into Pauline - Early Church, the Dark Ages, and the Modern Age brought about by the Reformation.[19]

> Deep and vigorous motives must have been at work when the mere reading of certain books written by a professor of theology could make men discard a nine-hundred-year-old method. "Reformation" must weigh heavier in the scales of history than "World Revolution" if we compare their achievements. It was no theologians' quarrel, no mere clergymen's dispute, but a revolution in the modern sense of the word: a breaking of all moulds, a pointing toward a new order of things, something totalitarian, universal in its aim, which had been unknown till then.
>
> Being a Reformation of the Church, it of course took every member of the human race to be a member of this Christian Church. Its gospel restored Christianity within the Church. Luther's greatest pamphlet announced "the freedom of every Christian."
>
> But since half the world was "church" in those days, the destruction of the visible church was nothing less then the reconstruction of the world.[20]

The Lutheran Reformation possessed some characteristics of all Revolutions. As Galtung[21] has shown in his discussion of the two models of social change — the Absolutist/Revolution Model and the Gradualist/Public Opinion Model — a revolution requires that there be a time of upheaval which results in a complete break with the old society, a period of chaos during which no clear norms or rules govern, and finally the establishment of the new society or the new age.

Rosenstock-Huessy set the first period, the time of upheaval, as that of 1517 - 1525, the time from the nailing of the Ninety-five Theses to the marriage of Luther. The chaotic time as that between 1525, when the Princes entered the Reformation in the war against the Peasants to 1555 the establishment of peace. The German Revolution continued in the Thirty Years War to the final settlement of religious and economic questions in 1648. In the end both the Church and German society had been restructured.

Similarly the Reformation had a slogan, as all revolutions must have slogans. Here the slogan was "Every Christian a priest." This can be compared with the slogans of the other revolutions: Russia - Every proletarian a capitalist; France - Every man of talent an aristocrat; and England - Every gentleman a King. As Rosenstock-Huessy pointed out in his discussion on the diseases of speech,[22] Revolution is brought about by deafness to old slogans and the shouting of new slogans to the detriment of past contributions to life.

As each of the other revolutions rejected forces which would have changed the structure of the new society, so Luther rejected the Anabaptists who would have reduced the revolution to one of individualism and small community. Luther sought reform for all the people within the Church. "... his new equation, 'every Christian a priest,' had to be fought through and secured, not for a single farm-house or a single village or town, but for the largest units of christendom then in existence. In those days this largest unit was the single State..."[23]

It was the character of Luther that he was a Gradualist and not a true Absolutist/Revolutionary.[24] The reason for this lay in his belief that Reform would be accomplished only through the action of the Word of God. "Our sword is the Word of God."[25] Luther believed that it was God working through the preaching of the Gospel which brought about change in the minds and lives of people. Thus the old ways were not to be cruelly destroyed or wrenched away from the people because change would come about through the work of the Word.

> When the Word took hold of their hearts, they forsook them [Luther is speaking here of idol worship and the early Christians] of their own accord, and in consequence the thing fell of itself. Likewise, if I had seen them holding mass, I would have preached to them and admonished them. Had they heeded my admonition, I would have won them; if not, I would nevertheless not have torn them from it by their hair or employed any force, but simply allowed the Word to act and prayed for them. For the Word created heaven and earth and all things (Ps. 22:6); the Word must do this thing, and not we poor sinners.[26]

Luther's approach to social change as expressed in this sermon is quite understandable to Canadians, but probably not to persons educated in the United States, since the Canadian experience is one of gradual social change instead of a revolutionary overthrow of the old society. Luther desired to bring the people along with him before changes were made in the existing social fabric. In this light his rejection of the Peasant's Revolt is understandable for he rejected all absolutist tactics.

Rosenstock-Huessy is well aware of this aspect of Luther's life and thought as shown in the following paragraph.

> For Luther, teaching and learning have nothing to do with the individual mind or soul. Love has created a stream of language, a Word, an inspiration, and sent it into the valley of tears, where men live blinded by their sins and in despair. First set this stream of instruction flowing, let love and spirit have their way; then all the chains of the oppressed, all the tears of the blind, will cease to be. For the preceding and preforming voice of the redeemer restores Creation to its old glory and true meaning. "And the Truth shall set you free" is the song of triumph of the Reformation. The stream of teaching and learning flows through the unworthy vessel of teachers and students; but since God *had pity* and *has pity*, all our misunderstanding cannot resist the pure, unmixed and genuine "Evangelium". Die *reine Lehre*, takes the place in Germany of the mere philosophical after-dinner reflection of a Bodin or a Montaigne.[27]

Given this teaching of Luther the German revolution was a more gradual revolution in which the old society was allowed to die down as the new society grew to replace it. This stability in the German revolution founded by Martin Luther led, according to Eugen Rosenstock-Huessy, to a) a strong civil service which maintained the stability of society, b) the development of academic freedom in German universities, c) the increased power of lay teachers in theology, German philosophy, law, and d) a new base for philosophy which cannot be understood except in the light of Luther's concept of the Living, Active Word of God which creates, sustains and renews human society.

Rosenstock-Huessy showed how, because of Luther's work, the civil service came to take the role played by the clergy in Medieval society. The effect of the Reformation was that "for the first time in history, the great prince and the little count, the diocese of Cologne on the lower Rhine and the small district of the Abbots of Sackingen on the upper Rhine, became equals in their responsibility for the religious salvation of their subjects."[28]

> Every High Magistrate became a pope in his own big or little territory. For most of the territories, because of their very smallness, the Reformation was a spiritual, religious and political movement; it was not a military or belligerent enterprise at all. On the contrary, the princes of central Germany, because they felt protected by the Emperor's colossal ring of countries, took up the Reformation in order to consolidate the administration of their own territories. Reformation to them was a

revolution for the purpose of co-ordinating all ecclesiastical institutions under the jurisdiction of one High Magistrate. The outcome was the creation of civil government and a civil service, to replace *ecclesiastical* government and the employment of the clergy in political office. The word "clerc" (clerk) can still be used in French and English. In German the word "clergy" was extirpated, because in Germany the civil servant appeared as a religious rival of the clergy. The civil power and Civil Law became sacred weapons against ecclesiastical power and against legislation by Canon Law.[29]

There are several main effects of the development of a concept of Civil Law and Civil Service. First, German princes became servants of the State instead of princes in the sense that Machiavelli understood Italian princes as existing above the State. Secondly, there was the separation of the military from the civil service. Before the Reformation one was either a layperson ruled by "martial, feudal, and canon law" or a member of the clergy. There was no Civil Law or Common Law. One was considered a soldier first and a peaceful citizen second. After the Reformation one was considered a citizen first and only in time of crisis a member of the military. The Reformation separated the military from the civil service.

"The High Magistrate, when he created a civil law and a civil service, separated his general from his civil servants and made them generals pure and simple, without any claim to be made governors, either then or later."[30] Whereas the French have had a MacMahon or a DeGaulle, the British a Duke of Wellington, and the Americans a George Washington, Andrew Jackson, U.S. Grant, or Dwight Eisenhower, Germany has only had two military leaders who attempted to lead the State — Wallenstein and Hindenberg. Wallenstein was assassinated on orders from Vienna after he tried to make peace during the Counter-Reformation, "thus restoring the control of the magistrate over the military."

But the Reformation abolished this confusion. From Luther's time down to 1890, ordinarily no German general was invested with civil power! Hindenberg was a great exception to the rule. German militarism consisted in the strict exclusion of generals from politics. This cardinal contribution of Germany to democracy and civilization was not adopted by the democratic countries.[31]

Another contribution of the Reformation is the development of the German university as an independent institution under the protection of the High Magistrate who provided for academic freedom. Luther taught at the University of Wittenberg which was regulated by Canon and Roman Law. The university had been established in 1502 and Luther went to teach there in 1512. When Luther defied Canon and Roman Law, the Elector of Saxony (who as Rosenstock-Huessy pointed out, "had a domain one ninth as large as England...parts of six different bishoprics were included in his territory," along with one hundred monasteries making at least one third of his land free of taxation)[32] acted to consolidate jurisdiction under his own hand and to maintain the university as an institution in which Luther was free to teach doctrine as God gave him wisdom to understand it.

Since universities were not old in Germany, the question was a new question indeed. But a prince who cherished his university as the apple of his eye could not admit the right of anyone else to pass judgment on its orthodoxy, since its very *raison d'etre* was to check other peoples' (that is to say, foreign-clerical) influences òver his territory.

Charles V perceived this obstacle. In framing his Edict of Worms he gave the right of censorship in all matters of religion, not to the bishops, but to the theological faculty of the universities. The Emperor himself thus implied a kind of exemption and sovereign privilege for the theological faculties of the universities. They were appointed as acting censors, and nobody else could officially rebuke them. This regulation in the Emperor's Writ outweighed his approval of the pope's decision in respect to Luther's past actions. For the future, men like Luther who, after all, was a member of a faculty, were acknowledged as competent judges of orthodoxy, public morals, and Christian principles.

Luther's prince, therefore, was not protecting Luther as a personal friend, he was standing for the right of a High Magistrate to harbour a sovereign university in his territories.[33]

When Luther married, he again placed himself outside Canon Law. Since this was linked with the problem of protecting the university it led to "the conclusion that certain chapters of Canon and Imperial Law could be abolished by the prince's decision..." The princes were informed that they were "bound in conscience to...act in this religious emergency."[34] This was not an economic emergency but one of restoring normalcy in religion and law to persons who had moved out of the established realms of law into a new realm.

The secular state of the Reformation was the result of an *emergency* in religion and law. The monk and the nun relied on someone's prerogative to give them back their rights of citizenship, of normality. He who had the power, and who used that power in order to make their

situation regular, was bound to be hailed as their sword
of justice, righteous governor, and true leader toward
prosperity and happiness.[35]

The power granted to the princes in this crisis evolved into the establishment of a stable civil service. The sovereignty given to the universities evolved into the strong role played by the university in German society. Just as the theologians were the first arbitrators of morality and law, so in later German society were the faculties of law; they played a role similar to that of the Supreme Court in our society. The effect of this was to establish the professorate as a valuable and prestigious calling for individuals in German society. It also gave rise to a systematic, logical approach to thought which one still finds in German philosophy but which dates back to Melanchthon's rejection of Scholasticism.[36]

Another contribution of the Reformation through Martin Luther was the development of music as a part of popular Christian worship and thus as an established part of the social fabric. Luther used music to evangelize, teach, and comfort. He considered his hymns to be as important as his catechism and Postils.

> The purified Church replaced pictures by music, bodily
> pilgrimages by singing. "Luther sang many millions out
> of Catholic Church"is an old saying. The German
> chorale is unequalled in beauty and variety. The German
> nation, robbed of its visible ornaments, takes refuge in a
> world of sound. In German an influential man does not
> "set the fashion," he "gives the tone" (i.e., the pitch).
> Music became a politicum, a religious institution in
> Germany. As in the field of learning, where three
> centuries were dominated successively by theology,
> law, and philosophy, so German music has three periods,
> from Luther to Bach, from Bach to Mozart, and from
> Beethoven to Wagner and Strauss. "Music and govern-
> ment are like church and state," wrote Luther himself.[37]

It is Wagner, according to Rosenstock-Huessy, who compromised the purity and power of German music first established by Martin Luther. Wagner brought into the German sphere influences of French and Italian thought and philosophy. Thus the spontaneity which called forth response in the works of Luther, Bach and Beethoven was replaced by a "mystifying and obscuring." The music of Wagner spoke to a German society which had lost the Lutheran vision. "But it had the great merit of giving to the isolated, weakened and nervous soul of a German 'Gebildeter,' who no longer went to church, a substitute for his lost religion."[38] Wagner desired a reconciliation of the disputing parties from the Reformation. "Wagner's background is not Lutheran Germany, but all Germany; hence his music goes beyond the split between Protestants and Catholics."[39]

Martin Luther also contributed to German society with his attack on Popular Religion and Popular Culture. The attack on the Priests was also an attack on all forms of witchcraft, sorcery, and popular religious beliefs. A recent article traces the development of Roman Catholic Popular Culture through the worship of Saints.[40] Vatican II changed Roman Catholic piety and popular culture by attacking the veneration of Saints and revising the liturgical calendar. The Reformation served the same reforming process in the sixteenth century.

> The struggle against the witches is a necessary feature of the Reformation. Wherever man tried to purchase safety too cheaply, to insure the issue without exposing his faith to God's intervention, he was the servant of the devil. Luther went against the sorcerers of Pharaoh who promised the life of happiness and plenty instead of preaching penitence. Men have to listen to God passively, and then to act for themselves. But between the hours of listening and of action there is a middle period to be endured where everything is uncertain...Suddenly darkening all the bright order of the Madonna, the Holy Family, apostles, Saints, Popes, Bishops, Luther extinguished all the friendly lights kindled for the night of life by faithful generations before him.[41]

Luther realized that the German people needed him to have something to replace the popular religious teachings with a proper understanding of God's Word. From the beginning of the Reformation his concern was a pastoral concern for the German people whom God had placed in his care. He expressed this in the letter he wrote to Cardinal Albrecht, Archbishop of Mainz, to explain his posting of the Ninety-five Theses.[42] It is the primary driving force of his work during a lifetime which saw the publication of hymns, postils, catechism, books and tracts all aimed at teaching people to live with the Holy Spirit.[43]

Conclusion

For Eugen Rosenstock-Huessy, Martin Luther is a central, privotal figure in human history. It was Luther who began the process which led to the development of the German nation and university. It was Luther who molded a revolution so great as to set the tone of history. "Luther really saved a world which was going fascist. About 1500 the decay of the Catholic Church had led to a blind struggle for power in Italy...In this decisive hour Luther's sermon on the freedom of the Christian broke in like the trumpets of the Last Judgement."[44]

Luther's contribution to German society went far beyond that of the ecclesiastical reformation within the Church. Luther wrote extensively on all topics of concern to the Germans of his day from money lending and profit making to education and the establishment of social welfare agencies. As Rosenstock-Huessy showed in his writings on Martin Luther the contributions of this German reformer go far beyond the simple protest against papal indulgences. The reformation of the Church led to the creation of a new German society.

The roots of Eugen Rosenstock-Huessey's own unique perspective can be found in the teachings of Martin Luther. Rosenstock-Huessy began not with human thought or human faith but with the living, vital Word which proceeds from the one who stands over against us. The necessity of response to the one who calls us forth and gives us being is central to both Luther and Rosenstock-Huessy's understanding of human reality. Luther would understand, I am sure, Rosenstock-Huessy's rejection of the Alexandrian grammar [I love, You love, He-She-It loves, We love, You love, They love] with a new grammar which teaches us the reality of Speech-thought. The grammar Rosenstock-Huessy taught, having learned from Luther was:

ama (amate)	Love!
ame (ameus)	that I may love! (that we may love)
amatus	loved (they love)
amavimus	we have loved[45]

Similarly the Cross of Reality, which he used to explain the structure of human existence, is based on this understanding of communication/response as the central reality of all life.

The study of the Reformation and the life of Martin Luther not only illuminates for us the roots of Western civilization but helps us to approach the problems which face us in modern society.

> The difficulties of Charles V are still our difficulties today. Censorship of movies or plays, controversies between fundamentalists and evolutionists, prohibition of books or news, occur daily. The function of the papacy has been taken over by nationalistic priests or communistic fanatics or elderly society ladies. And though the authorities are multiple, the result in any particular jurisdiction, in Russia or Tennessee, Italy or Germany, is as final and suffocating as it was in 1521![46]

As one reads Martin Luther and Eugen Rosenstock-Huessy's *Out of Revolution* modern day problems are illuminated. The censorship of the media is a problem facing Canadian society with a government which has withdrawn funding from the C.B.C., in the name of fiscal responsibility, because of a dislike for a national broadcasting system perceived to be critical of party policy and leadership. The presence of pornography and its control within our society is another problem which is being debated today. Whether Canada follows the United States example of total Free Speech or finds some middleground which allows for limitation on media content harmful to groups and persons within society thus promoting a limited concept of freedom of speech, still is unclear. On the world scene the United States withdrawal from U.N.E.S.C.O. is an attack on Freedom of the Press in the world and especially in developing countries. Canadians understand the necessity of a press policy which allows for the development of a national culture since it is a problem which they face in common with persons in the Third World. The United States has long attempted to camouflage a policy of media imperialism under the guise of promoting Freedom of Expression. Once again the arguments made by Luther in *Why The Books of the Pope and His Disciples Were Burned* become relevant in modern debate.

In *Out of Revolution* Rosenstock-Huessy showed how Hitler led an attack on Luther and the Protestant Reformation. Rather than seeing Luther as Hitler's Spiritual Ancestor, Rosenstock-Huessy understood clearly the antithesis between Hitler and Luther. "Hitler is a pre-Reformation type, by race, education and character. He is immune to the last four centuries of German history. He is neither a Protestant nor an academic person nor a civil servant nor an army officer... He himself has become pope, bishop, monk and council in one person."[47] By claiming Hitler as the new Messiah, the Christ, Nazi christians destroyed the German society which evolved out of the work of Martin Luther.

> The three essentials of the Reformation: civil service, universities, music, are of no importance any longer. They have been sacrificed, after the princes fell, by a young generation full of fear, full of superstitions, full of need for a simple, universal faith, and its personification in Hitler...The only thing continuing the experiences of the past is the army.[48]

It might be argued that the problems faced by Luther in separating the Canon and Civil Law during the Reformation and those faced by the members of the Kreisau Circle in Nazi Germany when a Nationalist/ Racist Law had overthrown Civil Law, are similar to those which are faced today when the Moral Majority of a Gerald Falwell and Ronald Reagan again attempt to provide the masses with a simplistic morality which under the guise of Religion attacks the freedom and responsibility of individuals before God. The links between the "Prime Time Preachers" or television evangelists with the possessors of political power have not been seriously examined yet.[49] These may prove to be as important to modern society as were the questions raised by Martin Luther about the power of the Pope and political forces in his world.

Martin Luther and his work are central to Eugen Rosenstock-Huessy's understanding of the Western World. The modern scholar has much to learn from both men. The questions which Luther faced are still relevant in our modern society. The answers which Luther gave have molded Western society and help us to understand the social forces in conflict in the modern world. At the same time the life and thought of Eugen Rosenstock-Huessy remind the scholar that one cannot withhold him or herself from the debate within our world. Taking seriously the rejection of Cartesian and Aristotelian thought the modern scholar cannot do Theology, Philosophy, History, Social Science in the same manner as before, whether from a Philosophical, Ethical, Rhetorical, Empirical, Phenomenological, Semantic, Linguistic, Semiological, or Critical perspective. Scholars of whatever discipline must sail forth, like Martin Luther, as an argonaut through uncharted seas, guided only by the Holy Spirit to provide new understanding for people in this hour.

PRINTING AND THE REFORMATION

George Wolfgang Forell

Anybody even superficially familiar with the events called "the Protestant Reformation" has heard of Luther's nailing of the 95 Theses on the door of the *Schlosskirche* in Wittenberg on October 31, 1517. Theses were propositions for debate or disputations which constituted an important aspect of the educational system in a medieval university. The particular church door in Wittenberg served as the bulletin board for the theological faculty of the university. Luther's dramatic nailing of his theses, which discussed the matter of indulgences, is part of the lore every schoolgirl or boy picks up in the course of their study of European history.

Thus it may come as somewhat of a shock to some of us that this nailing of the theses, one of the most famous events in the history of Christendom, probably never happened. About 20 years ago Erwin Iserloh, professor of medieval and modern church history at the University of Muenster in West Germany wrote a book whose English title states the message clearly *The Theses Were not Posted*. He showed that the story of the nailing of these propositions was never reported by Luther, who should have remembered it. Many years later Luther told how he had become involved in the indulgence dispute. After describing the offensive practices of the indulgence salesmen in some detail he added: "Then I wrote a letter with the Theses to the bishop of Magdeburg, admonishing and beseeching him to stop Tetzel (one of the most colorful indulgence salesmen) and prevent this stupid thing from being preached, lest it give rise to public discontent – that was the proper thing for him to do as archbishop. I can still lay my hands on that letter."[1] He comments again on the beginning of what he called "the Lutheran rumpus" in a table talk: "The monstrosities of Tetzel's preaching on indulgences moved me to oppose him ... Therefore I wrote suppliantly to the bishops of Brandenburg and Mainz, saying that if they did not suppress this evil I would write against it. But the bishops sent my letter to Tetzel."[2]

In a letter written to the Elector Frederick the Wise on November 21, 1518 recalling the events of a little more than a year ago he wrote:

> One thing vexes me greatly, and this is that the legate [Cajetan] should insinuate that I have acted as I have in reliance upon your Electoral Highness ... The fact is that not even my closest friends were aware of it, but only the archbishop of Magdeburg and Hieronymus, the bishop of Brandenburg. For I admonished in private letters these whose office it was to prevent scandal, most

humbly and respectfully, before I published my disputation theses. I knew quite well that I should not bring this
matter before civil authorities, but first before the
bishops. My letter is still extant; it has passed through
many hands and bears witness to what I say.[3]

The story of the public nailing of the 95 theses was never told during
Luther's lifetime. The source is Luther's close friend and colleague Philip
Melanchthon. In the preface to the second volume of Luther's collected
works, published after Luther's death he wrote: "Luther, burning with
zeal for true piety, issued indulgence theses which are printed in the first
volume of this series. He posted these theses publicly at the church near
the castle in Wittenberg on the vigil of All Saints Day in 1517." Since in
1517 Melanchthon was still in Tuebingen he could only have known
about the events from the reports of others. The posting of theses for
public debate at Wittenberg's church doors was the rule of the
university. It is logical to assume that Melanchthon thought that it had
been done in this instance as well.

But why introduce a paper on "Printing and the Reformation" with this
long unoriginal and controversial story about the nailing of the 95
theses? The answer is quite obvious. In spite of the publicity the alleged
nailing of the theses has received through the centuries it was of little
significance. The important occurrence was that after Luther had sent
his theses to the bishops and they had failed to act, these controversial
propositions were printed in Nuernberg, Leipzig and Basel. As Luther
himself told it: "So my theses against Tetzel's articles, which you can
now see in print, were published. They went throughout the whole of
Germany in a fortnight, for the whole world complained about
indulgences, and particularly about Tetzel's articles."[4]

Luther's success and the movement we know as "the Protestant
Reformation" is unthinkable without the printing press. As Arthur G.
Dickens told us:

> Between 1517 and 1520, Luther's publications pro-
> bably sold well over 300,000 copies.... Altogether in
> relation to the spread of religious ideas it seems difficult
> to exaggerate the significance of the press, without
> which a revolution of this magnitude could scarcely
> have been consummated. Unlike the Wycliffite and
> Waldensian heresies, Lutheranism was from the first
> the child of the printed book, and through this vehicle
> Luther was able to make exact, standardized and ineradi-
> cable impressions on the mind of Europe. For the first
> time in human history a great reading public judged the
> validity of revolutionary ideas through a mass-medium
> which used the vernacular languages together with the
> arts of the journalist and the cartoonist.[5]

No doubt Luther was aware of the importance of the printing press. In one of his Table Talks of 1530 he observed: "Printing is the last and also the greatest gift of God. By it He wanted to have the cause of the true religion become known and spread in all languages at the end of the world in all the countries of the earth."[6]

But how did the distribution take place? One must remember that a sixteenth century author received no royalties. There was no copyright law and the printer was generally an independent entrepreneur who lived from the popularity of his products and the speed of his production. Delay meant that the competition would reach the customer first and his product would be practically worthless.

Because of the demands of its technology most printing was done in larger cities which supplied the skilled workers and raw materials, especially paper, for this (for its time) high – technology enterprise. The printing establishment and the bookstore were usually the same place and the printer and book salesman the same person. One bought the books "hot off the press" at the printing plant. Editions were small consisting usually of about 1000 copies. Thus the number of well over 300,000 copies of Luther's writings published between 1517 and 1520 mentioned earlier, is based on 370 different known editions of Luther's thirty publications during this period.

Of course, in smaller towns book peddlers would sell books or more likely pamphlets, the so-called *Flugschriften*. Trade fairs and other public festivities were particularly good places to sell printed material in the vernacular languages. We read of people selling prints of Luther's hymns at such occasions and advertising them by singing them for potential customers.[7] Some salesmen were employed by the printer and some were independent, buying books wholesale and selling them at a profit.

In view of the importance of a support system to maintain a printer a town like Wittenberg would seem an unlikely place for a successful printer. The population of between 2000 and 2500 inhabitants in the 16th century[8] made it too small to support a printing establishment. Melanchthon described Wittenberg in one of his letters as "a spot which has no houses, but only tiny cottages, mere huts built of clay and covered with hay and straw."[9] One of Luther's archenemies, J. Cochlaeus, called it: "A miserable, poor, dirty village in comparison with Prague, hardly worth three farthings; yes, in fact, it is not worthy to be called a town in Germany. It has an unhealthy, disagreeable climate, is without vine-yards, orchards, or fruitbearing trees of any kind; a regular beerchamber; on account of its cold and smoke it is not an enjoyable place; it is very dirty."[10]

Nevertheless, because of the university, founded in 1502, it soon needed a printer and Johann Rhau-Grunenberg settled in Wittenberg in 1508. He had his plant in the Augustinian monastery where Luther also resided. Luther gave him some work but thought that he was a very poor craftsman. Rhau was later joined by other printers who because of their lack of capital were mainly supported by people like the painter Lukas Cranach. The investors could profit considerably from a successful printing establishment but could also lose their money very easily.[11]

The most serious problem for the Wittenberg printers, who had access to Luther's writings at no cost, was the practice of other printers everywhere to reprint whatever might appear profitable without asking the permission of the author or the printer. It even happened that printers from one town tried to steal manuscripts being processed by the printers of another town in order to publish a book first. On September 26, 1525, Luther wrote to the mayor and city council of Nuernberg asking them to stop the printers in that city from publishing Luther's manuscripts stolen from the Wittenberg printers. He claimed in this letter that the Nuernberg printers had actually managed to get their version of his manuscript into print ahead of those in Wittenberg. But he also complained that this had affected the accuracy of the books. He suggested that the Nuernberg printers should wait at least seven or eight weeks before they began their copying so that the Wittenberg printers whose work Luther could supervise, might also be able to make a living.[12]

The shady practices Luther had complained about, tempted the Wittenbergers to try very large editions so that the demand for a pamphlet or book could be supplied before the imitators had time to produce their copies. This, of course, added to the risk for the Wittenberg printer. According to Heinrich Kuehne thirty printers worked in Wittenberg during the 16th century and printed 746 different books and pamphlets. This does not include the work of Hans Luft who in the time from 1534 to 1584 printed 49 different editions of the Bible.

All this activity, however, depended on the academic reputation of the University of Wittenberg established by Luther and his colleagues, a reputation which eventually reached England and inspired Shakespeare to send Hamlet to Wittenberg for his studies at a time when such a university did not yet exist. After the death of Luther and Melanchthon the fame of Wittenberg soon dwindled until it was absorbed by the University of Halle in 1817.

The printers did not survive the university. Leipzig in Luther's time not much bigger than Wittenberg, became in the 18th century and until the Second World War one of the book and printing centers of the world. It surpassed all other German cities since it was free from the censorship which plagued earlier competitors, such as, Frankfurt, which was closer to the supervision of the emperor and his attempts to control publications.

We are now, perhaps, ready to draw some conclusions from our brief look at the effect of printing on the spread of the Reformation. In what way did the printing press and the resulting easy access to religious pamphlets and books, especially the Bible, affect the character of Protestantism?

First of all, religion and its formal articulation, theology, became a public concern. In the history of religion one observes that religious knowledge is frequently secret, reserved to a special caste and its possession a form of power or even property passed on among a distinct class of practitioners from generation to generation. Rituals and incantations, even the names of divine beings, may be a form of esoteric wisdom not shared with the general public.

Christianity from its beginning rejected this approach and was strikingly open to all kinds and conditions of men, women and children. To the amazement and even shock of the priests and philosophers of the time, Christians ignored in their religious life the distinctions between male and female, free and slave, Gentile and Jew as well as Greek and barbarian. This openness to everybody was, however, hampered at the time by the relative inaccessibility of the Christian's holy book, the Bible, and the Christian's theological tradition, the teachings of the fathers and mothers of the faith. (It may be worth pointing out that, for example the so-called Desert Fathers included women and that the great mystic Julian of Norwich was, indeed, female.)

Participatory theology, which would enable everybody to take part in religious discussion and contribute to the edification of the believers, depended on access for all to what Christians called "the Word of God," the Holy Scriptures, considered by them to be the source and norm of all true theology. The printing press made these documents available and the theological zeal of Protestant masses brought about the high level of literacy which made it real. The Reformers supported education for boys and girls in order that everybody might be able to read the World of God.

For the religious establishment of the time the access of all people to what was considered to be the fountain of all ultimate truth had some grave and unpleasant consequences. It undermined their position since their alleged expert knowledge appeared to be based on human traditions rather than the Bible and the early fathers and thus did not pass muster among people who wanted to get back to the sources. In 1521 Eberlin of Gunzburg wrote a satire illustrating the problem. Distraught functionaries of the religious establishment (*Pfaffen*) complain about the new developments. One says: "There are today so many German books and all divine and human wisdom is now available in the German language ... 15 year old boys possess knowledge based on their own reading which is better than what we learned from our Latin compendia."[13] Luther indicated his awareness of some of the problems which the new situation caused. The Reformation had made the conventional religious wisdom obsolete. This was illustrated by the popularity of Luther's writings. But the lack of interest in the publications representing the old ways created difficulties for the established religious leaders as well as for printers and booksellers who had supplied them with their compendia and sermon aids which they were no longer able to sell. In the letter to the mayor of Nuernberg mentioned earlier, Luther wrote: "I know, of course, that Koburger [a printer and bookseller in Nuernberg] has a lot of books he cannot sell, as happens to other printers. I cannot help it [that these books do not sell]. Should they revenge themselves [by stealing my manuscripts]? We did not try to harm them with our books." (WAB, 3, 578) The printing press had made possible a theology claiming to be based on the sources and made it available to anybody who desired to take advantage of it.

Secondly, this participatory theology led to pluralism. It became more difficult to manage theological differences since they were in permanent public form. It was very hard to back away from positions taken in print and distributed in thousands of copies, much more difficult than to deny oral statements. Thus what Pope Leo X, had described as a mere "monks' quarrel" with reference to Luther and the indulgence controversy, had become, thanks to the printing press, a hard and irrevocable reality that could not be managed in the customary manner. Even if Luther had been arrested and burned at the stake his books would have come to haunt his enemies.

Censorship which had served the established church well when it involved the destruction of a few copies of heretical writings generally found only in libraries became a herculean task when the censors were confronted by the printing press and a divided Christendom where one group's heresy was another group's orthodoxy. While censorship was tried most zealously by the Roman leadership with the establishment of the *Index Of Forbidden Books* it proved to be counterproductive. As Elizabeth Eisenstein in her *The Printing Press As An Agent Of Change* has pointed out: "Being listed as forbidden served as a form of publicity and may have spurred sales ... Given the existence of profit – seeking printers outside the reach of Rome, Catholic censorship boomeranged in ways that could not be foreseen. Lists of passages to be expurgated, for example, directed readers to 'book chapter and line' where anti-Roman passages could be found; thus relieving Protestant propagandists of the need to make their own search for anti-Catholic citations drawn from eminent authors and respected works.' Early copies of all original indexes found their way as soon as they were produced to Leiden, Amsterdam and Utrecht and were promptly utilized by the enterprising Dutch publisher as guides."[14] The author adds that the *Index of Forbidden Books* was also considered useful by Bodley's librarian." In 1627 he advised the curators of the Bodleian collection to look to the Index for those titles that were most worth collecting and preserving."[15]

The Reformation movement itself was profoundly affected by the trend towards pluralism which accompanied the printing press. While Luther would have wanted all readers of the Bible and the early Christian Fathers to see the truth his way, this was not to be. A vast variety of interpretations of the Bible was possible. The Protestant movement was not able to create any theological unanimity, precisely because it made access to the sources of all Christian theology so easy. Luther translated the Bible into an understandable German. His printers made the translation available. But it was open to a large variety of interpretations. The discouragement of Bible reading for the laity attempted by the Roman Catholic Church after Trent was not open to Protestants on theological grounds. The result was a proliferation of theological moral opinions leading to the formation of numerous communions or sects restrained only by the demands of the political leadership for a common civil religion. This led to *cuius regio eius religio* in Europe and to the uneasy coexistence of civil religion with denominationalism in the United States. Because of the multitude of Protestant options, religious censorship was not really tried. Whatever censorship there was in Protestant countries was based on political and general moral considerations rather than on theology.

And finally, the printing press made one of the Reformer's favorite teachings plausible. In his *Address To The Christian Nobility* Luther had insisted on the priesthood of all believers. For the Reformers baptism was ordination to the priesthood (thus making the argument about women priests moot, a point lost on Luther at the time). The ordained clergy, the pastor, was essentially a servant of the Word and the sacraments, no more priest than any other baptized Christian. This emphasis upon the priesthood of all believers achieved credibility because all of them, if able to read, had access to the Word, which for the Reformers constituted both church and sacrament. Of course, they believed that this Word was primarily and properly speaking the incarnate Logos, Jesus, the Christ and not a printed book. But the Reformers also never ceased to stress that access to the living Christ was by way of proclamation, the preaching of the Word, based on the words found in this book. For Luther the book is the "cradle of Christ", or as he will also say, the swaddling clothes in which Christ is wrapped. He did not want Christians to worship cradle or swaddling clothes but he did not know a Word separated from or at odds with the words of the Bible.

The entire life and substance of the church is in the Word of God and all baptized Christians must be given access to it. Nowhere is this emphasis on the power of the Word more clearly stated than in Luther's hymns. He sings, "God's Word forever shall abide, No thanks to foes who fear it." Or, "Lord, keep us steadfast in your Word."

In conclusion we may observe that in the sixteenth century the Reformation movement in its many expressions was able to make a successful appeal to the authority of what they all believed to be the Eternal Word because Gutenberg and his successors had made the printed word available to the masses and thus transformed the priesthood of all believers from a theological dogma to a practical possiblity.

HENRY MELCHIOR MUHLENBERG'S CANADIAN CONNECTIONS

Helmut T. Lehmann

Muhlenberg's connections with Lutheran congregations in Halifax and Lunenburg had their beginning in his communication with a man who had been pastor in Nova Scotia before coming to Pennsylvania. While serving as pastor of Trinity Lutheran Church in Reading, Pennsylvania from 1754-1757, Daniel Schumacher (1729-1787) recorded an entry in Latin in the congregation's record book saying that Muhlenberg had preached in Nova Scotia for three years before coming to Reading. In this entry, we are told that he had had to leave Nova Scotia because the poverty of the members of the congregation made it impossible for them to provide for their pastor's livelihood.[1]

It apears that Schumacher was the first pastor of the congregations in Halifax and Lunenburg to remain a Lutheran, though there is some doubt as to whether he was ever ordained or not; for while Peter Mischler (1732-1812) was being examined prior to possible reception into membership in the Ministerium of the United Congregations in Pennsylvania, June 24, 1769, he was asked whether anyone had ordained him. At this point Muhlenberg interjected, "Shame on such a Brutus who does not have ordination himself!"[2]

The lack of clarity as to whether Schumacher was the first Lutheran pastor in Nova Scotia is also due in part to the inducements the Church of England offered to Lutheran and Reformed clergymen to accept episcopal orders. If for the moment we can discount Muhlenberg's skepticism as to the ordination of Schumacher, then the latter is probably the first pastor who was and remained Lutheran. However, if we accept another report as accurate, namely, that Jean Baptiste Moreau accompanied 500 adherents of the Augsburg Confession from Montbeliard in late 1749 or 1750 to Halifax as missionary, and if Moreau was himself an adherent of the Augsburg Confession, then he may have been the first Lutheran pastor.[3] However, in the light of what G. Elmore Reaman says[4] it is most likely that Moreau was a Calvinist who subsequently received episcopal ordination in the Church of England. Christian Burger who was a Lutheran pastor in Halifax most likely died at sea on his return voyage from London, England where he had received episcopal ordination in the Church of England.[5] Mackinnon mentions the Rev. John Gottfried Turpel as one who had been a German minister and whose name appears in the records of St. George's congregation in Halifax. I was not able to find further information concerning him.

Mackinnon's reference to emigrants coming to Nova Scotia from Montbeliard is of more than passing interest. Located in the southwest portion of Elsace between the Voges and Jura mountains, Montbeliard (German: Moempelgard) belonged to the Dutchy of Wuerttemberg. As a result of the activity and preaching of the Calvinist, Charles Farel (1489-1565) and the reforming efforts of Duke Ulrich of Wuerttemberg (1498-1550) Montbeliard became Protestant. Consequently, among those who signed the Preface to the Formula of Concord in 1577, we find "Frederick, Count of Wuerttemberg and Montbeliard" representing the Lutherans.

Though Schumacher probably was the first Lutheran preacher in Nova Scotia with whom Muhlenberg had dealings, Muhlenberg's regard for him was not very high. In spite of the fact that Muhlenberg had recommended Schumacher to Trinity Church in Reading, Pa., as pastor he referred to him as "a scandalous vagrant preacher."[6] However, the editors of the *Hallesche Nachrichten* disagree with Muhlenberg's assessment of Schumacher's character saying he had been a learned and honorable man who lacked sympathy for the Hallensians.[7] Understandably such lack of sympathy contributed to Schumacher's decision not to seek membership in the Ministerium of the United Congregations in Pennsylvania but rather to follow an independent course of action in the many congregations he served in Pennsylvania in accordance with the inclination of his own nature.

Following Schumacher's departure from Lunenburg none other than the Lieutenant Governor of Nova Scotia, Charles Lawrence (1754-1756), issued a call in 1755 to Muhlenberg to come and serve the congregations at Lunenburg and Halifax. Muhlenberg, however, declined saying it was "made clear to me that it was not according to the will of God."[8] Unfortunately, Muhlenberg does not reveal what it was that prompted a negative response to the Lieutenant Governor's call.

At this point there seems to be a lapse of thirteen years in Muhlenberg's connections with the Nova Scotia Lutherans. Documentary evidence of a resumption of communications between Muhlenberg and these Lutherans surfaces at the synodical meeting of the Ministerium of the United Congregations in Pennsylvania in November, 1768. At that meeting a letter from the Lunenburg congregation was read. Dated June 27, 1768, the letter is omitted from the diary of Muhlenberg but included in an English translation of the record of that synodical meeting.[9]

Initially, the date of this letter is surprising, for two years prior to its writing Muhlenberg had recommended the Swedish Lutheran pastor, Paul Daniel Bryzelius (1713-1773) to the congregations in Halifax and

Lunenberg. Having left his congregations in New Jersey in the fall of 1766, Bryzelius sailed for London shortly before Christmas on the "Snow," Caspar Bertram, Captain, to receive episcopal ordination.[10] Our surprise at the date of the Lunenberg letter vanishes when we realize that the Lunenburg congregation did not want a pastor who had become an Episcopalian but one who was a Lutheran. In the view of the Lunenburgers, the acceptance of Episcopal ordination disqualified Bryzelius from occupying a Lutheran pulpit and from administering the sacrament of Holy Communion at a Lutheran altar.

Because they are heavily spiced with a mixture of sarcasm, satire, irony and discretion it is difficult to sort out Muhlenberg's judgment contained in his comments concerning the 1768 letter of the Lunenburgers. To some extent he seems to take this opportunity to chastise whose who "suppose that German was probably the language which Adam and Eve originally spoke in Paradise." He also seems to deride those who reduce the difference in doctrine between Lutherans who say *Vater Unser* and the Reformed who say *Unser Vater*. Throughout Muhlenberg's discussion of the plea of the Lunenberg congregation for a Lutheran pastor he is deferential to the point of appearing to be self-serving when speaking of the "reverend prelates, His Eminence the Archbishop of Canterbury and the Bishop of London." At the same time he is highly critical of the Anglican insistence on apostolic succession for ordination saying, "It seems that it [i.e. the English Church?] contends more for the empty shell or cicatrix of ordination in apostolic succession than they do for the kernel, the spirit of the great Shepherd and Bishop of souls, Jesus Christ, and of his dear apostles, which spirit is not locked up in a succession but is given to everyone who calls upon the Father and prays for it."

In spite of these strictures concerning apostolic succession Muhlenberg nowhere refers to the purpose of Bryzelius's journey to London to obtain episcopal orders. Nor does his having obtained these result in a break in communication between them. Nearly four years after the departure of Bryzelius for London and Nova Scotia Muhlenberg rather casually alludes to having received among his many letters one from Bryzelius.[11] That same batch of letters also contained one from "Squire Knaut, of Nova Scotia, concerning congregational matters."[12] But this entry is completely silent about the agony Lutherans in Lunenberg were experiencing because a preacher highly recommended by Muhlenberg had defected to Anglican ranks.

The distress of the Lutheran congregation in Lunenberg has been expressed in the tart comments of one of its own members, Andreas Jung. In his diary, Jung reported that Bryzelius took our children for instruction preparatory to confirmation and communion, from both Lutheran and *Reformirt* (sic), but instructed them in the Church of England doctrine, and administered to them the Sacrament according to the Church of England's form. That gave immediate cause for complaint and occasioned an open rupture in the congregation." This confessional eclecticism constrained the members of the congregation to meet in private homes where they conducted their devotions consisting of the reading of a sermon, singing and prayer.[13]

We do not know the contents of Knaut's letter concerning congregational affairs in Nova Scotia in 1770 but we may assume it familiarized Muhlenberg with the struggles going on in this British possession where civil and ecclesiastical authorities did as much as the law allowed to prevent the Lutherans from building their own church and from acquiring a minister who would not be deflected from faithfulness to his ordination vow to preach, teach and administer the sacraments in accordance with the Word of God, the ecumenical symbols and the Confessions of the Lutheran Church.

In view of the *status confessionis* in which the Lunenberg Lutherans found themselves Muhlenberg's response to their critical situation was nothing but short of astounding, though not unambiguously so. As has already been noted, on the one hand Muhlenberg was deferential and highly reverential when he adumbrated the ecclesial practices of "the English Church" i.e. the Church of England; on the other hand, as we have also seen, he was also highly critical of that self same church body. In the letter Muhlenberg addressed to the "Honored and Esteemed Sirs," in Lunenberg, dated November 15, 1771, the obsequious tone in relation to the Church of England is present to a degree which makes Muhlenberg appear to be a chattel in the hands of civil and ecclesiastical authorities whom he knew to be intentional roadblocks to the free development of the church life of the Lunenberg congregation. Written during the time when Bryzelius functioned as Anglican priest in Halifax and Lunenburg, Muhlenberg praised the English Established Church with its "upright, pious teachers, elders and members" as "our nearest and dearest friends and well-wishers."[14] Apparently with Bryzelius in mind, he admonished the Lunenbergers not to "judge a Church by one or another unworthy minister but by its Articles of Faith." Having acknowledged the validity of their request for a Lutheran minister and having expressed a willingness to honor it, Muhlenberg, nevertheless, exhorted his readers not on this account to "despise the English Mother or High Church and her ministers and missionaries," but to hold them "in just and proper esteem." "Do not judge them," Muhlenberg continued, "but be friendly and respectful toward them."

There is, however, reason to suspect the authenticity of this letter for the following reasons:

(1) Muhlenberg's diary for 1771 ends with an entry for October 2, thus making no reference to a letter written by him on November 15.

(2) The English translation of the letter appearing in *Acadie and the Acadians* seems to be based on what purports to be a copy of the German original text of the letter. This copy is signed by Heinrich Muhlenberg i.e.

without the umlaut. Whereas the copy of the letter is in Gothic German script Muhlenberg's signature is not. Nevertheless, the handwriting appears to be that of Muhlenberg or very good imitation of it. Furthermore, we know Muhlenberg had persons who acted as copyists of his diary and correspondence so that the difference in handwriting is not a compelling reason for its inauthenticity.

(3) An "N.B." appears at the end of the letter in handwriting identical with the letter itself. In translation this "N.B." reads, "Our lords, nevertheless, wanted to rob us of our right through trickery and bring us to that point through deceit. However, it is said that those who sought the child's life are dead." In the handwriting of another person – probably that of D. Luther Roth, author of *Acadie and the Acadians* – a note is entered in parentheses following the "N.B." The portion of the note which is legible reads in translation, "This P.S. has been omitted in the basic text (*Grundschrift*)." In view of this omission Roth did not include the "N.B." in his translation of Muhlenberg's letter of November 15, 1771.[15]

As is apparent from a reading of the *nota bene* of the letter, its content contradicts the letter to which it is appended. Though Roth's sympathies lay with the "N.B." more than with the letter in connection with which it appears, he chose not to include it in his narrative of the Lunenburg Lutherans. Perhaps he thought that the response of the Lunenburg Board of Elders[16] to Muhlenberg's letter expressed the sentiments of the presumably non-authentic "N.B." at the end of Muhlenberg's letter. For in that letter the Elders of Lunenburg said they had done all that Muhlenberg requested them to do without, however, succeeding in gaining the support of the authorities for securing a Lutheran minister of their own and proceeding with the erection of their own church building.

Reflection on the circumstances surrounding Muhlenberg's letter of November 15, 1771 and on the literary and textual problems to which the apparently extant manuscript copy gives rise suggests that a debate concerning its authenticity remains inconclusive.

Eventually, however, the persistence of the Elders of the congregation in Lunenburg bore fruit. In his "Notes on My Recent Journey to Lancaster and on the Synodical Meeting in That City, September 25 to October 8, 1772," Muhlenberg referred to a call from Lunenburg which appeared on the agenda of the synodical meeting. Like the German Reformed brothers and sisters, Muhlenberg reported, the German Lutherans, too had separated from the "English Episcopal Church," had built their own church and, having requested the Ministerium for years with unceasing prayers and petitions, once again were pleading for a preacher in accord with the Unaltered Augsburg Confession.[17] The Rev. Carl Friedrich Wildbahn, pastor of the scattered Pennsylvania congregations, had promised to heed the call to Nova Scotia in 1771 but reneged on it in the spring of 1772 much to the disgust of the man[18] who had come from Lunenburg to accompany him there. While on his way back to Lunenberg this man stopped in New York to see the Rev. John Siegfried Gerock, pastor of the German speaking congregation in New York (1767-1773), who himself at one time had been urged to accept the call to Lunenburg.[19] According to Muhlenberg the man from Nova Scotia "discovered little Mr. Friedrich Schultz." When Gerock presented the call to Schultz the latter immediately promised he would set out for Lunenburg and accept the call on a trial basis.[20]

It is perhaps impossible to establish whether Muhlenberg intended with the world, "little," to describe Schultz's physical stature or his character or both. In view of the negative judgments Muhlenberg expressed concerning Schultz the reference may be to his character, for Muhlenberg said of him that "it grieves and pains me that he was unable to break himself of his two faults, avarice and pride." William J. Mann, Muhlenberg's biographer, judged Schultz to be the least successful of all the missionaries sent from Halle in the times of Muhlenberg.[21]

When we consider that Schultz was without a charge when Gerock presented the call to Lunenburg to him and that Schultz did not enjoy the favorable estimate of his fellow Hallensian, Muhlenberg, it does not come as a surprise that Schulz set out for Lunenburg "at once," even though he did so "on trial." The temporary nature of his ministry in Lunenburg may be regarded as having become permanent because Schultz remained in Nova Scotia from 1772-1782, a period of ten years. Moreover, he did so without bowing to the blandishments of the Church of England, thus becoming the first pastor who was and remained a Lutheran in Nova Scotia, if one is inclined not to grant this distinction to Daniel Schumacher on the grounds that the latter was not a *rite vocatus* in the Church of the Augsburg Confession. What Schultz did after 1782, apart from perhaps having organized a congregation in Shelburne, Nova Scotia, has so far remained a mystery.

While Zion congregation in Lunenburg had the services of a Lutheran minister at least with some degree of regularity during the time of Pastor Schultz, St. George's congregation in Halifax to the north of Lunenburg had not yet enjoyed that privilege. St. George's had to be satisfied with the leadership of a schoolmaster and the intermittent services of Anglican rectors. Great therefore was the joy of the members of St. George's when in 1784 the Rev. Bernard Michael Hausihl (1727-1799), a Lutheran clergyman, came from New York to accept appointment as their pastor.[22] Although this well-educated, brilliant man from Wuerttemberg, having been ordained by the Consistory in Rotterdam, Holland, in 1752 and having begun his ministry in that same year in Frederickstown, Maryland, his first contacts with Muhlenberg and the Ministerium of Pennsylvania were not made until two years later at its Seventh Convention in New Hanover, Pa., in June, 1754.[23] Among those requesting an invitation to the convention, the report says, were Jacob Frederick Schertlin (1696-1768 (?) "and another, Hausihl by name, from

Frederickstown, Maryland." The nature of the reference to Hausihl seems distant and impersonal so that one suspects he was referred to in this fashion because he was not an Hallensian. However, that does not seem to be the case because in a letter to the Court Preacher in London, F.M. Ziegenhagen and G.A. Francke (1696-1769), the Director of the Institutions in Halle, Muhlenberg had high praise for Hausihl as a good friend of those associated with the Ministerium and as a preacher whose thoughts were well organized, edifying and penetrating. Muhlenberg, therefore, recommended him without qualification as a pastor for the congregation in Reading.[24] In the same year in which he had penned this encomium of Hausihl, Muhlenberg referred to a conference he had had on June 5 with "Pastor Hausihl (sic), *nota bene*," without explaining the reason for the cryptic *nota bene*.[25] Hausihl gained the confidence of members of the Ministerium sufficiently not only to merit membership in it but also to be included among those who examined others for membership. In his capacity as an examiner Muhlenberg was impressed enough with Hausihl to note on one occasion that Hausihl asked a candidate for ordination several "difficult questions in polemics".[26]

Though he succeeded in gaining the confidence of the Ministerium and impressed his peers with his brilliance, he did not remain in the congregations he served in Maryland, Pennsylvania, New Jersey and New York very long. We know he had difficulties with his congregation which led to a rather sharp exchange between him and Muhlenberg. When Hausihl requested Muhlenberg to counsel him as to whether he should or should not accept a call from some Lutherans who had become disenchanted with St. Michael's Church in Philadelphia Muhlenberg refused to do so on the ground that St. Michael's had had him and John Frederick Handschuh (1714-1764) as pastors. To request Muhlenberg under these circumstances to provide Hausihl with a written opinion would be like a friend asking Muhlenberg "whether he might sleep with my wife and ruin my family."[27]

The deterioration of relationships between Muhlenberg and Hausihl is evident in Muhlenberg's sarcastic reference to the former as "the great orator" who accepted the call to the dissident Lutherans in Philadelphia with a view to splitting and destroying the existing congregations.[28] Confessionally Hausihl's acceptance of this call was complicated when members of St. George's Reformed Church joined the Lutherans in the establishment of a new congregation. Consequently, at its meeting in Philadelphia, June 10-13, 1766, the Ministerium decided that Hausihl was no longer one of its members because his conduct did not conform to its rules and requirements.[29]

During the time Hausihl was pastor of the Old Dutch Lutheran Church in New York (1770-1783) his loyalist sympathies became apparent. The change in the spelling of his name from Hausihl to Houseal was symbolic of his affection for the English royal family. He became an ex officio governor of King's College, an incorporator of New York Hospital and, most significantly, "a signer of the address of New York loyalists to the British government in October, 1776," following the British occupation of New York.[30]

At the conclusion of the Revolutionary War in 1783 Hausihl and his family understandably left New York for Halifax with members of his congregation. In Halifax he became pastor of St. George's congregation. The joy of the congregation at having — at last! — a German Lutheran pastor after twenty-two years was short-lived. Francis Partridge, Hausihl's successor as rector of St. George's, has told us of the affinity Hausihl felt toward the Church of England. A year after his arrival in Halifax Hausihl sailed for England to be ordained a priest in that church. As Partridge said, it was a momentous step for Hausihl to take because it involved the admission of the invalidity of his previous ordination and a submission "to the imposition of Episcopal hands."[31]

The step Hausihl took was critical for St. George's congregation for as a consequence it lost its confessional identity. And from 1766 onward communication between Hausihl and Muhlenberg steadily diminished and, with the former's removal to Halifax, references to Hausihl in the latter's diary ceased.

Muhlenberg's connections were not limited to Nova Scotia. He also was in touch with a pastor who is regarded as a pioneer among Lutherans in a region formerly known as Upper Canada and is now a part of the province of Ontario. Like Hausihl he is numbered today among the United Empire Loyalists who settled in Dundas County following the American Revolution. John Samuel Schwerdfeger (1734-1803) became the pastor of Lutheran Loyalists in the town of Williamsburg in 1790.[32]

What prompted his removal to Williamsburg?

When reviewing his activity from the time of his arrival in Baltimore, Md., in 1753 and his ministry in numerous Pennsylvania parishes to the time he served congregations in Albany (1774-1784) and Feilstown (1777-1788), New York, one cannot escape the conclusion that Schwerdfeger did not possess the gift of accommodating himself with any degree of ease to his new environment and the people to and with whom he was called to minister. His personality manifested a penchant to involve himself in affairs in a infelicitous way. In the process of recording a number of unrelated news items and letters he had received on June 9, 1777, Muhlenberg also included an item concerning Schwerdfeger. He wrote in his diary "that Pastor Schw(erdfeger) has been imprisoned in Albany because he meddled in political affairs which did not belong to his office."[33] In evaluating this judgment of Muhlenbeg concerning Schwerdfeger one needs to bear in mind Muhlenberg's conscious and strenuous effort to remain publicly apolitical because he felt that posture to be the appropriate one for a pastor, especially in the turbulent times of the American Revolution.[34] Most likely, Schwerdfeger's meddling in political affairs consisted of his expression of his sympathies for the cause of the British crown, thus appearing to be disloyal to the colonists' side. However, his expressions cannot have been too volatile for he continued to serve his congregation in Feilstown for more than ten years after his imprisonment. But his "meddling in politics" probably contributed to his leaving Feilstown and moving to Williamsburg.

An inference from Schwerdfeger's move from Albany to Feilstown may give us a clue as to why he left Feilstown for Williamsburg. An item on the agenda of the Ministerium's convention in Lancaster, Pa., 1784, speaks of "a libellous writing of a vagabond against the Rev. Mr. Schwerdfeger."[35] In the very same year in which this item appeared on the convention agenda Schwerdfeger left Albany for Feilstown. In 1788, the year Schwerdfeger left Feilstown, the minutes of the Ministerium's convention report that Schwerdfeger excused himself in writing from being present at its sessions.[36] Does his absence from the convention signify difficulties experienced by him with the same vagabond or some other in his parish? Did he leave for that reason?

Why Schwerdfeger's ministry in Feilstown ended in 1788 and did not commence in Wiliamsburg until 1790 has remained a lacuna in tracing his activity. Information concerning this two-year period so far does not seem to be available. Since Muhlenberg died a year before this silent period in Schwerdfeger's ministry occurred, no data, of course, are available in his diaries. But the last entry we have in Muhlenberg's diary referring to Schwerdfeger tells us something about the character of both men. Writing to the Rev. Justus Henry, Christian Helmuth (1745-1825) who at the time was senior pastor at St. Michael's-Zion parish in Philadelphia, Muhlenberg referred in his memorandum to eleven guineas Schwerdfeger had borrowed on Muhlenberg's credit from the Rev. Dr. Gustav Anton Wachsel in London when Schwerdfeger was on his trip to Germany in 1769. "He is not so poor he cannot pay it," is Muhlenberg's lament after seventeen years!

In his accounting procedures Muhlenberg was scrupulous to the point of a fault. By way of contrast Schwerdfeger did not appear to be able to keep his head above water at any time.[37] The convention of the Ministerium of Pennsylvania in 1773 included an item in its agenda which read, "The necessary provision for Mr. Schw(erdfeger), because he has no place, has a wife and five children and does not have what his body needs."[38] In the light of this information we are not surprised to learn that while he was at Williamsburg "he tried to improve his still poor financial situation by claiming land grants from the British government on the strength of his stand as a loyalist during the revolution."[39]

CANADA'S LUTHERANS IN A MEDIATING ROLE?

E. Theodore Bachmann

"Make no small plans." With these words the University of Saskatchewan's president, Charles Spinks, concluded his comments to me. He was anticipating the favorable action of the University's Board of Governors to permit the Lutheran Theological Seminary to relocate on the University campus with a 99-year renewable lease. For the Board of Theological Education of the Lutheran Church in America, whose executive I then was, as well as for the Evangelical Lutheran Church of Canada and its parent body, The American Lutheran Church, this was good news indeed. And it was timed to the very day on which the merged seminary's new president, William E. Hordern, was being inaugurated.[1]

That Wednesday, January 4 in 1967 – the year of the Reformation's 450th anniversary – is a day for reflection. Here was a native of Saskatoon assuming the presidency of an improbably consolidated Lutheran theological institution. He had begun his studies at the University as a would-be chemistry major under the then new Professor Spinks. But he switched, and in due course graduated from St. Andrew's, the United Church's Theological College, located on that same university campus. Geographically he had traveled far, stayed away long, and returned full circle – yet on a different confessional wave-length. During his period of graduate study at Union Theological Seminary, New York, in the late 1940s, Bill Hordern was attracted to Luther, assisted in a Lutheran parish, and became Lutheran.[2]

To his new post in Saskatoon he brought the experience of teaching in Quaker (Swarthmore College) and Methodist (Garret Theological Seminary) schools as well as the broad concern for an informed Christian laity, as expressed in his widely used books, notably his *Layman's Guide to Protestant Theology*. But this return of the native to Saskatoon now engrafted him into a quite different context than the one in which he had grown up. Well that it was so. For his presidency, already begun in September 1966, gave a freshness of approach to the various groups of Scandinavian, German and other ethnic origins that comprised the seminary's still divided constituency. His sound theology and engaging ways, it was fervently hoped, would wear well. And so they have – down to his year of retirement, almost two decades later.

Lutheran Theological Seminary itself, now with an enrollment of about 90 students working for the first professional degree, is fully at home on the university campus. For everyone the excitement of the seminary's new beginning may well have vanished into the past, but it is worth remembering that this was – and with one exception to this day remains – the only Lutheran Theological Seminary in the Americas situated on a public university campus. Thanks to Canadian policy and practice, Anglican, United, Roman Catholic, and other communions share this kind of academic setting. For Lutherans not only in western Canada but also in many other places this juxtapositioning of Church and World can be confessionally and ecumenically creative. Indeed, it invites further reflection on what a friendly view from south of the border might call a peculiarly Canadian role of mediation. That is, of helping churches elsewhere to see themselves as others see them. Plenty of churches – and people generally – will continue to comment on Canada, or – worse – to take Canada for granted. This is particularly true of the United States. Our American Lutheran churches have a history of extending their missioning activities northward across the border. Until recent decades, at least, bigness has usually blighted a creative give-and-take between American and Canadian Lutherans. But times have been changing. And the merging of the Evangelical Lutheran Church of Canada and the Lutheran Church in America-Canada Section – January 1, 1986 – turns this particular Saskatoon story into a text for further thought. Here too, the theme recurs: Make no small plans.

I

Consolidation, like that culminating in the creation of the Evangelical Lutheran Church in Canada, as of January 1, 1986, presupposes purpose and implies greater power. Lest this sound like an overstatement, consider the context – the country in which this takes place. It is Canada, one of those nations others think of as an enabler; able to empower others without overpowering them. Giant in size, rich in resources, diverse in population origins, bilingual, member of the Commonwealth of Nations, active in the United Nations, good neighbor to the United States.

Such thoughts about Canada suggest that it has vantage points from which to help others see themselves more clearly and their place in a world of nations more confidently. If, as various occasions have demonstrated, Canada can help the weak grow stronger, it can – or should – also help the strong grow more understanding. This, as I see it, pertains especially to Canada's relations to the United States – a relationship too often taken for granted by Americans and too often found frustrating by Canadians – also in the church.

Yet here our thoughts are on church consolidation in Canada and on how the new Lutheran body – among its various functions – may also have an enabling, a mediating role. Will the new ELCIC, by virtue of being what it is and by what its predecessor bodies were, be able – as situations arise – to exercise a mediating service between, say, churches in the Two-Thirds World (they prefer that designation) and the churches in the United States or Europe? Make no mistake, the closer the churches worldwide are drawn together, the greater the need for mediating understanding as well as for enabling self-confidence to develop. The greater, also, is the need to recognize and act upon the way any mediating role in the church relates to Christ, the Mediator, and draws strength from God's boundless grace.

In the following sequence I hope that the several sections, in no strict order, may convey some thoughts that have come while thinking about Canadian Lutherans in a mediating role.

Consolidations of church bodies have, of course, a special connotation in Canada by virtue of the formation of the United Church in 1925. Aside from this event and its ecumenical implications in India, the United States and elsewhere, there is the perennial striving to bring together the churches of one confessional family, such as the Lutheran.

It is high time that Canada experiences this phenomenon. Although the prospective unanimous plan has had to settle – at least temporarily – for a two-thirds majority, the consolidation of the Evangelical Lutheran Church of Canada (1967) and the Lutheran Church in America-Canada Section (1962) carries much promise.

As consolidations go, this Canadian event has comparable developments which have taken place elsewhere earlier. Merely to name those emerging since the end of World War II excites the imagination. The Reformation's homeland led off with the formation of the United Evangelical Lutheran Church in German (VELKD, 1948). Next, the Evangelical Church of the Lutheran Confession in Brazil (1954); The American Lutheran Church (1960); Lutheran Church in America (1962); Japan Evangelical Lutheran Church (1962); Evangelical Lutheran Church in Tanzania (1963); Lutheran Church of Australia (1966); Evangelical Lutheran Church in Southern Africa (1975); and last, yet already a federation in 1926, United Evangelical Lutheran Church(es) in India (1975).[3]

The new Evangelical Lutheran Church in Canada deserves to feel at home in this company – and in much more besides. For it has long since earned its place internationally in a helping role second to none which the Canadian Lutheran Commission for War Service (1940) and then Canadian Lutheran World Relief (1946) – with its extensive resettlement activity – gratefully call to mind.

Partnership is what Canadian Lutherans, like those in other countries, have come to prize. For them, as for others – especially in the Two-Thirds

World – the early satisfactions of dependency have long turned to impatience. Politely but firmly Dr. Nils Willison spoke also for others when he reminded the United Lutheran Church already in 1941 of what he called Lutheran maturity in Canada. "I contend," he declared, "that the Lutheran Church in Canada and the Lutheran Church in the United States are, and of necessity have to be, two entities, and that the church in Canada is entitled to recognition on a basis of neighborly equality."

In almost the same breath he challenged his fellow Canadians to grow up "to a keener sense of the importance of [their church's] station in Canadian life." He urged them to "escape from that backwardness which has been the outcome of a feeling, more or less openly admitted, that Lutheranism in Canada is an exotic, a foreign element in the nation."[4]

Certainly the ecumenical movement, gaining momentum despite the war, helped also Anglican and other Protestants to emerge from their own provincialisms and to see beyond their Anglo-Saxon horizons. In time Lutheranism as well as Eastern Orthodoxy, and finally Roman Catholicism itself, would be seen as essential partners in the manifestation of Christian unity.

For Canadian Lutherans, meanwhile a new kind of supportiveness had come from the Lutheran World Federation. A quartet of delegates gave Canadians a strong representation at the federation's first assembly in Lund, 1947. I remember them well: John Schmieder, Kitchener, Ontario, pastor of St. Matthew's, the country's largest Lutheran congregation; Rex Schneider, president of Luther College, Regina, Saskatchewan; John R. Lavik, president of Luther Seminary, Saskatoon; and Nils Willison, president of Lutheran College and Seminary, Saskatoon. Lavik represented the Evangelical Lutheran Church (Norse); Schneider, the old American Lutheran Church; Schmieder and Willison, the United Lutheran Church. Together they prefigured by four decades the course of confessional unity in Canada.[5]

Two more points must be made for 1947. First, the LWF assembly adopted a policy of "encouraging as soon as practicable ... united Lutheran churches in the various mission fields." By so doing the federation strengthened the calls for unity in those countries mentioned above and in more besides. And second, Canada's own National Committee of the LWF was formed in August 1947, even though the nation as yet had no autonomous Lutheran church. The moment was opportune inasmuch as an attempt to form a Canadian Lutheran Council had just become stalled. Those of us at work in postwar Europe at the time realized how Canada's resettlement policies were ahead of those in the United States. A National Committee and World Relief reinforced each other. Characteristically, Willison thanked the ULCA Executive Board for sanctioning the formation of a National Committee and saw it as "an act of generous and farsighted statesmanship." The ALC's

Canada District was more skeptical, warning that the committee not be dominated by any general Lutheran body or agency "outside of Canada."[6] Who could that be?

Progress toward an independent Lutheran church in Canada has been more like a pilgrimage than a wandering in the wilderness. Though in either case it is possible to lose partners on the way. Norman Threinen's careful study, *Fifty Years of Lutheran Convergence: The Canadian Case* [1922-1972], covers the story perceptively. Aside from the fact that it ends before the plot explodes and the Lutheran Church-Canada retreats to prepared positions, there is so little apparent ground for a plot at all. Outsiders, and surely some insiders, must have marveled long how comparatively homogeneous and conservative Canadian Lutheranism is. The late Olaf G. Malmin, editor of *The Lutheran Standard* during the early 1960s, visited the Canada District of the ALC annually. "This is my most difficult trip," he confided as we stood near the peaceful border, "Theology is not the problem. It's ethics, custom, coffee, beer. Things like these trigger debate."[7]

The creation of actually or potentially independent church bodies gives particular significance to the decade following the LWF assembly in Minneapolis in 1957. The following year the Missouri Synod's districts north of the border were designated Lutheran Church-Canada. With the formation of the ALC in 1960, that body's Canada District was poised to become the Evangelical Lutheran Church of Canada (1967), latching on to the 1922 incorporation of its Norse antecedent district which had taken the name, Norwegian Evangelical Lutheran Church of Canada. Still farther back, the old United Norwegian Lutheran Church – the strongest missioning force in Western Canada – had formed its Canada District (1913). Even earlier, the Joint Synod of Ohio, pushing well beyond Regina, organized its own Canada District (1905).

The Lutheran Church in America-Canada Section (1962) has an interesting array of components in its background, all of them partners in the more conservative of the LCA's distant predecessor bodies. These components were the Canada Synod (1861), the German Manitoba Synod (1897), the Nova Scotia Synod (1907), and the other English-speaking unit, the Synod of Central Canada (1909) – whose initiative, as I'll mention again later, spearheaded the founding of Waterloo Lutheran College and Seminary. and the beginning of an indigenous Lutheran ministry in Canada. In addition, as an outgrowth of the Minnesota Conference, Ausgustana's Canada Conference emerged just prior to the first world war.

The distinction should not be over-rated, but the policy of the General Council to continue encouraging the formation of self-governing synods – as customary state-side since colonial times – set a tone hospitable to unity.

In its own way Missouri Lutherans picked up congregations earliest in Ontario and then extended its activity into the Prairies and on to British Columbia. Its Ontario District (1879) led the way; followed at a distance by the Alberta-British Columbia and the Manitoba-Saskatchewan Districts in 1920. These developments, interestingly paralleled others in South America, in the Missouri Synod's Brazil District (1904) and Argentine District (1928).

This spread-eagle effect over the Americas exported Missouri's spectrum of problems internationally. Australia, likewise, came into the picture. The improvement of inter-Lutheran relations that manifested itself also in Canada during the 1960s seemed particularly promising for Lutheran union. But then came the explosion in Missouri. Its effect in Canada requires an accounting.

Climate in the realms of thought and theology is sometimes as changeable as in nature's seasons. Here it suffices to note a few factors productive of change. Behind the laboriously fashioned *Affirmation and Appeal* (1970), to which the LC-C as well as the ELCC and the LCA-CS agreed, there lay 25 postwar years and a perceptible change in the "mind of Missouri." Among the factors were developments like these: the Bad Boll Conferences (near Stuttgart), convened by leaders of the Missouri Synod and of the Lutheran churches in Germany, showing exegetical study and theology in a new light;[8] the coming of a new generation of university trained faculty to Concordia Seminary, St. Louis, the brain center of the synod; a selective openness to the ecumenical movement, particularly in connection with Vatican II on the Roman Catholic side and also toward other Lutherans; participation in the formation of the Lutheran Council in the USA (1966), with its required involvement in theological study; declared pulpit and altar fellowship with the American Lutheran Church (1967-75); and sundry other developments. Inter-Lutheran relations in Canada benefited.

Unhappily, the change in the Missouri Synod was short-lived. A conservative laity, unable to understand, wondered what had happened to make traditional positions and restrictions obsolete. The ensuing revolt from the Right left the bearers of change with "no room in the brotherhood." In a book by that title, Professor Fred Danker, of Concordia, described vividly how the once huge theological seminary lost most of its faculty and student body.[9] Seminex – Concordia Seminary in Exile – became the centerpiece of the Association of Evangelical Lutheran Congregations (AELC) whose membership was nationwide but did not extend into Canada.

Instead, the 1971 convention of the Missouri Synod, meeting in Milwaukee, after animated debate and the airing of grave doubts about the situation in Canada, nevertheless voted by a wide margin to authorize a professorship on the faculty of Lutheran Theological Seminary at Saskatoon. But this is getting ahead of the story, especially with respect to the education of an indigenous ministry by and for the Lutherans in Canada – a matter of central significance.[10]

II

An indigenous ministry – native to and educated in a given country – has long been seen as a sign of the Christian church coming of age in that land. Where this indigenization happened already generations or centuries ago, it is taken for granted. But in many parts of the world, where the church is relatively new, or quite young, the subject rivets attention. Ask some veteran native Christian to tell about it on the spot, and the tale of how the first pastors were taught and called is likely to carry overtones of Jesus and his disciples. In fact, a striking aspect of the oneness of mission shows up. On the one hand, the subject is the painstakingly gathered constituency of converts from some other religion – traditionally called *foreign* missions. On the other, the eagerly assembled company of settlers, as ready-made Lutherans from elsewhere, comprise the field of *home* missions. They may be thousands of miles from home – in Australia, South Africa, Brazil or Canada – but to European as well as nearby American Lutherans – response to their need was seen as home mission.

For the Canadian scene the 1840s were a time of discovery, at least on the part of the American Lutherans. Fellows in the faith in Nova Scotia (1846, W.A. Passavant's brief visit) and in Ontario (1849, Adam Keffer's appeal) aroused the Pittsburgh Synod to action. Eventually the Canada and the Nova Scotia Synods referred to the Pittsburgh as their "mother synod."

In eastern as well as later in western Canada the initial supply of pastors was meagre. American demands for pastors far exceeded the supply, so that appeals from Canada faced stiff competition. Gettysburg (1826) was the first American seminary represented among pastors coming to Canada. Other seminaries – Philadelphia (1864), Chicago (1891) – followed suit. But especially for the German settlers in Canada – as for their larger counterpart in the States – the biggest suppliers of pastors (or ordainable graduates) came from the training schools of the major mission societies in Europe. Happily they agreed to route some of their graduates to the "home" fields in other continents whither Germans had emigrated.

Today it is well to recall that emissaries from mission institutes in Europe to South Africa assumed the dual role of reaching out to the blacks and of serving the newly settled whites. In Australia similar impulses, in reverse order, concentrated on the white Lutheran immigrants and soon thereafter included the Aboriginals and then, in 1886, pressed on to Papua New Guinea. In the Americas the mission school emissaries focused attention almost exclusively on their white fellow Lutherans, especially after some initial overtures to Indians proved difficult.

In Canada's case an initial source of ministerial supply came from Basel and some of the other major mission societies in Europe. After about 1885, and into the 1920s, an important source was the North German seminary in Kropp, Schleswig-Holstein – the institution favored by the General Council. Later on graduates from Breklum seminary – Kropp's neighbor and supplier for the more limited German-language needs of the General Synod – also found their way to Canada and, to name only Otto Heick in Waterloo, contributed significantly.[11] Graduates of American seminaries, however, took the lead in pressing for an indigenously trained Canadian ministry among the Lutherans. For example, the young English-speaking Synod of Central Canada (Ontario) in 1909 made known its decision to open a theological seminary "in federation with the University of Toronto." And immediately, from state-side, the warning lights flashed.[12]

Confessional integrity and an indigenous Canadian Lutheran ministry went hand in hand. The General Council's earlier (1907) prevention of a theological seminary being formed jointly on the Pacific coast by a synod of the Council and a synod of the General Synod (the more liberal Lutheran body) was presently repeated for Canada. At the behest of its president, Theodore E. Schmauk, the General Council had adopted the policy that no member synod should establish an academic institution except upon the Council's "Fundamental Principles"; and that "it is unwise for any synod to establish a Theological Seminary without the encouragement and definite endorsement of the General Council." The light was yellow, cautioning the Council's own regional home missionary, Milton James Bieber – also the first president of the Central Canada synod – to slow down.[13] When the seminary opened, it was not in Toronto nor in federation with the University, but in Waterloo some 40 miles away; yet it was in the heart of Ontario's Lutheran concentration. Its opening (1911) was a festival. And its direction followed the Council's advice to be wary. The danger of "unionism" with other Protestants was seen as a contributing cause of the large losses to Lutheranism in North America. Language barriers, while they lasted, were seen as safeguards. Schmauk reminded the Canadians, "The English [-speaking Lutheran] church is under a greater strain than the German in standing out for sound Lutheranism."[14]

Not the original faculty but the first graduate of Waterloo Seminary is widely remembered. Nils Willison graduated in 1914 at the age of 34. In effect he was a late vocationer in the ministry. As such, however, he brought much to it and embodied something of the creative diversity in Canadian Lutheranism. Born an Olsson in southern Sweden, raised in Ontario's Muskoka region – inland from Georgian Bay and Lake Huron – he was confirmed by the pastor of the local Norse Lutheran congregation.

Well educated (University of Toronto), he became a teacher and was a school principal prior to his call to the ministry. At the fledgling seminary – with its bilingual offerings – Willison was both a student and a tutor. As the first graduate of any Lutheran college or seminary in Canada, Willison served a parish four years. In 1918 he returned to Waterloo Seminary as professor for the next six years, whereafter he headed the Seminary's preparatory department until 1928. Returning to the parish ministry near Hamilton, he remained there until 1936. Then came his big jump to Western Canada. From 1936 to 1949 he was president and dean of Lutheran College and Seminary, Saskatoon. After three more years in the parish on Georgian Bay (Owen Sound and Wiarton), Ontario, he died in Waterloo in 1964.

Early in life Nils Willison envisioned Canada's Lutherans united into a single church. Even as his vision rose above the differences between Eastern and Western Canada, so his career unfolded and made him at home in the country as a whole.

A luminous part of his vision was the rise of an indigenous, Canadian-educated ministry. In 1940 progress in this direction reached a significant milestone. In that year, Willison reported, the halfway mark toward this goal had been attained by the three Canadian Synods of the United Lutheran Church in America. Of the then 168 pastors serving in these three synods, 51 were graduates of Waterloo, and 33 from Saskatoon. Confessional integrity and an indigenous Canadian Lutheran ministry, going forward hand in hand in the east, had already joined forces with those of like commitment in the west.[15]

The Saskatoon and Waterloo seminaries, though widely separated, have the same roots. Their rise within the same decade suggests a common sense of urgency. Their kinship stems from the Lutheran General Council and thus relates them also to the Council's other seminaries in Philadelphia, Chicago, Rock Island, and Seattle (now Berkeley). The deposits of time have obscured these roots, yet some notice of them helps us understand how it was possible for Lutherans of the three major strains to trust each other with a common education of their ministry and to do so earlier in western Canada than virtually anywhere else in North America. Indeed, mutual trust is the stuff which makes a mediating role possible.

At least for a while – beginning in 1971 – the professorship authorized by the Missouri Synod's Milwaukee convention enabled the Lutheran Theological Seminary in Saskatoon to be distinctively inclusive. This was not always the case, and the recent opening of two Canadian Concordia Seminaries – St. Catherines, Ontario (1978), and Edmonton, Alberta (1983) – may be seen as pointing to the past as well as to the future.

Happily, the history of the seminary in Saskatoon is soon to be available (a work by Professor Walter H. Freitag). Therefore it suffices here to note a few features of the past that play into the present and thus help interpret Saskatoon's significance state-side.

When Nils Willison in 1941 (above) mentioned that 33 Saskatoon graduates were then serving in the Canadian synods of the ULCA he expressed gratitude as well as impatience.[16] Gratitude that a school, opened in Saskatoon in 1914 and chartered in 1922 as Lutheran College and Seminary, had been solidly founded, well led, and faithfully supported, being thus enabled to survive through the depression of the 1930s. Perhaps it was the will to succeed – as personified in Juergen Goos, the school's first director – that made the human difference. Goos, a native of Schleswig-Holstein, in North Germany, came to America in 1887 as a graduate of the Kropp Seminary. Called and ordained by the Canada Synod, Goos served in Ontario until 1903. Responding to the perennial plea for pastors to serve in the Prairie Provinces, Goos and his family moved to Alberta, spending the next decade in congregations near Edmonton. The (German) Synod of Manitoba and adjacent Provinces, having decided in 1911 in favor of training future pastors on its own vast territory, entrusted the teaching task to Juergen Goos.[17] From the simplest beginnings (1912) in the Spruce Grove parsonage and then briefly in Edmonton, the school was relocated to Saskatoon in 1914. As its director until 1918, and one of its professors until 1939, Goos blazed the trail to an indigenous ministry.[18]

Other Lutherans no doubt had similar intentions, but trained their pastors in the States. The Norwegian Lutherans, perhaps the most numerous ethnic Lutheran constituency in Saskatchewan at the time, relied mainly on Luther Seminary of the United Norwegian Lutheran Church in St. Paul, Minnesota. The Joint Synod of Ohio – like the Manitoba Synod – was active among the various types of ethnic Germans, largely from eastern Europe and maintained a missionary seminary in Phalen Park, St. Paul. The Missouri Synod, ever ready to supply pastors to vacant German-speaking congregations, had its two large Concordia Seminaries in St. Louis, Missouri and Springfield, Illinois. For the Swedish settlers, pastors were trained at Rock Island. The indigenous venture in Saskatoon thus faced a difficult situation, but the ULCA board of Higher Education provided encouragement – also in modest financial grants as well as in the setting of standards.[19]

III

A new dimension of indigenous ministerial education opened in 1939 for the Lutherans in Western Canada. In that year the Norwegian Lutheran Church of America (1917) and the United Lutheran Church in America (1918) began to make common cause in a field still jealously guarded elsewhere as the nursery of a given church body's identity. As the Canadian counterpart to its own big Luther Seminary in St. Paul,

Minnesota, the NLCA (after 1946 the Evangelical Lutheran Church/ELC) opened Luther Seminary, Saskatoon.

True, there were various types of precedents worth recalling. The first American-trained pastors of the Norwegian Synod – after 1917 part of the NLCA – were graduates of Concordia Seminary, St. Louis. So, too, were the first pastors of the Icelandic Synod (1886) who, a decade earlier, had given Canadian Lutheranism its first doctrinal debate in Gimli, Manitoba. A little later, Norwegian as well as students of other nationalities attended the Chicago Lutheran Seminary in order to receive their theological education in the English language. Indirectly incidents of this kind benefited the Lutheran situation in Western Canada as well as in the United States. But the founding of Luther Seminary, Saskatoon by the NLCA as a church body, was triply significant. It departed from the policy of one-denomination-one-seminary. It recognized the special needs of fellow members in Canada. And it tacitly affirmed partnership – in Canada – with the ULCA, a much larger denomination with whom the NLCA was not officially in pulpit and altar fellowship.

"It is our pleasure," declared the officers of the ULCA Executive Board on October 12, 1939, "to report that arrangements have been fully consummated with the Norwegian Lutheran Church for cooperative activity in theological education at the institution in Saskatoon, Saskatchewan."[20]

At a time when Canada was already involved in the war effort, this ULCA description of the new situation in Saskatoon is particularly revealing. "The faculty there consists now of five men, two of them from the Norwegian Lutheran Church. The students all live on the [ULCA] campus and all attend the classes of all professors. Certain subjects are however specifically for the students of each general body. The financial arrangements are satisfactory to both general bodies. The charter and ownership remain as before. While there are two seminaries so far as the two Church Bodies are concerned, the faculties will operate under one schedule and a coordinated curriculum."[21]

Manifestly, this goal was attained only after long negotiations. In the process a person with the background of Dr. Willison played an important role. He as president of the College and Seminary generated mutual confidence. Not only this theological heritage but also his Swedish origin, his Norwegian confirmation, his German association and his Anglo-Saxon wife (Margaret White of Muskoka Falls) as well as his conversance with the English-oriented world made him an indispensable partner in this instance of Lutheran convergence.[22]

Space prevents commenting upon other participants, except for John R. Lavik. Named president of the newly founded Luther Seminary (Norse), his early ministry in Saskatoon preceded pastorates in Wisconsin and Colorado before he returned to where he started. It would be interesting to know how this Norwegian-Swedish, or Swedish-Norwegian presiding alliance of Willison and Lavik worked out back-stage. For his part, Willison had the strong support of the ULCA Board of Higher Education as well as of a church body which, by formal action at its 1932 convention, openly encouraged the eventual creation of a fully united Lutheran church in Canada.[23]

Affirming that "no church is greater than its schools", it remained for one like Dr. Gould Wickey, executive of the ULCA Board of Higher Education, to urge – already in the 1930s – that the Saskatoon College and Seminary be relocated on to the campus of the University of Saskatchewan. But in this he was decades ahead of his time.[24]

The extensive diversity of the Lutheran population in the Prairie Provinces both complicated and eventually accelerated the advance toward an indigenous ministry and a unified Lutheran church. On the German side, no doubt more so than on the Scandinavian, the subtlety as well as range of differences was enough to stagger many a younger pastor. What a wife of one of them wrote about parsonage life in Edmonton prior to about 1925, may be typical: "Our congregation was not large, but in the comparatively small group we had members from more than a half-dozen European countries, such as Germany, Austria, Russia, Hungary, Romania, Bessarabia, Poland, and a few from Ontario and the United States."[25]

Parenthetically, emigration was induced by the often drastic changes in living conditions in eastern European countries. Particularly after the war, the breaking-up of the Austro-Hungarian Empire and the rise of new nations, made many ethnic Germans (Volksdeutsche) as well as others ready to leave. For people whose forebears had once moved eastward to fertile farmland in Europe what could now be more daring than to emigrate westward to the Canadian prairies.

Among those of Scandinavian stock the lure of the vast expanse north of America's Great Plains was likewise strong. Unfolding in the 1890s, the movement northward from Minnesota and Dakota was dominated by Norwegians. Germans, to be sure, had already preempted many good regions in Manitoba and Alberta. But in between, Assiniboia held special promise, particularly when it was constituted as the Province of Saskatchewan in 1905. Jumping ahead with figures, by 1940 the provincial population was about 12 percent Lutheran, and most of these were of Norwegian descent.[26]

The Norse thrust into the Prairies was part of the North American westward movement. It interlinked the destinies of Canada and the United States, keeping separate by an invisible political boundary what nature had made in incomparable sweep of beckoning land. By the year 1900 four brands of Norwegian Lutherans were in the Prairie Provinces; the Synod, the Hauge, the United, and the Free. The most numerous were the United Norwegian Lutheran Church. In 1917, stateside, all but the Free had joined in forming the Norwegian Lutheran Church of America. That year its Canada District was organized, and in 1922 chartered as the Norwegian Lutheran Church of Canada.

Meanwhile, the Joint Synod of Ohio's strength among the Germans in Western Canada had increased considerably, Ohio, as we have seen, had its Canada District also. And by 1926 it had opened Luther (Junior) college in Regina. But this commitment to higher education was actually the last of several similar ventures. Five years earlier, the then newly formed Alberta-British Columbia District of the Missouri Synod opened Concordia College (1921), in Edmonton. And already in 1911 the Norwegian Lutherans in Alberta had founded Camrose (Junior) College, in Camrose.

This concern for an educated laity found various other expressions. One among them illustrates both the aspiration and frustration of the Norse rural folk. The Saskatchewan Norwegian Lutheran College Association (1911) became the supporting constituency of an academy located in Outlook, near the South Saskatchewan River and some 50 miles south of Saskatoon. John R. Lavik, then a young pastor, favored Saskatoon. The majority, however, were eager for a secondary school – and anticipated college – in the midst of the sprawling patchwork of farms and the environing congregations.[27] Today this is Lutheran Collegiate Bible Institute, Outlook, which includes coming Canadians – Chinese from Hong Kong and Taiwan – among its students. The horizon is global.

In 1911 the beginnings were slow. A young pastor, Omar Brenne, living on a homestead near Hanley, and caring for a string of new congregations, was promoter and fund raiser. By 1914 funds sufficed to begin construction. It was the same year that Lutheran College and Seminary, erstwhile in Edmonton, opened in Saskatoon. That summer, too, Canada was drawn into the first world war. In looking back, many people see 1914 as the actual end of the 19th century and the beginning of the 20th.

If global wars are, alas, the major marks of this century, the years of World War II were an agonizing period of change and adaptation. A very minor yet significant development was that during the war years three students of the old American Lutheran Church/Canada District attended and completed their studies at the two seminaries in Saskatoon – Lutheran College and Seminary, and Luther Seminary. By 1946 these three had done all their work under non-ALC faculty. The accomplished fact was an embarrassment to traditionalists in the ALC, but a new openness had prevailed. Even so, in 1948 the ALC placed one of its own men – William E. Nehrenz – on the Lutheran College and Seminary faculty and another on its board of directors.[28]

In time Missouri Synod students from the Canadian districts began attending in Saskatoon instead of St. Louis. As already mentioned, the authorization of a professorship and the placement of a Missouri man on the Saskatoon faculty (1971) marked a first for All-Lutheran theological education in North America.

There is no need at this point to rehearse the growing pains of the 1950s and early 60s. Both Luther Seminary and Lutheran College (given up after the war) and Seminary moved into new facilities – a mile apart but academically still delicately together.

Already in 1961 traces of a turning tide appeared. The will to stay together grew stronger. New facilities were needed. But on whose campus? Deadlock? The installation of Lutheran College and Seminary's new president – Walter H.P. Freitag, also professor of church history – coincided with a Saskatoon meeting (Sep. 26-27/62) of the new ALC Board of Theological Education, on which ALC President Fredrik Schiotz was a member ex officio. Their agenda included consideration of the University of Saskatchewan campus as a possible site for the ALC's Luther Seminary. This, as Dr. Schiotz told me at the time, was part of an overall ALC survey of theological institutions in Canada and on the west coast. The manifest partnership in Western Canada, he added, would also further cooperation with the newly constituted Lutheran Church in America in its Pacific Seminary in Berkeley.[29]

The LCA, meanwhile, had directed Dr. Conrad Bergendoff – executive secretary of its Board of Theological Education – to survey its multiplicity of seminaries, and to draft a master plan with recommendations. "The time should not be far off," he noted, "when the Canadian Lutherans take over the administration of their own seminaries, with the USA bodies giving such help as they can." The LCA would "concentrate for the present at Waterloo," while "it would appear the part of churchmanship to let the ALC administer a seminary in central Canada." He concluded, "We can best help Canadian Lutherans by letting them plan their work as a Canadian Lutheran Church."[30]

Acting upon this report, the LCA 1964 convention resolved that "the Lutheran Church in America approve the proposed merger of the seminaries at Saskatoon as a significant and promising move."[31]

This is a good place to pause for perspective. How dull and minor these developments among Lutherans in western Canada would be, were they not seen against a global background of ecumenical efforts to foster an abler indigenous ministry. The churches in Africa, Asia and Latin America – many of them organized and self-governing only since the end of World War II – were the outcome of earlier missionary effort and were themselves eager to spread the gospel. Only to name it is to remind ourselves that an agency like the Theological Education Fund (1958), in the exercise of its successive mandates, had made its impact also on Lutheran Seminaries in the Two-Thirds World. It would be interesting – for example, from the vantage point of present-day Saskatoon – to contrast the content of Yorke Allen's invaluable resource, *A Seminary*

Survey (1960), with the situation today.[32] The same is true of *A Theological Book List* (1960), compiled by Raymond P. Morris, and offering some 5,400 titles – suggested mainly by westerners – "to strengthen and improve the theological colleges and seminaries training for the Christian ministry in Africa, Asia and Latin America."[33] How different that inventory of seminaries or list of books would be today. Yet how striking are parallel efforts in North America. Only to mention the clustering of theological schools in some adequate university context, or to recall how Vatican II opened a new dimension of ecumenism in ministerial education, is sufficient to prompt a fresh look at what was happening during the 1960s in Saskatoon. The global, as they say, must be local to be real. So too, the local must be global to have vision.

Therefore, what was happening in Lutheran theological education in Canada during the 1960s – and which continues into the present day – has a breadth of implication – also south of the border. For it becomes clearer from the outside than, perhaps, from the inside how the course of events has placed the seminaries in Saskatoon and Waterloo as well in a mediating position.

With the merging of the two seminaries in Saskatoon came the decisive struggle over location. Pending a decision – June 18, 1965 – old anxieties again ran high. To move or not to move to the University campus, that was the issue. An autonomous Evangelical Lutheran Church of Canada was still two years away. Dr. Karl Holfeld, president of the ALC Canada District reminded the members of the newly formed board of Lutheran Theological Seminary in Saskatoon of the recent (1964) vote of the ALC convention against moving the school on to the University campus. He assailed "a small minority of nincompoops" for re-opening the question. He saw a university campus location as "status seeking." With great emphasis he told the board, "we don't need the university." Amost as if he were echoing Schmauk in 1911 against the synod of Central Canada's intention to locate a seminary on the University of Toronto campus, Dr. Holfeld warned a half-century later, that those presuming the University setting to be a place of witnessing to their faith will instead "actually lose the faith they still have." Looking back over four decades, he reminisced, "I have seen us have to fight for every inch of recognition, for every member. The other Protestants still don't know what Lutheranism is and don't, in most cases, care to know... Our danger is that we shall lose the little we have. Our business, therefore, is to stay where we are – here on 8th Street or on Wiggins... Our task is to train ministers here in this place."[34]

The board's vote to move to the University campus was nearly unanimous. A number of theological colleges – Anglican, United, Roman Catholic – were already there; others, like the Ukrainian Orthodox, nearby. Soon the search was under way for a president to head the seminary and to lead the transition from old setting to the new. William

Edward Hordern was the man to match the move, and to stay with it. Dedication of the new seminary complex took place at a service of thanksgiving on Friday, October 25, 1968.[35]

The relocation was, in effect, a re-founding of the seminary. And, in a larger sense, it foreshadowed a stronger as well as united Evangelical Lutheran Church in Canada. Besides, the very location of the seminary linked it not only with the wider world of learning but also – no longer in seclusion but in openness – with the church worldwide.

IV

Ever since the dedication in 1968 the thought has kept recurring to me that the seminary in Saskatoon exemplifies, in its own way, the mediating potential of the Lutheran Church in Canada. In 1976, while attending the annual meeting of the Lutheran World Federation's Commission on Church Cooperation, the thought came alive. I could not help but marvel at the repeated expressions of joy coming from African, Asian, Latin American, and eastern European participants. The meeting place – Saskatoon Seminary – seemed just right. Those who had come from afar found at least some things which reminded them of home. The setting on the great prairie was not over-powering with man-made structures. Nor was the country as daunting as the Super Power to the south. The host church, moreover, was no giant but of a more familiar size. Those who browsed in the library stack close by or scanned the journals or news releases in the reading room were reminded of still other aspects of the church worldwide. Yet for some all this was enough to excite envy since, comparatively, they had so little.

Commission chairman, Josiah Kibira, seemed particularly interested in learning more about the church, the people and the nation where we were meeting. He also had his own way of probing beyond the quickly given account of the Canadian scene. What, he asked a veteran synodical official, is your attitude toward and your country's treatment of its original inhabitants? How much justice have the Indians? For a moment it seemed as though this Tanzanian bishop was on visitation in his own Northwestern Diocese, by Lake Victoria, and not on business in western Canada. Yet for him – the later president of the Lutheran World Federation – the given context mattered as well as the agenda at hand.[36]

The theme of the commission meeting, "Self-reliance for Mission," was amplified from various sides. Whether in a major paper, by an astute staff member from India, or in the ensuing discussion, the theme recurred. In fact, it underlay many of the projects being reviewed by or proposed to the commission. Self-reliance was used as shorthand for a church striving, in whatever country, to become indigenous. Self-reliance was for a purpose: for mission. Self-reliance was emphasized as basic to full partnership among the churches, regionally and in all six continents. Only as partners, not simply as extensions, could there be true cooperation among the churches. Therefore it was African and Asian churches, most of them newly formed since the end of World War II, which had pressed the Federation in 1970 for the change of name from "World Mission" to "Church Cooperation."

Bishop Kibira had his own way of making the point. "The habit of breast feeding should be stopped. In my part of the world, when a mother wants to discourage a child from breast feeding, she smears 'pilipili' on the breast. This is pepper and it is hot. The child, after tasting this once or twice, decides to abandon sucking for good. The child becomes self-reliant. I think the time is not far off when God is going to use such hard methods to convince us to stop clinging to our old ways" – in mission and interchurch relations.[37]

Being editor at that time of *Lutheran World*, the Federation's quarterly journal, the meeting in Saskatoon seemed like a long succession of hinted but untold stories. The business moved from point to point *as if* the participants were already familiar with each other's churches and their stories. But they were not. Not really. Once a movement like the LWF has become an institution the malaise of assumption sets in. Pleasantries too easily obscure profundities. The agenda – what must be done – leaves too little room to convey who we are. Yet breaks come to the rescue, almost.

On the Sunday morning when we were deployed to congregations near and far around Saskatoon, I learned more than I had ever imagined about the Hungarian-speaking Lutheran minority church in western Romania. For Pastor Odon Deak was my partner that morning. As I interpreted his German into English, the minutes were all too few to convey to an interested congregation something of the promise as well as plight of his church. The people in Zion Church, Hague, were notably eager to hear, as follow-up conversations made clear. But they were also glad for the opportunity to think how their own faith and life was linked worldwide – a reality which the long trains awaiting the grain harvest suggested. But what happened to the story?[38]

From a different angle – outside the agenda again – came a story about Chinese students, newcomers in Saskatoon. Andrew Hsiao, president of the Lutheran Theological Seminary in Hong Kong, and a member of the commission, spoke excitedly to a few of us about the little group of Chinese Christians in Saskatoon and how they were making their way. They were typical of about 100 such groups in Canada and the United States. They gather for Bible study, and they eat together. There are Lutherans among them. Their host, an older man working as an assistant in one of the University labs, and a former classmate of Hsiao's in China, had come to Saskatoon several years ago. Later on he bought a house larger than he needed for his own family, ready to serve as a waystation for newcomers. He and some other Lutheran Chinese for a while attended one of Saskatoon's Lutheran churches but failed to feel at home. Now they are active in a non-denominational Chinese church – part of a missioning network across the continent and on to Europe as well as back to Asia.[39]

There were more stories like this. And stories behind the stories – if one kept asking – until it seemed that the continents were linked. The global suddenly became local. It was happening in Saskatoon, even as it had happened earlier in eastern Canada. That was 1967, Canada's centennial year – and also the Reformation's 450th anniversary – when the Lutheran World Federation Executive Comittee met in Waterloo. There, in the new facilities of Waterloo Lutheran University (now Wilfred Laurier) – complete with a striking new seminary structure – representatives had gathered from India, Tanzania, Namibia (South West Africa), Norway, Sweden, Germany East and West, Indonesia, Brazil and the United States. Three more churches were received into LWF membership: the Simalungun in Indonesia and the Lithuanian in the Soviet Union as well as the Evangelical Lutheran Church of Canada. The ELCC was warmly welcomed as the first autonomous Canadian Lutheran church body. Its president, Dr. Karl Holfeld, the featured speaker at the large banquet, shared highlights of the Canadian Lutheran story – especially that in western Canada.[40]

Nor was that all. In August that summer the ELCC also joined the World Council of Churches. Of the 11 church bodies received into membership at that time, two were Lutheran: the other one being the Evangelical Lutheran Church in Tanzania. The WCC Central Committee which acted upon these applications for membership was meeting at the time in Heraklion, Crete, Greece, on invitation of the Ecumenical Patriarch of the Eastern Orthodox Church. This also was the last time Dr. Franklin Clark Fry, president of the Lutheran Church in America, chaired the Central Committee. He had been chairman for an unprecedented dozen years, and vice-chairman since the formation of the WCC in 1948. Shortly before the next assembly in Uppsala, Sweden, he died (May 1968). At Uppsala the ELCC took its place as one of the six Canadian member churches, being represented by its president, Dr. Holfeld.

In looking back, Waterloo 1967 for the ELCC appears analogous to Lund 1947 for the LWF itself – or to Amsterdam 1948 for the World Council of Churches – inasmuch as these three events denote a chairos, a right time, a coming of age. All three events could only happen because of immeasurable preparatory work sprung from firm faith and – often through the silent deeds of diakonia – confessing Jesus Christ as God and Saviour. Indeed, the stories behind these three events included the infinite suffering and catastrophic destruction brought upon peoples of many nations by World War II. Therefore, that moment in 1967 fittingly stands out as the moment when Canadian Lutherans – as represented in the ELCC – took their place as identifiable members in the global fellowship of faith. In fact, Canadian Lutherans – like their counterparts in Brazil, Australia and elsewhere – had grown in number by their own readiness, and that of their country, to receive, welcome, and help resettle thousands of Europe's uprooted.

Those June days in Saskatoon, nearly a decade after the Waterloo meeting, brought home the fact that, in a distinctive way, theological seminaries are the conservators of the church's memory and the imparters of the church's story – especially in its more recent years. Unhappily, anyone who has taught church history knows how much time goes into the main stages of a distant past and how little time remains for the years within memory. Perversely, so it seems, the assumption is that "everybody knows what happened." But the assumption misleads, even as the often infinitely rich array of stories – also of God's wondrous leading and enabling die in obscurity. Was this perhaps true also of that little band of Chinese Christians in Saskatoon? And if so, then what has happened to the personal epics of those resettled from Europe? Has anyone outside their own kin been listening?

It is a truism – yet all too true – that the global must be local to be real. Conversely, the local must have a vision to be global – and responsible. This fact became weightier by the day in Saskatoon. It so happened that it was my responsibility at the time to write and edit a handbook which the following year came out under the title, *Lutheran Churches in the World*. To facilitate circulation, it was published as a double number of the LWF quarterly journal, *Lutheran World*. It contained brief accounts of over a hundred Lutheran churches across the world, including those not members of the LWF. Besides the current situation – which representatives from the Two-Thirds World urged be described first – each story brought the historical background and a reference to beginnings.[41]

Despite its bulk of 240 pages, it was shipped air-freight from Minneapolis (Augsburg Publishing House) to Dar-es-Salaam, Tanzania by Swissair in four days – which was said to be something of a record. The 350 copies sufficed to provide each delegate, the advisers, the staff, and most of the press with a copy. Its effect was like a large backdrop. But each reader instinctively turned to his or her own church first. Suddenly the assembly seemed like a corps of 350 proof readers, at least to the author. A sense of relief soon came in frequently overheard comments by delegates introducing themselves to each other with the help of the handbook. Typically one comment was often repeated: My church is the one on page (so-and-so).[42]

Soon the handbook came out in German translation. Copies in limited number reached the churches in eastern Europe. On a study trip in Romania in 1978 the comment of the district dean in Brasov was particularly moving. He read in the handbook every night, he said, about some church in another land, explaining, "This is my window on the world."[43]

V

By design, *Lutheran Churches in the World* included ecumenical cross-walks. Such walks, of course, were physically part of the University of Saskatchewan campus and led, as desired, to the Anglican, United Church, Roman Catholic or other schools. In Geneva such walks were the hallways of the Ecumenical Center. Even while the Lutheran handbook was in preparation, friends in the World Council of Churches took the cue. In fact, one of the Council's embarrassments was that – as a world fellowship of churches which "together confess Jesus Christ as God and Saviour" – the member churches really did not know each other.

Two things happened in close succession. In 1982, for the first time, there was published by the World Council a *Handbook of Member Churches*. Its model had been set by the earlier Lutheran handbook, and the write-ups of the Lutheran member churches were often verbatim or summaries of those that had appeared in 1977. But here at last was the worldwide context of Anglican, Orthodox and Protestant churches. Only the Roman Catholic church was missing. The timing of this publication was significant. The WCC handbook appeared just over a year prior to the 1983 assembly in Vancouver. To those who received copies this publication was not only of preparatory but also of more enduring helpfulness.[44]

The other thing that happened was the unprecedented program of worldwide church visitation. First suggested by Canada's Anglican Archbishop Edward Scott – he was moderator of the WCC Central Committee, 1975-83 – the program was carried out by teams. Deployed on brief visits to all continents, the teams comprised WCC staff members plus four or more representatives of churches in different parts of the world. This was costly and time consuming, but for many Christians it was the first time they had ever met with partners in the faith from distant lands. For those visiting as well as for those visited, the oikoumene revealed a new – and at the same time its oldest – dimension. It could be experienced as a movement, not simply as an institution.

Perhaps it is not an exaggeration to claim for fellow Christians in Canada – and for fellow Lutherans among them – a mediating role. Canadians know the feeling of being left out. They also know the joy of being included. And they are able, on occasion, to do something about it: to remind the majorities in traditional centers of numerical strength how they appear to others whom they often overlook; and to reassure minorities in younger, and sometimes much older, churches how their partnership in the gospel can count worldwide.

The 1983 WCC assembly in Vancouver did much to dramatize Canada's mediating and enabling role. The big gathering in Vancouver went beyond earlier assemblies in its balance of representation from

Asia,/Africa, Latin America, Europe and North America, as well as Australia, New Zealand and the Pacific Islands. Its mingling of Anglican, Orthodox and Protestant traditions, as well as the presence of a large number of Roman Catholic observers set Vancouver as a highpoint on the ecumenical scale. The accent on worship, climaxed in the Eucharist according to the recently completed "Lima Liturgy", set this assembly apart and embraced the sweep of the church catholic and evangelical as never before. For those present it was not an uncritical oneness, but a stirringly outgoing witness.

Earlier events in the ecumenical movement, as held in Canada, came to mind. The formation of the United Church of Canada (1925) appeared as an achievement almost before its time. The locating of theological colleges of various traditions on university campuses – even there on the campus of the University of British Columbia – stood out as an enabling ecumenical step. Its influence can be seen in India and in other lands where its adaptation has included Lutherans also. Events associated with continuing movements recalled other parts of Canada: Whitby (1947), when new directions were clarified for worldwide mission; Toronto (1950), when the Central Committee of the WCC adopted its ecclesial policy on "The Church, the Churches and the World Council of Churches"; Montreal (1963), when the WCC Commission on Faith and Order – joined for the first time by Roman Catholic observer-participants – achieved a break-through in the understanding of Tradition and the traditions in relation to Scripture. In this train of events the pre-Vancouver visitation program was in plausible progression. Nor should it be overlooked that ecumenical events – like those within a confessional legacy like the Lutheran – are best remembered geographically; where the local is host of the global.

POSTSCRIPT

More than we realize, the story is integral to the ecumenical movement – to that oneness mediated once by God's redeeming work in Jesus Christ and manifested endlessly in human response. In this context churches have their stories, and individuals have theirs. The two types of story – that of the group and that of the individual – interact and belong together. Busy times preoccupy us. The art of listening – not passively via the media but actively – is a listening-in-presence. It means *hearing each other out* and responding in person. For the telling and hearing, as churches and members go, is also under the Head of the Church who is present wherever two or three are gathered in his name.

With the newly formed Evangelical Lutheran Church in Canada, the January 1, 1986 date may become a durable reminder that also the partners – precisely because they are partners – need to have opportunity to tell each other their side of the story. They need ways of visitation and times set side in order *to hear each other out*, and to discover each other's identity in the larger setting.

To share your story you must know your story; and it is what it is only because of others. Which brings me back to the beginning of this narrative, and to the inauguration of William Hordern as the improbable first president of the Lutheran Theological Seminary in Saskatoon. Without some special recognition of him upon the occasion of his retirement being the prompter, the foregoing story would not have been told. That it is told with affection and admiration need hardly be added. But the personal motivation to write it has deep roots.

In my case, a Canadian bias spans three generations. It also joins eastern and western Canada. My maternal grandfather, John Jacob Brezing, a Basel man who wound up in Canada instead of Africa, became a pastor in the vilage of Heidelberg, near Waterloo, Ontario, in 1873. Early he drew the women in the parish into a mission study group. At the end of his first year in the parish he was able to send a gift of $34.00 to Basel for the work in Africa. In the mid-1880s he was even president of the Canada Synod of the Lutheran General Council in North America. My mother, Lydia, raised in Ontario, remained a loyal Canadian all her life; part of it in Buffalo, New York, but most of it in Philadelphia, where my father Ernest F. Bachmann was pastor of the Deaconess Motherhouse and was grateful for every Sister from Canada. Besides, the Deaconess Community's worldwide ties became a kind of advance preparation for rejoicing in the ecumenical advance during the present century.

Unexpectedly, Western Canada has strengthened this bias. My wife, Mercia, was born in Saskatchewan – not far from Outlook. The second daughter of Omar Brenne and Mary (Jensen), she was bundled off to the States already in 1914. But her father's Canadian career, launched as a home mission pastor among the Norse farm folk, and ending as the promoter of Outlook College, was mission-oriented ever after. This disposition rubbed off on the five daughters: one became a "foreign" missionary in China and the others remained "home" missioners.

In 1957, the lure of the Prairie Provinces drew Mercia and me, accompanied by our two children, to chart our way from Berkeley, California to the Lutheran World Federation Assembly in Minneapolis via the breadth of western Canada. In Saskatchewan we found roots.

So together, Mercia and I – two state-side loyal "Canadians" greet the Lutherans of Canada, and salute William Hordern whose retirement has given us the occasion to reminisce on a choice part of our heritage.

THE SEARCH FOR CHRISTIAN UNITY

Otto W. Heick

Numerically the Lutheran Church is the largest evangelical branch of the "one, holy, catholic and apostolic Church". Luther had no intention of destroying the unity of Western Christianity. The Reformer was neither a separatist nor a religious individualist. He did not want the Church to be called after his name.[1] The Church, he said, is the Kingdom of God in its earthly form. It is the first institution which God established before the home and the state. Christ and the Church belong together; neither will come to an end (I Cor. 15:24). Constituted by the preaching of the Word and the administration of the sacraments, the Church is both a visible institution and an invisible fellowship of believers. "God's Word cannot be present without God's people, and God's people cannot be without the Word of God".[2] The Roman Church too is a part of the one, holy, Catholic and Apostolic Church for "there remain in it baptism, the sacrament, the voice and text of the Gospel, the Holy Scriptures, the ministries, the name of Christ and the name of God."[3] This indicates that, in the eyes of Luther, order and liturgy are *adiaphora*. Unlike the fathers of the Anglican Church, neither Luther himself nor his followers ever composed a *Book of Common Prayer*, nor did they believe in "the apostolic succession of the ministry as essential for the unity of the Church." Instead, Luther's interest was centered in the succession of believers (*successio fidelium*). For Luther, the chief marks of the Church are the Word and the sacraments. Occasionally he added other marks such as the keys, ministry, prayer, suffering and to a lesser degree the effect of the Word in the lives of the People. Menno Simons and other radical Reformers however tried to make the Church a community of "visible saints."[4] In their eyes, the moral conduct of the human being is a dependable criterion of regeneration. Menno's rejection of infant baptism is basically motivated by this conception of the Church.

In the later Middle Ages, Germany was a highly decentralized state, political sovereignty resting not with the imperial government but rather with 300 odd territorial princes and the magistrates of the free independent city republics. Consequently, the emerging Lutheran Church was far from being an organizational entity. From bishops standing in alleged episcopal succession the emphasis shifted to the princes or magistrates as the most influential lay persons. The Augsburg Confession, for example, was signed by seven princes and the civil authorities of the cities of Nuremberg and Reutlingen.[5] The Reformation followed practically the same trend in Denmark and Norway. The success of the Reformation in these countries was the doings of King Christian III (1533-59). The Catholic bishops were imprisoned and deposed November 30, 1538. Their estates were confiscated; the King in turn assumed the payment of the salaries of the evangelical ministers.[6]

The rise of Lutheranism in Sweden was as turbulent as the success of the Reformation in England. Gustavus Vasa was chosen king in 1523. By royal decree he placed the Church directly under his personal authority (1538). In 1544 Sweden was officially proclaimed "an Evangelical Lutheran nation and both the king and parliament were pledged" never to depart from this doctrine which had now come to be. Anyone opposed to these reforms and evangelical doctrines was to be considered "a heretic and heathen."[7] But some ultra-Lutherans and some Calvinists refugees from France and Holland were to purge the Swedish church of every vestige of the papal church. Yet archbishop Laurentius Petri succeeded in maintaining evangelical freedom against both Roman traditionalism and Calvinist improverishment "in matters of organization and forms of worship".[8] Finally in 1593 all Swedish bishops officially recognized the Augsburg Confession. Ever since that time the Swedish Church has been an episcopally organized Lutheran Church. Yet this fact has not infringed upon full communion with other Lutheran churches throughout the world. Apostolic succession to the great majority of Swedish theologians is an *adiaphoron*. The unity which they confess is founded upon the Gospel. The Lutheran World Federation has its unifying principle in the Scriptures as summarized in three Ecumenical Creeds and in the Augsburg Confession of 1530, and Luther's small Catechism as a "pure exposition of the Word of God".

This liberal approach to church order makes it possible for Lutherans to hold membership in the World Council of Churches which is not a super church but rather a federation of churches with a diversity of ecclesiastical polity "confessing Jesus Christ as God and Saviour".

Article VII of the Augsburg Confession defines the Church as "the assembly of saints" or, according to the German text, "the assembly of believers" known by the preaching of the Gospel and the administration of the sacraments. This definition then unites the concept of the Church as a spiritual fellowship of believers and as an institution constituted by human activities. To obtain faith, Article V adds that "the ministry of teaching the Gospel and administering the sacráments was instituted."[9] The continuity of the Church therefore is to be seen in the succession of believers. "Thus an ambivalence of sorts seems to prevail in the Confession for the marks of the Church are limited to the Word and sacraments. Yet the ministry is regarded as essential for their operation."

This lack of precision has "caused considerable dispute among Lutherans on either side of the Atlantic."[10]

As has been said above, Luther put the administration of the church into the hands of the civil authorities. The prince was regarded as the *Summus Episcopus*. The unity of the emerging Lutheran church was strictly theological. Administratively each territorial church was independent. But this arrangement infringed upon the corporate character of the church, degrading it to a branch of government and making civil servants of the pastors. The formation of the Union in Prussia, 1817, was a striking example of a Reformed king forcing the Lutheran clergy to submit to his orders. This fact called for a re-examination of the traditional Lutheran teaching on the ministry. Some theologians began to include the ministerial office among the marks of the Church, maintaining that the Church is not only a spiritual fellowship but also a divine institution. Of ecumenical importance in this development were such German churchmen as, for instance, Wilhelm Loehe (1837-72) who founded in the village of Neuendettelsau, Bavaria, a deaconess motherhouse and a seminary for training missionaries for the foreign field and pastors for German immigrants to North America, August Vilmar (1800-1868) professor at Marburg and J.A.A. Grabau, founder of the former Buffalo Synod. Deposed from office and incarcerated by the Prussian King, he arrived with a band of followers in America, 1839, organizing in 1845 what later became known as the Buffalo Synod.

Minor differences notwithstanding, these men were agreed that a duly ordained ministry of presbyterial succession, belonged not only to the *plene esse* but rather to the very *esse* of the Church. Such a ministry, they maintained, was the guarantor of the historical continuity and unity of the Church throughout all ages. The call to the ministry, they said, was not extended to the candidate through the laity; instead, it was the clergy as a class which called and ordained young men to the Gospel ministry.

Concerning ordination, however, a divergency of opinions prevailed. Loehe regarded prayer including the congregation as the essential element of ordination. Vilmar held that ordination, though not a sacrament, is a "sacramental" function in which not the human being but God is operative for the redemption of the world. The apostolic practice of the laying on of hands "actually confers the Holy Spirit and the power to remit and retain sins, and to rule and govern the Church."[11] Grabau's view of ordination was still "higher". Opposing Missouri's congregational polity, he taught that ordination exists by divine command, that the ministry gave validity to the sacraments, and that the office of the keys was to be exercised by the ministry alone. Though called by the congregation, the pastor is by a legitimate call *"placed over the Congregation by God Himself"*, yet he has "no right to impose and execute excommunications alone without a previous verdict of the entire congregation".[12]

The various tendencies crystallized into a definite movement. In Germany the *Hochkirchliche Vereinigung* (High Church Association) was organized October 9, 1918 under the leadership of Heinrich Hansen (d. 1940) pastor of the Lutheran Church of Schleswig-Holstein. Previously, he had published a set of Ninety-Five Theses in commemoration of the fourth centennial of the Reformation. He denounced the Reformation as a deformation because most of its well-meant intentions had met with ill success. Concerning the problem under discussion, he said that "the Church as the visible kingdom of God in this world needs visible leadership and representation."[13] The most unique man of the movement was the Danish theologian, Nicholai F.S. Grundtvig (1773-1872). The source and norm of the Christian faith, he said, was to be seen in the life of the Church. The living Word has priority over the written Word for the Gospel was spread by the living word of the Apostles and the Church independent of the written Word. In the Apostles' Creed, we have the earliest confession which preceded the Bible and which is Christ's own confession imparted to the Apostles during the forty days after Easter. This view of the Apostles' Creed which Grundtvig called his "discovery" remained basic for him. The Church builds on history. Baptism and the Lord's Supper are the "life fountains" of the Church in which we meet the living Christ. The validity of the sacraments is not dependent upon episcopal succession; instead it is conditioned by the institution of Christ and the corporate life of the Church where Christ is present.[14]

A new approach to the problem under discussion is to be seen in Joachim Heubach's book *Die Ordination zum Amt der Kirche* (1956). The main argument of the author may be summarized as follows: a) The ministerial office belongs not only the *plene esse* but to the *esse* of the Church, for the Church is built through the Word and sacraments which must be proclaimed and administered. If these functions ceased the Church would pass out of existence. b) The office includes three different aspects: *vocation, benedictio, missio*. Jesus Himself is the *primus ordinator*. He calls men to the office inwardly through the Holy Spirit, outwardly through the Church, which includes both ministers and people. However, the Church speaks through its ministers. Consequently, an ordained man calls others to the ministry. c) Likewise, an ordained minister is also the *ordinator*. With respect to the latter, it is not a question as to who has the *potestas* (Loehe), or the "right" (Vilmar). Instead, every ordained man is under compulsion to call, ordain and commission, lest the Church should cease to exist. The *rank* or *position* of the *ordinator* is not a theological question but rather a matter of church order. It may be a bishop but it may also be any other minister whom the presiding officer may appoint.

The *benedictio* must not be understood, Heubach says, in the Roman sense with its underlying idea of *gratia infusa*. The grace of God is not graded. As to grace, no essential difference exists between the Blessing bestowed upon a bishop, pastor, or deacon, or even deaconess. The difference between these offices lies in the *vocatio* and *missio*. They are not all called nor commissioned to do the same type of work.

The *benedictio* does not impart an "indelible character", for ordination does not confer upon the person a new indestructible quality. Rather it commits to the person an "indelible Auftrag" (commission). Hence, ordination has a life-long meaning. To re-ordain a person who has been ordained in a church body that is faithful to the essentials of the Gospel is contrary to the nature of the office. Likewise, an ordained man cannot lay down the office without violating the commission he has received. Nor can a church or congregation retire a person. This is God's own privilege. But if through a sinful life an individual renders his service unacceptable the Blessing will turn into a curse. Like Luther, these people are united in regarding the ministry as an additional mark of the Church, likewise considering, as did Luther, episcopal ordination to be nonessential to church unity.

Though Lutherans in North America are still organically separated, they are theologically united in the Gospel as set forth in the Confessions of the Reformation. However, some orthodox Lutherans still deny that this spiritual unity is enough for church fellowship. They maintain that the Bible is not the Word of God "merely" for the Gospel. In their eyes unity in faith depends on an "errorless" Bible.[15]

Another issue is the ordination of women. While the majority of synods accepts it, the Lutheran Church: Missouri Synod rejects it as unscriptural. Theodore Jungkuntz at Valparaiso University opposes it as contrary to the creative and redemptive order of God. Commenting on Galatians 3:28, he says that Paul is referring to the spiritual equality of the sexes not to a functional equality of the male and female. W.E. Keller also at Valparaiso, rejoined in the next issue of the Cresset (January 1979) saying that the Lutheran confessions pose no barrier to women preaching and administering the sacraments. The redemptive work of Christ is more than a restoration of the order of creation. In Christ we are free from the restraint and sanctions of the order of creation. Both Walter H. Freitag and J. Robert Jacobson have eloquently defended the ordination of women in two issues of Consensus.[16]

Lutheran Union Movement

As has previously been mentioned, the fragmentation of the Lutheran church was especially pronounced in Germany. The suggestion to unite came from farsighted individuals such as F.K.D. Wyneken, a German-Lutheran pastor, affiliated with the Missouri Synod (d. 1878). The issue gained momentum when in 1866 Lutheran territories, Hannover, Schleswig-Holstein and others became Prussian and so passed under the rule of a Reformed king. This led to the founding of the General Evangelical Lutheran Conference at Hannover in 1868. The conference attracted the attention of leaders of the General Council and the Iowa Synod in the U.S.A. At its meeting in 1890, a representative from Sweden was present who presented an invitation to meet at Lund in Sweden in 1901. However, it was to be World War I that expedited the movement for closer fellowship. During the war the Lutheran synods progressively became English-speaking. They learned to co-operate in the Lutheran National Commission for Soldiers' and Sailors' Welfare. This Commission developed into the National Lutheran Council (1918) of which J.A. Morehead became the executive director. Since 1967 the organization has become known as The Lutheran Council in the United States of America. These events made the Lutheran people more world-conscious. After the war they felt constrained to undertake a ministry of mercy among the millions of suffering fellow believers in Europe. Thus a meeting of Lutherans on a truly international basis became a reality. It took place in 1923 at Eisenach at the foot of the Wartburg, Luther's "Patmos", when he had become an outlaw in 1521.

The second meeting at Copenhagen in Denmark, 1929, dealt specifically with the trials and sufferings of Lutheran minorities in eastern Europe. At the third meeting in Paris, 1935, the purpose of the Convention was declared to "bring the Lutheran churches and organizations of the world into an enduring relationship with one another in order to promote oneness of faith and confession and to ward off antagonistic and hostile influences." It also declared that the church "must help to bring about a better social order."[17]

After the Paris meeting, it was planned to hold the next meeting in Philadelphia, 1940, but the outbreak of war in 1939 made this impossible.

The first post-war assembly took place in Lund, 1947. Here the convention was re-constituted as the Lutheran World Federation. The famous theologian and bishop Anders Nygren was elected president. For the first time after the War, men from former enemy countries faced each other as brethren in a common faith. Most responsible for the formation of the Federation was S.C. Michelfelder, a pastor of the former American Lutheran Church (died 1951).

At the second assembly at Hannover, 1952, Bishop Lilje succeeded Anders Nygren as president. Its central theme was "The living Word in a responsible Church." Again Missouri sent an unofficial delegation, twenty in number.

On the third occasion, the Federation met at Minneapolis, 1957. Its broad ecumenical outreach was indicated by the presence of official representatives from the Lutheran Church: Missouri Synod, the World Council of Churches, and from the Presybterian, Methodist, Baptist and other Protestant bodies. President-elect F.C. Fry, president of the United Lutheran Church in America summarized the history of the Federation saying, "At Lund we learned to walk together, at Hannover we learned to pray together, at Minneapolis we learned to think together."[18]

The fourth assembly was held at Helsinki, 1963. It elected F.A. Schiotz, president of the new American Lutheran Church as president of the Federation. The meeting was attended by official visitors from the Missouri Synod, from the Roman Catholic Church and from a large number of other Protestant bodies. The assembly was marked by a larger and more vocal delegation from the Third World. As an important action, it was decided to make permanent the Institute for Inter-Confessional Research. "In summary, the federation has led the Lutherans of the world to lift their eyes above the limitations of language and nationality and ecclesiastical organization. It has brought them closer to unified intelligence and consciousness of solidarity than they have ever been before in the four centuries of their history. And it has enabled them to present a more effective witness to their common faith."[19]

The fifth assembly at Evian, 1970, in many ways was a turning point in the history of the LWF. Its theme "Sent into the World", directed the attention of the delegates to the social problems of Africa, Asia and Latin America whose representatives received full attention. As it should be, the next assembly was held on African soil at Dar-Es-Salaam, 1977. It elected Bishop Josia M. Kibira, of the Lutheran Church in Tanzania to be president of the LWF. Bishop Kibira regarded his election as a sign of confidence in the contribution of African Lutherans to the work of the LWF. In August 1984, the LWF met for the first time behind the Iron Curtain in Budapest. The Church exists, its was stressed, so that the Gospel of love may be voiced, but "real love is not always talk but action." Bishop Zoltan Kaldy was elected President to succeed Josia M. Kibira. His "theology of koinonia" seems to shun confrontation with the communist society in favor of the opportunity to do the work of the Church.[20]

Lutherans and Catholics in Dialogue

Following Vatican II a bilateral commission was organized. The fifth and final meeting was held at Malta in February 1971.

Concurrent with these meetings, American Lutherans and Catholics entered into a theological dialogue under the leadership of the late Paul C. Empie, General Secretary of the U.S.A. National Committee and then Bishop John T. Wright of Pittsburg. At successive meetings the committee discussed the Status of the Nicene Creed as Dogma of the Church (1965), Baptism (1966), The Eucharist as Sacrifice (1966-67), The Eucharist and the Ministry (1968-70), the Primacy of the Pope (1970-72), Teaching Authority and Infallibility in the Church (concluded in 1978), and Justification by Faith (1983).

Traditionally, Lutherans have understood justification as a declatory act of God by which he declares the sinner righteous, while Catholics following St. Augustine, regard justification as a transformative process, making the sinner righteous. Yet both churches are one in that man is saved by grace and Christ alone, though agreement on doctrine does not always imply agreement on the application of the criterion. The problem remains how to integrate the teaching of purgatory, and the expressions of Catholic piety (rosary, cult of saints etc.) in the Reformation teaching of *sola fide*?[21]

Concerning the ministry, both the Catholic and Lutheran traditions confess that the Church has the duty to proclaim the Good News to the world. While all Christians are called to minister to the needs of men, Christ has instituted a special Ministry as a particular form of service (Rom. 12:6-8, I Cor. 12:28-30, Eph. 4:7-12). In Catholic tradition there are the deacon, the priest and the bishop. In Lutheran tradition there is only one order called the pastor. Admittedly, there is in the New Testament no word congruent with the later distinction between priest, bishop or pope. The different concepts of ordination, whether sacramental or not, whether conferring an indelible character or simply affirming a call to service remains unresolved even among Lutherans themselves.[22]

Papal infallibility is a problematical issue even among Catholics. The Jesuit scholar Avery Dulles says that men who in good conscience fail to accept this dogma are not thereby excluded from the eucharistic communion of the Church. The dogma of Vatican I was culturally and politically conditioned by the liberalism of the nineteenth century. To retain its meaning, dogma can be reformulated when the environment of its origin has undergone a change. Yet the Lutheran participants made it clear that they would rather discard the term in preference to the "indefectibility" of the Church, i.e. that the Church can never fall away from Christ in its entirety.[23]

In discussing the place of Mary and the saints in the Church, German theologians from both churches tackled this problem in April 1983.[24] A Catholic representative pleaded for mutual recognition maintaining that the traditional teachings about Mary no longer justify the separate existence of the two churches. Both were agreed that Jesus was born of the Virgin Mary, and thus that Mary has a place in the divine economy of salvation. Though God is working in all, he has co-workers in his kingdom. In this way Mary may be called a co-worker with God. In order to avoid misunderstanding, however, it would be better to say that by grace Mary was active in the redemptive work of Christ. By consenting to the angel's message she became the first believer, the first Christian, the mother of the Church. The dogma of her Immaculate conception simply means that by the grace of God, Mary was pre-empted from the stain of original sin. She was in need of redemption like all men. Jesus is also her redeemer. As to the Assumption of Mary, passages like Matthew 27:52 and I Corinthians 15:23 indicate that some saints were taken up into heaven before the Second Coming and St. Paul says that believers are now seated in heavenly places with Christ (Ephesians 2:6).

Here it is appropriate to add a special note. In both Europe and America Lutherans have been engaged in a dialogue with other Protestant churches. In Germany a statement, the so-called Leuenburger Konkordie, was issued expressing mutual recognition as brethren in Christ. But on this continent, the dialogue between Lutherans and Anglicans, centering on the historical episcopate, is of special concern.[25]

In 1982, the Faith and Order commission of the WCC issued a statement on Baptism, the Eucharist and Ministry, approved at Lima, Peru.

By Baptism, men are brought into union with Christ and with the universal Church. It cannot be repeated. Both forms, "infant baptism" and "believer's baptism" embody the primacy of grace and express the response of faith within the believing community.

The statements on the Eucharist reflect the influence of the Eastern Church and of Calvinism stressing, as they do, that by the power of the Spirit the sacramental elements become the body and blood of Christ. The sacrament is a communion with Christ and at the same time communion with the believers of all time and places.

In order to fulfill its mission, the Church needs persons to publicly proclaim the Gospel. The New Testament does not describe a single pattern of ministry, but demonstrates that a variety of forms existed at different places. But during the second and third centuries a threefold pattern of bishops, presbyters and deacons became established. Churches maintaining this pattern "will need to ask how its potential can be fully developed for the most effective witness of the church." Churches which do not have this pattern will also need to ask themselves "whether the threefold pattern as developed does not have a powerful claim to be accepted by them." "Women's ministry is as fully blessed...as the ministry of men."

Concerning apostolic succession, the document says that a distinction ought to be made "between apostolic tradition" – emphasized by Lutherans – and "the succession of apostolic ministry." Churches practicing apostolic succession increasingly recognize that a continuity of apostolic faith, worship and mission has also been preserved in churches which have not retained the form of the historic episcopate. Yet these churches are being asked to realize that the continuity of the Church finds profound expression in the laying on of hands by bishops and that this sign will strengthen and deepen that continuity. Evidently the churches are moving toward unity on the basis of a reconciled diversity of doctrinal formulation and church polity.[26]

However, Pentecostals and the so-called "Born Again Christians" remain opposed to this line of thought. According to their theology, the charismatics are more important than ordained ministry. Spiritually nourished by the electronic evangelists, they are suspicious of the social concern of the established churches. They are political conservatives.

The Ecumenical Movement

Luther was no separatist nor an unyielding dogmatist. In his negotiations with Martin Bucer he was satisfied with saying that the body of Christ is present in the Supper "with" the bread (Wittenberg Concord, 1536, Engl.). The treaty of Augsburg, 1555, accepted Lutheranism as the territorial version of the Church (cuius regio eius religio).

Lutherans participated in a number of colloquies during the seventeenth century[27]. Calixtus (d. 1656) and Leibnitz (d. 1716) were working for a reunion of the churches.[28] The modern ecumenical movement has its roots in the nineteenth century, the century of world missions and of international and interconfessional youth and student organizations. The World Missionary Conference at Edinburgh in 1910 marked the beginning and that on several fronts. In 1920 Faith and Order was organized by Charles Brent, calling it "a pilgrimage to unity." The International Missionary Council became the co-ordinating agency of Protestant world missions, meeting at Jerusalem and ten years later at Tamaraam, India. In Jerusalem, the delegates wrestled with the rising tide of secularism and the uniqueness of the Gospel. At Tamaraam the delegates grappled with the implications of Hendrik Kraemer's preparatory volume, *The Christian Message in a Non-Christian World*.

Life and Work was conceived amid the anguish of World War I. It had its antecedents in the Christian social movement. Proposed by Archbishop Nathan Soederblom and seconded by the Ecumenical patriarch of the Universal Christian Conference, Life and Work was constituted at Geneva 1920.

The first plenary session was held at Stockholm, 1925, comprising complex opposites. Though basically Western, it included a large delegation from Eastern Orthodox churches. Admittedly, the absence of representatives from the Third World and Rome was a weakness. The two organizations merged into the World Council of Churches at Amsterdam, 1948. The meeting was attended by 450 delegates representing 147 churches. The Dutch theologian Visser 't Hooft was elected secretary general (he served till 1965). The International Missionary Council moved inevitably toward integration and became The Division of World Mission and Evangelization. Five official observers represented the Vatican at the third assembly at New Delhi, 1961.

Lutheran participation in the movement was rather cautious.[29] Lutherans represent a unique though minority group among Protestants who, minor differences notwithstanding, havé their roots in the Swiss Reformation. In the eyes of Lutherans, American Protestantism seems to lack something. As Dietrich Bonhoeffer said, "America has a Protestantism without Reformation". Nevertheless, F.C. Fry and Bishop Lilje played a significant part in the movement as members of the

Executive Committee of the WCC. The former was elected President at the second assembly at Evanston, 1954.

"Christ the light of the World" was the central theme of the third assembly at New Delhi, 1961. It was attended by five official observers of the Vatican. The assembly emphasized the need to manifest the unity of all Christians in each place. The fourth assembly at Uppsala 1968, stressed the need of common worship, Bible studies, ecumenical offerings and joint response to social needs at the level of local congregations. Yet unity in faith does not require uniformity in doctrinal definitions or liturgical practice. As a common confession of apostolic faith and a common witness to the world, the fifth assembly at Nairobi, 1975, was said to be of utmost importance. Without the unity of the Church, Christians cannot credibly champion the unity of humankind and of the cosmos. At the sixth assembly at Vancouver, 1983, worship was a highlight and focal point, but it was also marked by a heated discussion over WCC relations to the communist countries. Dorothea Soelle, a German theologian declared, "The bombs, I believe, are targeted to God...Militarism is humanity's supreme effort to get rid of God once and for all, to undo creation and prevent redemption leading to fullness of life."[30]

In conclusion, modern technology has created a global village. A confessional state, as envisoned in 1555, no longer exists. Not only are Christians of different persuasion rubbing shoulders with one another in daily life, but followers of the great religions of the world also are to be found on all continents offering a real opportunity for the churches to proclaim the Gospel to all nations by teaching and baptizing them in the name of the Father, and of the Son, and of the Holy Spirit.

FOOTNOTES

Abbreviations of works cited

CD   Barth, K., *Church Dogmatics*, Edinburgh, 1955-62. 3rd ed.

CRC   Carl Raymond Cronmiller, *A History of the Lutheran Church in Canada*. [Kitchener, Ontario]: The Evangelical Lutheran Synod of Canada, 1961.

CHG   Charles H. Glatfelter, *Pastors and People*, 2 vols. Breinigsville, Pa. The Pennsylvania German Society, 1980-1981.

DH   *Documentary History of the Evangelical Lutheran Ministerium of Pennsylvania and Adjacent States*, (ed.) A. Spaeth, H.E. Jacobs and G.F. Spieker. Mount Airy, Philadelphia: Board of Publication of the General Council of the Evangelical Lutheran Church in America, 1898.

DLR   D. Luther Roth, *Acadie and the Acadians*. Philadelphia Lutheran Publication Society, 1890.

EA   Luther's Works, Erlangen edition.

EF   *Existence and Faith, Shorter Writings of Rudolf Bultmann*, transl. by S.M. Ogden, London, 1961.

EPT   *Rudolf Bultmann, Essays Philosophical and Theological*, transl. by J.C.G. Greig, The Library of Philosophy and Theology, ed. R.G. Smith, London, 1955.

FU   *Faith and Understanding*, I, Rudolf Bultmann, ed. R.W. Funk, transl. by L.P. Smith, N.Y., N.Y., 1969.

GU   *Rudolf Bultmann, Glauben and Verstehen*, I-IV, Siebente Auflage, Tuebingen, 1972.

HN   *Nachrichten von den vereinigten Deutschen Evangelisch-Lutherischen Gemeinden in Nord-America absonderlich in Pennsylvanien*, (ed.) W.J. Mann, B.M. Schmucker, W. Germann. Allentown, Pa.: Brobst, Diehl & Co., 2 vols., 1886-1895.

IFM   Ian F. Mackinnon, *Settlements and Churches in Nova Scotia 1749-1776*. Halifax, N.S.: T.C. Allen & Co., [1930 ?].

JCT   Journal for Theology and the Church, II & IV, ed. R.W. Funk and G. Ebeling, Harper Torchbooks, N.Y., N.Y., 1965/7

KM I-II Keryma and Myth, A Theological Debate, ed. H.-W. Bartsch, transl. R.H. Fuller, London, 1972

LW   Luther's Works, American Edition

MJ   *The Journals of Henry Melchior Muhlenberg in Three Volumes*. (Ed. and trans.) Theodore G. Tappert and John W. Doberstein. Philadelphia: Muhlenberg Press, 1942; 1948; 1958. – Reprinted by the Lutheran Historical Society of Eastern Pennsylvania and Whipporwill Publications, Evansville, Indiana, 1982, together with the "Travel Diary of Henry [Melchior] Muhlenberg May 1-26, 1772 and July 20–August 17, 1773," translated by Helmut T. Lehmann and John W. Kleiner, vol. 2, pp. 773-808.

TK   Moltmann, J., *The Trinity and the Kingdom*, San Francisco, 1981.

WA   Luther's Works, Weimar edition

WJM   William J. Mann, *Life and Times of Henry Melchior Muhlenberg*. Philadelphia: G.W. Frederick, 1887.

C. Braaten

1. Gordon Kaufman, *Systematic Theology: A Historicist Perspective*, New York, 1968, p. 111.

2. James Gustafson, *Ethics from a Theocentric Perspective*, Chicago, 1981.

3. John Hick, *God Has Many Names*, Philadelphia, 1980.

4. Paul Knitter, *No Other Name? A Critical Survey of Christian Attitudes Toward Non-Christian Religions*, Maryknoll, New York, 1984.

5. Gene TeSelle, *Christ in Context*, Philadelphia, 1975.

6. Tom Driver, *Christ in a Changing World*, New York, 1981.

7. In my critical view this is a typical refrain in the contributions to the popular book, *The Myth of God Incarnate*, edited by John Hick, Philadelphia, 1977.

8. Eberhard Juengel, *The Doctrine of the Trinity*, Grand Rapids, Michigan, 1976.

9. Juergen Moltmann, *The Trinity and the Kingdom*, New York, 1981.

10. Robert W. Jenson, *The Triune Identity*, Philadelphia, 1982.

11. Juergen Moltmann, *The Crucified God*, New York, 1974, pp. 215-216.

12. Wolfhart Pannenberg, *Basic Questions in Theology*, Philadelphia, 1971, Vol. II, p. 139.

13. Juergen Moltmann, *The Crucified God*, p. 278.

R. Goetz

1. For an examination of the historical dynamics of the Theopaschite phenomena in modern theology, see the article which I have submitted to *The Christian Century*, "The Theopaschite Century".

2. A partial list of modern Theopaschite thinkers would include Barth, Berdyaev, Bonhoeffer, Brunner, Cobb, Cone and Liberation Theology generally, Küng, Moltmann, Reinhold Niebuhr, Pannenberg, Reuther and Feminist Theology generally, Temple, Teilhard, and Unamuno.

3. Barth, K. *The Humanity of God*, Richmond, Va., 1960, p. 51.

4. Surveying the widespread theopaschism in early 20th century England, J.K. Mozley (1926) observed that many defenders of divine impassibility had failed to think the issue through. K.J. Woollcombe (1967) still thought this was the case. See also Dawe, G., *The Form of a Servant: A Historical Analysis of the Kenotic Motif*, Philadelphia, Pa., 1963 and Lee, J.Y., *God Suffers For Us: A Systematic Inquiry into a Concept of Divine Passibility*, The Hague, 1974, for similar appraisals.

5. Dawe, *op. cit.*, p. 164.

6. *The Epistle to the Romans*, 6th ed., Oxford, 1933, p. 47.

7. Barth, K. *Church Dogmatics*, IV., 1, Edinburgh, 1956, p. 130.

8. If divine suffering is indeed the key to the real radicalism of 20th century theology, then it is Tillich, not Barth, who was theologically conservative. Woollcombe was the first to observe that Tillich barely touched the issue, and then only to warn that theologians should not ignore the matter. Tillich himself worked with an essentially 19th century liberal concept of deity.

9. CD, II, 2, (1957), p. 167.

10. Bauckham, R., "Juergen Moltmann," Cornerstone Books, P. Toon, & J.D. Spieland, eds., Westchester, Ill., 1980. Bauckham correctly indicates the importance of Moltmann's early criticisms of Barth's doctrine of the Immanent Trinity for Moltmann's doctrine of the eschatological character of God's ultimate being. This was published before Pauckham could have read "The Trinity and the Kingdom" which provides a further confirmation of his judgment.

11. The Trinity and the Kingdom, San Francisco, 1981, pg. 139-144.

12. TK, pg. 171-173, 190.

13. "By being the Father in Himself from eternity, God brings Himself forth from eternity as the Son. By being the Son from eternity, He comes forth from eternity from Himself as Father. In this eternal bringing forth of Himself and coming forth from Himself, He posits Himself a third time as the Holy Spirit, i.e., as the love which unifies Him in Himself. By being the Father who brings forth the Son, God already negates in Himself from all eternity, in His utter simplicity, existence in loneliness, self-sufficiency, self-dependence,", Barth, C.D., I. 1, pg. 552-553.

14. TK, pg. 141, 156

15. TK., pg. 55

16. TK, p. 167.

17. TK, p. 57.

18. TK, p. 172.

19. TK, p. 58.

20. TK, p. 218.

21. TK, p. 53.

22. TK, p. 106.

23. TK, p. 106.

24. TK p. 58.

25. Moltmann appeals to an essentially Augustinian doctrine of freedom to shore up his contention that God is in fact both free and under the pull of necessity. "True freedom is not 'the torment of choice', with its doubts and threats; it is simple, undivided joy in the good", TK, p. 55. This is ironic, because Moltmann must turn to the "modalistic" Augustine for a definition of freedom with which he attempts to buttress his own "tritheistic" trinitarian alternative which he claims is the only basis on which true freedom can be grounded. Yet, Moltmann begs the issue, for he leaves unanswered the question: is "the good" ontologically prior to God's loving freedom and thus the eternal criteria by which God Himself is judged? Is not the Bible suggesting the opposite? Namely, God in His loving freedom creates the good as a reflection of His own eternal goodness which He eternally wills.

26. TK, p. 55.

27. TK, p. 108.

28. TK, p. 106.

29. Moltmann's ambivalence in these matters leads to flat contradictions. He argues that "God loves the world with the very same love which He Himself is in eternity" (TK, p. 57). Yet in another context the love of the Trinity for Itself is incomplete and needs an "other" (the creature) to love in order to become "creative love." "But this inner-trinitarian love is the love of like for like, not love of the other...it is not yet creative love". TK, p. 106.

30. TK, p. 164.

31. TK, p. 106.

32. In light of the harshness of his criticism of Barth it is interesting that Moltmann's few references to Whitehead are quite benign and even appreciative. He also draws lines of contact between his own understanding of creation and that of Neo-Plotonism. TK, p. 113. Plotinus was clearly the greatest philosophic exponent of a limited deity the Western World has produced.

33. Cited in Hordern, W., *Experience and Faith: The Significance of Luther for Today's Experiential Religion*, Minneapolis, 1983, p. 90.

34. TK, p. 91-92.

35. Berkhouwer, G.C., *The Triumph of Grace in the Theology of Karl Barth*, Grand Rapids, Mich., 1956, p. 151-165.

36. Barth, *CD*, III, 2, 1960, p. 632.

37. CD, *IV*, 3, 1961, pg. 173-180.

38. It is true that Barth never began his eschatological volumes of the Dogmatics. Nevertheless, he would have had to have effected a major shift in order to answer Berkhouwer's criticism of the eschatology adumbrated in III/2.

M.J. Erickson

1. William Hordern, *New Directions in Theology Today*, Vol. I, Introduction, Philadelphia, 1966, pp. 141-42.

2. *Ibid.*, p. 143.

3. *Ibid.*, pp. 143-45.

4. *Ibid.*, p. 150.

5. *Ibid.*, p. 146.

6. *Ibid.*, p. 147.

7. Langdon Gilkey, *How the Church Can Minister to the World Without Losing Itself*, New York, 1964, p. 54n.

8. Hordern, *op. cit.*, p. 148.

9. Gabriel Fackre, "Narrative Theology, An Overview", *Interpretation*, Vol. XXXVII, No. 4, October, 1983, p. 340.

10. *Ibid.*, p. 343.

11. Belden C. Lane, "Rabbinical Stories: A Primer on Theological Method," *The Christian Century* Vol. 98, No. 41 (Dec. 16, 1981), p. 1307.

12. Gilbert Meilaender, "Theology in Stories: C.S. Lewis and the Narrative Quality of Experience" *Word and World*, Vol. I, No. 3 (Summer, 1981), p. 224.

13. Darrell Jodock, "Story and Scripture," *Word and World*, Vol. I, No. 2 (Spring, 1981), p. 133.

14. George Stroup, *The Promise of Narrative Theology: Recovering the Gospel in the Church*, Atlanta, 1981, p. 212.

15. *Ibid.*, p. 221.

16. Jodock, *op. cit.*

17. *T. Patrick Burke, "The Theologian as Storyteller and Philosopher," Horizons*, Vol. 4, No. 2 (Fall, 1977), p. 211.

18. *Ibid.*, p. 212.

19. Robert P. Roth, *Story and Reality: an Essay on Truth*, Grand Rapids, 1973, p. 9.

20. *Ibid.*, p. 11.

21. George Stroup, *op. cit.*, p. 17.

22. *Ibid.*, p. 201. It should be noted that in this chapter Stroup is using the term "hermeneutics" in a sense much broader than merely biblical hermeneutics.

23. *Ibid.*, p. 200.

24. Stephen Crites, "Unfinished Figure: On Theology and Imagination," *Journal of the American Academy of Religion Thematic Studies*, 48, No. 1, 1981, p. 172.

25. James. W. McClendon, Jr., *Biography as Theology: How Life Stories Can Remake Today's Theology*, Nashville, 1979, p. 37.

26. Michael Goldberg, *Theology and Narrative: A Critical Introduction*, Nashville, 1981, p. 38.

27. John S. Dunne, *A Search for God in Time and Memory*, New York, 1969, p. 170.

28. Robert Roth, *op. cit.*, p. 189.

29. *Ibid.*

30. *Ibid.*, p. 31.

31. *Ibid.*

32. *Ibid.*, p. 54.

33. *Ibid.*, p. 77.

34. Amos Wilder, *Jesus' Parables and the War of Myths: Essays on Imagination in the Scripture*, Philadelphia, 1982, p. 37.

35. Gabriel Fackre, *The Christian Story*, Grand Rapids, 1978, p. 14.

36. *Ibid.*, p. 15.

37. *Ibid.*, p. 18.

38. *Ibid.*

39. Stroup, *op. cit.*, p. 73.

40. James Barr, "The Interpretation of Scripture. II. Revelation Through History in the Old Testament and in Modern Theology," *Interpretation*, Vol. 17, No. 2 (April, 1963), pp. 196-97.

41. Eric Donald Hirsch, *Validity in Interpretation*, New Haven, 1967.

42. *New Frontiers in Theology*, Vol. II, *The New Hermeneutic*, James M. Robinson and John B. Cobb, eds., New York, 1964.

43. Hartt, *op. cit.*, p. 121.

44. *Ibid.*, p. 120.

45. E.g., Jerome Schaffer, "Existence, Predication, and the Ontological Argument," *The Many-faced Argument*, ed. John Hick and Arthur C. McGill, New York, 1967, pp. 226-45.

46. Soren Kierkegaard, *Concluding Unscientific Postscript*, Princeton, N.J., 1941.

47. Stephen Crites, "A Respectful Reply to the Assertorical Theologian," *Journal of the American Academy of Religion*, Vol. LII, No. 1 (March, 1984), p. 133.

1. For an account of black theology in South Africa, see Basil Moore (ed.), *Black Theology: The South African Voice*, C. Hurst & Co. 1973; Allan Boesak, *Farewell to Innocence: A Socio-Ethical Study on Black Theology and Power*, Maryknoll, NY, 1976.

2. For an account of this bus boycott, see Martin Luther King, Jr., *Stride Toward Freedom*, New York, 1958.

3. The best general history of the black church is Gayraud S. Wilmore, *Black Religion and Black Radicalism*, Mary Knoll, N.Y., rev. ed., 1983. See also Vincent Harding, *There is a River: The Black Struggle of Freedom in America*, Harcourt Brace Jovanovich, 1981.

4. *Black Religion*, Beacon Boston, 1964, pp. 142-143.

5. The best source for an introduction to Malcolm X's nationalist views is his *Autobiography* (1964).

6. The best analysis of black power is Stokely Carmichael and Charles V. Hamilton, *Black Power: The Politics of Liberation in America*, Random House, 1967.

7. This statement is found in Gayraud S. Wilmore and James H. Cone (eds.), *Black Theology: A Documentary History, 1966-1979*, Mary Knoll, N.Y., 1979. This is the most informative single volume on black theology.

8. *A Black Theology of Liberation*, Lippincott, 1970, p. 17.

9. See especially Jacquelyn Grant, "Black Theology and Black Women" and Pauli Murray, "Black Theology and Feminist Theology: A Comparative View" in G. Wilmore and J. Cone (eds.), *Black Theology: A Documentary History*, pp. 418-433 and 398-417. See also the important essay by Theressa Hoover, "Black Women and the Black Churches: Triple Jeopardy" in the same anthology, pp. 377-388.

10. An important account of black theology's contact with Third World theologies is found in G. Wilmore and J. Cone (eds.), *Black Theology: A Documentary History*, pp. 445-608. Black theologians have been involved in the Ecumenical Association of Third World Theologians' dialogues since its organizing meeting in Tanzania (1976). Since Tanzania, dialogues have been held in Ghana (1977), Sri Lanka (1979), Brazil (1980), and India (1981). An account of these meetings have been published by Orbis books: Sergio Torres and Virginia Fabella (eds.), *The Emergent Gospel* (1978); Kofi Appiah-Kubi and Sergio Torres (eds.), *African Theology en Route* (1979); Virginia Fabella (ed.), *Asia's Struggle for Full Humanity* (1980); Sergio Torres and John Eagleson (eds.), *The Challenge of Basic Christian Communities* (1981); Virginia Fabella and Sergio Torres (eds.), *Irruption of The Third World* (1983). For an interpretation of black theology's dialogue with African, Asian, and Latin theologies, see my "A Black American Perspective on the Future of African Theology" in *African Theology En Route*; "A Black American Perspective on the Asian Search for a Full Humanity" in *Asia's Struggle For A Full Humanity*; "From Geneva to Sao Paulo: A Dialogue Between Black Theology and Latin American Liberation Theology" in *The Challenge of Basic Christian Communities*; "Reflections from the Perspectives of U.S. Blacks" in *Irruption of the third World*.

11. Our first efforts to transcend the particularities of our respective continents and to create a Third World theology of liberation occurred at the New Delhi, India, conference (1981). See especially Virginia Fabella and Sergio Torres (eds.), *Irruption of the Third World*.

12. The classic description of this methodological point is found in Gustavo Gutierrez: "Theology is reflection, a critical attitude. Theology *follows*; it is a second step. . . . The pastoral activity of the Church does not flow as a conclusion from theological premises. Theology does not produce pastoral activity; rather it reflects upon it" (*A

Theology of Liberation, trans. Sister Caridad Inda and John Eagleson, Maryknoll, N.Y., 1973, p. 11.).

13. Black Theology emerged as a reflection upon the civil rights and black power movements. African theology's origin can be located as early as the 1950's and it was inseparable from the movement toward nationhood on that continent. A similar happening occurred earlier on the continent of Asia. An analagous comment can be made about feminist and other forms of liberation theologies as well. The distinctiveness of Latin theology is its careful formulation of this methodical point with the use of Marx's philosophy.

14. Again Latin Americans have been the most articulate in the formulation of this point regarding orthopraxis. See G. Gutierrez, *A Theology of Liberation*, p. 10.

15. Malcolm X, *By Any Means Necessary*, edited by George Breitman, New York, 1970, p. 155.

16. Archie Epps (ed.), *The Speeches of Malcolm X at Harvard*, New York, 1968, p. 133.

17. See especially, José Miranda, *Marx and the Bible: A Critique of the Philosophy of Oppression*, trans. John Eagleson, Maryknoll, N.Y., 1974 and his *Being and the Messiah: The Message of St. John*, trans. John Eagleson, Maryknoll, N.Y., 1977; Elsa Tamez, *Bible of the Oppressed*, Maryknoll, N.Y., 1982).

18. "Towards a Theology of Han" in Kim Yong Bock (ed.), *Minjung Theology: People as the Subjects of History*, Singapore: Commission on Theological Concerns of the Christian Conference of Asia, 1981, pp. 53-54. A further explication of this point is made by Cyris Hee Suk Moon, "An Old Testament Understanding of Mingjung" and Ahn Byung Mu, "Jesus and the Minjung in the Gospel of Mark" in *Ibid*. For black theology's use of the Bible, see my *God of the Oppressed*, New York, 1975, especially chapters 4-7. For African theologians view of the Bible, see Kwesi Dickson and Paul Ellingworth (eds.), *Biblical Revelation and African Beliefs*, Maryknoll, N.Y., 1969.

19. The questioning of the authority of the Bible was sharply expressed by several South African and feminist theologians at EATWOT's Geneva Conference (January 1983). While the attitude of many feminist theologians are well-known, the biblical questioning of South African theologians was new to me. Some North American feminists reject the Bible and Christianity as incurably sexist. For a variety of perspectives on white North American feminist theology, see Carol P. Christ and Judith Plaskow (eds.), *Womanspirit Rising: A Feminist Reader in Religion*, New York, 1979.

It is important to note that many Third World women theologians of Asia, Africa, and Latin America do not like the term "feminist" as a description of their theological work. They view it as western and thus not fully accountable to their cultural and political aspirations. They do, however, affirm the importance of women's experience in making theology. See especially Amba Oduyoye, "Reflections from a Third World Woman's Perspective: Women's Experience and Liberation Theologies" in V. Fabella and S. Torress (eds.) *Irruption of the Third World*, pp. 193-200. While black North American women do not reject the term feminist, they are not as negative in their attitude toward the Bible and Jesus as are many white feminists.

B.J. Smillie

1. William Hordern, "Political Theology," *Political Theology in the Canadian Context*, ed. Benjamin G. Smillie, Waterloo, 1982, pp. 43-60.

2. _____ "Liberation Theology in the Canadian Context," (Unpublished paper), Prairie Christian Training Centre, Fort Qu'Appelle: June 14-16, 1984.

3. Paul Lehmann, *Ethics in a Christian Context*, New York, 1963, p. 117, pp. 81f. Lehmann sees the goal of the Christian life to be maturity, not morality. Furthermore, central in every Christian life should be an "imaginative and behavioural sensitivity to what God is doing in the world to make and to keep human life." To know what God is doing in the world, says Lehmann, inevitably involves Christians in the "politics of God."

4. The Episcopal Commission for Social Affairs, Canadian Conference of Catholic Bishops, *Ethical Reflections on the Economic Crisis*, Catholic New Times, 1983.

5. *Ibid.*

6. *Ibid.*

7. 30th General Council of the United Church of Canada, Morden, Manitoba, August, 1984.

8. *Political Theology*, p. 52.

9. Roger Hutchinson, Canada/United States Consultation, "Struggle for the Church: Ideological Forces Shaping the Future and our Faith Reponses," Niagara Falls, Ontario, November 14-16, 1984. (Unpublished notes from a panel discussion)

10. *Ibid.*

11. Karl Marx, *German Ideology*, New York, (1844) 1977, pp. 52-56, p. 64. "Historical Materialism." Because Karl Marx has shaped the present discussion on historical materialism, it is important to understand his explanation. Marx starts by describing humans' "basic needs" as eating, drinking, a habitation, clothing and many other things. The first historical act is the production of the means to satisfy these needs – which means the production of material life. The second need, beyond this basic satisfaction, is the development of instruments or tools of satisfaction which create new needs. The third need is to recognise that the people who daily remake their own lives, begin to make other men and women to propogate their kind. This leads to the family. The act or procreation requires cooperation within the family which, in turn, leads to division of labour. The fourth need is the development of the modes of production to continue to satisfy demand which produces a materialist connection of men and women with one another. At this stage, with the development of the modes of production, there develops not only a more sophisticated consciousness, but also a "false consciousness." This is equated with power. Those who dominate have to create the illusion that they are superior. Says Marx: "The ideas of the ruling class are in every epoch the ruling ideas i.e. the class which is the ruling material force of society, is at the same time its ruling intellectual force." This quote is central to the theme of historical materialism because historical materialism, grounded in conrete reality, also stands in opposition to idealism.

12. Dan Westell, "Big Chunk of Business in Hands of a Few,": *The Globe and Mail*, Report on Business, August 25, 1984, p. B1.

13. *Ibid.*

14. *The Financial Post*, Toronto, May 15, 1982.

15. John Cavanagh, "Arms and the Bronfmans," *This Magazine*, August, 1983, Vol. 17, p. 15.

16. *Ibid.*, p. 16.

17. Norman Gottwald, ed. *The Bible and Liberation*, New York, 1983, p. 191.

18. *Ibid.*, p. 194.

19. Fernando Belo, *A Materalist Reading of Mark*, New York, 1981.

20. George V. Pixley, *God's Kingdom: A Guide to Biblical Study*, New York, 1977, pp. 64-87.

21. *Ibid.*, pp. 66-67.

22. *Ibid.*, p. 80.

23. *Ibid.*, p. 79.

24. *Ibid.*, p. 87.

25. Elizabeth Schussler Fiorenza, *In Memory of Her*, New York, 1984, pp. 182-183.

26. *Ibid.*, p. 6.

27. *Ibid.*, p. 350.

28. Marlene Dixon, *The Future of Women*, San Francisco, (1978), 1983, p. 43, p. 80.

29. Walter Stegemann, *The Gospel and the Poor*, Philadelphia, 1981.

30. Linda McQuaig, "Stalking the Rich in the Tax Jungle and Ending Up Being Mauled," *The Globe and Mail*, August 27, 1984.

    An Analysis of Federal Tax Expenditures for Individuals. Published under the authority of the Honorable Allan J. MacEachen, Deputy Prime Minister and Minister of Finance, November, 1981, by the Department of Finance, Government of Canada.

    GATT-FLY Report. "How to End the Depression: Self-Reliance and Economic Independence," Vol. IV, No. 5, December, 1983.

    GATT-FLY Report. "Self-Reliance for Canada," March, 1984.

31. Benjamin G. Smillie, "Alberta Religion and the Immoral Majority," *Signs of the Times*, Editors John Foster, Virginia Smith, Kitchener, 1984, pp. 17-21.

W. Wagner

1. The shift is clear also in statements, speeches and programs of the World Council of Churches, particularly at the 1983 Assembly held in Vancouver, B.C. Pope John Paul II spoke in the same vein during his 1984 visit to Canada, especially in Alberta. Social statements, study books and convention actions of the Lutheran Church in America, note its Seattle (1980), Louisville (1982) and Toronto (1984) conventions.

2. Mark 10:23-27f is paralleled at Matthew 19:16-30 and Luke 18:18-30. A growing number of New Testament scholars posit that the canonical gospels were written out of the experiences of and to strengthen particular communities of believers. The trend among these scholars is to identify the different communities supposedly addressed by the synoptic evangelists with poor and marginalized groups of Christians.

3. W. Wagner, "A Father's Fate: Attitudes Toward and Interpretations of Clement of Alexandria," *Journal of Religious History*, 1971, pp. 210-231. M. Hornschuh, "Das Leben Des Origenes und die Entstehung der Alexandrinischen Schule," *Zeitschrift Fuer Kirchengeschichte*, 71, 1960, part 1, pp. 1-25.

4. Clement may have been the first Christian writer to call a body of literature "the New Testament." He included I Clement and Shepherd of Hermas.

5. Clement may have agreed with the Valentinians that the human soul was female and would be completed in heaven with a male angelic counterpart.

6. That is, the highest rank of angels below the Logos.

7. The new level is not necessarily higher or more advanced. Depending on the soul's learning and discipline, she may enter a higher or a lower grade.

8. Whatever the socio-economic status of the original communities may have been, by the end of the first and into the second century church members included prosperous

and well-educated persons. Traces of this are in the canonical gospels (e.g., Zacchaeus and Joseph of Arimathea), other canonical works (James and Revelation), the apocryphal New Testament, and the writings of Justin, Tertullian and others.

9. *Who Is the Rich Man Being Saved* 2. Clement dealt in the treatise only with Christians. The lengthy account of John the Apostle and the repentant robber-youth may be a later addition to the text, and is not relevant to the study.

G. Watts

1. Juergen Moltmann, *Theology of Hope*, London, 1967, p. 15.

2. *Ibid.*, p. 16.

3. James Cone, *Black Theology and Black Power*, New York, 1969, p. 37.

4. Moltmann, *op. cit.*, p. 17.

5. Moltmann, *ibid*, p. 16.

6. *Basic Facts About Corrections In Canada 1984*, Ottawa: Communications Branch of the Correctional Service of Canada, 1984, pp. 8-12.

7. C.E.B. Cranfield, "Love", *A Theological Word Book of the Bible*, ed. Alan Richardson, New York, 1951, p. 134.

8. Reinhold Niebuhr, *An Interpretation of Christian Ethics*, New York, 1958, p. 188.

9. Reinhold Niebuhr, *The Nature and Destiny of Man: A Christian Interpretation*, New York, 1949, Volume II, p. 204. (hereafter cited as *NDM*.)

10. Niebuhr, *An Interpretation*, p. 123.

11. *NDM*, II, p. 85.

12. *NDM*, II, p. 85.

13. *NDM*, II, p. 85.

14. *NDM*, II, p. 191.

15. *NDM*, II, pp. 85-86.

16. *NDM*, I, p. 285.

17. *NDM*, I. p. 228.

18. William E. Hordern, *A Layman's Guide to Protestant Theology—Revised Edition*, New York, 1968, p. 161.

19. Ibid.

20. June Bingham, *Courage to Change*, New York, 1961, p. 383.

21. John Bennett, "The Contribution of Reinhold Niebuhr," *Union Seminary Quarterly Review* (Fall, 1968), Volume 24, p. 13.

22. Harry Davis and Robert Good, ed., *Reinhold Niebuhr on Politics*, New York, 1960, p. 199.

23. D.B. Robertson, ed., *Love and Justice*, Cleveland and New York, 1967, p. 270.

24. Moltmann, *Theology of Hope*, p. 17.

25. Moltmann, *Ibid.*, p. 16.

26. Moltmann, *Ibid.*, p. 227.

27. *NDM*, II, p. 290.

28. Juergen Moltmann, *Hope and Planning*, New York, 1971, p. 197.

29. Juergen Moltmann, "Foreword" in *Origins of The Theology of Hope*, by M. Douglas Meeks, Philadelphia, 1974, p. xi.

30. Juergen Moltmann, *The Passion for Life: A Messianic Lifestyle*, Philadelphia, 1978, p. 97.

31. Moltmann, *The Passion*, p. 95.

32. Moltmann, *Theology of Hope*, p. 324.

33. Juergen Moltmann, *The Crucified God*, New York, 1974, p. 70.

34. Charles Kegley and Robert Bertall, ed., *Reinhold Niebuhr: His Religious, Social, and Political Thought*, New York, 1961, p. 439.

35. Reinhold Niebuhr, "A View of Life from the Sidelines", *The Christian Century* (December 19-26, 1984), p. 1195. (A previously unpublished article written in 1967.)

36. Juergen Moltmann, *The Church in the Power of the Spirit*, London, 1977, p. 279.

37. Niebuhr, *NDM*, II, p. 99.

38. Moltmann, *The Church*, pp. xvi-xvii.

39. Moltmann, *Ibid.*, p. 279.

40. *Ibid.*, p. 89.

41. *Ibid.*, p. 112.

42. *Ibid.*, p. 191.

43. Moltmann, *The Passion*, p. 49.

44. Moltmann, *Theology of Hope*, p. 21

45. *Ibid.*, p. 9.

46. *Ibid.*, p. 48.

R. Hordern

1. Monastic vows evolved over time, beginning perhaps in the Third or Fourth Century. Some have located the critical theological shift around 410 AD in Augustine's writings against Pelagius, the Pelagians advocating that Christianity remain distinct from the Roman way of life, Augustine developing a theology of accommodation. The Pelagians were the last of the early church tradition that called for voluntary poverty as a way of life for all Christians. This was probably a more important question at that time than the matter of free will which is normally imputed to the Pelagians.

2. Gustavo Gutierrez, *A Theology of Liberation: History, Politics and Salvation*, trans. and ed. Caridad Inda and John Eagleson, Maryknoll, 1973, pp. 287-306 deals with this problem, and also suggests that voluntary poverty should be seen today as a form of solidarity with the poor in protesting poverty.

3. Martin Luther, *Ninety-Five Theses*, pp. 25-33, LW *31*: 29.

4. LW 31:30

5. LW 31:33

6. Martin Luther, *Trade and Usury*, in *LW, 45:286*

7. Martin Luther, *Explanations of the Ninety-Five Theses, LW 31:199*.

8. Luther, *Trade and Usury*, LW 45:286 n. 107.

9. *Ibid.*, pp. 287-288. This expands his comments in *Explanations of the Ninety-Five Theses*, LW 31:203, thesis 45.

10. Karl Holl, *The Reconstruction of Morality*, ed. James Luther Adams and Walter F. Bense, trans. Fred W. Meuser and Walter R. Wietzke, Minneapolis, 1979, pp. 125-126.

11. "Introduction" to Martin Luther, *Ordinance of a Common Chest, LW 45:161*.

12. The idea was later developed in *Ordinance of a Common Chest, Preface* (1523) and *Fraternal Agreement on the Common Chest of the Entire Assembly at Leisnig*; both in *LW 45*.

13. "He [the Pope] wears a triple crown, whereas the highest monarchs wear but one. If that is the poverty of Christ and of St. Peter, then it is a new and strange kind of likeness!"; Martin Luther, *To the Christian Nobility of the German Nation Concerning the Reform of the Christian Estate, LW 44:139-140*.

14. LW 44:189

15. LW 44:190, "As I see it, there is no other business in which so much skullduggery and deceit are practiced as in begging, and yet it could all be easily abolished."

16. Martin Luther, *Ordinance of a Common Chest, Preface, LW 45:172-173*.

17. "Introduction" to *Ordinance of a Common Chest*, p. 162.

18. *Ibid.*

19. Luther, *Ordinance of a Common Chest*, p. 192.

20. "Introduction" to *Ordinance of a Common Chest*, p. 166.

21. See Harold J. Grimm, *The Reformation Era: 1500-1650, Second Edition*, New York, 1973, p. 10 etc.

22. "Introduction" to Luther, *Trade and Usury, LW 45:233*. This viewpoint had been commonly accepted in the church for centuries.

23. Luther did feel that interest could be honestly charged in some situations, such as by a widow whose only means of income is lending, provided the interest rate was reasonable (4%-5%) and the lender would also share in any losses sustained by the debtor. Interestingly, Luther did not say that the practice of interest should be stopped entirely. See Paul Althaus, *The Ethics of Martin Luther*, trans. Robert C. Schultz, Philadelphia, 1972, p. 108.

24. Roland Bainton, *Here I Stand: A Life of Martin Luther*, New York, 1978, p. 183.

25. *Ibid.*, p. 184; also "Introduction" to *Trade and Usury*, p. 233.

26. Luther, *Trade and Usury*, pp. 247-248. Althaus, p. 109, writes that Luther saw "all business" as "dominated by an unlimited selfish desire for profit."

27. Holl, p. 123.

28. "Introduction" to *Trade and Usury*, p. 239. Althaus, p. 111, has a more limited conclusion: "However we may evaluate his individual judgments, the seriousness with which he criticizes economic life on the bases of love and equity remains a valid example."

29. Luther, *Trade and Usury*, p. 281.

30. Martin Luther, *The Sermon on the Mount (Sermons), LW 21:293*.

31. LW 21:14-15

32. See Holl, pp. 111-112.

33. Luther, *Sermon on the Mount*, p. 313. The Biblical backing for this statement is not solid.

34. Luther writes, "In God's sight everything which a man has left over and does not use to help his neighbor is an illegal and stolen possession; for before God one ought to give, to lend, and to let everything be taken away from him. Therefore the popular proverb says that 'the biggest big shots are the biggest thieves,' for they have the most left over and give the least," quoted by Althaus, p. 107 n. 8.

35. Martin Luther, *The Magnificat, LW 21:313*.

36. In symbols, a transcending meaning is developed only in reference to a material sign or reality; either the transcending meaning or the sign, alone, do not convey the message. As symbolic, the inward disposition of poverty is only understood with reference to the materially poor and oppressed. To develop a meaning of "poverty" that has no necessary connection with the poor and the oppressed is to develop an allegorical meaning.

37. Luther, *The Magnificat*, p. 340.

38. James H. Cone, *My Soul Looks Back, Journeys in Faith* (series) ed. Robert A. Raines, Nashville, 1982, p. 105.

39. Frederick Dale Bruner and William Hordern, *The Holy Spirit: Shy Member of the Trinity*, Minneapolis, 1984, p. 65.

40. William Hordern, "Liberation Theology and the Canadian Scene," lecture at Prairie Christian Training Centre, Saskatchewan, June 14, 1984 (xerox), pp. 7-8.

41. This is the observation of Einar Billing, as reported by Edgar M. Carlson, *The Reinterpretation of Luther*, Philadelphia, 1948, p. 97.

42. Most revolutionary movements, be they the peasants of 1525 or modern Marxists, tend to envision the coming new society as a return to some previous form of social justice that existed prior to the introduction of a distorting injustice.

R.E. Miller

1. The validity of this appraisal was borne out once again for the writer during a Lutheran World Federation sponsored speaking tour to 25 Lutheran theological institutions around the world in 1982-1983. It became clear that even third world seminaries and divinity schools, generally following western patterns, had not entirely come to grips with the issue; yet a great desire to do so was also evident.

2. Jaroslav Pelikan's definitive, multi-volume work, *The Christian Tradition: the Development of Doctrine*, Chicago, 1971ff. examines in detail the development of Christian doctrine in the West, in relation to its religious and philosophic environment. The rise of a scholar with the comprehension and technical skills to understake a similar task for the church in Asia is awaited!

3. Eric J. Sharpe, *Comparative Religion: A History*, New York, 1975, p. 7. Sharpe's balanced study and fine bibliography provide a useful entry into the history of the science of religion.

4. J.W. Sweetman, *Islam and Christian Theology*, Vol. I of Part One, London, 1955, pp. 63-65. Timothy went so far as to eulogize Muhammad, saying that "he also walked in the way of the prophets," Cf. Laurence E. Browne, *The Eclipse of Christianity in Asia* New York, 1967, repr., p. 112, *et passim*.

5. R.W. Southern, *Western Views of Islam in the Middle Ages*, Cambridge, Mass, p. 3.

6. Pelikan, Vol. II, pp. 241ff.

7. Al-Ghazali's attack on Ibn Rushd, titled *The Incomprehensibility of the Philosophers*, came from deep personal religious experience, but the premier Muslim theologian's

position also symbolized the closing of the door of private interpretation in Islam (*ijtihad*) in favour of the principle of tradition (*taqlid*), which in the course of time turned Islam into the path of intellectual stagnation. Ibn Rushd's spirited response, *The Incomprehensibility of the Incomprehensibilities* did not have a major impact; the torch of learning had been passed to the Christian West!

8. For an excellent introduction to the life of Lull, cf. E. Allison Peers, *Fool of Love*, London, 1946.

9. James Kritzek, *Peter the Venerable and Islam*, Princeton, 1964, p. 47.

10. Will Durant, *The Age of Faith*, Vol. IV in *The Story of Civilization*, New York, 1950, p. 709.

11. For Ziegenbalg see Stephen Neill, *History of Missions*, London, 1964, pp. 228ff. With respect to William Carey, it may be noted that he fitted his research into an extremely active ministry. One of the results, in collaboration with his colleagues, Marshman and Ward, was the translation of the whole Bible into five languages and the New Testament into 23 languages! Carey's personal diary, located at Serampore College, Calcutta, which contains his daily schedule, reveals his secret: intense, sustained effort!

12. Richard C. Martin, "Symbol, Ritual, and Community: An Approach to Islam," in J. Raitt, ed., *Islam in the Modern World. 1983 Paine Lectures in Religion*, Columbia, 1983, p. 56.

13. Jacques Waardenburg, *Classical Approaches to the Study of Religion*, Vol. I, The Hague, 1972, p. 480.

14. For brief summaries of the development, cf. J.M. Kitagawa, "The History of Religion in America," in J.M. Kitagawa and M. Eliade, eds., *The History of Religions: Essays in Methodology*, Chicago, 1959, pp. 1-30; Philip H. Ashby, *History and Future of Religious Thought*, Englewood Cliffs, N.J., 1963, pp. 1-47; and Kitagawa, "Humanistic and Theological History of Religions with special reference to the North American Scene," in P. Slater and D. Wiebe, eds., *Traditions in Contact and Change. Selected Proceedings of the XIVth Congress of the International Association of the History of Religions*, Waterloo, 1983, pp. 552-563.

15. Durant, *Rousseau and Revolution*, Vol. X in *The Story of Civilization*, New York, 1967, p. 512.

16. We have consistently used the phrase "religions and religion" in this essay for the simple reason that religion can only be met with and only becomes visible in the religions.

17. Waardenburg, Vol. I, p. 93.

18. *The Future of Religions*, New York, 1966, p. 91.

19. Quoted from a speech in Staten Island, New York, 1954, by Hans Werner-Gensichen, "The Legacy of Walter Freytag," in *International Bulletin, Vol. 5, No. 1, January 1981, p. 17. First reported by Max A.C. Warren, "The Thought and Practice of Missions: Notes on Walter Freytag's Contribution," in J. Hemerlink and H.J. Margull, eds., Basileia. Walter Freytag zum 60. Geburtstag*, Stuttgart, 1959, p. 146. Freytag's Gospel *The and the Religions: A Biblical Inquiry*, I.M.C. Research Pamphlet No. 5, London, 1957, is a small jewel.

20. It cannot be gainsaid that a well-rounded curriculum in theological education for today would also include exposure to these "isms" of our society, as well as to the classical religions. The place of the pseudo-religions in *religionswissenschaft* is regularly debated; the discussion must be placed against the background of the distinction between the sacred and the profane.

21. The writer recalls an earnest discussion with Dr. Martin Scharlemann of Concordia Seminary, St. Louis, in the mid-1960's, in which the latter affirmed that every divinity

school should desirably have a department of philosophy and religion alongside the classical divisions of learning in theological studies.

22. Paul Tillich, *The Future of Religions*, p. 88. Tillich also deals with this point in his *Christianity and the Encounter of the World Religions*, New York, 1963, pp. 90ff., where he remarks that "the Bible is God's fight against religion," and in his *Systematic Theology*, Vol. III (Chicago; University of Chicago Press, 1967), pp. 104ff., where he rephrases the thought to say: "One can read the history of religions, especially of the great religions, as a continuous struggle against religion for the sake of the holy itself. Christianity claims that in the Cross of Jesus Christ the final victory in that struggle has been reached..."

A. Leske

1. William Hordern, *Living by Grace*, Philadelphia, 1975, pp. 33, 38.

2. This article constitutes an expansion of my paper, "Covenant Implications in Paul's Concept of Justification by Faith," delivered to the Canadian Society of Biblical Studies in Ottawa, 1982.

3. E.R. Achtemeier, "Righteousness in the OT," *The Interpreter's Dictionary of the Bible*, New York, 1962, IV, 80-84.

4. As it is elsewhere in a number of places, e.g. Is. 1:24: 11:5: Jer. 4:2.

5. The verb *yadae* is used often to imply intimacy in the covenant relationship. Cf. Jer. 9:24; 22:16; 31:34; Is. 5:13; 53:11.

6. The punishing aspect of God's righteousness is really the other side of the coin and is not as rare as Carl Graesser, Jr. states in his fine article, "Righteousness, Human and Divine," *Currents in Theology and Mission*, X/3(June, 1983), p. 139.

7. W.D. Davies, *Paul and Rabbinic Judaism: Some Rabbinic Elements in Pauline Theology*, New York, 1948, p. 261.

8. G.E. Mendenhall, "Covenant," *The Interpreter's Dictionary of the Bible*, I, 721.

9. E.P. Sanders, *Paul and Palestinian Judaism: A Comparison of Patterns of Religion*, Philadelphia, 1977, p. 180.

10. *Ibid.*, p. 204. I must agree with Sanders that the Rabbis still saw salvation as dependent on God's mercy in the covenant relationship and that their good works did not *earn* salvation but *maintained* that relationship. However, in the popular theology the continual emphasis on obedience to the law may very well have been understood as meritorious.

11. Cf. Matt. 6:1-20.

12. Cf. Sanders, pp. 421-422.

13. I find myself in complete disagreement with the thesis of Benno Przybylski, *Righteousness in Matthew and his World of Thought*, Cambridge, 1980, p. 87, who defines *dikaiosyne* in this passage as "conduct according to a norm which in this case is the law." He goes on to say that the disciples are exhorted "to live according to a different interpretation of the law, namely, an extremely meticulous and strict interpretation which appears to be based on a [rabbinic] principle related to making a fence around Torah." He is saying that a higher form of legalism is being advocated.

14. Cf. C.B. Caird, *Principalities and Powers: A Study in Pauline Theology*, Oxford, 1956, pp. 43-45. See also H. Berkhof, *Christ and the Powers*, translated from the Dutch by J.H.Y. Scottsdale, Pennsylvania, 1962, p. 16.

15. Against Sanders, pp. 496-497, who makes the Gentile question and the exclusivism of Paul's soteriology the reason for Paul's rejection of the law.

16. Ernst Käsemann in his *New Testament Questions of Today*, London, 1969, pp. 177-178 sees the idea of covenant faithfulness in the term "righteousness" and defines the latter as conveying the sense of a relationship (p. 172). But it goes beyond that. For him, God's righteousness is "God's sovereignty over the world revealing itself eschatologically in Jesus." (p. 180)

17. Davies, pp. 221-222.

Freitag

1. An Attempt to Understand Him, *KM II*, p. 123.

2. The article may conveniently be found in *KM I*, p. 1 ff.; a new translation is contained in *Rudolf Bultmann, New Testament Mythology and Other Basic Writings*, ed. and transl. by S.M. Ogden, Philadelphia, Pa., 1984, p. 1 ff. (hereinafter Ogden).

3. W. Hordern, *Layman's Guide to Protestant Theology*, N.Y., N.Y., (rev. edit.), p. 191.

4. *Luther's Vorlesung ueber den Roemerbrief, 1515/16, Die Scholien*, (hereinafter J. Ficker).

5. *Paulus und Luther ueber dem Menschen*, Guetersloh, 1938, 2nd edit., 1951.

6. *Der Christ und die Bergpredigt nach Luther's Deutung*, 1933.

7. *Die Verkuendigung Jesu Christi*, 1948.

8. Christ the End of the Law, *EPT*, p. 49.

9. The Significance of 'Dialectical Theology' for the Scientific Study of the New Testament (1928), *FU*, p. 154.

10. Bultmann, R., *Jesus Christ and Mythology*, N.Y., N.Y., 1958, p. 54.

11. Grace and Freedom (1948), *EPT*, p. 175: Luther, Scholia on Rom. 8:26 – "Semper ita fit, ut opus nostrum intelligamus, antiquam fiat, Dei autem opus non intelligimus, donec factum fuerit." Latin text again in Humanism and Christianity (1948), *EPT*, p. 157. A slightly different English version in The Question of Wonder, *FU*, p. 256, ftn. 9.

12. What Does It Mean to Speak of God?, (1925), *FU*, p. 53fff.

13. On the Question of Christology (1927), *FU*, p. 117; see also Theology as Science (1941), *Ogden*, p. 51ff.

14. *Ibid.*

15. Grace and Freedom, (1948), *EPT*, p. 175.

16. Cf. R. Bultmann, *Jesus Christ and Mythology*, p. 63/4.

17. Echte und saekularisierte Verkuendigung im 20. Jahrhundert, (1055), *GU III*, p. 124ff. See also Theology as Science (1941), *Ogden*, esp. p. 58 ff. Also, General Truths and Proclamation (1957), *JTC 4*, p. 154.

18. On the Question of Christology (1927), *FU*, p. 124-7.

19. Liberal Theology and the Latest Theological Movement, *FU*, p. 28ff. Bultmann deals with these areas in another way when he set the various Weltanschauungen in the sharpest contrast to faith in the article, The Crisis in Belief (1931), EPT, p. 8f.

20. The Question of Wonder, *FU*, p. 253, ftn. 6. Luther on Rom. 8.26 in J. Ficker, p. 204, lines 11ff.

21. Question of Natural Revelation (1941), *EPT*, p. 113. ftn. 1. Luther on Rom. 3:5, J. Ficker II, p. 67, 21-23. Latin in text is: Et ita Deus per suum exire nos facit ad nos; ipsos introire et per sui cognitionem infert nobis et nostri cognitionem. A different English version in R. Bultmann, *Jesus Christ and Mythology*, p. 76. See also *Ogden*, p. 115.

22. Liberal Theology and the Latest Theological Movement (1924), *FU*, p. 47.

23. What Does It Mean To Speak Of God? (1925), *FU*, p. 63.

24. *Ibid.*

25. The Significance of Jewish Old Tradition for the Christian West (1950), *EPT*, p. 271; cf. Humanism and Christianity, *EPT*, p. 157f., and The Significance of the Idea of Freedom for Western Civilization, *EPT*, p. 309. The point is made much earlier in Historical and Supra-Historical Religion in Christianity (1926), *FU*, p. 110.

26. Grace and Freedom, *EPT*, esp. p. 174/5. Frequent references in Bultmann's articles on this point.

27. The classic statement is found in Bultmann's preliminary remarks on Paul's theology in *New Testament Theology*, N.Y., N.Y., 1951, transl. by K. Grobel, p. 190f. Refer also to Liberal Theology and the Latest Theological Movement, (1924), *FU*, p. 51; The Meaning of Christian Faith in Creation (1936), *EF*, esp. 249ff. Man Between the Times, (1952), *EF*, and The Historicity of Man and Faith, (1930), *EF*, p. 106ff., the last from the angle of existential analysis.

28. On the Question of Christology (1927), *FU*, p. 139, citing Luther, EA, vol. 10, p. 162f.

29. See, for example, The Crisis in Belief, (1931), *EPT*, p. 11: "For Christianity belief in God is not belief and trust in God as a general principle, but belief in a definite Word, proclaimed to the believer. The event is *Jesus Christ*, in whom, as the New Testament says, God has spoken, and whom the New Testament itself calls 'the Word'." Bultmann cites pungent statements of Luther in this connection. Bultmann deals at length with the idea in The Concept of the Word of God in the New Testament, *EPT*, p. 286fff. See also On the Question of Christology, *FU*, p. 122f, 137ff., and for Luther citations, p. 143.

30. The Primitive Christian Kerygma and the Historical Jesus (1962), *The Historical Jesus and the Kerygmatic Christ, Essays on the New Quest of the Historical Jesus*, transl. and ed. by C.E. Braaten and R.A. Harrisville, N.Y., N.Y., 1964, p. 42.

31. H.W. Bartsch's article on The Present State of the Debate (1954), *KM II*, treats the various positions of scholars and the ecclesial reaction to Bultmann's program. See also specific articles by such authors as K. Jaspers and F. Buri.

32. Rudolf Bultmann, Bultmann Replies to his Critics, *KU I*, p. 191ff. clearly demonstrates the parallels between his own theology and that of Luther. Cf. to On the Problem of Demythologizing, (1952), *Ogden*, p. 119.

33. Both citations in the article On the Question of Christology, *FU*, p. 138.

34. What Does It Mean To Speak of God? (1925), *FU*, p. 64.

35. *Op. cit.*, p. 138.

36. *Ibid.*, p. 143. Fides non ideo iustificat aut salvat quia ipsa sit opus per se dignum, sed tantum quia accepit misericordiam promissum. Apol. Conf., II, p. 56.

37. On The Problem of Demythologizing, *Ogden*, p. 119; cf. to R. Bultmann, *Jesus Christ and Mythology*, p. 78 and Bultmann Replies to His Critics, KM I, p. 206.

38. What Does It Mean To Speak Of God? (1925), *FU*, p. 64.

39. Transl. by K.E. Crum, Richmond, Va., 1967, p. 23.

40. *Ibid.*

41. *Ibid.*, p. 31, ftn. 9.

42. Christ the End of the Law (1940), *EPT*, p. 63. But Bultmann also insists upon the *verbum externum*, that is, that it "is God's word only as the word that is happening here and now and not because of its content of ideas – not because, say, it talks about God's grace and kindness (however rightly) but only because it confronts me here and now as judgment or grace." On the Problem of Demythologizing, *Ogden*, p. 119. On the following page of the same article he writes: "As the word of God Christ is *ante me et extra me*, although not as a fact that can be objectively stated and chronologically ante me, but as Christ pro me, who encounters me in the word."

43. *Ibid.*

44. The Crisis in Belief, (1931), *EPT*, p. 18; cf. to Forms of Human Community, *EPT*, p. 301, and The Significance of the Idea of Freedom for Western Civilization, *EPT*, p. 323.

45. The Crisis in Belief (1931), *EPT*, p. 17f.; Humanism and Christianity (1948), *EPT*, p. 151ff.; The Idea of God and Modern Man, *JTC 2*, p. 83.

46. Jesus Christ and Mythology, p. 38.

47. See New Testament and Mythology (1941), *Ogden*, pg. 23, 25, 28; and The Problem of Hermeneutics (1950), *Ogden*, p. 82.

48. The Historical Jesus and the Theology of Paul (1929), *FU*, p. 235-246; Points of Contact and Conflict (1946), *EPT*, p. 133ff. Church and Teaching in the New Testament, *FU*, p. 211; The Question of Wonder, *FU*, p. 260; The Christology of the New Testament, *FU*, p. 278f.

49. Classically articulated in the chapters on Paul in Bultmann's *New Testament Theology*.

50. The Meaning of Christian Faith in Creation, *EF*, esp. p. 216 ff.

51. *Lighten Our Darkness, Toward an Indigenous Theology of the Cross*, Philadelphia, Pa., 1976, p. 203.

52. Humanism and Christianity, *EPT*, p. 157. He goes on in citing Luther as follows: "Assuredly this is a difficult undertaking, and it mightily shatters a man. For that the soul should be without a stirring of comprehension and will means that it goes into darkness and, as it were, ruin and annihilation; and in face of that starts back violently." J. Ficker, Scholia, p. 205.5f., 202.5ff., 206.10 ff.

53. R. Bultmann, The Old and New Man, p. 53.

54. Jesus Christ and Mythology, p. 84.

55. *Ibid.*, p. 85.

56. Bultmann – An Attempt to Understand Him, *KM II*, p. 123.

E. Grislis

The author's gratitude is expressed to the Faculty Fellowship Division of the Social Sciences and Humanities Research Council of Canada which has enabled the research for this study.

1. Paul Althaus, *The Theology of Martin Luther*, Philadelphia, 1966, p. 3

2. Lennart Pinomaa, *Der existentielle Charakter der Theologie Luthers*, Helsinki, 1940, pp. 143-147.

3. Cf. Daniel Olivier, *Luther's Faith: The Cause of the Gospel In the Church*, St. Louis, 1982

4. For an account of current bibliography, see Egil Grislis, "Luther in Review: Approaches in Major Studies – A Bibliographical Perspective, "*Word and World*, 3, 4 (1984):442-443

5. LW 35:49; WA 2:742:7-10

6. LW 35:50; WA 2:742:33 – 743:1

7. LW 35:50; WA 2:743:7-8

8. LW 35:51; WA 2:743:11-12; Paul Althaus, *Communio Sanctorum: Die Gemeinde im lutherischen Kirchengedanken*, Muenchen, 1929, pp. 75-79

9. LW 35:53; WA 2:744:25-30

10. LW 35:53-54; WA 2:745:5-7

11. LW 35:54; WA 2:745:11-14

12. "What is most remarkable is the rigorous and living view of the church which undergirds Luther's interpretation of the Lord's Supper. Holy Communion is not something which the individual guest enjoys in isolation." Gustaf Aulén, *Eucharist and Sacrifice*, Philadelphia, 1958, p. 70, cf. pp. 74-75

13. Werner Betcke, *Luthers Sozialethik: Ein Beitrag zu Luthers Verhaeltnis zum Individualismus*, Guetersloh, n.d.., pp. 64-77; Donald Ziemke, *Love for the Neighbor in Luther's Theology*, Minneapolis, 1963

14. LW 35:54; WA 2:745:25-30

15. LW 35:58; WA 2:748:24-26

16. LW 35:59; WA 2:748:29-35

17. Egil Grislis, "The Manner of Christ's Eucharistic Presence According to Martin Luther," *Consensus: A Canadian Lutheran Journal of Theology*, 7,1 (1981):3-15; for a detailed study of medieval sources, see Hartmut Hilgenfeld, *Mittelalterlich-traditionelle Elemente in Luthers Abendmahlsschriften*, Zuerich, 1971

18. LW 35:60; WA 2:749:37 – 750:1

19. LW 35:61; WA 2:750:4

20. Helmut Appel, *Anfechtung und Trost im Spaetmittelalter und bei Luther*, Leipzig, 1938, pp. 116-124; Horst Beintker, *Die Ueberwindung der Anfechtung bei Luther*, Berlin, 1954; Paul Buehler, *Die Anfechtung bei Martin Luther*, Zuerich, 1942, pp. 104-105; Egil Grislis, "Martin Luther's View of the Hidden God", *McCormick Quarterly*, 21,1(1967):81-94

21. LW 35:61; WA 2:750:8-11

22. Ragnar Bring, *Das Verhaeltnis von Glauben und Werken in der lutherischen Theologie*, Muenchen, 1955; George W. Forell, *Faith Active in Love: An Interpretation of the Principles Underlying Luther's Social Ethics*, New York, 1954; Martin Seils, *Der Gedanke vom Zusammenwirken Gottes und des Menschen in Luthers Theologie*, Guetersloh, 1962; the sermonically profound interpretation by Gerhard O. Forde entitled *Justification by Faith – A Matter of Death and Life*, Philadelphia, 1982, pp. 39-59, begins with a priceless vignette: "There is an old story about a Lutheran pastor who on his deathbed declared his confidence that he would go to heaven because he could not remember ever having done a good work in his life!"

23. LW 35:61; WA 2:750:11

24. LW 35:61; WA 2:750:15-18

25. LW 35:66; WA 2:753:17-19

26. LW 35:66; WA 2:753:19-22

27. Egil Grislis, "Ernest L. Hazelius: Ecumenical Theologian of the Southern Lutheran Church", *Lutheran Theological Seminary Bulletin*, 45,3 (1965): 22-39; For the high praise of this treatise, see Paul Althaus, *The Theology of Martin Luther*, p. 378, and Gustaf Aulén, *op. cit.*, p. 78

28. "... when Erasmus read the tract, he ejaculated: "The breach is irreparable." Roland H. Bainton, *Here I Stand: A Life of Martin Luther*, New York and Nashville, 1950, p. 137

29. Cf. Adolf Hamel, *Der junge Luther und Augustin*, 1938, rpr. Hildesheim and New York, 1980

30. LW 36:19; WA 6:502:14-15; St. Augustine, *Sermo* 112, cap. 5; Migne 38:645

31. Helmut Gollwitzer, "Zur Auslegung von Joh. 6 bei Luther und Zwingli", *In Memoriam Ernst Lohmeyer*, Stuttgart, 1951, pp. 143 ff.

32. LW 36:20; WA 6:502:24-26; St. Augustine, *Contra Julianum*, 11, cap. 36; Migne 44:699-700

33. LW 36:32; WA 6:510:20-24

34. LW 36:33; WA 6:510:34

35. Carl F. Wisloff, *The Gift of Holy Communion*, Minneapolis, 1964, pp. 41-55; Wolfgang Schwab, *Entwicklung und Gestalt der Sakramententheologie bei Martin Luther*, Frankfurt /M, pp. 170-173

36. LW 36:36; WA 6:512:30-34; yet – "Luther war bereit anzuerkennen, dass auch in der roemischen Kirche trotz aller Miszbraeuche das Abendmahlssakrament erhalten geblieben sei". Werner Elert, *Morphologie des Luthertums*, Muenchen, 1952, vol. I, p. 264

37. Oswald Bayer, *Promissio*, Goettingen, 1971

38. LW 36:38; WA 6:513:24-25

39. LW 36:38; WA 6:513:34-35

40. Hans Grass, *Die Abendmahlslehre bei Luther und Calvin*, Guetersloh, 1954, pp. 87-92; Heinrich Bornkamm, *Das Wort Gottes bei Luther*, Muenchen, 1933, p. 18 and *Luther: Gestalt und Wirkungen*, Guetersloh, 1975, p. 175

41. LW 36:39; WA 6:514:19-20

42. LW 36:40; WA 6:515:28

43. Hans Bernhard Meyer, S.J., *Luther und die Messe*, Paderborn, 1965

44. LW 36:43; WA 6:517:20-21

45. LW 36:43; WA 6:517:27-28

46. LW 36:44; WA 6:518:17

47. Rudolf Hermann, *Luthers These "Gerecht und Suender zugleich"*, Guetersloh, 1960

48. LW 36:48; WA 6:521:8-11

49. Paul Althaus, *The Theology of Martin Luther*, p. 381

50. LW 36:134; WA 8:482:32-483:4

51. For Luther's hermeneutical principles, see Gerhard Ebeling, *Evangelische Evangelienauslegung: Eine Untersuchung zu Luthers Hermeneutik*, Darmstadt, 1962; Willem Jan Kooiman, *Luther and the Bible*, Philadelphia, 1961; as Paul Althaus put it precisely in regard to the Marburg Colloquy: "Luther is bound neither by a theory of verbal inspiration of the Scripture nor through grammar", *The Theology of Martin Luther*, p. 382, cf. also pp. 383-389

52. LW 36:134; WA 8:483:4-8

53. Bernhard Lohse, *Ratio und Fides: Eine Untersuchung ueber die Ratio in der Theologie Luthers*, Goettingen, 1958; B.A. Gerrish, *Grace and Reason: A Study in the Theology of Luther*, Oxford, 1962; Karl-Heinz zur Muehlen, *Reformatorische Vernunftskritik und neuzeitliches Denken*, Tuebingen, 1980

54. LW 36:336; WA 19:484:6-7

55. LW 36:336; WA 19:484:13-14

56. LW 336 ftn. 2; WA 19:457 ftn. 2

57. LW 36:336; WA 19:484:18-19

58. LW 36:336-337; WA 19:484:20-25

59. Friedrich Beisser, *Claritas Scripturae bei Martin Luther*, Goettingen, 1966

60. LW 36:337; WA 19:484:26-27 and 30-31

61. LW 36:337; WA 19:485:6-11

62. LW 36:337; WA 19:485:12-19

63. LW 36:338; WA 19:485:27-28

64. LW 36:338; WA 19:486:14-20

65. Walther von Loewenich, *Luther's Theology of the Cross*, Minneapolis, 1976; Regin Prenter, *Luther's Theology of the Cross*, Philadelphia, 1971; William Hordern, *Experience and Faith: The Significance of Luther for Understanding Today's Experiential Religion*, Minneapolis, 1983, pp. 85-105

66. Hermann Sasse, *This Is My Body*, Minneapolis, 1959, pp. 187-294

67. LW 38:301; WA 54:153:10-18

68. Ulrich Asendorf, *Gekreuzigt und Auferstanden: Luther's Herausforderung an die moderne Christologie*, Hamburg, 1971, pp. 291-356; David Loefgren, *Die Theologie der Schoepfung bei Luther*, Goettingen, 1960; Gustaf Wingren, "Das Problem des Natuerlichen bei Luther", pp. 156-168, and Gerhard Ebeling, same title, pp. 169-179, in *The Church, Mysticism, Sanctification and the Natural in Luther's Thought*, ed. by Ivar Asheim, Philadelphia, 1967

69. LW 36:339; WA 19:488:9-12

70. LW 36:339; WA 19:488:22-25

71. LW 36:339; WA 19:488:26-28 and 489:5

72. LW 36:341; WA 19:490:14-23

73. LW 36:342; WA 19:492:19-24

74. Hans-Martin Barth, *Der Teufel und Jesus Christus in der Theologie Martin Luthers*, Goettingen, 1967, pp. 114-115. Cf. also Ulrich Becke, *Die Welt voll Teufel: Martin Luther als Gegenstand Psychologischer Betrachtung*, Marburg, 1981

75. LW 37:13; WA 23:64:6-14 (manuscript) and 65:4-14 (printed text)

76. LW 37:18; WA 23:70:29-32 (manuscript); 71:29-32 (printed text)

77. LW 37:23; WA 23:78:13-15 (manuscript); 79:13-15 (printed text)

78. Mark U. Edwards, Jr., *Luther and the False Brethren*, Stanford, 1975, and *Luther's Last Battles: Politics and Polemics 1531-46*, Cornell Univ., 1983; Harry Loewen, *Luther and the Radicals*, Waterloo, 1974

79. LW 37:35; WA 23:98:3 (manuscript); 99:3 (printed text)

80. LW 37:56; WA 23:132:2 (manuscript); 133:2 (printed text)

81. LW 37:68; WA 23:148:31-32 (manuscript); 149:31-32 (printed text)

82. LW 35:59; WA 2:749:7-10

83. LW 36:28; WA 6:508:1-6

84. LW 36:28-29; WA 6:508:7-26

85. LW 36:30; WA 6:508:27

86. LW 36:57; WA 6:526:25-27

87. LW 37:85; WA 23:178:7-9 and 179:7-9

88. LW 37:28; WA 23:86:22-35 and 87:22-35

89. LW 37:216; WA 26:329:27-29 and 32-33

90. LW 37:224; WA 26:337:9-14 and 21-23

E. Tate

1. In 1982 an international conference was held at the University of Waterloo to focus the attention of the academic community on the work of Eugen Rosenstock-Huessy. The collected papers of the conference appear in Darrell Bryant, *The Ever Growing Word*, Toronto, in press 1985.

2. Eugene Tate, *Contributions of Eugen Rosenstock-Huessy to the Development of Communication Theory: Some Preliminary Suggestions*, Unpublished paper, presented to International Conference on Eugen Rosenstock-Huessy, University of Waterloo, June 1982. See also: Eugene Tate, Eugen Rosenstock-Huessy: Revolutionizing Communication Theory, in Darrell Bryant, *op. cit.* Eugene Tate, *The Communication Theorist as Pirate and Argonaut: Eugen Rosenstock-Huessy and Communication Theory*, Unpublished paper presented to Annual Conference of the Canadian Communication Association, Guelph, Ontario, June 1984. See also: Eugene Tate, Developments in Communication Theory, *Canadian Journal of Communication*, 1981, **7** (3), 57-71. Eugene Tate, Review of Eugen Rosenstock Huessy, *The Origin of Speech*, and Clinton Gardner, Letters to the Third Millennium, *Canadian Journal of Communication*, 1982, 8 (3), pp. 86-89.

3. A more complete biography will be found in *I Am An Impure Thinker*, Norwich, Vermont, 1970, pp. 182-190, and in Harold Stahmer's introduction to *The Christian Future: Or the Modern Mind Outrun*, New York, 1966, pages vii-lvii.

4. Eugen Rosenstock-Huessy, *Judaism Despite Christianity*, University, Alabama, 1969.

5. Harold Stahmer, *op. cit.*, page xxxiii.

6. Quoted in Stahmer, *op. cit.*, page xxviii.

7. Jack J. Preiss, *Camp William James*, Norwich, Vermont, 1978.

8. Thomas Kuhn, *The Structure of Scientific Revolutions*, Chicago, 1962.

9. Charles David Axelrod, *Studies in Intellectual Breakthrough: Freud, Simmel, Buber*, Amherst, Mass, 1979.

10. Axelrod, *op. cit.*, page 60.

11. *Ibid.*, page 69.

12. Sydney and Beatrice Rome, *Philosophical Interrogations*, New York, 1964, page 32.

13. Eugen Rosenstock-Huessy, *Out of Revolution: Autobiography of Western Man*, Norwich, Vt., 1969, page 758.

14. Clinton C. Gardner, *Letters to the Third Millennium*, Norwich, Vermont, 1981, pp. 64-65.

15. Eugen Rosenstock-Huessy, *The Christian Future . . . .*, New York, 1966, page 5.

16. Clinton Gardner, Introduction to *Speech and Reality*, Norwich, VT, 1970.

17. Rosenstock-Huessy, *I Am An Impure Thinker*, pp. 65-67.

18. *Ibid.*, pp. 14-15.

19. *Out of Revolution*, page 362.

20. *Out of Revolution*, pp. 363-364.

21. Johan Galtung, Foreign Policy Opinion as a Function of Social Position, in J. Rosenau, Editor. *International Politics and Foreign Policy*, New York, 1969, pp. 551-572.

22. Eugen Rosenstock-Huessy, *The Origin of Speech*, Norwich, Vermont, 1981, page 17.

23. *Out of Revolution*, page 366.

24. For a further discussion of this point see: Eugene Tate, *Martin Luther as a Spiritual Director*, Unpublished M.A. Thesis, Northwestern University, 1964. Eugene Tate, Canada and U.S. Differences in Similar TV Story Content, *Canadian Journal of Communication*, 1978, 5 (2), 1-12.

25. Martin Luther, *Commentary on Deuteronomy 7:22.*

26. Martin Luther; Sermon at Wittenberg, 10 March 1522, Monday after Invocavit, *LW*, 51:77.

27. *Out of Revolution*, page 411.

28. *Ibid.*, page 370.

29. *Ibid.*, page 371.

30. *Ibid.*, page 373.

31. *Ibid.*, page 373.

32. *Ibid.*, page 374.

33. *Ibid.*, pp. 380-381.

34. *Ibid.*, page 384.

35. *Ibid.*, page 385.

36. For a detailed discussion of this aspect of German society see pages 391-450 in *Out of Revolution*.

37. *Ibid.*, page 417.

38. *Ibid.*, page 421.

39. *Ibid.*, page 422.

40. Richard Kieckhefer, The Cult of Saints as Popular Religion, *Explor*, 1984, 7, 41-48.

41. *Op. cit.*, page 391.

42. Letter to Cardinal Albrecht, Archbishop of Mainz, 31 October 1517, *LW*, 48:46.

43. See my discussion of Martin Luther as a Spiritual Director, M.A. Thesis, Northwestern University, 1964.

44. *Out of Revolution*, page 406.

45. *Speech and Reality*, page 100.

46. *Op. cit.*, page 379.

47. *Ibid.*, page 443.

48. *Ibid.*, pages 444-445.

49. Some attempts have been made in this direction as in Jeffrey K. Hadden and Charles E. Swann, *Prime Time Preachers*, Amherst, Mass, 1980.

G.W. Forell

1. Iserloh, E., *The Theses Were Not Posted*, Boston, Mass. 1968. p. 48

2. *Ibid.*, p. 53

3. *Ibid.*, p. 58

4. Against Hanswurst, 1541, *LW* 41, p. 234

5. *Reformation and Society in Sixteenth Century Europe*, London, 1966, p. 51, (repr. N.T., 1968.)

6. *WA, Tischreden*, 1, p. 1038

7. *WA* 35, 9

8. E.G. Schwiebert, *Luther and His Times, the Reformation from a New Perspective*, St. Louis, 1950, p. 209.

9. *Ibid.*, p. 207

10. *Ibid.*, p. 206

11. Cf. Heinrich Kuehne, "Der Wittenberger Buch und Papierhandel im 16 Jahrhundert", *450 Jahre Reformation*, Berlin, 1967, p. 301 ff.

12. *WA, Briefe*, 3, p. 578

13. Johann Eberlin von Junzburg, *Saemtliche Schriften*, ed. Ludwig, Enders, Halte a.s., II, p. 69.

14. Cambridge U. Press, 1979, I. 416

15. *Ibid.*

H.T. Lehmann

1) HN 1, 415. – For more information concerning Schumacher see CHG 1, 127-129. – WJM, p. 325. – Apparently unaware of Muhlenberg's reference to Schumacher's ministry in Nova Scotia (MJ 2, 244) Roth consigns Mann's inclusion of Schumacher's statement concerning the latter's ministry in Nova Scotia to the realm of the apocryphal because "no record, at least, of any such person as Schumacher, has been found to show he had ever been pastor at Lunenburg." DLR, pp. 304-305.

2) MJ 2, 408.

3) IFM, p. 65 n. 3

4) *The Trail of the Huguenots in Europe, the United States, South Africa and Canada*, Baltimore, 1966, pp. 206-207.

5) CRC, p. 38.

6) MJ 2, 453.

7) HN 1, 415.

8) WJM, p. 325. Unfortunately, Mann does not provide the source of his information. – MJ contains no material for 1755. – DLR erroneously identifies the lieutenant

governor's call as occurring in 1775. CRC follows DLR and consequently misplaces and misinterprets Muhlenberg's call to Nova Scotia in 1755. – Mann, Roth and Cronmiller mistakenly attribute Muhlenberg's call to the governor of Nova Scotia. In 1755 Lawrence was still lieutenant governor. He did not become governor until 1756.

9) DH, pp. 96-99, where the letter from Lunenburg together with an extended discussion of it may be found. – See also MJ 2, 370-372.

10) CHG 1, 24; MJ 2, 317.

11) MJ 2, 441.

12) *Ibid.*

13) DLR, pp. 270; 280.

14) *Ibid.*, pp. 295-301.

15) The copy of this letter is in the Lutheran Archives Center in Philadelphia having the call number PM 95/DI, 1771.

16) DLR, pp. 301-302. – The letter is dated Lunenburg, January 1, 1772.

17) MJ 2, 511-512; CHG 1, 164-165.

18) There seems to be some confusion concerning the identity of this man. CRC, p. 48, identifies him as Mr. Kaulbach. In his report Andreas Jung identifies him as Lorenz Conradt. DLR, p. 292.

19) HN 1, 632.

20) MJ 2, 512; CHG 1, 124-125. – For Schultz's ministry in Nova Scotia see also V. Eylands, *Lutherans in Canada*, Winnipeg, Canada, 1945, p. 37.

21) WJM, p. 287. – HN 1, 262 – CHG says Schultz only served eight years in Lunenburg, 1772-1780.

22) For more details concerning Hausihl (later Houseal) see CRC, pp. 43-44; CHG 1, 52-53; DLR, pp. 134-144, where Roth reproduces the account and estimate of Hausihl as person and pastor by his Anglican successor. A reconciliation of some of the discrepancies between these various accounts of Hausihl as a person, pastor and British patriot remains a task for the future.

23) Letter of Johann Friedrich Handschuh (1714-1764) in HN 1, 646-647; DH, p. 41.

24) Letter of February 27, 1759 in HN 1, 732-733.

25) MJ 1, 390.

26) MJ 1, 451.

27) MJ 2, 145.

28) MJ 2, 249-253.

29) MJ 2, 310.

30) CHG 1, 53; Harry Julius Kreider, *Lutheranism in Colonial New York*, New York, 1942, p. 146.

31) DLR, p. 142.

32) Various spellings of Schwerdfeger's name occur: Schwerdtfeger and Schwertfeger. According to HN 1, 956 Schwerdfeger did not only have the two given names, John Samuel but a third, namely, Wilhelm. – This is also the place to state that HN 1, 428 notes that Schwerdfeger died in Feilstown, N.Y., in 1788. Apparently the editors of HN were unaware of Schwerdfeger's ministry in Upper Canada. WJM, p. 411 repeats this error.

33) MJ 3, 50.

34) Helmut T. Lehmann, "Heinrich Melchior M ühlenberg als Mann, Kirchengr ünder und Seelsorger," *Der Synodalbote* 14(1942), pp. 2-6.

———— – ————, "The American Revolution in the Experience of Henry Melchior Muhlenberg,"

———— – ————, "Henry Melchior Muhlenberg; Patriarch or Patriot?" *Mr. Airy Parish Practice Notebook*, March, 1976, pp. 1-4.

Theodore G. Tappert, "Henry Melchior Muhlenberg and the American Revolution," *Church History* 11(1942), pp. 284 – The credit for showing Muhlenberg's neutral posture during the American Revolution belongs to Tappert. Prior to the appearance of this article William J. Mann, for example, made Muhlenberg appear to be a patriot.

35) DH, p. 192.

36) DH, p. 220.

37) MJ 3, 720.

38) DH, p. 141.

39) CHG 1, 131.

E. Theodore Bachmann

1. Notes 86:40 (Jan 4/67). Reference hereinafter to Notes indicates the personally kept notebooks, consecutively numbered and paged, in which I entered information on conversations and events as they happened or very soon thereafter. The current series dates from October 13, 1960 and now numbers over 350 pocket-size volumes. As aide-mémoire they have proven indispensible, also for the writing of this account.

2. From various conversations with William Hordern. Cf *Directory of American Scholars*, 7th edn., New York & London, 1978, IV:218.

3. *Lutheran World* 1977/2-3 = "Lutheran Churches in the World. A Handbook. 1977." Geneva, *passim*.

4. "Lutheran Maturity in Canada," by N[ils] Willison, *The Lutheran Church Quarterly*, XIV (October 1941), 4, 351.

5. *Proceedings of the Lutheran World Federation Assembly*, Lund, Sweden, June 30-July 6, 1947, p. 163.

6. *Ibid.*, 95. United Lutheran Church in America, 1948 Convention *Minutes, 687-88*. Norman Threinen, *Fifty Years of Lutheran Convergence:* The *Canadian Case-Study*. Publication No. 3, Dubuque, 1983, p. 141.

7. From a vividly recalled conversation with this old friend and former editor of *The Lutheran Herald*. Now he had to move discretely not only among the varieties of Norse but also of German custom. A kind of post-merger malaise.

8. The best is a first-hand account of the Bad Boll conferences by Karl Arndt, their initial planner. His "Missouri and Bad Boll, 1948", *Concordia Historical Institute Quarterly*, vol. 52 (Spring 1979), No. 1, pp. 2-22, is choice. So also is his sequel, "Missouri and World Lutheranism at Bad Boll, 1949," CHIQ, vol. 54 (Summer 1981), No. 2, 50-62. – Arndt was one of my colleagues in the Religious Affairs Branch of the U.S. Military Government in Germany after the war.

9. Frederick W. Danker, *No Room in the Brotherhood. The Preus-Otten Purge of Missouri*, St. Louis, 1977 has become the classic account by a participant on the Seminex side.

10. Notes, 30-31 (Friday, July 16/71). President Philip Fry, Manitoba-Saskatchewan District – formerly of Nebraska – held off until a string of state-side champions of the negative had displayed their anxieties as well as ignorance. Then Fry straightened them out and convinced the convention. – I felt it fortunate to be present.

11. A card index of the Basel men who came to North America during the 19th century is in my possession and was prepared at my request in Basel in 1947.

12. General Council, *Minutes* of the Thirty-second Convention, Minneapolis, 1909, p. 51, cf. p. 54.

13. General Council, *Minutes* of the Thirty-first Convention, Buffalo, N.Y., 1907, p. 215. – On Milton James Bieber, see *Biographical Record of the Lutheran Theological Seminary at Philadelphia, 1864-1962*. Class of 1894.

14. Carl R. Cronmiller, *A History of the Lutheran Church in Canada*. Volume I. Prepared at the Request of the Evangelical Lutheran Synod of Canada to Mark its Centennial, July 1961. p. 214.

15. Willison, LCQ (1941), pp. 359, 360.

16. *Ibid.*, p. 359.

17. General Council, *Minutes* of the Thirty-third Convention, Lancaster, Pa., 1911. References to Manitoba Synod's college: pp. 17, 46, 50, 183, 216. General Council, *Minutes*, 1909. Resources seem too weak to venture a theological seminary, p. 211. General Council, *Minutes*, 1913. Juergen Goos reports from Manitoba Synod, p. 47.

18. Valdimar J. Eylands, *Lutherans in Canada*, Winnipeg, 1945, pp. 249-50.

19. ULCA 1932 Convention *Minutes* (Philadelphia) bring the report of a special commission to study the situation of the Canadian Synods. The findings were positive and the recommendations looked toward the day of one Evangelical Lutheran Church in Canada. Pp. 72-83, 294.

20. ULCA 1940 Convention *Minutes* (Omaha), pp. 106-7.

21. *Ibid.*

22. Cronmiller, p. 215.

23. ULCA 1932, p. 83.

24. Dr. Gould Wickey, executive secretary, ULCA Board of Higher Education, to me in 1961.

25. Bessie Lee Rehwinkel, M.D., wife of the Rev. Alfred M. Rehwinkel, who narrated also her career in Alberta in *Dr. Bessie*, St. Louis: Concordia, 1963, p. 163.

26. "Saskatchewan", in Encyclopedia Britannica (1954 edn.).

27. Harold Engen, *History of the Evangelical Lutheran Church of Canada*, Saskatoon: Luther Theological Seminary, 1955, pp. 61-62. This work, a B.D. dissertation, apparently draws most of the historical information from the extensive coverage in Olaf Morgan Norlie, *Norsk Lutherske Menigheter I Amerika*, Minneapolis, 1918, Vol. II includes the congregations in western Canada, pp. 394-491. See also Norlie, *History of the Norwegian People in America*, Minneapolis, 1925, pp. 315-28, for the Norse settlement in western Canada in a still wider context.

28. Threinen, *Fifty Years*, p. 115.

29. Notes 31:105 (Wed, Sept 26/62). Besides President Schiotz, the group with whom I spoke (over breakfast in the "KG" Hotel) included Alvin Rogness (president, Luther Seminary, St. Paul); Edward C. Fendt (dean, Evangelical Lutheran Seminary, Columbus, Ohio), Casper B. Nervig, parish pastor, Williston ND, an architecture buff and keen on housing a merged Lutheran seminary enterprise on the Luther Seminary campus, Wiggins Ave.

30. "The Lutheran Church in America and Theological Education. A Report to the Board of Theological Education," by Conrad Bergendoff, Executive Secretary (New York: BTE/LCA, 1963), pp. 47, 48. Usually called the "Bergendoff Report," this study laid the groundwork and set the direction of much to follow.

31. Lutheran Church in America, 1964 Convention Minutes, Pittsburgh, p. 589.

32. Financed by the Theological Education Fund and published in New York, 1960, 640 pp.

33. Likewise financed by the TEF, this immense work by the Yale Divinity School librarian – aided by a large advisory group (mainly North American and European theologians and churchmen) – was widely circulated. Paperback, 8½ x 11, mimeographed. – While teaching in Brazil (1959), we on the Lutheran Faculdade de Teologia filled out the forms circulated by this library inquiry according to our field; and I learned at first-hand under what limitations students and faculty even in a privileged Latin American seminary must operate. Later I was to discover the same elsewhere in the Two-Thirds World; e.g. in Ethiopia, Tanzania, India, Indonesia, Papua New Guinea, The libraries in Bangalore, India; Singapore (Trinity); Suva, Fiji; Hong Kong (the two Lutheran Seminaries would be stronger if united!); and Tokyo (the Lutheran adjacent to Tokyo Union Seminary on the International Christian University campus), set an excellent pace. Today there is a noticeable similarity between the Canadian (Lutheran) and Australian (Lutheran) seminary libraries; and the Faculdade in Brazil (at Sao Leopoldo) has come up greatly since 1959. It is now said to have the largest collection on Latin American church history, exceeding even that in Union Seminary, Buenos Aires (now called ISEDET).

34. Notes 57:19, 25, 27 (Fri, June 18/65).

35. Notes 122: 121-41 (Fri, Oct 25/68). The text for the dedicatory sermon, Rom 15:13, moved me to accentuate hope. The present; the long road from the past; the pull of the future. It was a thrill to have been invited to preach on this day of dedication and thanksgiving. The building was as yet unfinished. It brought back recollections of the dedication in Sao Leopoldo, Brazil, nearly a decade earlier, where – on dedication day – the fine new building of the Faculdade was not yet finished. But that kind of condition has its own come-on.

36. Notes 274:6 (Fri, June 4/76), ff.

37. *Lutheran World* 4/76, p. 300. (As part of the annual round-up of LWF activities.)

38. 274:153 (Su, June 6/76).

39. *Ibid.*, 67 (Mon, June 7). – A couple of days earlier, in a stimulating conversation, (the late) Don (Donald H.) Voigts referred back to his article in *Lutheran World* (1972) on "twinning". He saw in the current meeting on Church Cooperation a rare opportunity to give twinning a try: that is, e.g. relating Lutheran Collegiate Bible Institute/Outlook with a comparable school in Cameroon – perhaps with the seminary in Meiganga. Why not try it? At least have the representative from Cameroon meet the president from Outlook, since both are presently in Saskatoon. Similarly, twin-up Christ Church/Waldersee and a parish in Leipzig/East Germany, since both are at the moment represented by persons at this meeting. Similarly, why not initiate a linkage between Ascension Church/Edmonton and the city church in Porto Alegre/Brazil – the pastors of both parishes (Daniel Berg and Godofredo Boll) are attending the CC meeting. And so Voigts continued. An enormously appealing idea, its possibilities are without limit. Yet the followthrough is demanding. Who will keep it up? Others joined us. The circle widened. Finally there were 25 of us – 15 from overseas – trading ideas. Voigts had thought things through well; was calm, clear, persuasive. We saw this as a kind of follow-up on "Mission in Six Continents" – as set forth by the World Council's Mexico City conference nearly 15 years ago. This was mediating oikoumene at the prairie-grass roots. (17-19).

40. Eric Modean's first article – news report – from Waterloo. Lutheran Council in the USA/News Bureau 1967/47, p. 6 (June 13).

40.a WCC/CC *Minutes*, Heraklion, 1967, pp. 42-43. The Uppsala '68 Report, pp. 421, 445.

41. *Lutheran World* 77/2-3, pp. 113-352. This procedure had been worked out in a small committee at the 1974 meeting of Church Cooperation in Lund, Sweden (Notes 245:37ff [Wed May 22/74]).

42 Notes 288:55ff (Wed June 1/77). As I subsequently traveled on to Geneva, Swissair kept me informed by telex every time the shipment was transferred; in Chicago, Zurich, and finally on arrival in Dar-es-Salaam. The venture proved what could be done via planning and persistence. Omar Bonderud, Chief of Publications at Augsburg, as I thanked him, said, "We've never worked such a close deadline." I had come over from Geneva May 6 with the nearly completed MS; checked out some stories still in the making, like the formation of the Missouri split-off, the AELC; worked with designers, composers, pressmen; supervised everything; shared the proof-reading; did the index; secured the copyright; and best – stimulated a sense of teamwork. Exhilarating. Notes 287:87-153 (May 6-20/77).

As to the reception of the handbook by individual members of the assembly, this was most encouraging. Notes 288:146. Ironically, however, on recommendation of the Federation's own Communications Committee, the Executive Committee – convened prior to the assembly – in Dar-es-Salaam voted to discontinue *Lutheran World* and its slightly older German edition, *Lutherische Rundschau*. This 25-year long record of LWF thought and action was thus terminated in favor of more emphasis on the electronic media and their outreach into the Two-Thirds world. Yet, ironically, in March 1977 the Ethiopian government had seized the Federation's pivotal communication center, Radio Voice Of the Gospel (RVOG), Addis Ababa. (LW 77/2-3, 126)

43. Notes 306:155 (Oct 24/78). Helmuth Herberth, dean of the Brasov (Kronstadt) District of the Evangelical Church of the Augsburg Confession in the Socialist Republic of Romania. The church roots are in the pre-Reformation era when the Hungarian rulers brought in settlers from the German Rhineland to till the soil as well as to guard the frontier against Turkish and other incursions. With the coming of the Reformation, these now numerous Germans turned Lutheran. But the gothic style of their churches – as the Black Church in Brasov – recalls the 12th and 13th centuries during which the Germans came here. After 800 years large numbers of them are now being lured back to the "good life" in West Germany; much to the sorrow of those who remain.

44. *Handbook. Member Churches, World Council of Churches*. Ed. by Ans J. van der Bent, Geneva: WCC, 1982. 283 pp. In the words of General Secretary Philip A. Potter, this volume "is the World Council's first ever attempt to gather in one readily accessible form an overview of all its member churches." Together the member churches comprise "a treasure-house of tradition and inspiration." This handbook, then, "is to ensure that these riches are seen and shared." (vii)

O. Heick

1. *EA*, 41:127.

2. "On the Councils and the Churches", *LW* 41, III, 3-178.

3. *Commentary on Galatians*.

4. Cf. O.W. Heick, *History of Christian Thought*, Vol. II, 17 ff., Philadelphia, 1966.

5. Cf. *Confessio Tetrapolitana* (The Confession of the Four Cities, Strassburg, Constance, Memmingen and Lindau) presented to Charles V at Augsburg, 1530.

6. Cf. *Encyclopedia of the Lutheran Church*, Julius Bodensik, ed., Vol. I, 678 ff., Philadelphia, 1965.

7. *Ibid.* III, 2287 f.

8. *Ibid.* II, 1430.

9. *The Book of Concord*, T.G. Tappert, ed., Philadelphia, 1959.

10. E.A. Sortland, "High Church Tendencies in Lutheranism", *The Ecumenist*, Vol. 20, No. 4, May/June, 1982.

11. The quotations are from the writer's article, "High Church Tendencies in Nineteenth Century Lutheranism", *Augustana Quarterly*, Vol. 25, April 1946, pp. 99-111.

12. E.C. Nelson, ed., *The Lutherans in North America*, Fortress Press, 1975, p. 227—In the Theses on the Church Ministry Walther taught that the office is "conferred by God through the congregation...by its call prescribed by God." Ordination on the other hand, "is not by divine institution." It is "merely a public confirmation of the Call." *Walther and the Church*, trans. by Wm. Dallmann, W.T.H. Dau and Th. Engelder. St. Louis, 1938, pp. 71-86.

13. For an inclusive translation of the Theses. cf. *Augustana Quarterly*, pp. 109 f. and Sortland, p. 50.

14. Heick, *op. cit.* II, 216 f.

15. Cf. "The 'Merely' Gospel of the Indiana Majority", *Missouri in Perspective*, Vol. 7, No. 20, Sept. 8, 1980.

16. "Perspective on Women's Ordination", *Consensus*, Vol. 3, No. 4, 1977, and "Women in the Ministry of the Contemporary Church", *ibid.* vol. 4, No. 1, January, 1978.

17. Bodensik, *op. cit.*, II, 1424.

18. Nelson, *op. cit.* p. 512—For a penetrating analysis of the LWF, cf. Ulrich Duchrow, Conflict over the Ecumenical Movement, pp. 51-296, Geneva 1981.

19. Wentz in Bodensik, *op. cit.*, ii, 1430.

20. R.E. Mueller, "Lutherans at Budapest", *The Cresset*, November 1984.

21. Cf. The critical review by G.A. Lindbeck, *Partners*, December 1984/January 1985.

22. Cf. "Toward a Fuller Doctrine of Ministry", *Partners*, August 1982 and subsequent editions.

23. *Dialogue* VI, 25.

24. *Lutherische Monatshefte*, June 1983, pp. 266-271.

25. *Lutheran Episcopal Dialogue*, 1980 and *Anglican Lutheran Dialogue*, 1982.

26. "Baptism, Eucharist and Ministry", *Faith and Order Paper*, No. 111, Geneva, 1982.

27. Cf. J.L. Neve, *Lutherans in the Movement for Church Union*, 1921.

28. The clime at the court of Hannover was very favorable to such endeavors. Linked by marriage to the Catholic house of Hapsburg, the Electress Sophia, friend of Leibnitz, herself of Calvinist training, became in 1713 heir apparent to the throne of Great Britain. Her son, George I, ascended the throne in 1714. Because of his dual reign, he was head of the Lutheran church of Hannover, of the Anglican establishment in England and of the Presbyterian church in Scotland.

29. Cf. the penetrating discussion of the relation of the Lutheran World Federation to the Ecumenical Movement by Ulrich Duchrow, *Conflict over the Ecumenical Movement*, Geneva 1981.

30. *Partners*, December 1983, p. 8.

Publications of William Hordern

Books

Christianity, Communism and History, Abingdon Press, Nashville, N.Y., 1954

A Layman's Guide to Protestant Theology, MacMillan, N.Y., 1955 (revised 1968)

The Case for a New Reformation Theology, Westminster Press, Philadelphia, 1959

Speaking of God, MacMillan, N.Y., 1964

New Directions in Theology Today, Volume I: Introduction, Westminster Press, Philadelphia, 1966

Living by Grace, Westminster Press, Philadelphia, 1976

Experience and Faith, Augsburg, Minneapolis, 1983

Edited Series, *New Directions in Theology Today*, Westminster, Philadelphia.

Contributed to *How My Mind Has Changed*, 1961
                 Theologians of Our Times, 1966
                 A Dictionary of Christian Theology, 1969

                 Co-Author with Dale Bruner
                 The Holy Spirit - Shy Member of the Trinity, Augsburg, Minneapolis, 1984.

Articles

1948   **Christianity and Crisis**, Dec. 13, 1948 pp. 164-166
            New York, N.Y.

            "In Search of a Prophetic Voice".

1950   **Christianity and Crisis.**, April 17, 1950 pp. 45-46
            New York, N.Y.

            "Some Reflections on Euthanasia".

            The World Christian Digest. Sept., 1950 pp. 17-20

            "Hastening Death" condensed from **Christianity and Crisis**.

1950-51	**Religion in Life**. Winter Number, 1950-51 New York, N.Y.
	"The Relevance of the Fall".
	"His reflections on the Fall are an outgrowth of his work on a doctoral Thesis at U.T. Sem, N.Y. City, entitled *"The Relationship of Christian and Marxian Interpretations of History."*
1952	**Friends Intelligencer**., Second Month 2, 1952 pp. 59-60. Philadelphia, Penn.
	"The Christian and Other Faiths"
	Friends Intelligencer., Fifth Month 3, 1952 pp. 248-250 Philadelphia, Penn.
	"Modern Trends in Theology."
	The Christian Century., March 12, 1952 pp. 306-307 Chicago, Ill.
	"Young Theologians Rebel."
1953	**Friends Intelligencer**, Second Month 21, 1953 pp. 95-97. Philadelphia, Penn.
	"Why Theology?"
	*This is the first of a series of articles dealing with modern theology. Subsequent essays deal with the theologies of R. Niebuhr, K. Barth, E.J. Carnell, and M. Buber.
	Friends Intelligencer. Third Month 14, 1953 pp. 136-138 Philadelphia, Penn.
	"The Theology of Reinhold Niebuhr"
	Friends Intelligencer. Fifth Month 2, 1953 pp. 240-242 Philadelphia, Penn.
	"Niebuhr's Gospel for Society"
	Friends Intelligencer. Sixth Month 13, 1953 pp. 323-325. Philadelphia, Penn.
	"The Barthian Challenge"
	The Christian Century. July 8, 1953 pp. 792-794 Chicago, Ill.
	"Hope: Here and Hereafter".
	Friends and Intelligencer. Seventh Month 25, 1953 pp. 399-401 Philadelphia, Penn.
	"Fundamentalism Revived."

Episcopal Churchnews. August 30, 1953 pp. 12-13, 15-17.
Richmond, Va.

"A Prologue to Christology."

1954   **Friends Intelligencer**. Second Month 6, 1954 pp. 76-77
Philadelphia, Penn.

"'I and Thou' in the Thought of Martin Buber"

1955   **Friends Intelligencer**. Fourth Month 23, 1955 pp. 237-239
Philadelphia, Penn.

"A Forgotten Quaker Prophet"

The Journal of Bible and Religion. July, 1955 pp. 187-192
Brattleboro, Vermont.

"Communicating Theology to the Laity"

1956   **The Pastor**. February 1956 pp. 10-12
Nashville, Tennessee.

"The Theology of Nels Ferre"

Christian Life. April, 1956 pp. 20-22
Chicago, Ill.

"Is Liberal Theology Changing?"

*"...conclusions resulting from a special **Christian Life** study."*

The Christian Century. Dec. 19, 1956 pp. 1476-1477.
Chicago, Ill.

"What's Right With Christmas?"
     W. Hordern's comments used in article.

1957   **The Lutheran**. June 19, 1957 pp. 12, 15.
Philadelphia, Penn.

"The Church Never Had it so Good."

The War Cry, Saturday, June 22, 1957 pp. 3, 15
Atlanta, Georgia.

"America's Religious Revival: Asset or Liability?"

The Lutheran Companion. June 26, 1957 pp. 4-5, 16
Rock Island, Ill.

"Our Colleges and America's Religious Revival."

The Chaplain. August, 1957 pp. 7-13
Washington, D.C.

"America's Religious Revival: Asset or Liability?"

Lutheran Standard. August 24, 1957 pp. 8-10.
Columbus, Ohio.

"America's Religious Revival: How Deep Does it Go?"

The Cumberland Presbyterian. August 27, 1957 pp. 8-9.
Memphis, Tenn.

"Is this an Asset or Liability?"

The Cumberland Presbyterian. Sept. 3, 1957 pp. 9, 14-15
Memphis, Tenn.

"America's Religious Revival"

The New Christian Advocate. Oct. 1957 pp. 44-48
Chicago, Ill.

"America's Revival: Asset of Liability?"

The Lutheran. Oct. 30, 1957 pp. 11-13
Philadelphia, Penn.

"You can't save yourself"

The Presbyterian Record. Nov. 1957 pp. 4-5, 35.
Toronto, Canada.

"Religious Revival: Asset or Liability?"

1959   **The Chaplain**. Oct. 1959 pp. 21-28
Washington, D.C.

"Karl Barth: The Preacher's Theologian."

Journal of Bible and Religion. Oct. 1959

Review *"Triology on Protestant theology; a triple review of three books."* (listed as such in index).

1960   **The Journal of Bible and Religion**. April 1960 pp. 222-228
Brattleboro, Vermont.

"Theology in Prospect"

Christian Advocate. July 21, 1960 pp. 5-6
Chicago, Ill.

"Neo-Orthodoxy: Child of Liberalism"

The Christian Century. Nov. 23, 1960 pp. 1370-1373
Chicago, Ill.

"The Primacy of Faith"

Lutheran Herald. Dec. 13, 1960 pp. 4-5
Minneapolis, Minn.

"What's Right With Christmas?"

1961   **Canadian Journal of Theology**, April 1961 pp. 82-90
Toronto, Ontario.

"Recent Trends in Systematic Theology"

Christian Century, Sept. 13, 1961 pp. 1080-1081

"Psychiatry discovers sin"
Chicago Review of *"The Crisis in Psychiatry and Religion"*
    by O. Hobart Mowrer.

How My Mind Has Changed, pp. 148-158.
Cleveland, Ohio.

"William Hordern"
*note "the contributions to this book were first published
as articles during the 1959-60 publishing year." p. 7
(In Christian Century Nov. 23, 1960 *"The Primacy of
Faith"*)

Adult Teacher. March 1961 pp. 20-21.
Nashville, Tenn.

"Advanced Studies"

"A Layman's Guide to Protestant Theology" (a study guide)

Worldview. Nov. 1961 pp. 4-8.
New York, N.Y.

"A Perspective on Foreign Affairs"
(Frame of Reference for ethical judgment)

Religion in Life. Autumn 1961 pp. 547-554.
Nashville, Tenn.

"Neo-Orthodoxy or Post-Neo-Orthodoxy?"

1962   **Christian Advocate**. March 29, 1962 pp. 7-8.
Nashville, Tenn.

"Is there a New Barth?"

The Chicago Theological Seminary **Register**. April 1962
pp. 6-15.
Chicago, Ill.

"Sanctification and Politics in the Theology of Karl Barth"

Christianity & Communism. 1962.
New York, N.Y.

(an elective study) Reprinted from **Christian Action**, May &
June, 1962. Meth. Pub. House (book).

The Church and Broadcasting. April 30, 1962 pp. 7-11.
Chicago, Ill.

"The Church and Broadcasting: The Churchman's View"
(an address by William Hordern - booklet)

Workers With Youth. May 1962 pp. 10-12.
Nashville, Tenn.

"The Radical"
(Is the leftist with ties to Russia a true radical? Background for *"Christianity and Communism,"* in **Christian Action** for May and June.)

Christian Action. May 1962 pp. 16-36.
Nashville, Tenn.

"Christianity and Communism"

Christian Action. June 1962 pp. 15-35.
Nashville, Tenn.

"Christianity and Communism"

Adult Teacher. Sept. 1962 pp. 2-4.
Nashville, Tenn.

"Christianity, Communism, & History"

The Christian Century. Dec. 5, 1962 pp. 1482-1484.
Chicago, Ill.

"Heidegger: King Without Clothes"
Review of **Being and Time** by Martin Heidegger.

1963 **The Expository Times**. March 1963 pp. 177-180.
Edinburgh.

"Theologians of Our Time IV. Karl Barth To-day"

The Methodist Story. May 1963 pp. 2-7.
Evanston, Ill.

"Chosen by God"

Dialog. Summer 1963 pp. 196-200.
Minneapolis, Minn.

"The Image of Communism in America"

Christian Advocate. June 6, 1963 pp. 7-8.
Nashville, Tenn.

"Truth as Encounter"
A review article of Emil Brunner.

The Lutheran. Aug. 28, 1963 pp. 12-16.
Philadelphia, Penn.

"What Happens to Christian Faith at College?"

The Episcopalian. Sept. 1963 pp. 10-13.
Philadelphia, Penn.

"When a Christian Goes to College..."

Presbyterian Life. Sept. 1, 1963 pp. 6-9, 35.
Philadelphia, Penn.

The College Student and Religion/Part One

"What Happens to Christian Faith in College?"

The Lutheran. Sept. 11, 1963 pp. 11-15.
Philadelphia, Penn.

"The Jittery Generation"

The Lutheran. Sept. 25, 1963 pp. 14-19.
Philadelphia, Penn.

"What Sort of Leaders Will we Have in 1990?"

Presbyterian Life. Sept. 15, 1963 pp. 12-15, 42.
Philadelphia, Penn.

The College Student and Religion/Part Two

"The Seeking Generation"

Presbyterian Life. Oct. 1, 1963 pp. 20, 36-38.
Philadelphia, Penn.

The College Student and Religion/Part Three

"What of the Future?"

The Episcopalian. Oct. 1963 pp. 19-21.
Philadelphia, Penn.

"The Seeking Generation"

The Episcopalian. Nov. 1963 pp. 37-40.
Philadelphia, Penn.

"Veterans of a new age..."

1964   **Dialog**. Summer 1964 pp. 220-222.
            Minneapolis, Minn.

            "A Theological Critique of the Psychedelic Experience"

1965   **Christianity Today**. March 26, 1965 pp. 3-7.
            Washington, D.C.

            "Faith, History, and the Resurrection"

            Church of the Brethren Leader. May 1965 pp. 9-12.
            Elgin, Ill.

            "What Happens to Christian Faith in College?"

            Church of the Brethren Leader. June 1965 pp. 1-4.
            Elgin, Ill.

            "The Seeking Generation"

Dialog. Summer 1965 pp. 227-229.
Minneapolis, Minn.

"Response to Albert Anderson's Review"

Church of the Brethren Leader. July-August 1965 pp. 1-5.
Elgin, Ill.

"Veterans of a new age"

Class Mate. Sept. 1965 pp. 28-30.
Nashville, Tenn.

"The Difference Between Faith and Religion"

1966 **Arena**. Feb. 1966 pp. 10-11.
St. Louis, Mo.

"The Difference Between Faith and Religion"

Christian Advocate. June 2, 1966 pp. 11-12.
Nashville, Tenn.

"Our New Denominationalism"

The Shepherd. Sept. 1966 p. 6.
Saskatoon, Sask.

"Training Ministers Today"

Lutheran Quarterly. Nov. 1966 pp. 329-336.
Gettysburg, Penn.

"Renewal in the Seminary" (Review Article)

Theologians of our Time. 1966 pp. 77-85.
Edinburgh, G.B.

From 1962-65 there appeared in **The Expository Times** a
series of articles entitled 'Theologians of our Time'

"Karl Barth To-day"

1967 **The Baptist Program**. Nov. 1967 pp. 16-17, 19.
Nashville, Tenn.

"The Myth of 'Modern Man'"
(Reprinted from **Christian Advocate**, June 2, 1966)

The Shepherd. January 1967 pp. 6-7.
Calgary, Alberta.

"Can We Be Heard?"

The Shepherd. February 1967 pp. 6-7.
Calgary, Alberta.

"Blinded by the God of This Passing Age"

1968	**The Christian Century**. May 29, 1968 pp. 713-715. Chicago, Ill.

1968   **The Christian Century**. May 29, 1968 pp. 713-715.
Chicago, Ill.

"Canada's New Prime Minister"

The Shepherd. January 1968 p. 14.
Calgary, Alberta.

"Reformation: 450"

The Shepherd. July 1968 pp. 5, 21.
Calgary, Alberta.

"The Work of Christian Ministry Today"

The Shepherd. August 1968 p. 12.
Calgary, Alberta.

"The General Convention: A Reaction"

1969   **The Christian Century**. March 29, 1969 pp. 411-413.
Chicago, Ill.

"Barth as Political Thinker"

Lutheran Quarterly. Nov. 1969 pp. 342-351.
Gettysburg, Penn.

"The Theology of Hope in America"

1970   **The Shepherd**. May 1970 p. 11.
Calgary, Alberta.

"Warming Up For Elections"

The Shepherd. June 1970 pp. 9-10.
Calgary, Alberta.

"Confirmation and Baptism"
(1st publish. in **Podium**, Vol. 2, No. 5)

The Shepherd. Sept. 1970 p. 4-6.
Calgary, Alberta.

"The Old and the New"

1971   **The Christian Century**. Sept. 15, 1971, pp. 1079-1080, 1085.
Chicago, Ill.

"Dialogue on Black Theology" James Cone & W. Hordern.

The Shepherd. Sept. 1971 p. 6.
Calgary, Alberta.

"Good News or Bad?"

1974-75   **Studies in Religion**. pp. 233-236.
Toronto, Ontario.

"Responses to Charles Davis"

Proclamation. Series B. Lent 1975.
Philadelphia, Penn.

Homiletical Interpretations. W. Hordern and John Otwell.

1975   **Augsburg Sermons**. 1975. pp. 93-98.
Gospels series B 1st Sunday on Lent.
Minneapolis, Minn.

"The Humanity of Christ and Our Lives" Mk. 1:12-15.

Consensus. April 1975 pp. 7-14.
Winnipeg, Manitoba.

"Canadian Culture and the Gospel"

("This article is a condensed form of a paper presented to the Division of Theological Studies, Lutheran Council in Canada, May 27, 1974, in Winnipeg, Manitoba. Single copies of the unabridged version are available free upon request as long as present supply lasts." p. 14)

1976   **Augsburg Sermons**. 1976. pp. 280-283.
Epistles Series C
Minneapolis, Minn.

"Lord of All Creation"

The Shepherd. 1976 p. 20.
Saskatoon, Sask.

"Response to the Joint Committee on voting rights for all clergy" by William Hordern and Erwin Buck.

1977   **The Lutheran Standard**. Jan. 18, 1977 p. 5.
Minneapolis, Minn.

"Evangelism-love without strings"
(excerpt from Living by Grace)

1978   **Consensus**. April 1978 pp. 21-28.
Winnipeg, Manitoba.

"The Christian and Civil Disobedience"

1979   **Chelsea Journal**. January-February 1979 pp. 40-47.
Saskatoon, Sask.

"Religion's Right to 'Dabble'"

1980   **Partners** (LCA). April 1980 pp. 13-14, 33.
Philadelphia, Penn.

"Will Our Children Have Faith?"

1982   **Political Theology in the Canadian Context**. Book. pp. 43-60.
Waterloo, Ont. Ed. Benjamin G. Smillie.

"Political Theology"

Theological Education. Spring 1982 pp. 234-240.
Vandalia, Ohio.

"Response"
Response to Robert T. Handy.

The Shepherd. Sept. 1983 pp. 30-31.
Saskatoon, Sask.

"Response to Book Review"

The Shepherd. December 1982 pp. 14-15.
Saskatoon, Sask.

"The Justice Statement"

1983   *"Evangelism, Luther and the Augsburg Confession"*
Saskatoon, Sask. 1983.
Publication of a lecture; booklet, 32 pp.

Central Canada Lutheran. May 1983 pp. 6-8.
Steinbach, Manitoba.

"The Priesthood of All Believers"

1984   **Prairie Messenger**. May 1, 1984 p. 13.
Meunster, Sask.

"Christian Divisions deny the value of Baptism"

Western Catholic **Reporter**. March 12, 1984 p. 9.
Edmonton, Alberta.

"God has found us before we look for him"

Augsburg Sermons 2. 1984 pp. 129-133.
Minneapolis, Minn.

"The Resurrection Today"

1985   **Touchstone**. Vol. 3, Jan. 1985 No. 1 p. 22.

"Creationism...A Problem in Biblical Authority"

INDEX
List of persons named or cited in articles

Abu Qurra, T., 111
Achtemeier, E., 126
Albrecht of Mainz, 174
Al-Kamil, Malik, 113
Allen, R., 41
Allen, Y., 207
Althaus, P., 138
Anselm, 167
Antony, 65
Aquinas, T., 112
Aristotle, 100, 112, 114
Auden, W.H., 162
Augustine, 10, 111, 151
Axelrod, 164

Bach, 173
Bachmann, E.F., 215
Bachmann, Lydia, 215
Bachmann, Mercia, 215
Barr, J., 36
Barth, K., 6, 7, 13, 17, 18-25, 27, 28, 41, 138, 146, 163
Beethoven, 173
Belo, F., 58
Bennett, J., 3
Bergendoff, C., 207
Berkhouwer, G.C., 27
Bertram, Capt., 187
Beyer, H.W., 138
Bibliander, T., 114
Bieber, M.J., 201
Bonhoeffer, D., 6-8, 225
Braun, H., 7
Brenne, O., 206
Brent, C., 225
Brezing, J.J., 215
Bronfman, E.M., 56
Bronfman, S., 56
Bryzelius, P.D., 186-188
Buber, M., 163-165
Bucer, M., 225
Bultmann, R., 38, 41, 138-144, 146
Burcke, 32
Burger, C., 185

Cajetan, 178
Calixtus, 225
Calvin, 17, 21
Carey, W., 114-115
Carmichael, S., 42
Charles V, 113, 172, 175
Clement of Alexandria, 64, 66-77, 111
Cochlaeus, J., 180

Comte A., 8
Cone, C., 44
Cone, J., 104
Confucius (Kwang Fu Tse), 114
Cox, H., 162
Cranach, L., 181
Crites, S., 33, 36-38
Cyrus of Persia, 129

Danker, F., 199
Davies, W.D., 136
Dawe, D.G., 18
Deak, O., 210
DeGaulle, 171
Descartes, 166
Dickens,, A.G., 179
Dixon, M., 60
Driver, T., 12
Dulles, A., 223
Dunne, J.S., 34

Eberlin of Gunzburg, 182
Eck, J., 97, 100
Ehrenberg, H., 163
Ehrenberg, R., 163
Eisenhower, D., 171
Eisenstein, E., 183
Empie, P.C., 222

Fackre, G., 30, 35, 36
Falwell, G., 176
Farel, C., 186
Feuerbach, 8, 20, 49
Ficker, J., 138
Fiorenza, E., 60
Fosdick, E., 3
Francis of Assisi, 65, 112-113
Francke, G.A., 191
Frederick of Wittenberg, 186
Freitag, W., 202, 207, 220
Freud, 8
Freytag, W., 122
Frick, H., 116
Friedman, M., 61
Fry, F.C., 211, 221, 225

Gardner, C., 165
Garnet, H.H., 41
Gerock, J.S., 190
Gilkey, L., 30
Gogarten, F., 138
Goos, J., 203
Gottwald, N., 57, 58
Grabau, J.A.A., 218

Graham, Billy, 90
Grant, J., 44
Grant, U.S., 171
Gretzky, W., 54
Grundtvig, N.F.S., 219
Gustafson, J., 12

Hall, D., 145
Hammarskjold, D., 34
Handschuh, J.F., 34
Hansen, H., 219
Harnack, A., 14
Hartt, 37
Hausihl, B.M., 190-192
Hegel, 18
Heick, O., 201
Heidegger, 144
Helmuth, C., 193
Henry, J., 193
Herder, 117
Hermann, 140
Heubach, W., 219
Hick, J., 12
Hieronymus, bp of Brandenburg, 178
Hinderberg, 171
Hitler, 176
Holfedt, K., 208, 211
Holl, K., 100
Hordern, Bob, 5
Hordern, W., 29, 30, 38, 51, 53, 63, 78-9,
   82-3, 104, 125, 194, 208-9, 215
Howell, L., 54
Hsaio, A., 210
Huessy, Margrit, 162
Hume, D., 116, 117
Hutchinson, R., 54

Ibn Rushd (Averroes), 112, 113
Ibn Sina (Avicenna), 112
Irenaeus, 25, 111
Iserloh, E., 178

Jackson, A., 171
Jacobson, J.R., 220
James, H., 163
James, Freya, 163
Jensen, 14
Joan of Arc, 167
John of Damascus, 111
John Paul II, 76
Jones, M., 43
Jordan, C., 34
Juengel (Jüngel), 14
Julian of Norwich, 182
Jung, A., 187
Jungkuntz, T., 220

Kaldy, Z., 222
Kamper, D., 162

Kant, I., 10
Karlstadt, 99
Kaufman, G., 9, 10
Keffer, A., 200
Keller, W.E., 220
Kibira, J., 209, 210, 222
Kierkegaard, S., 37
King, M.L., Jr., 34, 40-42
Knaut, Squire, 187-8
Knitter, P., 12
Koburger, 183
Kraemer, H., 225
Kuehne, H., 181
Kuhn, 164

Lane, B., 31
Lavik, J.R., 197, 204-6
Lawrence, C., 186
Leibnitz, 225
Leo X, Pope, 183
Lessing, G., 117
Lewis, C.S., 31, 36
Lightfoot, G., 54
Lilje, 221, 225
Loehe, W., 218-9
Luft, H., 181
Lull, R., 112
Luther, M., 7, 8, 13, 15, 17, 21, 25, 82, 94-
   108, 113, 125, 138-9, 141-143, 145,
   147-161, 162, 168-184, 216, 218, 220,
   221, 225

Mackinnon, 186
MacMahon, 171
Malcolm X, 40, 42, 47
Malmin, O.G., 198
Mann, W.J., 190
Marty, M., 35, 162
Martyr, J., 111
Marx, K., 8, 49, 55
McCarthy, J., 8
McClendon, 33, 34
Meilander, G., 31
Melanchton, P., 114, 173, 179-181
Meredith, J., 42
Michelfelder, S.C., 221
Mischler, P., 185
Moltmann, J., 14, 16, 17, 21-28, 79-81,
   86-88, 90-93
Moreau, J.B., 185
Morehead, J.A., 221
Morris, R.P., 208
Mozart, 173
Mueller, M., 117, 121
Muhlenberg, 185-193
Mulroney, B., 61
Murray, A., 54
Murray, P., 44

Nam-Dong, S., 48
Nehrenz, W.E., 206
Niebuhr, Reinhold, 3, 4, 78-83, 85-88, 90-92
Niebuhr, H.R., 12, 14
Nygren, A., 221

Oekolampadius, 154
Origen, 111
Otto, R., 6, 118

Pannenberg, W., 15
Partridge, F., 192
Pascal,, B., 10
Passavant, W.A., 200
Peter the Venerable, 112-4
Petri, Lauentius, 217
Picht, W., 163
Pixley, G., 58-9
Pleutschau, H., 114

Reagan, R., 60-61, 176
Reaman, G.E., 185
Rhau-Grunenberg, J., 180
Ricci, M., 114
Robert de Nobili, 114
Roberts, J.D., 43
Robert of Ketton, 114
Rosenstock-Huessy, E., 162-177
Rosenzweig, F., 163
Roth, D.L., 189
Roth, R., 33, 34, 38
Rousseau, 117

Sanders, E., 131
Scherer, P., 3
Schertlin, J.F., 190
Schiotz, F., 207, 222
Schleiermacher, F., 6, 13, 14, 18, 38
Schmauk, T.E., 201, 208
Schmieder, J., 197
Schneider, F., 197
Schultz, F., 190
Schumacher, D., 185-6, 190
Schwerdfeger, J.S., 192-3
Scott, E., Archbp., 213
Simmel, 164
Simons, Menno, 216
Soederblom, N., 118, 225
Soelle, D., 226
Southern, R.W., 111
Spinks, C., 194
Stahmer, H., 162, 164
Stegemann, W., 61
Strauss, 173
Stroup, G., 32, 33, 35, 36, 38
Suleiman the Magnificent, 113

Tertullian, 67, 111
TeSelle, G., 12
Tetzel, 178
Thatcher, M., 61
T'Hooft, V., 225
Threinen, N., 198
Tiele, C., 117
Tillich, P., 3, 7, 20, 78, 121
Timothy, Patriarch Mar, 111
Tracy, D., 11, 13
Tubman, H., 44
Turner, H.M., 41
Turner, N., 41, 44
Turpel, J.G., 186
Twain, M., 8

Ulrich, Duke of Wittemberg, 186

Vahanian, G., 7
Vasa, G., 217
Vilmar, A., 218-9
Voltaire, 117
Von Weizsacker, V., 163

Wachsel, G.A., 193
Wagner, 173
Waldo, P., 65
Wallenstein, 171
Washington, G., 171
Washington, J., 40-42
Weismantel, L. 163
Westell, D., 55
Whitehead, A.N., 8, 15, 17-19, 26
Wickey, G., 205
Wildbahn, C.F., 189
Wilder, A., 34
Willison, N., 197, 201-205
Wilmore, G., 44
Wingren, G., 8
Wittig, J., 163
Wright, J.T., 222
Wyneken, F.K.D., 220

Ziegenbalg, B., 114
Ziegenhagen, F.M., 191
Zoroaster, 118
Zwingli, 156